EXPOSITION OF GENESIS

By
H. C. LEUPOLD, D.D.
*Professor of Old Testament Exegesis
in the
Capital University Seminary
Columbus, Ohio*

VOLUME I
CHAPTERS 1-19

BAKER BOOK HOUSE
GRAND RAPIDS, MICHIGAN

Library of Congress Catalog Card Number: 55-11417

COPYRIGHT, 1942

THE WARTBURG PRESS

Standard Book Number: 8010-0533-7

First Printing, December 1949
Second Printing, January 1953
Third Printing, March 1956
Fourth Printing, October 1958
Fifth Printing, October 1960
Sixth Printing, January 1963
Seventh Printing, April 1965
Eighth Printing, April 1967
Ninth Printing, December 1968
Tenth Printing, January 1970
Eleventh Printing, June 1971

PHOTOLITHOPRINTED BY CUSHING - MALLOY, INC.
ANN ARBOR, MICHIGAN, UNITED STATES OF AMERICA
1971

INTRODUCTION

1. Name of the Book

The name universally used in English for this book is "Genesis." This name is a transliteration of the Greek word γένεσις, which constitutes the regular title from of old in the Septuagint and was taken over by Jerome into the Vulgate — *Liber Genesis.* Luther made a new departure when he substituted in his German Bible the title "The First Book of Moses" — a designation requiring no further commentary. In the Hebrew Bible the book constitutes the first part of the Pentateuch. As a distinct part it so naturally stands out as a unit that there can be no doubt that it was designed to be just such a unit; and so even criticism from its point of view is ready to accept the division of the Pentateuch as a whole into five parts and that the book of Genesis in particular was a part of it at so early a date as at least four centuries before the Christian era. Though no evidence is available, we are inclined to believe that the Jews discerned the fivefold division of the Pentateuch from the time that the work was put into their hands. They are wont to refer to the book by the title of *Bereshith,* the very first Hebrew word, meaning: "in the beginning."

2. Author

Genesis contains no statement as to who its author was. Yet we hold very definitely to the conviction that Moses wrote Genesis as well as the rest of the Pentateuch, except Deut. 34. In our day such a position is regarded as so utterly outmoded that we must indicate, at least briefly, what grounds we have for standing thus. Our grounds are those which have satisfied conservative scholarship in the church throughout the ages. Neither is the group of those who still accept these arguments so inconsiderable as critics would have us believe.

The internal evidence of the Pentateuch runs as follows. In Exodus the passages 17:14; 24:4; 34:27, if rightly construed, indicate that Moses wrote more than the specific passages that appear under immediate consideration, in fact, all of Exodus. In like manner the numerous statements of Leviticus to the effect that "the Lord spake unto Moses" ("and unto Aaron"), such as 1:1; 4:1; 6:1, 8, 19, 24; 7:22, 28; 8:1, etc., again, if rightly construed, lead to the same result, in fact, cover Leviticus. For why should the exact nature of the revelation be emphasized, unless it be presupposed that this revelation was immediately conserved in writing in each case? In fact, the assumption that these directions were not committed to writing is most unnatural. The same argument applies to much of what is found in Numbers; but in this book the special portion that came by immediate revelation requires the background of the rest of the historical material of the book. Numbers 33:2 is the only passage that refers to the fact that Moses wrote, a statement inserted at this point in order to stamp even what might seem too unimportant to record as traceable to Moses. In Deuteronomy a comparison of the following passages establishes the Mosaic authorship: 1:1; 17:18, 19; 27:1-8; 31:9; 31:24. If, then, on the basis of the evidence found in these four books we may very reasonably conclude that they were written by Moses, the conclusion follows very properly that none other than the author of these later four books would have been so suitable as the author for Genesis also. Certainly such a conclusion is far more reasonable than that Genesis — or for that matter the entire Pentateuch — is to be ascribed to another one of these genial Nobodies of whom criticism has a large number in reserve as authors.

We shall not now trace down how the Old Testament in its later books — historical as well as prophetic — strongly supports the idea of the Mosaic authorship of the Pentateuch and by implication also of Genesis. The critic, misreading the evidence, misdates all these books, and so the argument means nothing to him. The man who is not affected by critical arguments can find proof more ample than we can here reproduce in the writings of Hengstenberg, Keil, Rupprecht and Moeller.

The support that the New Testament lends to our position is singularly strong and, for that matter, even decisive on the whole issue, at least for him who believes in the plenary inspiration of the Scriptures. It is sufficient in these introductory remarks merely to list the major passages as such, passages that all refer to the Mosaic authorship of the whole or of parts of the Pentateuch. In the Gospels we find: Matt. 8:4; 19:7, 8; 23:2; Mark 1:44; 7:10; 10:3, 4; 12:26; Luke 5:14; 16:29, 31; 20:37; John 3:14; 5:45; 6:32; 7:19; 7:22, 23. Aside from these passages which are from the lips of Christ Himself there are the remarks of the evangelists found Luke 24:27, 44; John 1:17. To the apostles must be ascribed the following words: Acts 3:22; 13:39; 15:1, 5, 21; 26:22; 28:23; Rom. 10:5, 19; I Cor. 9:9; II Cor. 3:15. To attribute ignorance on matters involved in literary criticism to Christ or to inspired apostles is unwarranted assumption. To class Christ's attitude as accomodation to prevalent opinion grows out of failure to apprehend the fact that Christ is absolute Truth. Any two or three of the above passages are sufficient to indicate to him that weighs their evidence that to Christ and to His apostles the Torah (the Pentateuch) was Mosaic.

In answering the question, At what time was Genesis written? we are, of course, entirely in the field of conjecture. It seems highly probable that the bulk, if not practically all of Exodus, Leviticus and Numbers, was written after the fashion of a kind of journal, especially those parts embodying specific words of direction given by God. This would naturally suggest some introductory work like Genesis, which could easily have been written by Moses during the time of the Wilderness Wanderings, which extended over thirty-eight years.

Since all the things recorded in Genesis transpired before Moses' day by more than four hundred years at the least, the question arises, Did Moses have sources available for compiling the Genesis account as we have it? We cannot deny the possibility that God may have revealed to Moses the entire subject matter of Genesis. On the other hand, since sources were, no doubt, available and reliable, we see no reason why Moses should not have used all available material and, being guided in his task by the Spirit of inspiration, have produced an essential portion of divine revelation. For it seems highly probable that godly men preserved a reliable record of God's revelation and dealings with men, and that with most painstaking care. The Creation record was obtainable only by revelation, which revelation would have seemed essential for Adam. This as well as all other truth that was left to him, as well as a record of his own experiences required but few links in the chain of tradition to bring it down to Joseph's time. For a careful examination of the Biblical genealogies (Gen. 5 and 11) reveals that Adam lived till the time of Lamech; Lamech to the time of Shem; Shem to the time of Jacob; Jacob would, without a doubt, transmit what he knew to Joseph. Since even Abraham already lived in a literary age, and Judah carried a seal (Gen. 38:18), and Joseph was learned in all the wisdom of the Egyptians, it seems utterly impossible that these men should have refrained from committing this valuable and reliable tradition to writing. Such tradition in written form Moses might well have found in his day and made extensive use of, nor would such use conflict with inspiration in as much as later historical books, especially Kings and Chronicles, testify to the abundant use of source materials.

3. Purpose

The purpose of Genesis may be formulated thus: the book aims to relate how Israel was selected from among the nations of the world and became God's chosen people. Since, however, this choice was not made because of the merit or the excellence of Israel's ancestors but wholly because of God's unmerited and unmeritable mercy, the book may also be said to be the story of God's free grace in establishing Israel for Himself as His people.

4. Text

Two major considerations deserve attention under this head. First, the matter of the state of the purity or the integrity of the Hebrew text. No one in our day errs in the direction of the one possible extreme, namely of venturing to claim that the Hebrew text is in a state of virgin purity, exactly as it appeared in the original manuscripts. But many err in the opposite extreme of considering the Hebrew text to be utterly unreliable and in need of continual correction. Such an attitude is dangerous and ungrounded. Occasional errors may be detected, a few may be surmised. The Jewish marginal corrections, the *Keris,* may occasionally prove suggestive. But on the whole we have a text which is quite pure and satisfactory. It is not to be tampered with or modified according to the far less reliable Septuagint, the Targums, the Peshitto, or the

Samaritan Pentateuch, though occasionally these versions (or transliterations) may contribute a bit of material valuable from the standpoint of textual criticism.   The text is, furthermore, not to be modified according to subjective principles, such as critical theories or clever conjectures, which are anything but scientific.   Modern critical editions of the Hebrew text, such as Kittel's *Biblia Hebraica,* Stuttgart, (1929), contain much misleading material and must apart from the Masoretic text be used with great caution.   The traditional Masoretic text is in a good state of preservation and deserves far more confidence than is usually accorded to it.   In our Hebrew Bibles we have a very good Hebrew text.

The other matter that may be considered in this connection is the question whether Genesis is a poem and therefore to be considered as Hebrew verse.   On the question, which are the poetical books in the Canon, the Jews have always had a very reliable tradition.   It would be strange if they themselves should have lost sight of the poetic character of the first one of their sacred writings if it had actually been poetic. The method by which outstanding exponents of this unusual hypothesis, like Sievers, arrived at their conclusions is enough to make anyone suspicious of the idea.   This method involves abandoning the first principle of Hebrew poetry (parallelism) ; it necessitates changes or substitution of the divine name; it includes occasional textual alterations merely for the sake of securing the desired meter; and even then the type of meter which seemingly was discovered is not in evidence as clearly as we are led to believe.   Neither the present text nor the original sources, as others claim, were ever cast in verse form, with the exception of such minor portions that bear the earmarks of poetry (4:23, 24; 9:25-27; 49:2-27).   But we are perfectly ready to admit that Genesis has many portions of very fine rhythmical prose that rise almost to the level of exalted strains of poetry (cf. 1:27, 28; 12:1-3, and many other passages).

5. Historical Character of the Record

The issue involved briefly stated is: Have we history or legend in Genesis? A notable array of famous scholars can be cited in support of what the great majority of writers on the subject in our day regard as the only tenable view, namely Genesis is legend. From Wellhausen down outstanding names are Gunkel, Jeremias, Driver, Skinner, Procksch, etc., etc. However, we are not impressed by this array of learning, which we must without reservation class as pseudo-science on matters of this sort. Strong dogmatic presuppositions are too definitely displayed by these scholars: miracles are considered as practically impossible; so is plenary inspiration; Israel's history can rise to no higher levels than the Babylonian or the Egyptian; an arbitrary evolutionary standard is to be employed in measuring historical evidence. Besides, the following facts of Israel's history are overlooked: a) the utter dissimilarity of the Genesis record and the legends of the nations (the sober common sense of average Christians has always been able to detect this difference much more clearly than the over-trained scholar, who often loses entirely his sense of perspective); b) the clear distinction preserved by Israel's sacred records of the successive stages of revelation (4:26; 17:22-27; Exod. 6:3; Exod. 20; Deut. 18:15-19; I Sam. 3:1, etc.); c) the accuracy of Israel's historical tradition (13:10; chapter 14; 20:20-24; chapter 25; 26:1; cf. also chapter 5 and chapter 10); d) distinct efforts by the patriarchs to perpetuate the remembrance of events of outstanding religious importance (12:7; 13:18; 21:33; 33:20); e) the sober tone displayed in recording the most exalted revelation (we refer to the following chapters 12, 15, 18, 22, and 32:23-32); f) the utter impartiality displayed in

recording the history of those who are the patriarchs
and the fathers of tribes (12:10 ff; 20:1-18; 26:1-17;
30:1-43; chapter 34; chapter 38). Koenig's *Commentary* (p. 80 ff.) gives additional material on this
score.

A proper evaluation of the facts enumerated above
leads definitely to the conclusion that Genesis gives a
sober, accurate, historical account of the events that
led to the separation of Israel from among the nations
and to her establishment as a new nation with a divinely given destiny. If the other nations of this period
are known to have had no records that for accuracy
and sound historical pragmatism can begin to compare
with the Biblical accounts, that cannot in any wise
impugn the singular merit of the latter. Criticism has
shown itself singularly weak in the direction of evaluat-
ing comparatively the merit of Biblical history. Attempts to cut everything of superior merit found in
Israel's Sacred Writings down to the level of contemporary literature is still the bane of scholarship in
the Old Testament field.

We may at this point take issue with the claim
commonly raised in our day that Genesis, *as to its con-
tents,* as well as other older Biblical books falls in the
category of *poetry* rather than history. Apparently,
they who take this position are reluctant about claiming that such books are legendary in character. That
would seem derogatory to their distinctive character.
Yet they would prefer not to be bound to accept the
Creation account, the record of the Fall, and the like
as literal history. Then these ancient tales would be
a grand poetic conception, involving a deeper view of
truth yet allowing for a great variety of interpretations such as may be suited to the fancy of the individual. We are utterly out of sympathy with such an
attitude; for it does not conform to the facts of the
case. Nothing in the book warrants such an approach.
It is rather a straightforward, strictly historical ac-

count, rising, indeed, to heights of poetic beauty of expression in the Creation account, in the Flood story, in the record of Abraham's sacrifice of Isaac, in Judah's plea before Joseph, and the like. But the writer uses no more of figurative language than any gifted historian might, who merely adorns a strictly literal account with the ordinary run of current figures of speech, grammatical and rhetorical.

The various other types of construction put particularly upon the patriarchal stories, like the tribal or ethnological theory; the astral myth theory; the purely mythical theory, and the like are evaluated at the beginning of the patriarchal record (Gen. 12).

Rather closely tied up with the question of history is that of *chronology*. The prevailing attitude on questions of chronology is to discard the Biblical data and to accept as authoritative the far more difficult and uncertain Babylonian and Egyptian systems of reckoning, as they are computed in our day. Barton, *Archaeology and the Bible,* (Philadelphia, 1937), p. 56-61, gives the beginner a good idea how these computations are made and how far back they reach with a fair measure of accuracy. But it must be said with emphasis that the Biblical chronology excels all others in completeness, simplicity and accuracy; and, though, indeed, there are unsolved chronological problems, the Biblical chronology deserves our fullest confidence also for the pre-Mosaic age and for the earliest history of mankind. Michell, *The Historical Truth of the Bible,* (London, 1926) shows excellently how Babylonian and Egyptian chronology, rightly construed, agrees with the Biblical system of chronology.

6. Criticism

Unfortunately, in the field of the Mosaic writings negative literary criticism — higher literary criticism so called — has wrought incalculable confusion and still is the bane of fruitful investigations in this field.

Therefore it behooves us, first of all, very briefly to summarize the critical position in reference to Genesis or, for that matter, in reference to the entire Pentateuch. This summary is designed primarily for non-theologians and, therefore, makes no claim to completeness.

Critics speak with much assurance, as though the proof for their position were unassailable, of the various sources that have been worked into the Pentateuch as we now have it; and they assure us that this composite work was finally compiled by an editor — commonly called Redactor (R) — after the time of the Exile perhaps as late as 400 B. C. The four major documents that have been worked into the Pentateuch are not only occasionally discernible in the work as a whole, but the cord has, as it were, been unravelled, and the four strands that compose it are laid before us side by side. The names given to these four documents or their authors are: a) the Elohistic document, written by the Elohist — abbreviated designation E — ; b) the Jahvistic or Yahwistic document — described as J; c) the Priestly document or P; and d) the Deuteronomic document — or D. Some critics consider E, J, D, and P as persons, others regard them as literary schools.

The reasons advanced for the separation of the whole into four major documents are again mainly four. First and foremost to this day the use of the *divine names* is a mark of authorship. Thus: the Jahvist (or Yahwist) uses the divine name Jehovah or Yahweh almost exclusively; the Elohist uses Elohim, the common name for God in the Hebrew; the Priestly writer also prefers Elohim; the Deuteronomist is marked by other characteristics. Secondly, each of these writers is said to have developed a *vocabulary* which is distinctly his own. However, in the case of J and E this is not as prominent a feature as in reference to P and D. Thirdly, certain *types of subject matter* are found quite regularly in certain of

these original documents: J likes narratives whose
scenes are laid in Judah; E prefers those that played
in the territory of the Northern Kingdom; P deals
with matters of legislation; and D is hortatory in his
treatment of all he presents. Lastly, the *style* of these
four presents quite naturally four different aspects:
"J excels in picturesque 'objectivity' of description";
"E, on the other hand, frequently strikes a vein of
subjective feeling, especially of pathos"; P is precise
and formal; D is the orator. It must be admitted
that an imposing array of arguments confronts us
here. Certainly, an immense amount of labor has
been expended on these studies. Many of the issues
involved are of a so highly technical nature as to confuse the layman, especially when Hebrew terms multiply, that he believes the issues must be left to pro-
fessional theologians and is all too ready to follow
their guidance if they adopt, as is often the case, a tone
of utter finality.

First of all, on the matter of the use of the divine
names, are we not taking a higher and more reasonable ground if we assume that they were used primarily according to their specific meaning and not
merely because the writer in question knew only the
one or tried to reflect a period where only the one
was known, or was addicted to the stylistic peculiarity
of the use of the one rather than the other? A good
parallel on the New Testament level is the fine distinction observed by all the writers between the personal
name "Jesus" and the official title "the Christ." Surely, if the one or the other had used the one of these
names exclusively, it would have been a failure to
appreciate deeper and vital issues. So on the Old Testament level "Elohim" is the generic name for God from
the root which signifies "to fear" or "reverence."
Therefore Elohim is the divine being whose power
and attributes inspire mortals with due fear. "Jehovah," more correctly written "Yahweh," signifies the

Abiding, Changeless, and Eternal One, and therefore describes God as the one true to His covenant relationship in reference to His people. When the writer desires to express the thought that the one or the other aspect of the divine character was *especially* displayed in a certain event, he uses the name appropriate to this purpose. That does not say that the other·aspect of the divine character was not in evidence at all. In fact, we might in some instances even have been inclined, but for the author's suggestive use of the divine name, to think the other of the two characteristics predominated. In the following exposition of Genesis we hope we have demonstrated the fine propriety that from this point of view is discernible in the use of the divine names according to their sense.

This approach of ours to the problem of the use of the divine names is by no means in conflict with Exod. 6:3: "I appeared unto Abraham, unto Isaac, and unto Jacob as God Almighty; but by My name Jehovah I was not known to them." For, in the first place, of course, "name" according to the Hebrew significance of *shem* means about as much as "character." The statement, however, though made absolutely, is meant relatively, as are many other statements in Scripture (Hos. 6:6; Matt. 5:34; I John 3:9 by way of example). The revelation of God's Yahweh-character given to the patriarchs is so far below the revelation of the same character that is about to be displayed in the Exodus that by comparison one would say that now this character is first really being manifested. The critics had better not press the literal meaning of this passage (Exod. 6:3) too much, for then it becomes a sharp two-edged sword. For when they use it to prove that there was an earlier period where Elohim was used and not Yahweh, this passage is having a new element foisted upon it by them. Exodus 6:3 does not set *Elohim* and *Yahweh* in contrast but *'El Shadday* (God Almighty) and *Yahweh,* a thought which the critical position cannot use at all, in fact, a very embarrassing thought. It militates directly against the earlier use of *Elohim.*

The seemingly formidable argument from vocabulary, separate and distinct vocabularies for the four source documents—especially where long lists of words appear used only in the one document — this argument we say loses its imposing character when we discern on what ground it is built. Leaving J and E aside because the argument carries little convincing weight under this head, we notice what happens in the case of P and D. Everything of a priestly legislative character is primarily assigned to P as well as everything that is presented after a more or less formal pattern like Gen. 1 as well as summaries. From these portions primarily deductions are made as to P's vocabulary. Naturally quite a substantial list results. Then other passages in the Pentateuch that use these distinctive terms are stamped as coming from P, whenever possible. Note how in the last analysis in legislative portions like Leviticus, where matters of priestly interest certainly predominate, a distinctive vocabulary *has* to be used and can very readily be listed. The fact of the matter really is not that a different writer is at work but that the same writer is dealing with an entirely different subject. No man can write a law book with the vocabulary of a book on history. From another point of view the argument practically amounts to this that one man could not write E or J and also P, because one man could not write both history and law. In like manner D's style, which is supposed to involve "a long development of the art of public oratory," covers the major part of the book of Deuteronomy as well as of later books whenever they contain hortatory passages after the manner of Deuteronomy. One can quite readily build up a separate vocabulary out of such sections. In the final analysis this is tantamount to saying that Moses could not have written such admonitions and exhortations as well as laws and history. The critics operate on the assumption that such flexibility of style is beyond the range of the capabilities of one man.

The other peculiarities that these major sources are supposed to display are most readily understood on the following assumption: take any longer work and divide it up into four portions on the basis of an approach that groups kindred things together, and the resultant four parts will naturally each have something distinctive.

There are other failings that mark the critical approach to the problem. The argument in a circle is, for example, employed frequently. We shall draw attention to quite a number of instances in the course of the following exposition. Passages having a certain type of vocabulary are assumed to belong to one source; when that type of vocabulary is discovered, the proof that there is such a source is treated as complete. Again, when added details appear that were not indicated at the commencement of a narrative, these added details, though they are merely supplementary to the original statements, are construed as being at variance with the original, and so evidence for the existence of two or more separate sources is manufactured, whereas, in reality, other sides of the matter are merely coming to the surface, as every unbiased reader can readily detect.

Again and again the critical approach gives evidence of being guided by purely subjective opinion instead of by valid logical proof. The critic expected that the writer would proceed to follow up a certain approach by a certain type of statement — at least the critic would have followed up by such a statement. The author's failure to offer what the critic expected is supposed to constitute sufficient proof that the case in point is an instance where two documents have been welded together rather crudely. Equally common is the critical practice of conjecturing how the Hebrew text may originally have read, especially if the Hebrew text offers material conflicting with the critical theories, and the Septuagint happens to disagree more or less with the Hebrew. Strangely, in such cases the conjectures as to the original form of the text always offer support to the critical position.

Analogous to the above point is this: when the different aspects of a case are presented, critics quite regularly fail to discern the deeper harmony that prevails in spite of the surface disagreement. So very frequently, after one motive for a deed has been indicated, the mention of a second motive is treated as proof of a divergent approach by a different writer, as though life were always so simple a thing, as to allow for the operation of but one motive at a time, instead of the complex thing that it is, where motives, countermotives, and subsidiary motives run crisscross through one another.

Of the failings of the critical approach perhaps the greatest of all is the failure to evaluate rightly the attitude and the words of Christ and His apostles in reference to books like those of Moses. As Christ treated Moses' writings so should we. His clear words attributing them to Moses dare not be ignored. This is not treating the Old Testament without regard for the distinction between the Old and the New Testament. This is following the excellent Reformation principle: "Interpret Scripture by Scripture"; and a sounder principle cannot be found. Critics dismiss the Savior's attitude with a shrug of the shoulder.

Unfortunately, it is impossible to treat the Old Testament in an expository way without taking the major features of the critical approach into consideration, especially since these critical findings have been popularized and appear on the shelves of public libraries, as does Dummelow's *One Volume Commentary*.

Surely, the main errors of criticism should be shown in order to combat the evil at its source. Those who do not stand in need of the aid that a refutation may offer or are not impressed by the critical claims may, of course, leave those paragraphs that deal with critical matters·aside. We have sought to let this apologetic material occupy a place of very inferior importance. Hardly five per cent of the total deals with critical problems.

We shall leave aside all the very able constructive works that orthodox teachers of the church have provided under this head: the works of Haevernick, Hengstenberg, Keil, Rupprecht, and Moeller. These men have ably refuted all critical contentions; only the critics fail to discern that they have been answered. Those who would specialize on these matters will find most ample treatment of the subject in the works of these men. We for our part prefer in this exposition to follow the course of showing in our own way the beautiful and the consistent harmony of the individual accounts, a harmony which is in itself the strongest index of single rather than of composite authorship. Occasional critical questions naturally come in for their share of attention. Our treatment will show that we have drawn upon the above mentioned Old Testament scholars, a fact that we have acknowledged wherever feasible. It will also appear that much can be learned from the more recent Eduard Koenig, though in a number of cases his works must be used with caution.

7. Outline

Of course, the book naturally is divided into two halves: the first (chapters 1-11) dealing with the general history of mankind; the second (chapters 12-50) with the special history of God's people. Going into greater detail, we could devise many other subdivisions. However, the author himself has provided an outline indicated by special headings, for he uses the heading *'elleh toledôth,* "these are the generations" (A. V.) = "this is the story," ten times and actually treats under this heading the story indicated by the heading, as of Adam, 5:1-6:8, etc. This is more than a formal division. If the inferior elements receive but scant consideration, viz. Shem, Ishmael, and Esau, in some cases, in fact, only about seven verses, that merely indicates that there are things of minor as well as of major importance to be treated in a work such as this. If the author provides an outline and clearly indicates what it is, why reject it and try to devise a better one especially in an inspired book? In the following outline we have merely shown the subdivisions of the ten *toledôth* or the Ten "Histories."

Introduction (1:1-2:3)
    Introduction — the Creation Account.

  I. *The First History — that of Heaven and Earth* (2:4-4:26).

    a) Supplementary details of the Creation account (2:4-25).

    b) The Temptation and the Fall (chapter 3).

    c) The Early Development of the Sinful Human Race (chapter 4).

  II. *The History of Adam* (5:1-6:8).

    a) The Separate Development of the Godly (chapter 5).

    b) The Commingling of the Two Races (6:1-8).

  III. *The History of Noah* (6:9-9:29).

    a) Noah's Piety (6:9-12).

    b) How Noah was preserved (6:13-9:17).

    c) The Future of the Races of Mankind Foretold (9:18-29).

IV. *The History of the Sons of Noah* (10:1-11:9).

    a)   The Sons of Japheth (10:1-5).
    b)   The Sons of Ham (10:6-20).
    c)   The Sons of Shem (10:21-31).
    d)   The Tower of Babel, or The Confusion of Tongues (11:1-9).

V. *The History of Shem* (11:10-26).

VI. *The History of Terah* (11:27-25:11).

    a)   The Life of Terah (11:27-32).
    b)   The Life of Abraham (12:1-25:11).

    1.   The Call of Abraham and the Exodus from Haran (12:1-9).
    2.   A trip to Egypt during a Famine (12:10-21).
    3.   Separation from Lot (13:1-18).
    4.   The Defeat of the Kings by Abraham (14:1-24).
    5.   God's Covenant with Abraham (15:1-21).
    6.   The Birth of Ishmael (16:1-16).
    7.   The Covenant Sealed by New Names and by Circumcision (17:1-27).
    8.   The Manifestation of Yahweh at Mamre (18:1-33).
    9.   Guilt and Destruction of Sodom (19:1-38).
        Sequel: Lot's Degeneration.
    10.   Abraham and Sarah at Gerar (chapter 20).
    11.   Birth of Isaac and Expulsion of Ishmael (21:1-21).
    12.   Abraham's Covenant with Abimelech at Beersheba (21:22-34).
    13.   The Sacrifice of Isaac (22:1-19).
    14.   Nahor's Descendants (Rebekah) (22:20-24).
    15.   Death and Burial of Sarah (23:1-20).
    16.   Isaac's Marriage (16:1-67).
    17.   Abraham's Second Marriage and His Death (25:1-11).

VII.   *The History of Ishmael* (25:12-18).

VIII.   *The History of Isaac* (25:19-35:29).

1.   Birth and Early History of the Twin Brothers (25:19-34).

2.   Various Scenes from Isaac's Life (chapter 26).

3.   Isaac blesses Jacob (27:1-45).

4.   Jacob's Dismissal from Home and His First Vision (27:46-28:22).

5.   Jacob's Double Marriage (29:1-30).

6.   Jacob's Children and His Increasing Wealth (29:31-30:43).

7.   Jacob's Flight from Laban; their Treaty (31:1-54).

8.   Preparations for Meeting Esau (31:55-32:32).

9.   Reconciliation with Esau; Settling in Canaan (33:1-20).

10.   The Outrage on Dinah Avenged by her Brothers (chapter 34).

11.   The Last Events of Isaac's History (35:1-29).

IX.   *The History of Esau* (chapter 36).

X.   *History of Jacob* (37:2-50:26).

1.   Joseph Sold into Egypt (37:2-36).

2.   The Danger that Threatened Jacob's Sons (chapter 38).

3.   Joseph's Imprisonment because of his Steadfastness (chapter 39).

4.   Interpretation of the Prisoners' Dreams by Joseph (chapter 40).

5.   Joseph's Exaltation (chapter 41).

6.   The First Journey of Joseph's Brethren to Egypt without Benjamin (chapter 42).

7.   The Second Journey to Egypt with Benjamin (chapter 43).

8. The Test Successfully Met by Joseph's Brethren (chapter 44).

9. Joseph Revealed to his Brethren; The Family Summoned to Egypt (chapter 45).

10. The Temporary Emigration of Israel to Egypt (chapter 46).

11. Israel Established in Goshen; Egyptian Famine Measures (47:1-26).

12. Jacob's Preparations for his End (47:27-49:32).

13. Jacob's Death and Burial (50:1-14).

14. Conclusion of Joseph's History (50:15-26).

8. Mode of Interpretation

There are several modes of interpretation current in our day that deserve to be stigmatized as inadequate and unsatisfactory. Some still prefer to *allegorize* portions of Scripture, rejecting the literal sense and seeking a hidden spiritual meaning, although hardly any would venture to follow this procedure exclusively and consistently. In rejecting this type of interpretation we do not question the validity of the interpretation that sees types of Christ in outstanding Old Testament characters especially where the New Testament suggests such a use. Much more common in our day is the fault of attempting *to press Old Testament Scriptures down to the level of the sacred writings of the heathen,* making them to be works patterned particularly after Babylonian source material. This type of interpretation includes what for want of a better name must be described as "debunking"—interpretation that speaks irreverently of venerable Old Testament characters, imputes the lowest possible motives to them, and so utterly fails to understand their ofttimes great and heroic faith. This approach often attempts nothing less than to discredit these sacred Scriptures as unworthy of use by the New

Testament church — an approach common in Germany at the present. Of course, there still is need of reminding that sound interpretation dare not disregard the difference between the Old and New Testament levels of revelation. Good exegetes, even up to the Reformation age, failed to reckon with the fact that the unchanging truth was revealed with ever increasing clearness and fulness, a revelation culminating in Christ Jesus. The fuller revelation of a later age was at times imputed to an earlier word that did not as yet embody the fuller expression. Of course, we do not for a moment imply any such thing as man's progressive achievement. Our principle of interpretation is to unfold the fulness of revealed truth by careful examination of the grammatical statement as well as of the historical circumstances of the inspired text in dependence upon the Spirit of revelation, who alone is able to lead us into all truth.

9. Value and Importance of Genesis

In a general way it would be correct to say that this book is singular in its kind, for it offers the only correct and satisfactory information that we possess concerning prehistoric times and the *Urgeschichte* ("history of the primitive ages"). It goes back beyond the reach of available historical sources and offers not mythical suppositions, not poetical fancies, not vague suggestions, but a positive record of things as they actually transpired and, at the same time, of matters of infinite moment for all mankind.

But more specifically, all this material relative to prehistoric times and the *Urgeschichte* really provides the most substantial and even fundamental theological concepts. The major theological concepts are incomplete and leave much to be desired, if the content that Genesis offers should be subtracted. Before God can be known as Savior, He must be understood as the Creator of humankind and of the world.

Just what manner of Father and Creator He is we find displayed in the two Creation chapters, Genesis 1 and 2. In like manner no adequate and correct conception of man is possible without a knowledge of the essentials concerning his creation, his original state, the image of God, and the like. Again, the problem of sin will constitute much more of a problem if the origin of sin, that is to say, the Fall into sin be not understood. With that fact correctly apprehended, we achieve a correct estimate of the degree of depravity that is characteristic of fallen men. Without the promise of ultimate victory through the Seed of the Woman all further revelations concerning the salvation to come must stand minus an adequate base upon which they can successfully build. In other words, certain vital questions in reference to the type of revelation that mankind needs find a satisfactory answer in Genesis and nowhere else.

Concerning some of these matters the legends and the traditions of mankind offer a bit of material, most of which is distorted by error; some of which, in the elements of truth that it contains, is too weak to be of any actual value. An illustration of the extent to which this material is available is the vague report current among the ancients that there once had been a Golden Age. The unreliability of such material is demonstrated by the utter absence of any tradition concerning a Fall into sin.

Disregarding the material relation to matters theological, we find that Genesis also provides the much needed foundations for all history. The vague surmises as to man's past prior historic times all stand corrected by the story of the beginnings of the human race in Adam, or by the story of the second beginning in Noah. Equally important are the very valid data concerning the unity of the human race as provided basically in Genesis 1 and in greater detail in chapter 10, incomplete though this latter chapter may be in regard to a few matters. So, too, the question as to the origin of the multiplicity of languages is disposed of by the account concerning the confusion of tongues. Similarly, the singular position of Israel among the nations, a challenge to every historian, finds an adequate explanation in the Call of Abraham. Of course, from that point onward Genesis no longer records general history but only the history of the Kingdom of God.

If at this point we append a summary of certain of the better known cosmogonies, or at least of those which have a certain affinity with the Biblical account, anyone can judge for himself whether the Biblical account in any sense seems to be a derivative.

The most famous of the non-biblical cosmogonies is the Babylonian or the so-called "Chaldean Genesis," which created such a stir at the time of its publication in 1876 after it had been unearthed as a part of the library of Ashurbanipal at Nineveh by George Smith in 1873. The several tablets on which the account is written are in a fairly good state of preservation. The story begins with an account that is a theogony — an account of the origin of the gods — in itself already an indication of a far inferior level. The true God did not come into being by a certain process, nor were there originally several deities. Now of these various deities one stood out as particularly aggressive and ferocious, the unsubdued Tiâmat — again a decidedly inferior point of view. For the struggle that impended Tiâmat, the old mother of gods, enlists as many of the old gods as she can and a whole crew of horrid monsters. The resulting conflict for supremacy (note the low moral level even among gods) is a truly titanic struggle in which the forces of the opposition are led by the great Babylonian deity Marduk. Marduk proves himself the stronger. He prevails over Tiâmat, cleaves her into two montrous halves, the upper of which he fixes in place as the heavens, in which in turn he fixes the heavenly bodies; and the lower of which halves, on the other hand, he sets in place as the earth. Then he compounds material of his own blood for the creation of man, the chief purpose of whose creation is "that the service of the gods may be established." This account of creation is so pronouncedly different from the Biblical account that the points of difference completely overshadow the incidental points of resemblance. To speak of a "striking resemblance between the two cosmogonies" certainly is a partisan overstatement of the case; and to go on to say that "the cosmogony of Genesis 1 rests on a conception of the process of creation fundamentally identical with that of the *Enuma elis* (the opening words of the Chaldean Genesis) tablets" is simply a distortion of the truth.

Of the Phoenician cosmogony it is sufficient to remark that it contains the idea of the world-egg, hatched out to produce the world. Analogous to this from this point of view is the Indian conception. The uncreated Lord appeared in chaos. The next step was to render this world visible by means of the five elements, by shining forth in brightest light and dispelling darkness. Into the water, which he creates first, he lays a germ cell. This becomes a gleaming egg in which Brahma is found, the source principle. A protracted period of hatching brings him to light. Aside from fantastic and confused elements it may well be that even this cosmogony carries within it certain echoes of the Genesis account which are all but forgotten.

The Parsee Genesis, appearing in a late book of the Bundehest, has at least this sequence of created things: 1. heaven, 2. water, 3. earth, 4. planets, 5. animals, 6. man. Nothing is said concerning the creation of light. The partial correspondence with the account of the Bible is obvious. But since this is a late book, this correspondence may have resulted from an acquaintance with the Biblical record.

Still more nearly parallel to the Biblical account is the cosmogony attributed to the Etruscans by the writer Suidas, who lived in the tenth century A. D. For the sequence runs thus: 1. heaven and earth, 2. firmament, 3. sea and water, 4. sun and moon, 5. souls of animals, 6. man. To the six items six periods of a thousand years each are assigned. Yet the influence of the Bible record is so very likely in the case of a writer of the tenth century of the Christian era that there is great likelihood that the writer's Christian ideas will have led him to find these successive items, which another might not even have noticed in the same material. Or else the ancient Etruscan tradition had absorbed a high percentage of Biblical thought on matters such as these.

One would expect the Persian cosmogony to be radically different and in conformity with the principles of dualism. In the Avesta time and light and darkness are uncreated. These constitute the true spiritual world. They are eternal because Mazda, the god of light, is himself eternal.

Hesiod informs us how the Greeks conceived of the origin of things. First there existed Chaos; thereupon the earth; next Tartarus; then Eros (Love), the most beautiful of the deathless gods. Out of Chaos night is born. The earth begets the heavens; then the ocean comes into being. After these Saturn, father of gods, existed. The rest of the pantheon follow him.

To the Egyptians several views on the origin of the earth are to be attributed. Some regarded the god Ptah as the craftsman who built the world. Others held that it was the goddess Neith who wove its fabric. The fundamental principle from which all things take their origin was thought to be water, for in it were fancied to be the male and the female germs of life.

Even the great god Ra was supposed to have sprung from it, though others believed that he had been hatched out of an egg.

We may well say that these cosmogonies are the best available outside the Genesis account. A man does not need any supernatural enlightenment to discern that not one of all these can compare even remotely with the scriptural account for depth of thought, simplicity, propriety and beauty. All the others disappoint us by their incompleteness, or by their confusion, or by their lack of sequence, or as being the embodiment of some deep-seated error. Their conception of God is most unsatisfactory and unworthy. Or if they rise to a higher level, we have reason for believing that the better element is traceable to the Bible as the source.

10. Bibliography

A. *Commentaries*

Delitzsch, Franz, *Commentar ueber die Genesis,* Leipzig: Doerffling and Franke, 1872.

Dillmann, August, *Die Genesis,* Leipzig: S. Hirzel, 4. edition. 1882.

Dods, Marcus, *The Expositor's Bible* (Genesis), New York: George H. Doran Co. No date.

Gunkel, Herman, *Handkommentar zum Alten Testament,* W. Nowak, editor. Goettingen: Vandenhoeck and Ruprecht. 1901.

Jamieson, Robert, *A Commentary Critical and Explanatory,* (Jamieson, Fausset and Brown). New York: George H. Doran. No date.

Keil, C. F., *Biblical Commentary on the Old Testament* (Genesis), (Keil and Delitzsch), Edinburgh: T. and T. Clark. 1875.

Koenig, Eduard, *Die Genesis,* Guetersloh: Bertelsmann. 1919.

Lange, J. P., *Bibelwerk* (Genesis), Bielefeld: Velhagen und Klasing. 1864.

Luther, Martin, *Saemtliche Schriften* (Genesis), St. Louis, Mo.: Concordia Publishing House. 1881. (2 vol.)

Procksch, Otto, *Kommentar zum Alten Testament* (Genesis), Ernst Sellin, editor. Leipzig: Deichert. 1913.

Skinner, John, *International Critical Commentary* (Genesis), Driver, et al editors. New York: Charles Scribner's Sons. 1925.

Strack, Hermann L., *Kurzgefasster Kommentar* (Genesis), Strack and Zoeckler, editors. Muenchen: C. H. Beck. 1905.

Vilmar, August Fr. C., *Collegium Biblicum* (Genesis), Christian Mueller, editor. Guetersloh: Bertelsmann. 1881.

Whitelaw Thomas, *The Pulpit Commentary* (Genesis), H. D. M. Spence, editor. London: Kegan Paul, Trench and Co. 1882.

References to these commentaries have been made exclusively by the author's name, as Delitzsch. Quotations appear, of course, under the verse that is being treated. Consequently, reference to pages was consistently omitted.

As to the position taken by these commentaries, works such as those of Dillmann, Dods, Strack may be classed as moderately critical. Gunkel, Procksch and Skinner belong into the class of the extremely critical. Delitzsch finally yielded to the blandishments of the critical approach and accepted at least the source theory in its major features but still put the critical work into the category of secondary importance. Jamieson disregards critical issues. Keil, seconded in many a case by Lange, did very substantial work in the direction of establishing the validity of the conservative approach. Whitelaw works in a similar spirit. Luther's comments naturally have a very different purpose but are still to be read with profit. Koenig does the most constructive work among modern writers, but unfortunately, he yielded to the source theory, though even in this his position is moderate.

B. *Dictionaries*

Buhl, Frants, *Gesenius' Handwoerterbuch ueber das alte Testament*; Leipzig: F. C. W. Vogel. 1905.

Brown, Driver, Briggs, *A Hebrew and English Lexicon of the Old Testament* (based on Gesenius). New York: Houghton Mifflin Co. 1907.

Koenig, Eduard, *Woerterbuch zum Alten Testament*. Leipzig:Dieterich. 1922. (2. and 3. edition.)

C. *Versions*

Holy Bible, Revised Version, American Standard Edition. 1901.

King James Version.

Luther's *German Bible.*

Smith, J. M. Powis, *The Old Testament, An American Translation* (Genesis by Theophile J. Meek). Chicago: University of Chicago Press. 1927.

Rahlfs, Alfred, *Septuaginta.* Stuttgart: Privilegierte Wuertembergische Bibelanstalt. 1935.

Onkelos, *Targum,* New York: Hebrew Publishing Co. No date.

D. *Other Helps copiously used*

Bailey and Kent, *History of the Hebrew Commonwealth* (revised edition). New York: Charles Scribner's Sons. 1935.

Barton, George A., *Archaeology and the Bible* (seventh edition). Philadelphia: American Sunday School Union. 1937.

Edersheim, Alfred, *Bible History* (The World before the Flood. Vol. I). New York: Fleming H. Revell Co.

Hengstenberg, Ernst Wilhelm, *Beitraege zur Einleitung ins Alte Testament* (Die Authentie des Pentateuches), Berlin: Oehmigke. 1836.

Hengstenberg, E. W., *Die Buecher Moses und Aegypten*, Berlin: Oehmigke. 1841.

Hengstenberg, E. W., *Christologie des Alten Testaments*, Berlin: Oehmigke. 1854.

Hengstenberg, E. W., *Geschichte des Reiches Gottes unter dem Alten Bunde*. Berlin: Schlawitz. 1869.

Hofmann, J. C. K., *Weissagung und Erfuellung*. Noerdlingen: Beck. 1841.

Jeremias, Alfred, *Das Alte Testament im Lichte des Alten Orients*. Leipzig: Hinrichs. 1904.

Kittel, Rud., *Biblia Hebraica* (Genesis), Stuttgart: Priv. Wuert. Bibelanstalt. 1929.

Kœnig, Eduard, *Geschichte der Alttestamentlichen Religion*. Guetersloh: Bertelsmann. 1912.

Kœnig, E., *Geschichte des Reiches Gottes*. Berlin: Warneck. 1908.

Kœnig, E., *Die Messianischen Weissagungen des Alten Testaments*. Stuttgart: Belser. 1923.

Kœnig, E., *Theologie des Alten Testaments*. Stuttgart: Belser. 1922.

Michell, G. B., *The Historical Truth of the Bible*. (Part I. The Comparative International History of the Old Testament) London: Marshall Bros. 1925.

Moeller, Wilhelm, *Biblische Theologie des Alten Testaments*, etc. Zwickau: Herrmann.

Oehler, Gust. Fr., *Theologie des Alten Testaments*, Stuttgart: Steinkopf. 1882.

E. *Grammars*

Gesenius, Wilhelm, *Hebraeische Grammatik* (revised by E. Kautzsch). 27. ed. Leipzig: Vogel. 1902.

Kœnig, Eduard, *Lehrgebaeude der Hebraeischen Sprache*. (Part II. Syntax.) Leipzig: Hinrichs. 1897.

F. *Abbreviations of the titles of the above works commonly used*

A. V. = King James Version.

A. R. V. = American Standard Edition of the Revised Version.

B. D. B. = Gesenius' Lexicon by Brown, Driver, Briggs.

B. T. = Moeller's *Biblische Theologie.*

G. A. T. = Kœnig's Geschichte der Alttestamentlichen Religion.

G. K. = Gesenius' *Grammatik* rev. by Kautzsch.

G. R. G. = Kœnig's *Geschichte des Reiches Gottes.*

K. C. = Kœnig's *Kommentar* on Genesis.

K. S. = Kœnig's *Syntax.*

K. W. = Kœnig's *Woerterbuch.*

T. A. T. (K.) = Kœnig's *Theologie des Alten Testaments.*

T. A. T. (O.) = Oehler's *Theologie des Alten Testaments.*

CHAPTER I

The Introduction — The Creation Account (1:1-2:3)

The object of this double title is to indicate that on the one hand, this is the Introduction which Moses has provided for the entire book of Genesis as well as, on the other hand, that this Introduction is given in the form of an account of creation.

It requires no deep insight to discern the basic character of this Introduction, both for the book as well as for all revelation. Man will go back in his thinking to the point where the origins of all things lie; he will desire to know how the world as well as all that is in it, and, most particularly, how he himself came into being. Here is the record, complete and satisfactory from every point of view, even if it does not perhaps answer every question that a prying curiosity might raise. He, however, who will ponder sufficiently what is here actually offered, will find facts of such magnitude as to stifle unseemly curiosity as to secondary matters.

Enthusiastic have been the comments of all who have read this account in an attitude of faith. Believing hearts are moved to devout praise of God and to adoration of His unbounded wisdom, power and mercy. Over against the criticism of our day even moderately critical writers offer comments such as Skinner (p. 11): "It is a bold thing to desiderate a treatment more worthy of the theme, or more impressive in effect, than we find the severely chiselled outlines and stately cadences of the first chapter of Genesis." Procksch, contrasting the basic thought of the chapter with all other literatures, advances the claim: "That the universe rises out of nothing by the almighty creative power of God is a thought so broad in its poetic as well as in its theological scope found nowhere in such clear-cut outlines in world literature before P."

The Scriptures themselves treat this account as pure history. Note the following passages: Exod. 20:9-11; 31:17; Ps. 8 and 104; Matt. 19:4-6; II Pet. 3:5; Heb. 4:4.

When the question is raised as to the sources of the truths set forth in this Introduction, we must freely admit that we know nothing about them. There are several possibilities. That Moses himself received the whole chapter by direct revelation is possible. Equally, if not more, reasonable is the assumption that divine revelation communicated to our first parents the account of creation. From them it came by tradition to Moses, who recorded the whole under divine inspiration, purging it from errors or inaccuracies, should any have begun to creep into the traditional version of it by this time. That, however, such tradition may have continued relatively, if not entirely, pure appears from the following three facts: first, the number of links in the chain of persons from Adam to Abraham was very few because of man's longevity at this time, and Abraham's time was already one of intense literary activity; secondly, godly men who perpetuated this tradition would have employed extreme care to preserve it correct in all its parts; thirdly, the memory of men who trusted more to memory than to written records is known to have been unusually retentive. But whatever explanation an individual may devise to make plain to others that tradition may have played a part in bringing this priceless record to us, and even if he grant the possibility of written records of this tradition prior to the time of Moses, all such supposition dare never be construed as conflicting with the very basic fact that Genesis 1 is revelation.

Suppositions like that of Dillmann and many others that the Israelitish mind was equipped with a better understanding of God and let the light of this insight be trained on the problem of the origin of all things and devised this which is to date still the best solution, are not satisfactory. Such claims are an attempt to dispose of immediate revelation as well as of plenary inspiration and are besides hardly reasonable. How could human ingenuity ever have penetrated into the divine order and manner of creation, when no witness to these works could ever be found? In any case, such explanations as to how the account was derived make of it a series of surmises and remove entirely the possibility of the objective correctness and the complete reliability of this record. All that remains is that of all speculations man ever elaborated about the origin of the world this is still by all odds the best. The claims and the attitude of the Scriptures, however, are met only by the explanation that says: This chapter was received by divine revelation; it contains full and absolute truth and only truth.

In order to make this scriptural account appear as just one more cosmogony it has become a common procedure to make more or less extensive comparisons with other cosmogonies as they are found here and there in the records of the traditions of the nations. We offer, however, a more extensive examination of these so-called "creation accounts" above in our Introductory Remarks (p. 27). A fair comparison with such materials makes our remarks above appear all the more reasonable.

Taking this creation account as a whole, how shall we arrange the work of the six days? Is there any possibility of grouping within the six days? Most schemes that are advanced are not entirely perfect, but they may yet contain a generous element of truth. It seems as though the best pattern or the categories that man employs are not of a big enough

mold to serve for the creation as God brings it about.
Let a few of these subdivisions be submitted. Thomas
Aquinas (1225-1274), mentioned by Strack, suggested
two triads of days, the first three concerned with works
of division, the second three with works of embellishment. Yet the third day's work in its second half
certainly comes under the head of embellishment. A
second suggestion notices the manifest parallel between the two triads of days, pointing to the fact that
both the first and the fourth days are concerned with
a work that begins on high with light (or light
bearers). Then in the work of the second and the
fifth days the work drops to a lower level, namely,
to the firmament and to the birds of the air. Lastly,
on the third and the sixth days the creative work
moves on the level of the earth and accomplishes a
double objective, namely on the third, separation of
dry land and water and the production of green things,
whereas on the sixth day comes the creation of land
animals and man. The correspondence of the two
triads from this point of view cannot be denied, but
to try to imagine it as entirely adequate would overlook the work of the fifth day, which is double in character and drops not only to the level of the creation
of the birds of the air but also, unfortunately, to the
submarine level of the creation of fishes of the sea.
More satisfactory is Kœnig's arrangement which sees
four deficiencies or four instances of relative incompleteness listed in a definite order and sees the successive creative acts as removing these four in inverse
order, as we shall presently demonstrate.

But quite apart from such attempts to fit the
whole creation into a pattern of our own devising it
is immediately apparent that the account as a whole
proceeds from the lower to the higher, providing first
the basic essentials for existence as well as for plant
and for animal life, then running to a climax in the
creation of man for whose well-being and well-ordered

existence all previous steps in creation provide the adequate setting. So the account abundantly displays that God is a God of order. The very general formula devised by Driver (quoted by Skinner) is as satisfactory as any: "The first three days are days of preparation, the next three are days of accomplishment."

1. **In the beginning God created the heavens and the earth.**

The phrase "in the beginning" (*berêshîth*) refers to the absolute beginning of created things, to the *Uranfang*. This fact is supported by the following arguments in the face of many and strong claims to the contrary. 1. The corresponding phrase in Greek, ἐν ἀρχῆ, which the Septuagint translators used here and which appears at the beginning of John's Gospel, is plainly a reference to the absolute beginning. 2. The noun *rêshîth* appears without the article, appearing in use practically as a proper noun, Absolute Beginning (K. S. 294 g). The Greek Hexapla of Origin supports this, for its transliteration with few exceptions gives βρησιθ, seldom βαρησηθ. 3. The rendering which takes the expression as referring to the absolute beginning of things makes for a simple, natural progression of thought and avoids that peculiar periodic sentence structure, which shall presently be discussed as highly unnatural.

Because this noun *berêshîth* is without the article, that does not allow for its being taken as a genitive or construct case, viz. "in the beginning of God's creating," etc., for with that rendering attention is at once centered on the second verse and no reason appears for mentioning "the beginning" at all.

Here, then, at the opening statement of sacred Scripture we are taken back to that point to which the human mind naturally will revert and in reference to which it asks: "What was the beginning of things?" This solemn and pithy statement gives man the information: the beginning was made by God in His creation of heaven and earth. As far as this world is concerned, it simply had no existence before this time.

He that did the creative work is said to be God, *'elohîm*. This Hebrew name is to be derived from a root found in the Arabic meaning "to fear" or "to reverence." It, therefore, conceives of God as the one who by His nature and His works rouses man's fear and reverence. It is used 2,570 times (KTAT-(K) p. 144). This name is not a characteristic mark of a particular source as E, or in a measure also P, as Old Testament criticism is in the habit of claiming. It is used by Moses in accordance with its meaning. The work recorded in chapter one in a very outstanding way sets forth God's mighty works of power and majesty. God's omnipotence outshines all other attributes in this account. Omnipotence rouses man's reverence and holy fear rather than his love. In other words, it brings the Creator to man's notice rather as *'Elohîm* than from any other point of view. In stressing this we are not blind to the fact that this chapter also shows forth God as Yahweh, the faithful, merciful one. The claim, however, that *Yahweh* might just as well be employed as *'Elohîm*, if the meaning of these names is to be considered, really ignores the facts we have just emphasized above — facts which criticism, by the way, gives heed to far less carefully than conservative writers give attention to the arguments in favor of the various sources, E, J. P, D, etc.

A thought by Procksch should be noted here: "It so happens very appropriately that the first named subject of Genesis as well as of the Bible is 'God'."

The verb describing God's initial work is "created" (*bara'*). This verb is correctly defined as expressing the origination of something great, new and "epoch-making," as only God can do it, whether it be in the realm of the physical or of the spiritual. The verb *bara'* does not of itself and absolutely preclude the use of existing material; cf. Isa. 65:18 b: "Behold I create Jerusalem a rejoicing, and her people a joy." Also note v. 27 of this chapter. However, when no existing material is mentioned as to be worked over, no such material is implied. Consequently, this passage teaches *creatio ex nihilo*, "creation out of nothing," a doctrine otherwise also clearly taught by the Scriptures; Rom. 4:17; Heb. 11:3; cf. also Ps. 33:6, 9; Amos 4:13. The verb is never used of other than DIVINE activity.

The *berō'*, which Kit. proposes in the margin in conformity with the claims of many, for *bara'*, i. e. the infinitive for the finite verb, and which yields the translation, "in the beginning of God's creating," etc., is not only entirely unnecessary but, unfortunately, leads to an involved and confused sentence structure in place of a simple and a clear one. Besides, such a change is born entirely out of the desire to make room for a particular interpretation, viz. the interpretation that claims long ages of the earth's existence prior to the creative work here to be described. To use this change of vowels is the equivalent of substituting a confused road for a straight and a simple one.

The object of God's creation was "the heavens and the earth." We should have said, He created "the universe." Since the Hebrew has no word for the universe and can at best say: "the all" (cf. Jer. 10:16; Isa. 44:24; Ps. 103:19; 119:91; Eccles. 11:5), certainly the far more colorful "heavens and earth" is to be preferred. Besides, there is a deeper truth involved. In reality the world is bipartite; it is not a unit as far as we are concerned. The two parts constituting the world or the universe were originally in perfect harmony with one another. Now there exists a deep breach between the two. The term *shamáyim* signifies the "upper regions" (K. W.) and is a plural form, a plural of intensity (K. C.), pointing to the heavenly spheres or regions which rise one above the other.

This explanation is to be preferred to the other (e. g. K. S.) which makes this a dual in reference to the two halves of the heavens which stretch each from the zenith to the horizon. The word for "earth," *'érets,* bears a meaning which may be "that which is lower," *das Niedere.*

Over against the claim that "the heavens and the earth" may well be the equivalent of "the universe" it is contended that "heavens" here can only mean the "firmament," as in v. 8, and "earth" can only refer to the "dry land," as in v. 10. But then the very proper question arises: why single out "heaven and earth" in this sense at all and mention their creation in v. 1? Besides, in this creation account another word is used in a broader and in a narrower sense; cf. "day" in 5a with "day" in 5b with "day" in 2:4 — actually *three* meanings.

Now is this first verse a heading or a title? By no means; for how could the second verse attach itself to a heading by an "and"? Or is this first verse a summary statement akin to a title, after the Hebrew manner of narrative which likes to present a summary account like a newspaper heading, giving the gist of the entire event? Again, No. For if creation began with light and then with the organizing of existing material, the question would crowd persistently to the forefront: but how did this original material come into being? for v. 1 could not be a record of its origin, because it would be counted as a summary account of the things unfolded throughout the rest of the chapter. Verse one is the record of the first part of the work brought into being on the first day: first the heavens and the earth in a basic form as to their material, then light. These two things constitute what God created on the first day. The Hebrew style of narrative just referred to may or may not be employed on occasion, depending on the author's choice. Here it does not happen to be used.

Here also the statement may be disposed of which says: The initial creation was a chaos. Such an assertion is misleading. It may be meant in a way which would be entirely wrong. If it implies that as the record stands v. 1-2 show an unsatisfactory state of achievement, it is all wrong. However, if the disorganized state of the first steps of creation is called "chaos," with the reservation that this implies no criticism but is necessarily only the first and unavoidable step from lower to higher forms, then the statement may be used. Or if it is only intended as a statement which covers what v. 2 covers with other terms, it cannot be said to be wrong.

Before dropping this verse we should take issue with the question: "Does the term *'Elohim,* being a plural, embody a reference to the Holy Trinity?" Two extremes must be guarded against in submitting an answer. He goes too far who sees in this plural a direct and explicit reference to the Holy Trinity. The plural is a potential plural (K. S. 263 a-c) indicating the wealth of the potentialities of the divine being, chiefly in so far as God by His very nature and being kindles man's deepest reverence. However, what all the wealth of this reverence-inspiring Being is, is not fully revealed in all detail by the Old Testament, least of all in the time of Moses. The term *'Elohim,* however, allows for all that which the fuller unfolding of the same old truth brings in the course of the development of God's Kingdom. When, then, ultimately the truth concerning the Trinity has been revealed, the fullest resources of the term *'Elohim* have been explored, as far as man needs to know them. Consequently, he who would claim that the term can have no connection with the truth of the Holy Trinity goes too far. Nor dare it be forgotten, as we shall show in connection with v. 2 and 3, that the text itself introduces references to the persons of the Trinity without definitely indicating, of course, that they are distinct

persons in the Godhead. In that connection certain
New Testament words will be seen to have bearing
upon the case. Consequently Luther's statement, made
in reference to v. 2, is quite in order when he says:
"Consequently the Christian Church on this point displays a strong unity that in this description is to be
found the mystery of the Holy Trinity." Even a
second statement of Luther's may be accepted, if it
be construed in the sense of the first: "But we have
clear testimony that Moses aimed to indicate the
Trinity or the three persons in the one divine nature."

Before we examine v. 2 by itself it is necessary
to see how v. 1-3 stand related to one another. There
would be no occasion for giving attention to this matter if the familiar English versions (King James or
A. R. V.) and the German are followed, for these very
correctly indicate that the sequence of clauses is as
natural as it can be. But two translations, diverging
from the familiar form, have thrust themselves to the
forefront, leaning for support on eminent Hebrew
scholars. As representative of the one may count what
Meek submits (*The Old Testament, An American
Translation*) : "When God began to create the heavens
and the earth, the earth being a desolate waste, with
darkness covering the abyss and the spirit of God
hovering over the waters, then God said: 'Let there
be light.' " This translation makes v. 2 a parenthesis,
or it would practically have it set off by dashes and
makes of v. 1 the protasis and of v. 3 the apodosis.
The second makes v. 1 protasis and v. 2 apodosis,
thus: "When God created the heavens and the earth,
then the earth was, etc. . . . and God said, etc."
(Raschi et al.). A third might be listed here, although
it has been disposed of above. It is that which makes
v. 1 the heading and then proceeds with v. 2 and 3
as follows: "Now as the earth lay there, a waste
and empty mass — and darkness, etc. — then God said,
etc." (Procksch). The last mentioned having been

refuted, we shall dispose of the details involved in
the first two as we examine v. 2 and v. 3 more fully.
For a summary refutation let the following points be
noted. Grammatically such translations as Meek and
Raschi offer are possible but in this case highly improbable. The Hebrew does co-ordinate clauses where
we prefer subordination. Longer sentences of involved structure are found also in 5:1 and Num.
5:12-15; Josh. 3:14-16 and in many other instances.
But a chapter marked throughout by very simple sentence structure would never begin with so complicated
a structure as any of the ones noted above. Besides,
against the first combination it must be noticed that
the first word of v. 2 could hardly be *ha'arets* but
would have to be *wattehî,* in spite of occasional exceptions noted here and there for emphasis' sake.
Wellhausen's dictum in regard to this modern translation is worthy of being preserved; he called it a
"desperately insipid construction" (*verzweifelt ge-
schmacklose Construction*).

2. **And now, as far as the earth was concerned, it was waste and void, and darkness was
upon the face of the deep; and the Spirit of God was
hovering upon the face of the waters.**

Of the two parts of the universe mentioned the
author abandons the first, "the heavens," as lying
outside of the sphere of the present investigation,
for of its creation we need not know or perhaps could
not understand its details. Moses definitely limits himself to the second of the two parts by emphatically
setting "the earth" first in the sentence. This yields
a shade of thought which our translation above tries
to reproduce by saying: "And now, as far as the
earth was concerned." Or one might render: "Now
this earth," etc. As has been remarked, from this
point onward the point of approach may be said to
be geocentric.

By an outstanding double expression (cf. for similar combinations 18:27 and 21:23) an almost onomatopoeic effect is secured to describe the utmost of an unformed and unshapen mass: "waste and void" — *tóhû wavóhû*. *Tóhû* is really a noun used as an emphatic adjective (K. S. 306 r), as is also, of course, *bóhû*. The verb "it was," *hayethah*, cannot bear the emphasis in a sentence where two such significant predicates follow (K. S. 326 b). It must merely serve as a copula (K. S. 338 q). Consequently, all attempts to put into this verb some thought like: the earth then was there, or lay thus for quite a time, are grammatically quite inadmissible. Now *tóhû* as such means originally *unformedness* (K. W.) and so can come to mean a "waste" only in the sense of being not yet put into shape, not in the sense of having been laid waste by some catastrophe, as all those would postulate who try at every point to make room for geologic periods of development. All later usage of the word points in the same direction. It occurs once again with *bóhû*, Jer. 4:23. In Deut. 32:10 the parallel thought is "wilderness." Isaiah uses it to describe the unreality of idols. In 41:29, where it is rendered "confusion," its parallel is "wind," and similar terms are "vanity" and "nought." Similarly, Isa. 40:17 offers as parallels: "nothing" and "less than nothing." Cf. also 40:23; 49:4; I Sam. 12:21. The passage Jer. 4:23 is not at variance with these claims, for though it pictures a state of desolation by the quotation of the whole phrase *tóhû wavóhû*, it evidently means that the land is again to be reduced to a state like unto the primeval chaos. Isa. 24:10 is analogous. *Bóhû* is derived from a root "to be empty," therefore "emptiness." It is applicable to a region without inhabitants of any kind. Its thought is clearly distinct from *tóhû*. Both terms together then indicate two directions in regard to which the newly created world will undergo further changes: first, it must be shaped and formed into definite molds; secondly, it must be peopled with all kinds of inhabitants or beings.

The next sentence, "and darkness was upon the face of the deep," indicates the last two deficiencies or incompletenesses characteristic of this newly formed earth — "deficiencies" being here taken not in the sense of a positive defect but negatively as mere want of those things which in the purpose of God were consecutively to be supplied. The verb "was" carries over from the preceding clause and need not be repeated here. All of what had thus far come into being was wrapped in complete and absolute darkness. This is the first deficiency. The second touched upon in this sentence is that that which lay under the darkness was "the deep." Yet even here the expression used is not merely *"upon the deep"* but *"upon the faces of the deep."* This "deep" had a variety of aspects, "faces." In fact, since "deep," *tehôm,* from the root *hûm,* "to resound," signifies the surging, raging primeval waters, the term implies anything but a monotonous peace and uniformity. Besides, the absence of the article stamps the word as a kind of proper noun, viz. that one and only primeval deep. Whether now this original form is characteristic of the whole earth or merely of its surface; whether it involved an earth that had, as it were, a solid kernel but merely a disturbed surface; or whether solid matter and water were originally churned up into one vast conglomerate neither solid nor liquid, no investigation on our part will ever determine.

In fact, whatever efforts are made to throw light upon the matter by drawing upon Babylonian myths, and particularly upon the monstrous deity Tiâmat, only confuse the issues. Those who at once identify *tehôm* with *Tiâmat* do so without any warrant. The mere similarity of names does not make the Biblical account a derivative from Babylonian sources. As

K. W. rightly remarks: "The spirit of the Old Testament has disavowed the personification of the term as well as its mythological implications." The holy writer was not going afield among the grotesque mythological figures of the Babylonian pantheon. His statement is too sober and the term employed quite uncontaminated by crude heathen notions. If any connection exists between the true, sober Biblical term *tehôm* and the mythological *Tiâmat,* the latter in the sober light of facts must be a derivation form the former during the process of the degeneration of the original truth possessed by mankind. *Tiâmat* lies so much farther down the scale as to appear as a very manifest corruption. That mere "waters" are meant here by *tehôm* is also apparent from the next clause, where the term "waters" is actually substituted for it.

Note well that we have above carefully avoided that rendering of the last clause of v. 2 which makes the verb involved to mean "brooding." A good example was set by the Septuagint translators who used the term ἐπεφέρετο, "was borne along"; "moved" (A. V.) is less colorful but not wrong. The verb *rachaph* from which the piel participle is used, *mera(ch)chépheth,* signifies a vibrant moving, a protective hovering. No single instance of the Biblical usage of the verb would suggest "brooding," a meaning which was foisted upon the word in an attempt to make it bear resemblance to various old myths that speak of the hatching out of the world egg — a meaning specially defended by Gunkel, the strong advocate of mythical interpretation. Deut. 32:11 surely will not allow for the idea of "brooding." An eagle may brood over eggs but not over "her young." The fact that the Syriac root does happen to mean "brood" cannot overthrow the Biblical usage, which takes strong precedence over mere similarity of root in kindred languages. Kœnig (K. W.) rightly shows how such similarity may mislead. The Syriac and the Aramaic *melakh,* which is the Hebrew

malakh, means in Syriac and Aramaic "to give counsel" and incidentally "to rule," but in Hebrew it signifies "to be king." Comparative philology has its limitations. Or the Arabic *hálika,* "to perish," appearing
as the Hebrew verb *halakh* signifies "to go."

But what exactly is "the Spirit of God"? Since
in this account the noun for God *'elohîm* is without
a doubt definite, the word "spirit" also becomes definite,
according to a simple rule of Hebrew syntax. Consequently, the thought must be ruled out that we are
dealing with some such concept as "divine Spirit."
It must definitely be rendered "the Spirit of God."
Nor is there any warrant for rendering *rûach* as
"wind" in this instance. The verb with which it is
construed implies too much to let the statement merely
mean that a wind fanned the face of the waters. Since,
then, it actually is God's Spirit, the question might
definitely be formulated thus: "Does *rûach 'elohîm*
mean God's spirit or God's Spirit? Is it a mere
potency in God or is it the Holy Spirit who is involved? Or does the term refer to a principle or to
a person?" We must guard against overstatement
of the case, but we maintain very definitely: the Spirit
of God is the Holy Spirit, the third person in the
Trinity. For all the attributes ascribed to this divine
person in the Old Testament agree fully with what is
revealed in the New Testament concerning His person
and His work. Absolutely none other than the Holy
Spirit is here under consideration. Yet it would be
inaccurate and premature to claim that this passage
alone conveys this fact clearly to the mind of man. It
may have been much later in the course of the fuller
unfolding of divine revelation that the truth came
home distinctly to the mind of believers that God's
Spirit was God, a separate person or *hypostasis.* Yet
the harmony of the Word within itself and its inspiration by this same Holy Spirit necessitated that the
statements made in earlier stages of revelation, never-

theless, are in accurate and full conformity with the truth. It may require the full light of New Testament revelation to enable us to discern that the Spirit of God here is the same as He who in the New Testament is seen to be the Holy Spirit; but having that light, we need not hesitate to believe that it sheds clear light back on the Old Testament usage of the expression. Davidson and Kœnig in their Theology of the Old Testament may deny this. Even Oehler may hesitate to make a clear-cut assertion. This explanation, nevertheless, does better justice to the facts. Does it not seem reasonable that the Spirit of inspiration should have so worded the words that bear upon His activity that, when the full New Testament revelation has come, all statements concerning the Spirit are in perfect harmony with this later revelation?

We could never believe that this hovering of the Spirit over the face of the waters was idle and purposeless. From all other activities that are elsewhere ascribed to the Holy Spirit we conclude that His work in this case must have been anticipatory of the creative work that followed, a kind of impregnation with divine potentialities. The germs of all that is created were placed into dead matter by Him. His was the preparatory work for leading over from the inorganic to the organic. K. C. feels impelled to interpret this "hovering" as "an intensified and vitalized type of vibration." We should not be averse to holding that the foundation for all physical laws operative in the world now was laid by this preparatory activity. Other passages relative to the Spirit as "the formative cause of all life" are to be found: Job 26:13; 27:3; Ps. 33:6; 104:30; 143:10; Isa. 34:16; 61:1; 63:11.

From the grammatical point of view it may be remarked that the participle *mera(ch)chepheth* refers to the past in a context which refers to the past (K. S. 237 a). Besides, as a participle it embodies the thought of continuation as well as the idea of repetition (K. S. 238 a). This "hovering" was not a single and instantaneous act. It rather describes a continued process. *Máyim*, "waters," is plural of extent not dual (K. S. 259 d). The article before "waters" is the article of "relative familiarity."

3. And God said: Let there be light! and there was light.

Nothing could be more uncalled for and unnatural than to try to make this verse a part of a complicated sentence structure. The simple statement *wayyó'mer*, "and He said," is apt to be estimated too lightly in this connection. It shows the manner in which God worked — by His Word. Heb. 11:3 gives the clearest expression of this fact. That in reality this creation was in and through the Son of God, who is also called the Word, appears from Col. 1:16; John 1:3; I Cor. 8:6; so that the second Person of the Holy Trinity is seen to be involved in the work of creation. True, this is but obscurely taught at this point, but it becomes a matter that is clearly confirmed by the New Testament. In the light of these later passages we must admit that the truth itself is provided for by the nature of the statements found in this basic record. All this serves to explain and to confirm more fully what we said above on v. 1 as conveying a reference to the Holy Trinity.

But besides it is here very clearly taught in what manner the creative work proceeded. It was all wrought by God's omnipotent word, not by mysterious emanations from the divine being, not by natural processes, not by self-causation, but in a manner worthy of God and revealing the character of God. He is at once discerned to be divinely powerful, intelligent, and far above the level of His poor creatures: "He speaks and it is done; He commands and it stands fast" (Ps. 33:9). Nothing is altered in reference to this fact if it be pointed out that as we now read the record the primal substance, "heaven and earth," was not said

(v. 1) to have been made by a divine word. To argue that it was not is to use the poor argument from silence. We do not know how this was made. But that for all the works that follow God is said to have spoken simply aims to bring that mode of the process more strongly to our attention.

After the primary substance on the first day the most ethereal of all things is brought into being, "light." It is at the same time the most essential prerequisite for life and existence. Since God proceeds in an orderly fashion, He begins at the natural startingpoint. We may not be shooting wide of the mark if we infer that with light that other form of energy, heat, must have sprung into being. How inextricably both are interwoven in the sun we all clearly see.

The Hebrew is really more expressive than the English for the word spoken by God which we render: "Let there be light." It is a vigorous imperative of the verb *hayah*, "to become": "Become light" and "became light." The German comes closer to the original: *Es werde Licht und es ward Licht.* He who notices at once that there was no sun to serve as a vehicle for the light observes the truth. But it ill behooves man to speak an apodictic word at this point and to claim that light apart from the sun is unthinkable. Why should it be? If scientists now often regard light as merely enveloping the sun but not as an intrinsic part of it, why could it not have existed by itself without being localized in any heavenly body? If, then, another hasty deduction is based upon this observation in reference to the length of the first three days, as though they could not have been twenty-four hour days because they were not regulated by the sun, the serious limitations of this argument are palpably apparent. The last three days are clearly controlled by the sun, which is created on the fourth day, and all of them are described in the same terms used for indicating the nature and the course of the first three — a strong argument that the first six days were alike in length and in nature and normal days of twenty-four hours.

No one need think it strange that an inanimate object is addressed as animate when God speaks to the light. The situation is really even stranger: God speaks to the things that are not that they might be. The nature of creation requires just that. K. C. need hardly list instances where inanimate objects are addressed; they do not constitute real parallels, for in every case objects already in existence are referred to: Isa. 43:6; Amos 9:3 f.; Nah. 1:4; Hag. 1:11.

So of the four deficiencies listed above one has been removed, "darkness."

A certain order prevails in regard to significant terms employed in this account. Delitzsch first drew attention to it. He finds ten creative words introduced by "and He said." Seven times the expression "and there was" is found, chronicling the result. "And He called" is found three times; "And He blessed," three times; "good" is used seven times. Whether these numbers were designed and counted by the author we cannot say. In any case, they tally with reality as it actually appears in the account: just so many times God spoke, blessed, etc. Even as in the world of nature certain things now appear in stated sequence or uniformity according to regular patterns, so God Himself, being a God of order, operates after a pattern of order in harmony with His own being. For seven is the number of divine works and operations; three, the mark of the divine person; ten, the mark of completeness. In God there is nothing that is accidental. Even the number of steps taken by Him in His work are in fullest harmony with His nature and being.

4. **And God saw that the light was good, and God separated the light from the darkness.**

Any account may be misread, and thoughts may be imputed to it that are utterly unworthy of it. So here it would surely be beneath the level of the pure and worthy conception of God which pervades the account to make this verse yield the thought that upon inspection God discerned that the work had turned out well, and so He promptly expressed His approval. Rather, this is, on the one hand, for our definite information that we might note that all works wrought by God were actually good and perfect and in every sense adequate for their purpose. There was no experimentation of an unskilled craftsman. There was no trying and testing after the fashion of toiling men. In fact, another very noble conception pervades it all; since there are no other beings to herald the Creator's praise, He, having achieved so praiseworthy a work, in this account Himself voices His approval that all men might know that in the very highest sense His work merited praise. The word for "good," *tobh,* is perhaps best rendered as "excellent" in these instances (B D B).

The construction of the first clause is marked by a slightly unusual order of words. It literally runs thus: "God saw the light that it was good" (A. V.), the noun "light" being taken into the first clause by "anticipation," also called *antitopsis* (K. S. 414 b). Besides, the conjunction *kî* is used more commonly than *'asher* to introduce such object clauses (K. S. 384 f).

It had better also be noted that we have thus far had two so-called anthropomorphisms: "God said" (v. 3) and "God saw" (v. 4). This should be remembered over against those who attempt to set chapter one to 2:3 over against the rest of chapter two as though two divergent accounts were being presented by different authors, who held variant conceptions of God, the author of chapter one being usually regarded as having a more exalted conception of God, and the author of chapter two as presenting a more anthropomorphic and less exalted view of the divine nature. Anthropomorphisms are certainly found also in chapter one.

When the next clause states, "God separated the light from the darkness," this does not mean "separated" in the sense of "disentangled." They were not commingled together. *Wayyabhdel* means literally, "and he caused a division," that is in point of time, one functioning at one time, the other dominating at another. One is as much an entity or principle as the other. "Darkness" is not cancelled and put out of existence. We can perhaps go so far as to claim that a *"spatial"* separation was also involved according to the terms of this account. Job 38:19 f., though largely a poetic statement, seems to give warrant for such a deduction. To make the idea of separation still more prominent the preposition "between" is repeated before the second noun, and both nouns are given the article. "Light" appeared already at the beginning of the verse with the article of relative familiarity (K. C.).

5. **And God called the light day and the darkness He called night. Then came evening, then came morning — the first day.**

On "came evening" see v. 8; also on the derivation of "evening."

To appreciate what this act means it is necessary to bear in mind what the Hebrew idea of giving a name or "calling a name" to an object implies. For this includes not only finding a convenient label to attach to a thing that it might thereby be identified, but especially the idea of expressing the very nature of a thing. In this act God did not find names for man to use when speaking of ʾay and night; there was not even a man present to hear these names. But this act reports that God fixed day and night separately for their respective purposes. This concluded the first day's work, for now the light prevailed that man might put it to the uses for which God intended it, and night was fixed to fit the general scheme.

In the interest of accuracy it should be noted that within the confines of this one verse the word "day" is used in two different senses. "Day" (*yôm*) over against "night" (*láyelah*) must refer to the light part of the day, roughly, a twelve hour period. When the verse concludes with the statement that the first "day" (*yôm*) is concluded, the term must mean a twenty-four hour period. If any attempt is made to fix the time of the year when the creative work was done, the vernal equinox seems most likely to fit the needs of the case.

Extensive discussion has centered around the last statement of v. 5: "Then came evening, then came morning — the first day." To try to make this mean that the day began with evening, as days did according to the later Jewish reckoning (Lev. 23:32), fails utterly, because verse 5 reports the conclusion of this day's work not its beginning. Or again, to make this statement refer to two parts of a long geologic period: the first part a kind of evening; the second a kind of morning; both together a kind of long period, runs afoul of three things: first, that "evening" nowhere in the Scriptures bears this meaning; secondly, neither does "morning"; thirdly, "day" never means "period."

One major difficulty lying in the path is the attempt to make this whole statement like a problem in addition: evening plus morning, result: one day. Luther's translation, somewhat free at this point, seemed to support this view: *da ward aus Abend und Morgen der erste Tag,* i. e. "evening and morning went to make up the first day." In reality, a vast absurdity is involved in this point of view. An evening may be stretched to include four hours, a morning could be said to be four or even six hours long. The total is ten, not twenty-four hours. The verse, however, presents not an addition of items but the conclusion of a progression. On this day there had been the creation of heaven and earth in the rough, then the creation of light, the approval of light, the separation of day and night. Now with evening the divine activities cease: they are works of light not works of darkness. The evening (*'erebh*), of course, merges into night, and the night terminates with morning. But by the time morning is reached, the first day is concluded, as the account says succinctly, "the first day," and everything is in readiness for the second day's task. For "evening" marks the conclusion of the day, and "morning" marks the conclusion of the night. It is these conclusions, which terminate the preceding, that are to be made prominent. They are "the terminations of the two halves of the first day" (Procksch).

There ought to be no need of refuting the idea that *yôm* means period. Reputable dictionaries like Buhl, B D B or K. W. know nothing of this notion. Hebrew dictionaries are our primary source of reliable information concerning Hebrew words. Commentators with critical leanings utter statements that are very decided in this instance. Says Skinner: "The interpretation of *yôm* as aeon, a favorite resource of harmonists of science and revelation, is opposed to the plain sense of the passage and has no warrant in Hebrew usage." Dillmann remarks: "The reasons advanced by ancient and modern writers for construing these days to be longer periods of time are inadequate." There is one other meaning of the word "day" which some misapprehend by failing to think through its exact bearing: *yôm* may mean "time" in a very general way, as in 2:4 *beyôm*, or Isa. 11:16; cf. B D B, p. 399, No. 6, for numerous illustrations. But that use cannot substantiate so utterly different an idea as "period." These two conceptions lie far apart.

References to expressions like "the day of the Lord" fail to invalidate our contentions above. For "the day of the Lord," as B D B rightly defines, p. 399, No. 3, is regarded "chiefly as the time of His coming in judgment, involving often blessedness for the righteous."

Other arguments to the contrary carry very little weight. If it be claimed that some works can with difficulty be compressed within twenty-four hours, like those of the third day or the sixth, that claim may well be described as a purely subjective opinion. He that desires to reason it out as possible can assemble fully as many arguments as he who holds the opposite opinion. Or if it be claimed that "the duration of the seventh day determines the rest," let it be noted that nothing is stated about the duration of the seventh. This happens to be an argument from silence, and therefore it is exceptionally weak. Or again, if it be claimed that "the argument of the fourth (our third) commandment confirms this probability," we find in this commandment even stronger confirmation of our contention: six twenty-four hour days followed by one such day of rest alone can furnish a proper analogy for our laboring six days and resting on the seventh day; periods furnish a poor analogy for days. Finally, the contention that our conception "contradicts geology" is inaccurate. It merely contradicts one school of thought in the field of geology, a school of thought of which we are convinced that it is hopelessly entangled in misconceptions which grow out of attempts to co-ordinate the actual findings of geology with an evolutionistic conception of what geology should be, and so is for the present thrown into a complete misreading of the available evidence, even as history, anthropology, Old Testament studies and many other sciences have been derailed and mired by the same attempt. We believe that writers on the subject like Price and Nelson deserve far more consideration than is being accorded them.

Now follows in v. 6-8 the creative work of the second day, the creation of the firmament or the lower heavens (*Erdhimmel*).

6. **And God said: Let there be a firmament in the middle of the waters, and let it be causing a division between waters and waters.**

Again a creative word having the same power as the one of the first day, in reference to which Luther said: "God does not speak grammatical words but real things that actually exist." The "firmament" that results is called *raqîa'*. It comes from the root meaning "to hammer" or "to spread out." Therefore, by some the word is rendered "expanse." Our "firmament" is from the translation of the Vulgate, *firmamentum*, which involves the idea of something that is firmly put in place. The Greek στερέωμα conveys the same idea. Yet the *raqîa'* is the vault or dome of the heavens, or "that immense gaseous ocean, called the atmosphere, by which the earth is encircled" (Whitelaw). That so widely differing definitions as "dome" and "gaseous ocean" can be given in one breath is due to the fact, that that whole set of physical laws is involved which makes the lower heavens possible: an air space encircling the earth, evaporation of waters, rising of gaseous vapors, etc. For the purpose of the firmament is declared to be that it be "in the middle of the waters" and "causing a division between waters and waters." Apparently, before this firmament existed, the earth waters on the surface of the earth and the cloud waters as we now know them were contiguous without an intervening clear air space. It was a situation like a dense fog upon the surface of the waters. Clear vision of all except the very nearest objects must have been impossible. Free activity unhampered by the fog blanket would have been impossible. Man would not have had an appropriate sphere for activity, nor could sunlight have penetrated freely to do its beneficent and cheering work. Now the physical laws that cause clouds and keep them suspended go into operation. These clouds constitute the upper waters. The solid masses of water collected upon earth constitute the lower waters. He who has observed that the heavens may pour down unbelievable quantities of waters will not hesitate to call these upper lighter cloud masses "waters" also. The languages familiar to us have the same viewpoint as v. 8, which calls this firmament "heavens." The cloud heaven is the one we mean. The English word "heaven" is from the root "to heave" or "lift up."

Very queer constructions have been put upon this *raqîa'*. A. Jeremias wrapped up in his speculations on Babylonian mythology and the great importance the signs of the zodiac played in Babylonian thought, identifies the *raqîa'* with the zodiac (*Tierkreis*). A sober reading of the definition v. 6-8 gives of the "firmament" ought to make such an attempt impossible. Far more common is that view which imputes singular crudities to the Biblical narrative at this point. Let Dillmann furnish the picture: The *raqîa'* "was in olden times conceived of as made out of more or less solid matter, firm as a mirror of glass, . . . supported by the highest mountains as by pillars . . . having openings," namely the windows of heaven through which rain might be dropped upon the earth. But in spite of passages like Rev. 4:6; 15:2; 22:1 there is no doctrine of the Scriptures to the effect that there were "ethereal waters," and though the "windows of heaven" are referred to (7:11; Ps. 78:23; cf. II Kings 7:2; Isa. 24:18), these purely figurative expressions (also e. g. Job 26:11) are such as we can still use with perfect propriety, and yet to impute to us notions of a crude view of supernal waters stored in heavenly reservoirs would be as unjust at it is to impute such opinions to the writers of the Biblical books. The holy writers deserve at least the benefit of the doubt, especially when poetic passages are involved. Again: the view expressed in this verse is not crude, absurd, or in any wise deficient. Its simple meaning has been shown above.

The expression *wihî mabhdîl,* "and let it be causing a division," presents a very strong case where the participle is used to express duration or permanence of a certain relationship (K. S. 239 b; G. K. 116 r). *Yehî* is repeated to make the separate parts of the process stand out more distinctly (K. S. 370 s).

7. And God made the firmament and He caused a division between the waters under the firmament and the waters above the firmament: and it was so.

With a certain measure of circumstantiality the author reports in detail that God actually made those things that He had bidden come into being. This now does not imply that the initial word (v. 6), "Let there be a firmament," was inadequate to cause it to come into being, and so God actually had to "make" (*'asah*) it. This mode of statement of v. 7 merely unfolds in greater detail that the initial command to come into being involved the full exercise of God's creative power, which continued operative after the word had been spoken until the work was brought to completion. For "he made" (*'asah*) dare not be construed as involving a mode of operation radically different from creating (*bara'*), for a comparison of the use of the two verbs in v. 21 and in v. 25 shows that they may be used interchangeably. From one point of view one and the same task is *created,* i. e. is one of those marvelous, epoch-making achievements characteristic of God; from another point of view this task is *made,* i. e. God employs His almighty power and energy to carry it through till it is completed.

A textual problem needs to be considered here. Kit. in the margin suggests removing the "and it was so" (*wayhi khen*) from the end of v. 7 and appending it to the end of v. 6 after the example of the Septuagint translators and after the analogy of v. 9, 11, 15, 24, 30, where it is inserted before the actual carrying out of the thing ordained is reported. However, though a certain quite stereotyped pattern is followed by the author throughout the account in recounting the work of the individual days, the adherence to fixed forms need not be so rigid as to preclude the slightest departure from them. The situation at the close of v. 26 is the same as that of our verse. There the Greek translators did not insert the *wayhi khen,* proving themselves inconsistent in their corrective endeavors. The text here needs no improvement.

No effort should be made to render literally the compound preposition *mittáchath le,* "from under to." *Mittáchat* alone means only *"under."* Compound prepositions are wont to be followed by *le* (K. S. 281 p, and G. K. 119 c²).

8. **And God called the firmament heavens; and came evening, and came morning — second day.**

Again, the giving of the name to the object just created is more than an outward thing. What the term "heavens" implies, that is what the new arrangement will serve to be for man. All this, especially the term "heavens," gives us warrant for describing this creative work as we did in connection with v. 6.

Our rendering, as in v. 5, "then came evening" is not as exact from one point of view as it might be. *Wayhî* is not the verb "come," but is from *hayah,* "to be," or even better "to become." This latter idea to show the progression of time we felt could well be marked by the English idiom, "then came evening," etc. The word for "evening," *'érebh,* is commonly derived from the corresponding Hebrew root whose Arabic parallel means "to enter," "to go in." So, apparently,

a poetic thought is involved in that the sun is thought
of as going into its chamber, a thought found also
in Ps. 19:5.

After "one" the ordinals are used, "day the
second" (K. S. 315 n).

There follows in v. 9-13 the double work of the
third day.

9. **And God said: Let the waters under the
heavens be gathered together unto one place, and
let the dry land appear; and it was so.**

The second day's work may still be regarded
from one point of view as being connected with the
work of the first day. The light of the first day
requires a free space, the clear atmosphere, in order
that it might make its life-giving work felt upon plants
and upon man. So "the heavens" (v. 6-8), i. e. the
firmament, aids in the distribution of light. But
three of the deficiences noted under v. 2 still prevail.
The *tehôm* is now to be disposed of in the work of
the third day.

The expression "waters under the heavens" must
be taken in the light of the preceding division made on
the second day. The "waters above the heavens" are
the clouds. The waters on the unformed surface, perhaps seething and surging as *tehôm* suggests, are here
under consideration. Waters are to be gathered together to be by themselves; dry land is to assemble
by itself. If the waters are to be gathered together
"unto one place," this expression may be regarded
as sufficiently general to cover all oceans, or "the seven
seas" for that matter. These water are by themselves;
that is their "one place." So again "the dry land,"
hayyabbashah, literally: "the dry," involved a limitation in the figure of synecdoche; the term really means
continents, but continents are primarily "dry land."
The verb "let be seen," *tera'eh*, is an imperfect used
as an optative (K. S. 183 b).

The verse concludes with the customary "and it was (or became) so" to indicate that that which is bidden to come into being at once forms itself.

As to the method followed in the separation of dry land and water we can say little. Did depressions form and the waters rush down into them? We might think so. Or did elevations and mountains thrust themselves upward in the process of the congealing of the dry land and shed the waters as they rose? Ps. 104:7-9, in describing the work of this day, seems to imply the latter course, though the expressions used may be poetic rather than exact. No one, it seems, will ever be able to speak a final verdict in regard to this question.

But, surely, in the course of these gigantic upheavals, not catastrophic in nature because they involve organization rather than disruption, there was a tremendous amount of geologic formation. In fact, it would be perfectly safe to assume that all basic and all regular formations were disposed of in this day's work. As a result, indeed, no record of the rapidity with which certain formations took place is written upon the various formations, for vast as these formations were, they were controlled by the orderly operations of divine omnipotence and by these potentialities, no doubt, which the Spirit "hovering over the face of the waters" had implanted. Even these basic forms might, therefore, offer to him who acts on the assumption that there never were any accelerated formations the appearance of things laid down by the slow process of nature that we see in operation at this late day. But this ninth verse surely teaches that what we call geologic formations took place in titanic and gigantic measure at a vastly accelerated pace in a truly miraculous creative work as astounding as the rest.

As far as the expression *yammîm*, "seas," (v. 10) is concerned, it must be noted that it is used in a loose sense so as to include every body of water, like inland lakes and also the rivers. But since the area of the seas is vastly in excess of that of the smaller bodies, the name is taken from the outstanding part, *a parte potiori.*

Just because the Greek translators misread the word *miqweh,* "collection," for the word *maqôm,* "place," that does not give any better reading or occasion for a textual change (Kit.). To call the newly assembled waters "the collection of waters" is most appropriate (v. 10); to say that they are to collect in "one place" is equally appropriate (v. 9). The clause added by the Septuagint is a pedantic attempt at improvement.

10. **And God called the dry land earth and the collection of waters He called seas; and God saw that it was good.**

The meaning of the word "earth" was discussed under v. 1. The propriety of the use of the term "sea" was treated just before this verse. What God's calling signifies was shown in connection with v. 5.

Here is the place for discussing what reasonable explanation may be offered for the fact that at the conclusion of the work of the second day the customary approval of the Creator is not recorded (v. 8); but that it does appear now at the conclusion of the work of the third day (v. 10). As was shown at the beginning of the explanation of v. 9, the work of the second day reaches back and completes the work of the first day from one point of view. In a more decided sense the work of the third day reaches back and completes the work of the second in reference to the separation of water. The second day merely raises the surface fogs making them clouds, but the earth waters are still entangled with the solid matter. So the work of the second day was relatively incomplete, so much so that the divine approval, "it was good," was withheld, but it is in reality included in the approval bestowed upon the third day.

Note the chiasmus of v. 10: verb, object — object verb (K. S. 339 o).

11. And God said: Let the earth produce grass, and herbs yielding seed, and fruit trees bearing fruit after their kind whose seed is in them upon the earth; and it was so.

The second half of the work of the third day is here recorded. This work attaches itself quite naturally to the preceding work: the dry land just formed is at once to bring forth all forms of vegetation. The work of this half of the day is not immediate creation in the sense of the works preceding. For in the instances that went before the word was spoken and the result followed. In this instance the earth is the mediate agent, being bidden to produce whatever vegetation is necessary by a process of highly accelerated growth. Such a work is neither of a higher nor of a lower character than are the other works. Upon closer reflection this verse is seen to answer a question often asked, whether the plant preceded the seed, or the seed the plant. Since the seed is not bidden to bring forth but the earth is, and since the things brought forth are first to produce seed, and since nothing indicates the prior creation of seed, the only possibility left open to us is to believe that plants and herbs came first. This still leaves room for the possibility that the Spirit in His hovering implanted the potentialities that here unfold themselves.

How do the things produced by the earth differ from one another? The three orders mentioned are: 1) grass, 2) herbs, 3) trees. Some put the three items down as independent classes in an ascending scale (e. g. Delitzsch). Some make 2) a genitive dependent on 1), having as a result a pair of doubles: "grass of herb" and "tree of fruit," as the Greek version βοτάνην χόρτου and ξύλον κάρπιμον. Still others make

1) the general term covering all and 2) and 3) subdivisions of 1). We feel that the first point of view
alone is correct and does justice to the meaning of
the words employed. "Grass" represents the word
déshe', whose root signifies "to be damp." Whatever
grows in a well-watered spot will be of a fresh green,
therefore the word is rendered *frisches Gruen*. Since,
no doubt, these three classes aim to cover all vegetation in so far as it is of interest to man, the word
déshe' may well be said to include such things as
mosses and other plants designed to carpet the earth.
The second term, "herbs," is a singular collective
noun *'ésebh*, also translated "herbage." That the word
is really distinct from *déshe'* in meaning appears
first from its use in passages like II Kings 19:26 and
Isa. 37:27 where in an enumeration both are mentioned
separately. Again the characteristic mark ascribed
to it in this verse is noteworthy: *mazría' zéra'*, literally, seeding seed, therefore "yielding seed." Grasses,
for that matter, yield seed too, but if specific mention
of the seed is made only in the second class, apparently
this refers to something like seed-bearing pods which
make the seed more prominent as a separate feature.
According to scriptural usage man eats *'ésebh*; see
1:29 and 3:18. So do cattle, Deut. 11:15. This being
a broad class name, it must include things such as vegetables, or at least, generally speaking, everything between grass and trees and, without a doubt, the various
grains.

So, too, the last term must be used in a very broad
sense. "Fruit-bearing trees," again a singular collective *'ets peri*, must include both trees that bear fruit
as well as trees yielding nuts and cones and, surely,
all bushes yielding berries. For the expression translated literally means only "tree of fruit." Two other
marks, however, are appended to this class: first,
these fruit trees bear fruit "after their kind," a
peculiar and definite limitation, which all those under-

stand best who have seen how the "kind" sets limitations upon all who would mix kinds and cross them.
Nature itself here is seen to have definite limits fixed
which appear as constant laws or as insurmountable
barriers. The last mark stamped upon this third class
of vegetable growth is "whose seed is in them upon
the earth." The seed needed for the propagation of
the particular kinds is seen to be in the fruit. So
whether the fruit be edible or not, as long as it has
seed qualities, it meets the requirements of this mark.
The concluding phrase for this mark, "upon the earth,"
might perhaps better have been rendered as "above the
ground." For to try to make this phrase modify the
verb *tadhshe'* at the beginning of the sentence certainly removes it far from the word modified. Besides,
the characteristic thing about this "fruit-bearing
seed" is that it usually hangs at some distance above
the ground. Then, too, *'erets* does mean "ground,"
and *'al* does mean "above."

These three broad classes of vegetation may not
coincide with botanical distinctions as science now
makes them. But, assuredly, they are seen to be a
general and a very appropriate type of division as
far as man's use of them is concerned, and in some
ways the distinctions made are seen to be very apt.
The lines of demarcation drawn at creation are just
as sharp now as they were then.

This verse closes with an, "and it was so," to
indicate again how immediate was the fulfillment of
the thing commanded.

Tadshe' is, of course, a jussive or a *yakteel
elevatum* (K. S. 189), and *déshe'* and *zéra'* are cognate
objects.

We should yet draw attention to the fact that the
things mentioned in 2:5 are not to be included in the
above classification, and so reservations must be made
in reference to our use of the terms "vegetables" and
"bushes" in the above discussion.

If above in v. 7 the "and it was so" stood after
it had been reported that the individual things to be
created had actually come into being, here in v. 11
the "and it was so" precedes this latter statement,
(K. S. 369 b).

**12. And the earth produced grass and herbs
yielding seed after their kind and trees yielding fruit
whose seed was in them after their kind; and God
saw that it was good.**

The accomplishment of the things ordered in v. 11
is reported in this verse in terms that are not a wooden
repetition of v. 11; for after "seed" is inserted "after
their kind" to emphasize how the "kind" limitation
also applies to the herbs, though this had not been
mentioned previously. So, too, after "trees" the word
"of fruit" is omitted, since this idea is covered by the
qualifying phrase "bearing fruit." The work of the
second half of the third day is also to be found "excellent" in divine approval, so that the statement, "and
it was good," appears for each of the two halves of
this day.

**13. Then came evening, then came morning,
— the third day.** On this verse compare above v. 5.

It is true that the first three days have no sun
and no moon to furnish and to measure the needed
light. But that fact does not in any wise warrant
trying to make these days appear as different from
the following three or four, for the pattern into which
all six days of work fall is consistently the same for
all, "then came evening, then came morning." It is
the author's purpose by this means emphatically to
declare the six days alike as to length and general
character — regular twenty-four hour days. Nothing
but the desire to secure harmony with the contentions
of certain physical sciences ever could have induced
men to tamper with this very plainest of exegetical
results.

Follows the work of the fourth day in v. 14-19.

Since this has to do with the appointment of luminaries, we see, first of all, how this day's work attaches itself to the work of the third day, as well as how it reaches over to the works that are yet to follow. For the vegetation that was brought into being by the work of the preceding day needs not only light but also seasons with modification of light. Consequently, that intricate set of operations that brings seasonal changes for vegetation and for man now appropriately follows.

14, 15. And God said: Let there be luminaries in the firmament of the heavens to divide the day from the night, and let them be for signs and seasons and for days and years; and let them be for luminaries in the expanse of the heavens to give light upon the earth; and it was so.

It at once stands out in reference to the work of this day that the purpose of the things that are made to function is stated in a far more detailed fashion than is the case in regard to any other of the creative works. Nothing in the text explains this greater fulness of statement, but the suggestion advanced by Dillmann and others may be as satisfactory as any: "Is there perhaps a silent contrast involved with the superstition of the heathen that is wont to attach itself to the stars?" The statement, therefore, is unusually exhaustive in order to show what purposes the Almighty fixed for the heavenly bodies and to leave no room for heathen misconstruction.

At once now the next problem suggests itself: how do the "luminaries" stand related to the light which was created on the first day? With this is involved a second question: how do these luminaries stand related to the heavens, which were created on the first day (v. 1)? The analogy of "the earth" created simultaneously with "the heavens" (v. 1) and its equipment and arrangement up till this point through v. 2-13 points in the proper direction. In other words, the earth is created in the rough, subject to certain deficiencies or incompletenesses which are removed one by one through the following days; similarly the heavens are created in the rough, heavenly bodies in vast spaces, not yet functioning as they shall later. What still remains to be done in and with them is now completed on the fourth day. The sun, moon and stars were in existence but were not yet doing the work which gets to be theirs in the fourth day's work. Light was in existence, but now these heavenly bodies come to be the ones that bear this light in themselves — "light-bearers," "luminaries," *me'ôrôth.* Heavenly bodies were in existence, but from this point onward they begin to serve a definite purpose in reference to the earth. Consequently, we are out of keeping with the plan according to which the course of creation has been proceeding if we separate the elements of 14 a so as to make a definite pause after the statement, "let there be luminaries." This would imply the initial creation of all heavenly bodies. Rather, translating still more literally, the thing that is to transpire is this: "Let there become luminaries in the expanse of the heavens to divide the day from the night," etc. This really involves a double achievement: the non-luminous heavenly bodies become bearers of light, and this for the purpose of dividing the day from the night. The expression, "let there be *lights*" (A. V.) and *Lichter* (Luther) is inaccurate and misleading. "Light" in Hebrew is *'ôr*; here stands the word *ma'ôr*, "light-bearer." This does not, however, now mean that "the atmosphere being completely purified — the sun, moon and stars were for the first time unveiled in all their glory in the cloudless sky" (Jamieson), for such a result would have been achieved automatically without divine fiat by the work of the second day. More reasonable is the assumption that the existing light, by being allocated

to the sun, was tempered specifically to the needs of
plant and animal life upon our planet. In any case,
the purposes following are definitely tied up with having the sun in particular function as the primary
light-bearer.

Consequently, though day and night following one
another in rotation function satisfactorily as day and
night without sun and moon, from this point onward
the dividing of day and night is tied up specifically
with these luminaries. So this purpose is stated first.
The adverbial modifier "in the firmament of the
heavens" shows the relation of the fourth day's work
to that of the second. The firmament prepared in
advance had to be thus prepared, otherwise the light
of these luminaries would have failed to benefit the
earth. The singular verb *yehî* is followed by the masculine plural (feminine only as to form) *me'ôrôth,*
according to general Hebrew practice of letting the
most general form of the verb begin the thought (G.
K. 145 o).

But the luminaries have functions other than to
divide day and night. The fourteenth verse alone expresses two more general functions. The first of these
two is so broad in scope as to cover four items, expressed by the terms, "and let them be for signs and
for seasons and for days and years." A wide diversity
of opinion exists as to the actual enumeration here
given: are these two, three, or four distinct objects?
Nothing very vital hinges on the answer. For though
we stated above that *four* purposes are here listed,
we could readily from one point of view consent to
reduce them to *three.* For the preposition "for" (*le*)
is used but three times and has a double object in the
last instance — the closely related terms: "days and
years." Others, like Kœnig, make a double hendiadys,
thus, "for signs, as well for seasons as also for days
and also years." This again, depending on the individual's viewpoint, might mean either three or two

purposes. But though hendiadys is a common enough figure, we feel that nothing definitely indicates its use here; and also we notice that such translations push the independent meaning of the word "signs" too much into the background.

Now "signs" (*'ôthôth*) is here used in the broadest possible sense. Indeed, the luminaries are signs from various points of view. They are "signs" to devout faith, declaring the glory of their Creator (cf. Ps. 8 and 19). They are "signs" by which men get their bearings, or the point of the compass by day or by night. They may convey "signs" in reference to future events (Matt. 2:2; Luke 21:25). They furnish quite reliable "signs" for determining in advance the weather to be expected (Matt. 16:2, 3). They may be "signs" of divine judgments (Joel 2:30; Matt. 24:29). That they may well serve in all these capacities is clear both from Scripture and from experience. Dwelling only on one scriptural parallel, Skinner, pointing to Jer. 10:2, where "astrological portents" are referred to, misconstrues the use of the word when he claims to find a similar use here, "though it is not quite easy to believe the writer would have said, the sun and moon were *made* for this purpose." But Jer. 10:2 does not identify the expression "signs of heaven," with "astrological portents." These signs become such portents only by the fact that the "nations," who are "dismayed at them," make them to be considered such. Skinner construes the forbidden abuse of "signs of heaven" as the normal meaning of the expression. How Procksch injects the meaning "epochs" into the term is more than we can discern. The fact remains that men always have and in manifold ways still do regard and use luminaries for signs.

Besides, the luminaries are "for seasons." A certain brevity of expression obtains here. We could supply the implied term quite readily, for "*fixing* seasons, days and years." But without this added term the expression is not unclear. But "seasons" are called *mô'adhim*, from the root *ya'adh*, "to appoint"; therefore, "appointed time." The luminaries do serve as "indicators" (Meek) of such fixed, appointed times, whether these now be secular or sacred. To attempt to exclude what we are specifically wont to call seasons is unwarranted and grows out of the assumption that the hypothetical author P has a special interest in things ritual. Therefore, "seasons" or times in the widest sense are to be thought of: agricultural seasons (Hos. 2:9, 11; 9:5), seasons for seafaring men, seasons for beasts and birds (Jer. 8:7), as long as they are times that are fixed and come with stated regularity.

To complete the list of the things determined by the luminaries the divine command adds "days and years." These are respectively the shortest and the longest measures of time definitely fixed by the movement of the heavenly bodies. What "day" *yôm*, is (here the whole twenty-four hour day) every one knows, and yet the etymology of the term is entirely unknown. The word for "year" (*shanah*) seems to be traceable to the Assyrian root "to change."

Note that after the imperative "let there be" there may follow a converted perfect *wehayû* (K. S. 367 c).

When now v. 15 says distinctly that these luminaries are to be "in the expanse of the heavens to give light upon the earth," this plainly indicates that from the time of this creative work onward all light that the earth receives is to be mediated through the luminaries. How light functioned in the universe prior to this time we shall never know. How the regular alternation of day and night was regulated will for ever escape our discernment. What we know is only that as day and night now follow upon one another due to the light centered in luminaries, is an arrangement which God ordained on this day. It all certainly is a marvelous and praiseworthy work, but that is all that these luminaries are appointed for, as far as we are able to discern.

16. And God made the two great luminaries, the greater luminary to rule the day and the lesser luminary to rule the night — and also the stars.

The previous verse closes the initial command of the work to be done on the fourth day with the customary notice that "it was so," that is, what God commanded came into being. According to the almost invariable rule of this chapter we should now expect an account in detail as to how God actually wrought what He had ordained, beginning like all the others with either *wayyá'as*, "and He made," or with *wayyibhra'*, "and He created." This is just what we have with the usual situation that the account of how the original order was carried out affords sufficient variety of form to serve as a commentary upon the first statement of v. 14, 15. Stereotyped repetition would be both mechanical and wearisome. However, critics fail to see this clear situation in a number of instances. Skinner brings an indictment against the account: "The labored explanation of the purposes of the heavenly bodies is confused, and suggests overworking (the difficult 14 b and 15 a ᵅ). The functions are stated with perfect clearness in v. 16-18." Yet we have found both v. 14 and 15 perfectly simple and plain. The only difference between the initial command v. 14, 15 and the account of its being done v. 16-18 is that of the supplementary but entirely harmonious statements of purpose, the first gives greater prominence to the secondary purpose of serving for "signs, seasons," etc.; the second stresses particularly the primary function of controlling day and night and giving light.

So v. 16 is supplementary in mentioning for the first time the chief luminaries — "chief" as far as the earth is concerned. They are "the two great luminaries" in reference to the earth and also in view of how they appear to man. Naturally, a simple account such as this will not attempt to give to man the useless information as to which of the heavenly bodies are the largest in the absolute sense. Besides, in the very nature of the case the expression, "the great luminary," must be understood as a comparative, "the greater." Likewise "the small" (*haqqaton*) means the smaller (K. S. 308 a). Because the definite and very specific use of "the stars" in reference to the earth is very much inferior to that of sun and moon, they may well be added as a kind of afterthought, "and also the stars." Now man at least knows how important they are and how they originated — a type of account which is the complete negative of all astrological conceptions. So as a whole v. 16 is seen to be a very helpful commentary upon what preceded.

17, 18. And God set them in the firmament of heaven to give light upon the earth and to rule over the day and over the night and to separate the light from the darkness; and God saw that it was good.

Lest anyone be inclined to attribute any other or further purpose to these luminaries, v. 17 reasserts what was stated v. 15 b, they are in the expanse of the heavens "to give light upon the earth." It would be a crude interpretation of the opening verb "and he put," if this were understood to mean that God first fashioned the luminaries in one place and then took them and set or suspended them in the firmament. For a literal translation of *wayyitten* is "and He gave" in the sense of "appointed." Yet the original idea of "to give" is also very appropriate here inasmuch as the luminaries are one of God's good gifts to mankind.

Verse 18, in stating again what v. 14 said, "to separate the light from the darkness," prefixes the supplementary statement, "to rule over the day and over the night." This allows for that control of day and of night which expresses itself in their varying length as indicated and regulated by the sun and the moon.

This work also is so excellent (*tobh*) as to merit divine approval.

19. **Then came evening, then came morning — the fourth day.**

Cf. v. 5 and 8.

In this connection one particular problem still requires our consideration, and that is the computation of the light years by which the distance separating the earth from certain stars is measured. Some claim that then, of necessity, certain stars now visible could not yet have appeared to our first parents. If the astronomical calculations involved are correct, what if all stars were not at once visible but have only become apparent as time went on? Such a situation is not out of harmony with the Creation account; it would indicate merely a greater vastness to creation's work than man had first surmised. Where, however, it is claimed that this situation involves a greater antiquity of the earth than our construction of the Mosaic accounts allows for, we on our part still believe that the laws of light refraction in the interstellar spaces cannot be asserted to be identical with those prevailing under conditions as we know them. There still is the possibility that the tremendous spaces and the times resulting from certain astronomical calculations are based on assumptions whose correctness will always be only in part demonstrable.

The claim of Skinner must yet be disposed of when he maintains that the Genesis account presents a "religious advance to pure monotheism" over against "the idea of them (the heavenly bodies) as an animated host" as it "occurs in Hebrew poetry (Judg. 5:20; Isa. 40:26; Job 38:7); but here it is entirely eliminated." We do not grant that the passages cited are earlier than Genesis I. But they are poetic and, when rightly construed, offer no other view than that which any enlightened Christian now holds. They are far from teaching anything about heavenly bodies as "an animated host." The attempts of the critics to prove evolution of ideas where no such evolution occurs are unconvincing.

20. **And God said: Let the waters swarm with swarms of living souls, and let birds fly above the ground across the face of the firmament of the heavens.**

The work of the fifth day is also in a sense a double one, but its double character is by no means as pronounced as that of the third and the sixth days. For to have the waters and the skies filled with such creatures as these parts are best adapted to is in reality a work whose two parts are practically identical in nature. However, here the situation is not analogous to the work of the third day, where "the earth brought forth." Here it is not the waters that bring forth. A. V. is in error when it translates: "Let the waters bring forth abundantly." Luther did not make this mistake. The optative of the verb *sharats* followed by the cognate object *shérets* here must mean: "Let the waters swarm with swarms." Meek is more idiomatic: "Let the waters teem with shoals," but he loses the cognate object. We simply do not know from what source fish and birds sprang. They are simply bidden to people their respective domains. In apposition with the cognate object *shérets* stands the expression, "living souls" or literally, "souls of life." The word "soul" (*néphesh*) is here used for the first time — a collective singular — as a designation of these aquatic creatures, because the soul is the most important part of them, and at the same time the term definitely points to the new and distinctive thing involved. This is the first time that life in souls or living souls appears. Accord-

ing to the Biblical viewpoint plants have no life. But
the life of living creatures is present in their "souls,"
and so they have souls ascribed to them. But this
"soul" again is regarded as nothing more than "that
which breathes" (B D B) in any being. A kindred
form of life to that of fish is that of birds. Each
type has its special element. The *polel* form
ye'opheph is intensive and so implies: birds shall
"fly back and forth." Their element is described as
being "above the ground across the face of the firmament of the heavens." The firmament is regarded
as having a face, that is a side turned toward and,
as we say, "facing" the earth. Across this the birds
are to disport themselves. *Shérets* used in reference
to the fish is a graphically descriptive term. All forms
of life that love to move in continual agitation through
one another, like shoals of fish and the like, are
involved. This pronounced gregarious instinct marks
these creatures to this day. By this work the emptiness (*bóhû*) of the heavens and the waters is cancelled.

21. **And God created the great sea monsters
and each one of the creeping creatures with which
the waters teem after their kind and every winged
bird after its kind; and God saw that it was good.**

Verse 21 in its relation to v. 20 furnishes a very
excellent example as to how the account of what
actually was done furnishes an invaluable commentary
upon the original command of what was to be done.
We ourselves would, as a rule, not have discerned what
the original commands involved if the following statements had not made the full breadth of the original
command plain. As far as the "swarms of living
souls" of v. 20 are concerned, we are given to understand, first of all, that these swarms included not only
the smaller fry among the fish but also "the great sea
monsters" (*tannînîm*), a word whose root indicates
a creature of some length. In this category are found

not only "whales," as A. V. translates, but all larger marine animals like sharks and, no doubt, also crocodiles. Nor do we hesitate to include under this head amphibians like the saurians of every class and description. Then the account specifically mentions what we have translated, "each one of the creeping creatures!" For here, apparently, *néphesh* has the common meaning of "individual" or "one," and what the account wishes to emphasize is that of the teeming multitudes of these marine creatures each one owed its existence to God's creative work. On this meaning of *néphesh* see K. S. 302 a. The term rendered "creeping" (*roméseth*) literally implies "moving lightly about" or "gliding about" (B D B). Difficulty in fitting in these terms led to our rendering "creeping," which strictly does not apply to movement in the water. Another distinctive thought conveyed by this half of the verse is the added assertion that these creatures appeared "after their kind," a phrase not new but as important in its bearing as above (v. 12) and allowing for no transmutation of species. In the second half of the verse it is applied also to the birds.

The expression "winged bird" is literally "bird of wing," *kanaph*, "wing," being a genitive of quality and the phrase as a whole what is known as an "ornate epithet" (K. S. 335 a) similar to our expression "yellow gold." Of course, birds have wings. But here, besides, where the very broadest of class distinctions are being made, without a doubt, the expression is meant to include every type of being that has wings — the small and the large, and not only what we call birds.

But on the whole an entirely new type of being has come into existence, creatures that breathe and are animated and have power of their own volition to go from place to place. To give existence to such is the peculiar prerogative of God and is a monumental, epoch-making achievement that deserves to be described by the verb "and He created" (*way-yibhra'*) as the opening verse does.

22. And God blessed them, saying: Be fruitful and multiply and fill the waters in the seas and let the birds multiply on the earth.

That this which was last made now actually represents a more important form of life is also made manifest by the fact that God bestows a blessing upon these creatures, a blessing by virtue of which the needed powers for continuance and for multiplying are imparted. The very idea of an initial single pair of creatures of this type is excluded by the statements of v. 20 and 21 where, when called into being, these creatures are bidden "to swarm" and the waters to "teem." But from these copious beginnings these creatures are to keep on multiplying until they fill the earth. Every vestige of emptiness is to be ultimately cancelled. This blessing of God, however, is not a mere wish or a wishing-well on the part of the Almighty. It is a creative word of power which makes possible the things that it commands, and it continues in power to this day. The Creator is glorified by the multitudes of beings which His creative word makes.

It will be worth our while to make a check-up upon what is supposed to be an index of the style of P, to whom critics assign this chapter (P is the author of all that criticism calls the Priestly Codex). Skinner remarks about the double expression "be fruitful and multiply," *perû ûrebhû*, that it is "highly characteristic of P" and is used "only three times elsewhere." By such unwarranted remarks are the unwary misled, and by such insubstantial arguments is the case of the source criticism of the Pentateuch supported. B D B lists all the instances of the use of this double expression. The fictitious P is said to have it Gen. 1:22, 28 and 9:1 as well as 35:11 and 47:27, yet the last two expressions differ in that one is singular and the other not imperative but future. Yet Jeremiah uses these two verbs jointly in 3:16 and 23:3; so does Ezechiel in 36:11. Is it not an overstatement to call a phrase that one author uses five times and others three, "highly characteristic" of the one? It is not so much a characteristic of style but a case of having the author describe several situations that of themselves demand such a statement. By his statement of the case Skinner would lead men to believe that the so-called P must have used the phrase at least a dozen times.

In trying to make the fictitious P as real a figure as possible and to invest him with distinct characteristics Procksch remarks on this verse: "A tone of solemn joy pervades the knowledge that it is ordained that life should increase; P is in no sense a pessimist." The same note of "solemn joy," if you will, can be discerned just as plainly in chapter 2:4 ff, which is not ascribed to P.

23. **Then came evening, then morning — the fifth day.** Cf. v. 5 and 8.

24. **And God said: Let the earth bring forth living creatures after their kind, domestic animals, reptiles, and wild beasts of the earth after their kind; and it was so.**

We have come to the work of the sixth day. The nobler and higher forms of animal life are to be brought forth and finally man himself. We have a kind of mediate creation as on the third day (v. 11), for the earth is bidden to produce them or bring them forth — *tôtse'* = "cause to come forth." The situation is really very simple, as far as the text is concerned. God could have called forth these creatures by His mere word; instead He speaks the word that enables the earth to bring them forth. They are to have such kinship with the earth that they may again be able to return to the earth. There is no confusion here of two points of view, which P here fails properly to reconcile with one another: namely an old view, which is the outgrowth of some ancient natural philosophy, and a higher conception of pure creation by the word (Procksch). That both types of creation here flow into one is the simple fact noted by the text. To create artificial difficulty and to pose as having ability to detect strains of older and imperfectly assimilated elements of tradition, merely serves to make the unlearned suspicious without reason and is proof on the critic's part of not having fully comprehended what the author said.

On the shortened form *tôtse'* see K. S. 189.

The "living creatures" brought into being on this day are first described by this general title, which we have noted above (v. 20) to mean literally "soul of life," because the animating thing, the soul (*néphesh*), is the most prominent feature about them. Let it be remarked separately at this point that according to the Scriptures not only man has a soul but also all living creatures even down to fishes and birds. However, the soul as such is then regarded merely as the animating principle, the thing that causes them to breathe. Yet the soul of other creatures is not the same as that of man; it originated in a manner which makes it inferior by much to the animating principle in man, as a comparison with 2:7 indicates.

These "living creatures" now are of three classes. First we find "domestic animals," *behemah*, which may also be translated "cattle." According to its root, "to be dumb," this classword describes these creatures as dumb brutes. Used sometimes in reference to all animals, it is here employed in reference to cattle or domestic animals because of its manifest contrast here with the wild beasts. Yet "cattle" is still a bit too narrow a term; "domestic animals" (Meek) is better. The second class is described as *rémes*, which comes from the root meaning "to move about lightly" or to "glide about." "Creepers" almost covers the term,

however, "creeping things" is too narrow (A. V.), for
it does not seem to allow for bigger creatures like
reptiles. "Reptiles" (Meek) again is too narrow, for
it does not allow for the smaller types of life.
Everything, therefore, large or small, that moves upon
the earth or close to the earth, having but short legs,
may be said to be included. The third class comes
under the head of "wild beasts of the earth"
(*chayyath ha'árets*). This is an appropriate designation from two points of view: the original comes from
the root *chay*, to live, for these beasts are wild because "of their vital energy and activity" (B D B),
an abundance of life throbs in them; then the modifying phrase "of the earth" is added to their name, because in a sense different from the other two classes
these beasts have freedom of movement upon the earth.
The first time this name is used in v. 24 we have the
archaic connective, a remnant from an old case ending
chaythō and the word *'érets* without the article —
poetic — making a more solemn and dignified double
term coming from the lips of the Almighty (K. S.
268 a and 292 a). When the narrator continues his
own account, he lapses into the unarchaic prose
chayyath ha'árets (v. 25). A double "after their
kind," first applying to "the living creatures" as a
whole then to the three classes separately, impresses
this distinctive limitation upon all these creatures —
a truth amply confirmed as not to be eradicated, as
all who have engaged in crossbreeding of animals can
abundantly testify.

The three class names are in the singular, collective (K. S. 255 d).

An unwarranted critical verdict in regard to the
three classes just mentioned is rendered by Procksch,
who calls this classification "very imperfect, based half
on the history of civilization half on natural history."
It certainly is uncalled for to expect a writer of hoary
antiquity to operate with the specific scientific nomen-

clature of the twentieth century. Without a doubt, all readers who perused the accounts in a sympathetic spirit clearly detected that this popular grouping was sufficient to call to mind all types of living creatures as men not trained scientifically are wont to think of them.

25. And God made the wild beasts of the earth after their kind and the domestic animals after their kind, and the reptiles of the ground after their kind; and God saw that it was good.

The report as to how God proceeded to carry out the thing He ordains in v. 24, in v. 25 inverts the order of the classes — a merely chiastic inversion — and provides a comment upon "reptiles" by calling them "reptiles of the ground." Strictly speaking, the inverted order of names changes from 1, 2, 3 to 3, 1, 2. Then the expression "after their kind" is separately added to each class. The word for "ground," *'adhamah,* used with "reptiles" (for reptiles creep on the ground) most likely is to be associated with the root *'adhom,* meaning a "reddish-brown," a term descriptive of the covering of topsoil found wherever "ground" covers the rock layers. Lest anyone suppose that perhaps portions of the animal world may originally have been characterized by some defect, we find that all meets with divine approval: "God saw that it was excellent" (cf. v. 4). No blessing is specifically mentioned as in v. 22, apparently because the writer is hurrying to the climax.

26. And God said: Let us make man in our image, after our likeness, and let them have dominion over the fish of the sea and over the birds of the heavens and over the domestic animals and over the whole earth and over every thing that moveth about upon the earth.

A divine counsel precedes the creation of man. By this means the singular dignity of man is very strongly stressed. From every point of view man is seen to be the crown and climax of God's creation.

The hortative "Let us make" (*na'aseh*), is particularly striking because it is plural. Though almost all commentators of our day reject the view that this is to be explained in connection with the truth of the Holy Trinity and treat this so-called trinitarian view as a very negligible quantity, yet, rightly considered, this is the only view that can satisfy. Kœnig (K. C.) may brush it aside with the very briefest remark to the effect that "the number three cannot be expressed by the plural," yet he like many others labors under a misunderstanding of the trinitarian view. Those that hold that a reference to the Trinity is involved do not mean to say that the truth of the Holy Trinity is here fully and plainly revealed. But they do hold that God speaks out of the fulness of His powers and His attributes in a fashion which man could never employ. Behind such speaking lies the truth of the Holy Trinity which, as it grows increasingly clear in revelation, is in the light of later clear revelation discovered as contained in this pural in a kind of obscure adumbration. The truth of the Trinity explains this passage. It would not occur to us to call this an express and unmistakable, clear presentation of the full trinitarian truth. So also, in substance, Keil. So practically also Luther, after he has valiantly championed the trinitarian view even beyond what we might deem the legitimate statement of the case, goes on to remark: "Therefore what is first presented more or less dark, difficult and obscure, Christ has all made manifest and clearly commanded to preach. Nevertheless, the holy fathers held this knowledge through the Holy Spirit, yet by no means as clear as we now have it."

Some have seen the solution of the difficulty to lie in calling this the majestic plural, such as sovereigns are wont to employ in edicts. This type of plural, however, cannot be demonstrated as used in the Scriptures. Luther's somewhat ironical remark should also be considered here: "The Holy Spirit is not wont to employ the courtesies employed for royalty" (*kanzleiische Hoeflichkeit*). Rightly speaking, a kind of *potential plural* is involved (K. S. 260 a-e), as the fullness of the potentialities that lie in God is expressed by the plural of *'elohim,* which may even be used with a plural form of its predicate adjective (Judg. 24:19; Ps. 58:12), but abstract plurals like these are not yet quite the same thing as a verb used in the first person plural, hortatory, as Strack tries to persuade himself to believe.

The common explanation, perhaps the most popular at present, that God is addressing the angels has been shown up in its deficiencies by Kœnig (K. C.). It cannot be denied that on occasion God addressed the angelic host before His throne; Isa. 6:8; I Kings 22:19-22. Angels are found standing in His presence Job 1; 38:7; Dan. 4:14; 7:10. But never once does God actually counsel with them. The distance between God and angels is seen to be a very pronounced one. Even in Isa. 6:8 this important difference stands out: "Whom shall *I* send?" God acts independently without angelic counsel. Besides, it must be considered that neither here nor by the time 3:22 is reached has anything been revealed about the creation of angels. And lastly, man is not considered in the Scriptures to have been made in the image of angels. If this remark included angels, man would be made in an image which blurred the divine and the angelic into one. The Old Testament does not muddle such important concepts.

Kœnig's interpretation deserves mention (K. S. 207 a). He claims that an individual reflecting upon a course of action to be followed may appear to himself both as giving orders and as carrying out these orders. He claims such a thing would happen "quite naturally and easily" (*naturgemaess leicht*). We can hardly imagine any explanation more stilted and artifi-

cial. It is a figment of the clever brain, invented to
extricate its inventor out of a predicament.

We should yet especially emphasize that the trinitarian view, presented in modified form above, is not,
as many charge, transferring the New Testament back
into the Old. We have emphasized above that the
New Testament marks an advance upon whatever the
Old offers under this head. What the Old Testament
offers here would never have been fully grasped if
clearer and more elaborate revelation had not thrown
its light upon this passage from the New Testament.

The being to be made is called *'adham*, a term
whose root significance must very likely be sought in
the cognate word *'adhamah* (see v. 25) which refers
to the soil capable of cultivation. *'Adham* would,
therefore, be "the cultivator of the soil."

The double modifying phrase, "in our image, after
our likeness," requires closer study. It is in the last
analysis nothing more than a phrase which aims to
assert with emphasis the idea that man is to be closely
patterned after his Maker. This feature in man's
being is a second mode of setting forth prominently
the singular dignity of man: Man is not only made
after the deliberate plan and purpose of God but is
also very definitely patterned after Him. In making
both phrases practically result in an idea which is
one composite whole we are not erasing the distinction between the terms. "Image" is for the word
tsélem, whose root means "to carve" or "to cut off."
We cannot go so far as to apply this idea to the
physical similarity of man with God, as some have.
But, at least, the term refers to more concrete similarity, whereas the second word *demûth*, "likeness,"
refers more to similarity in the abstract or in the
ideal. But here again we cannot venture with the
Greek fathers to apply the term to man's inner or
spiritual resemblance to God. Nor dare we press the
change of prepositions; *be* "in" and *ke* "as." For

though *be* describes man as being *within* a certain mold as it were, it yet must also be called a kind of *Beth normae* (K. S. 332 r), for Exod. 25:40 it is used practically like *ke*. To this must be added the fact that v. 27 considers the use of *tsélem* without *demûth* sufficient to express what God did, "image" being used twice. Again it 5:1 *demûth* with *be* and not with *ke*, as in our passage, is thought to be an adequate statement of the case. So we shall have to regard the second phrase, "according to our likeness," as merely supplementary to or explanatory of the first. Of course, the possessive "our" in connection with these two nouns is to be explained like the plural of "let us make" above.

But yet we have not defined what the term "the image of God" implies. Those who would rule out the clear passages of the New Testament and construe a picture only by the help of what this chapter offers, fail to discern the true unity of scriptural revelation and are bound to arrive at a misleading conception. True, the author of the account may himself not have had a full apperception of what all was involved in this concept, but here most especially the principle must be applied: Scripture must be explained by Scripture. Especially such passages as Eph. 4:24 and Col. 3:10 must be drawn upon. The reformers clearly saw that the most important thing involved was a proper attitude of heart in faith. Luther says: "I understand this image of God to be . . . that Adam not only knew God and believed in Him that He was gracious; but that he also led an entirely godly life." Cf. also *Apology* II, 17-22. As adequate a summary of all features involved as any is that of Kœnig in TAT, p. 226 ff. He lists the following items as belonging to the outward side of the divine image: a) man's countenance which directs his gaze upwards; b) a capacity for varying facial expressions; c) a sense of shame expressing itself in the blush of man;

d) speech. It cannot be denied that all these are physical features which are noticeably absent in all animals. To the inner side of the divine image the same author assigns the following items: a) on the material side of man's inner make-up stands immortality; b) on the intellectual side is self-consciousness, reason and *Vernunft;* c) on the voluntative-moral side is the ability to discern good and evil, the freedom of the will, conscience, and the right use of his moral capacities — the most important of all. We understand Kœnig to make this last statement in the sense of the reformer's quoted above.

To sum up from a slightly different angle we should like to append the thought that the spiritual and inner side of the image of God is, without a doubt, the most important one. It will hardly be safe to say that the body of man is also patterned after God, because God, being an incorporeal spirit, cannot have what we term a material body. Yet the body of man must at least be regarded as the fittest receptacle for man's spirit and so must bear at least an analogy to the image of God, an analogy that is so close that God and His angels choose to appear in human form when they appear to men (Strack). In fact, we are justified to go even so far as to say that whatever this man is said to have is in a far more real sense a reality in God. Here lies the basis for the propriety of all anthropomorphisms. If man has a hand, an ear, an eye, a heart, not only may these also be possessions of the Almighty; in a far truer sense such potentialities lie in God. Yet, let it be well marked, in saying this we in no sense ascribe corporeality to the Eternal One.

Skinner confuses all basic concepts and departs far from revealed truth, glorifying man and his native ability in an unscriptural fashion, when he remarks: "The 'image' is not something peculiar to man's original estate, and lost by the Fall." He justifies this radical departure by the further remark: "Because P, who alone uses the expression knows nothing of the Fall, and in 9:6 employs the term, without any restriction, of post-diluvian mankind." What an untenable assumption even from the standpoint of criticism! Just because what is ascribed to P does not happen to mention the Fall, we at once know what P actually knew or did not know about the Fall. The critic is coming to the point where in his mind *the document P* and *the person P* are identical. The passage 9:6 is, of course, to be taken in the light of all that precedes, namely in the light of the Fall, which intervenes between chapters 1 and 9.

When evidence fails to support pet theories — in this instance the theory of the derivation of Israelitish knowledge from Babylonian sources — pure suppositions such as the following are resorted to: "The origin of the conception ('image') is probably found in the Babylonian mythology" (Skinner).

What follows is one direction in which the possession of the image of God on the part of man expresses itself — dominion over the earth. "Let them have dominion" is the verb *radhah* signifying "to trample down" or "to master." The breadth of the domain to be ruled by man is expressed by the various spheres of man's dominion that are now enumerated. They are, first of all, the classes previously described as having been brought into being, listed with a slight modification of terminology. The "swarms" or "shoals" previously created (v. 20) are referred to by a term covering the chief members of this class, *daghah*, "fish" in a collective sense. "The birds of the heavens" are the second group mentioned. Though we have translated *behemah* "domestic animals," we cannot deny that it might here, as a broader term often so used (cf. Exod. 9:25; 12:12), include all larger animals, wild and domestic, because man's dominion certainly covered the wild beasts as well, as appears from the remaining terms, yet the wild beasts are not separately mentioned. For the list goes on to mention "the whole earth," which cannot, as Kœnig suggests (K. C.), here be taken to mean "all beings upon the earth" (*Erdlebewesen*), for then the very last term in the list would duplicate this; nor can it mean "the dwellers upon earth," a meaning which "earth" sometimes has, for then the idle statement would result: let man rule over himself. Consequently, we take "the whole earth" in its simplest meaning, as the inanimate earth proper, which man is to master and subdue. We then list, as belonging in this department of his activity, man's mastery of the powers of nature, physical, electrical, chemical, physiological and the like. Whatever true scientific endeavor has produced comes under this broad charter which the Creator has given to man. Since, however, man's dominion is to find most frequent expression in the direction of the control of living creatures, the closing statement, the broadest of all, mounts to a climax in the words "over everything that moveth about upon the earth." Every type of being is to be subservient to man. The word employed for this last class is *rémes,* which appears here in the broadest application of its root sense "to move about" and less in the specific sense of "moving about *lightly.*" The verb used (*yirdû*) is a jussive (K. S. 364 h) and actually establishes as a divine word the situation it outlines. Man in reality became the controlling power. Yet there remains — even in the primeval state there remained — much to be achieved by way of a perfect mastery of his whole territory.

Taking the verse as a whole, we cannot but notice that it sets forth the picture of a being that stands on a very high level, a creature of singular nobility and endowed with phenomenal powers and attributes, not a type of being that by its brute imperfections

is seen to be on the same level with the animal world,
but a being that towers high above all other creatures,
their king and their crown.

**27. So God created man in His image, in the
image of God He created him, male and female He
created them.**

The higher strain of diction is made apparent
by a threefold parallelism of the statement — a kind
of solemn chant is here inaugurated in the creation
narrative. And well might any man who writes an
account of the subject write in a manner that betokens
his joy, for the honor bestowed upon man is indeed
great. In fact, none could be greater than that a
created being be made in the image of God.

The threefold use of the verb "create" (*bara'*)
is significant in this connection. To bring things into
being that had no previous existence is well described
by this word (v. 1). To bring into being creatures
endowed with life and a soul is also covered by this
word (v. 21). To do so outstanding a thing as to
call into being a creature like unto man is in every
sense "to create." However, whether the threefold
use of the term is to be accounted for by the fact
that the triune God is the Creator, is a question that
we feel inclined to leave open. To us such a conclusion
seems to lay more into the statement here made than
it can justly bear.

Rather important is the possessive pronoun
attached to the word "image," namely the *singular*
"his." As much as God, on the one hand, speaking
out of the fulness of His powers in the persons of the
Holy Trinity, is able to say, "Let *us* make," and *"our*
image," just so much is it a valid and proper statement for Him to say that He created "in *His* image."
One accords fully with the other in the mystery of the
Holy Trinity: there is but one God. The Septuagint
translators removed a difficulty in a portion of revela-

tion which they should not have tampered with when they simply omitted the phrase "in His image." The notes in the Hebrew Bible of Kittel should not have suggested the deletion of the word.

The change from "His image" to "the image of God" shows the attempt on the writer's part to make his statement as strong and as dignified as possible. Then, since the second statement, telling of the carrying out of the original command, usually serves in a measure as a commentary of the former, so here a very necessary suggestion is offered. Though from one point of view it is entirely proper to say that God on the sixth day created "man" (*'adham*), yet, as the rest of the account at once indicates, this term is meant generically; and, since by a special work of the Almighty woman is brought into being, this first statement of the case amplifies itself into the more exact statement of the case that "the man" (the article of relative familiarity, K. S. 298 a) was created "male and female" (*zakhar*, from the root meaning *male*; *neqebhah*, from *naqab*, meaning *to perforate*). In other words, all queer speculations about the first man are cut off as well as the quaint heresy that he was created androgynous, half man and half woman — a notion offered in crudest form by the Jewish speculation which had the two halves of the double creature attached back to back, and then had the Almighty saw them asunder. This account, then, of chapter one shows that its writer knows chapter two and writes in full harmony with the facts of that chapter. As will appear more and more clearly, the first two chapters are in perfect harmony with one another and by no means represent divergent or discrepant accounts. So, according to very permissible different viewpoints, yet without contradiction, the writer may well say: "He created *him*" and "He created *them*," even as *"our* image" and *"His* image" blend into perfect unity.

Procksch says on this verse: "Man, God's image, man, the crown of creation, man, male and female — we, too, have not been able to advance beyond these thoughts." A characteristic utterance of modern theology and a — platitude. Of course, we have not been able to advance beyond this thought; we never advance beyond revealed truth or God's thoughts. This account is not an achievement of the religious genius of P; it is revelation pure and simple.

28. **Then God blessed them, and God said to them: Be fruitful, and multiply, and fill the earth, and subdue it, and have dominion over the fish of the sea, and over the birds of the heavens, and over every living creature moving about upon the earth.**

That there is a similarity as well as a dissimilarity between man and all other living creatures is indicated by various means, here particularly by the fact that man's perpetuation of the human race is made to depend upon an effective divine blessing, as in the case of other creatures (v. 22), and by the use even of similar terms: "Be fruitful and multiply and fill." This last expression, therefore, is not a stylistic peculiarity but a historical fact indicative of the similarity just mentioned.

"Subdue," the new word in the account of man's dominion, is *kabhash*, and it differs from "have dominion" (*radhah*) in that its root rather implies "to knead" or "to tread," whereas the latter is the stronger according to parallel roots, meaning "to stamp down." Yet this difference is not to be pressed. The statement of the things to be ruled is a bit more condensed than in v. 26, for the last statement summarizes, "every living creature moving about upon the earth." This expression covers everything beyond "birds" and "fish," namely everything mentioned in addition in v. 26 with the exception of "all the earth." Again the text needs no correction or addition of "over the cattle" as Kittel suggests after the pattern of the

Septuagint and of the Samaritan Pentateuch. This would merely secure a kind of wooden uniformity plus an idle repetition. The statement in the text covers all this. This broader meaning of the verb *ramas,* "to move about," (B D B) is assured by the passages: 7:21; 8:19; Ps. 104:20. "Subdue it," the verb with the object suffix (*kibhshúha*) offers the only instance in this chapter of an object without the sign of the accusative (*'eth*).

A very important institution is brought into being at this point, the institution of marriage. Here is another point of correspondence between chapter one and chapter two, though the latter gives greater detail. After v. 26 has now given the summary account of the creation of one pair, "male and female," v. 27 proceeds to have the divine command laid upon this one pair: "Be fruitful and multiply and fill the earth." The primary purpose of marriage is here indicated. On "fill the earth" Whitelaw remarks: "This clause may be regarded as the *colonist's charter"* — a very proper observation.

29, 30. **And God said: Behold, I have given you all herbs yielding seed which are upon the face of all the earth, and every tree upon which there is seed-bearing fruit — to you it shall be for food. And to all the wild beasts of the earth, and to all the birds of the heavens, and to all the land reptiles in which there is a living soul (I have given) all the green herbs for food. And it was so.**

Such basic directions as man needs for guiding his steps in this world which is entirely new to him are here given in the matter of food (v. 29), and at the same time it is revealed to man what manner of food is to provide sustenance for beasts (v. 30). Besides being a very welcome direction, this word is also another indication of the rich and abounding love that the Heavenly Father bears to His creatures, made in His image.

The opening "behold" imparts a certain vigor to this gracious bestowal. The verb "I have given" (*nathátti*) stands in the perfect, the usual construction in ordinances or abiding decrees. The perfect gives the impression of a rule firmly fixed and already unwavering. (G. K. 106 m; K. S. 131). Man is permitted to use a great variety of things comprising a vegetable diet. Two great classes are laid open to him: "herbs yielding seed" and "fruit trees which have seed-bearing fruit." The classes are indicated and the distinguishing marks that are to be observed are stated. This marks two of the three classes of v. 11 as adapted to man's use. Since there is the possibility that since the Fall vegetation may have suffered a very material change, perhaps we are no longer in a position fully to appreciate how apt the the descriptive marks mentioned really are. However, the word "all" is indicative of the rich bounty bestowed. In a marvelously rich and beautiful world the rich bounty of very many different kinds of herbs and trees provided the finest proof of the Creator's goodness.

Without a doubt, this word covering what food is permissible was intended to be a complete guide as to what man might eat. If 9:3 be held at the side of this word, the contrast implies that animal food was not permitted. It will hardly do to point to man's dominion over the beasts of the field, over fowl, and over fish (v. 26), for this word (v. 29) very definitely shows man what he may use for food. We believe that sincere regard for the very letter of God's command will have led our first parents to stay strictly within the limits of this word. As to the question, whether any men ventured before the Flood to eat animal food, we can only offer surmises. Not all men continued in the right relation to God, and so there may have been some of the ungodly who ventured to transgress this original permission. But we cannot

venture to call such procedure common. Least of all
could any true believer have disregarded the restriction implied in this word.

Certainly, a measure of latitude is allowed to man
in respect to what may be permissible and wholesome
food for him. This broad allowance was never intended to be exhaustive. So it has been pointed out
(Dillmann) that nothing is said, for example, about
the use of milk and of honey, which may be thought
of as lying on the borderline between animal and
vegetable food. The critically minded should not forget that a being endowed with the high intelligence
that we find in the first man needed no more than a
broad outline to guide him to a choice pleasing to God
and beneficial for himself.

30. So it will also be observed that the directions that obtain for the other living creatures are not
exhaustive. Fish are not mentioned. But, no doubt,
this word was merely to inform man in reference to
the creatures with which he had the more immediate
contact. So all living creatures are summed up in this
verse in three classes: wild beasts of the earth, birds,
and reptiles — and, summing up still more, comes the
closing phrase applicable to all, "in which there is
a living soul." The food, however, that by God's ordinance is appointed for all these is described as "all
the green herbs." It is taken, therefore, from the
second of the three classes of v. 11 and the restrictive
modifier preceding *yéreg*, yielding the expression
"greenness of herb," which we have rendered "the
green herbs." That cannot be identical with everything that comes under the class of "herbs." Meek,
therefore, renders quite appropriately "all the green
plants." The verb of the main clause of this verse is
missing; "I have given" is best supplied from the preceding verse.

In brief, this verse is an indication of the perfect
harmony prevailing in the animal world. No beast

preyed upon the other. Rapacious and ferocious wild beasts did not yet exist. This verse, then, indicates very briefly for this chapter what is unfolded at length in chapter two, that a paradise-like state prevailed at creation.

Skinner pronounces v. 29 and 30 to be an indication of one of the sources which P worked into his account, because these verses, as he says, "differ significantly in their phraseology from the preceding sections." The trifling difference of an abbreviated summary is exaggerated into what is said to "differ significantly." The critics need far more substantial arguments than untenable exaggerations. The same author claims that we have in these verses an "enrichment of the creation story by the independent and widespread myth of the Golden Age." Why, pray, cannot the simple unadorned account merely be a narrative of things as they actually transpired? Answer: the critics have decreed that such accounts cannot exist; all such narratives must be patchwork in which a generous measure of myth has been incorporated. But decreeing that it must be as the critics surmise is not proof. We refuse to be intimidated by claims which lack actual substance.

Let the student of the original note in v. 29 an instance where the relative is not separated from its adverbial term belonging to it *'asher-bō* (K. S. 58).

31. And God saw all that He had made and behold it was very good. Then came evening, then came morning — the sixth day.

The writer says with emphasis that no imperfection inhered in the work God had wrought up till this point. For after all preceding statements to the effect that individual works were good comes this stronger statement to the effect that it was "very good," making a total of seven times that the word is used — seven being the mark of divine operation. The thought that God might be the author of evil and imperfection must be guarded against most strenuously (Strack). The "behold" moves the expression "very good" prominently into the foreground (K. S. 341v). *Kol* before *'asher* lies on the borderline between partitive genitive and appositional genitive (K. S. 337 h). "The sixth" has the article with the numeral for the first time (G. K. 126 w), meaning: "*the* sixth day," that last memorable creative day of God.

The next three verses had best be taken as the conclusion of the summary creation account of the first chapter, because the record of this account cannot be complete till all of the seven days have passed in review. More appropriate would have been the chapter division at 2:4.

HOMILETICAL SUGGESTIONS

There is so much matter in every line of this chapter that perhaps the chief danger encountered is the tendency to use too short a text. We personally believe that here for once it might be permissible to use as a text one verse such as v. 1 or v. 27. But to treat such a Scripture properly requires true homiletical skill. We feel that it might be best to treat the work of each of the creative days separately in six distinct texts, always stressing how each day's work displays primarily God's great power but then also very manifestly His wisdom and His mercy. The apologetic approach should be avoided. Attempts to harmonize science and religion lie too much in the realm of apologetics and usually are not handled very successfully. A warning should be offered here against allegorizing the chapter, as is done by all those who see in the successive stages of creation a picture of the successive steps in the process of conversion. Attractive as the parallel may be, it does not lie in the purpose of the chapter and should not be injected. In sermons on other texts it may be appropriate to use material from Genesis Chapter One incidentally as providing a kind of illustration—a use found in II Cor. 4:6. But allegorizing as such does violence to the purpose of this chapter. Talley's *A Socratic Exposition of Genesis* as well as Rimmer's books tend toward this unwarranted allegorizing.

CHAPTER II

1. Thus the heavens and the earth were finished and all their host.

Though the first word literally reads *"and* they were finished," yet the idea of retrospect involved in the verse was caught very beautifully by Luther, who rendered "and" *also*; "thus" is an equally correct rendering of A. V. Attention is particularly drawn to the elaborateness and completeness of this work by the added subject "and all their host" *(tsebha'am).* Without a doubt, this expression includes all the works found in heaven and on earth as a result of the creative work thus described. "Host" *(tsabha')* may refer to the stars; cf. Neh. 9:6; Deut. 4:19: 17:3; II Kings 17:16, etc. It may refer to angels: I Kings 22:19; Neh. 9:6; Ps. 148:2. Here its connection determines its reference to the things just made. Since the creation account has up to this point said nothing about angels, it will hardly be safe to advance the claim that the angels are meant to be included in this term. The time of the creation of angels is as little fixed by this account as falling on this day as it is assigned to the fourth. We simply know nothing definite as to the time of their creation.

2. And on the seventh day God declared His work on which He was engaged, finished, and He desisted on the seventh day from all the work on which He had been engaged.

After the first verse has plainly stated that all was finished, the statement of v. 2 to the effect that not until the seventh day God finished His work (A.

R. V.) is, to say the least, misleading. A. V. evaded
the problem by subsituting "ended" for "finished" (v.
1), although the same verb root is involved: *yekhullû*
(v. 1), *yekhal* (v. 2). But the verb used in v. 2 is
of the *Piel* stem, which is sometimes declarative in
sense, as *tiher* means "to declare clean," Lev. 13:6-
14:48, and *timme'* means "to declare unclean," Lev.
13:8; 20:25. So here we may have the meaning,
"He declared finished." Thus the difficulty, which
prompted the Septuagint translators and many since
(cf. K.) to alter "seventh" to "sixth," is satisfactorily
removed. Cf. K. C. The pluperfect, adopted from
Meek, "on which He *had been engaged*," is not a necessary translation. Pluperfect renderings should be
employed with great caution. The meaning is the
same when the imperfect is used: "on which He *was
engaged*."

Since the primary meaning of the verb *shabhath*
is "to cease" or "to desist," we are freed of all misconceptions which may attach to God's activity if we
adopt this meaning. If God desisted from labor on
this day, then no more work was done on it, then
nothing had to be completed, then no unseemly thought
about God's being weary needs to be rejected. The
verse then amounts to an emphatic statement to the
effect that just as on the preceding days a marvelous
creative work was in progress, so now that type and
that manner of working on God's part came to an end:
He declared all finished, He desisted from all. The
"work" that He desisted from is described by the term
mela'khah, meaning a special task He had set for Himself and afterward "used regularly of the work or
business forbidden on the Sabbath" (Driver quoted by
Skinner) Exod. 29:9, 10; 35:2; Jer. 17:22, 24 *et al.*
Incidentally, in this connection Skinner makes the
very sane observation that "the actual Jewish Sabbath
as we know it (is) without any point of contact in
Babylonian institutions." However, the thing under

consideration in these verses is not the Jewish Sabbath but the creation Sabbath.

3. **And God blessed the seventh day and sanctified it, for on it He desisted from all His work which He had created by making.**

Creatures have been blessed (v. 22), man has been blessed more richly (v. 28). The summary creation account which began at 1:1 is aptly concluded by an act of divine blessing, which, however, in this case attaches itself to the seventh day. The object of this rather unusual procedure is twofold: on the one hand, such an act serves as an indication to man that rest such as the divine rest is noble and holy and by no means to be lightly esteemed; in the second place, those blessings of the Sabbath that are later to flow forth for the good of man are potentially bestowed on it. For on the one hand, the verb "he sanctified it" (*qiddesh*), being a *Piel* stem, has the connotation of a causative — as the *Piel* often does (K. S. 95) — and on the other hand, it at the same time has a declarative sense: "He declared holy, or consecrated." However, it should be well observed that no commandment is laid upon mankind at this point. Procksch remarks rightly and pointedly: "for the present the Sabbath stays in heaven." Yet this does not make the Sabbath a futile abstraction, but, as was remarked above, its connection with the divine rest or cessation from labor is made to stand forth as a worthy divine act.

At the same time the entire groundlessness of the critical assumption becomes apparent, where the arrangement of works according to days is attributed to clever and purposeful manipulation on the part of the author. For, having eight major works, he (it is said) nevertheless compresses them within six days, to be followed by a seventh rest day, in order to secure a divine parallel to the Hebrew week. This is not a week ordained for man. It is entirely a divine week. Nor is there clever editorial manipulation, but simply an accurate and straightforward account of things as they actually took place.

With a certain fulness of expression this part of the account comes to a dignified close with the causal clause, "for on it He desisted," etc. The adjective clause "which He had created by making" conveys the thought that, though it was creative work (*bara'*), yet at the same time this creative work was accomplished by work which was done through successive steps: "by making" (*la'asóth*). This gerundival use of the infinitive is explained in K. S. 402 y and G. K. 114 o.

Before leaving this initial account we must yet take definite issue with one problem involved in the account as a whole. On the one hand, is this a strictly factual account, reporting what actually transpired in the manner in which it transpired? Or have we here a picture devised by human ingenuity, which picture seeks to convey truth by its general outlines or by the basic thoughts which are here expressed in terms highly figurative? Though this latter view has come to be held almost universally, it is still by no means true. We have not in this chapter a marvelous product of the religious creative genius of Israel. Such efforts would merely have produced just one more trivial and entirely worthless cosmogony. The account as it stands expects the impartial reader to accept it as entirely literal and historical. The use made of it in the rest of Sacred Scriptures treats every part referred to as sober fact, not as a fancy-picture. Compare on this chapter the dozens of marginal reference passages found in almost any Bible.

By answering this question we have answered a second one: Does the value of this account lie "in the broad basic truths it embodies" (K. C.), or in the details by which these truths are conveyed? The form of this question is unfortunate. It should not

postulate an "either – or," but a "both – and." The
details are truthful, exact and essential, being in all
their parts truth itself. Only since this is the case,
are the broad, basic truths conveyed by the account
also of infinite moment and in themselves divinely
revealed truth. Faith in inspiration, as taught by the
Scriptures, allows for no other possibility.

II. The First History (Toledôth)
viz., that of Heaven and Earth (2:4-4:26)

Unfortunately, every inch of this chapter is a
battleground. Instead of accepting its simple revelation as harmonious in itself and with what precedes,
an unbelievable amount of ingenuity is displayed in
an effort to prove certain preconceived critical contentions, which are not only misleading but entirely
erroneous and mischievous, for their acceptance breaks
down all possibility of firm faith in these portions of
revealed truth.

These erroneous contentions center around the
major critical error of the various sources of the
Pentateuch: the author of this portion is no longer
P but J, the Jahwist. The amount of supporting
arguments advanced by the critics is truly imposing.
Their arguments are set forth in four or five major
claims, which Dods sums up: two chapters "glaringly
incompatible in details."

1. It is asserted that the different divine names
employed are in themselves almost convincing proof
of material from the pen of quite a different writer
than he who submitted 1:1-2:3. It is true that the
divine name *Yahweh* (or *Jahweh*) appears regularly
in this chapter in conjunction with the name employed
heretofore, *Elohim*. However, by way of refutation
let the following facts be noted. In the first place,
the critical assumption is a very narrow one, nor has
it ever been proved, namely, the supposition that the

writers of the various source-documents knew for the most part but *one* of the divine names, at least J and P for the most part knew but one name. It was blithely assumed that the earliest writers, of whom J was one, could know God from only one aspect. Secondly, all manner of arbitrary assumptions bolster up the initial assumption, so, for example, when in 3:5 *Elohim* alone appears, this is supposed to be a portion of another source which J used. Or when *Elohim* and *Yahweh* appear jointly in chapter two, i. e., regularly as *Yahweh Elohim,* this is supposed to be explained by the activity of some later redactor, not J, who combined the two to smoothe over the transition from the one name to the other, and so aimed to teach that in reality both authors believed in one and the same divine being. Such claims can never be proved.

Mœller, B T, p. 67, draws attention to a very remarkable parallel in this connection. He makes a count of the divine names in 1:1-2:3 and then of the divine names in 2:4-4:26 and presents these findings: "In 2:4-4:26 it must be observed that *Yahweh 'Elohim* is used successively *twenty* times, with the name *'Elohim* interrupting *five* times, but always for a very definite reason, and the name *Yahweh* is used *ten* times, making a total of *thirty-five* (built up out of the sub-totals 20 + 5 + 10). Furthermore it must be observed that these thirty-five correspond exactly to the *thirty-five 'Elohim* found in 1:1-2:3, which thirty-five names are again contained in the tenfold expression *"and God said"* (*'Elohim*) and therefore also resolve themselves into 25 + 10. Consequently, the *seventy* divine names of 1:1-4:26 can in no wise be regarded as being used in a purely arbitrary sense . . . . "

2.   It is also asserted that the writer of this portion uses a vocabulary different in many other noticeable aspects from that of the author of the first

chapter. It certainly cannot be denied that quite a number of different words occur in this chapter. But the far simpler and very evident reason is not change of author but change of subject matter. When a new subject is taken in hand, new words must needs be employed to describe it. Self-evident as this is, we have never seen a critic face this argument squarely.

3. It is furthermore asserted that the difference in point of view between the two authors involved goes so far as to make very prominent a noticeably different conception of God: the Yahweh Elohim of 2:4 ff. is much more anthropomorphic than the God of chapter one. He "forms" man (v. 7); He "plants" a garden (v. 8); He "takes" the man whom He has formed and "puts" him into the garden (v. 15); He experiments with man to find a helpmate for him (v. 19); He "builds" a woman out of the rib (v. 22); He "walks" in the garden (3:8); He "drives" man out of the garden (3:24). So e. g. Dillmann. Other items are occasionally cited; there may suffice. More detailed refutation of these points will be offered as they occur. It should, however, be borne in mind that chapter one, as we pointed out, offered certain very prominent anthropomorphisms, which may very well be classed as arguing a conception of God no different from that of the next two chapters. A trifling difference, which may not even be worthy to be called a difference of style, is exaggerated to the point of being made to appear as a radical difference. Practically identical with this argument, from another point of view, is the claim that was considered above under 2 as "different vocabulary." On the negative view consult especially Skinner.

4. Then, with practical unanimity the critics point to what on the surface looks like a different conception of the sequence of the works of creation. For in this chapter the sequence of events is claimed

to be: man (v. 7), trees (v. 9), beasts (v. 19), woman.
If this were actually what J claims, there would certainly be a radical difference between the first two
chapters. The difference would be so violent as in
no sense to allow for merely divergent points of view.
One account would of necessity rule out the other. A
flat contradiction would prevail. Oehler (J A T, p.
76) has rightly remarked under this head: "It is
just as unlikely as it can be that the author should
have been such a dunce (*so borniert*) as to set down
at the very outset two mutually exclusive records
of creation." The truth of the matter, however, is
simply this: the account of chapter two does not aim
to present a complete creation story, nor is the time-
sequence followed by the author, Moses. Rather, those
supplementary facts, essential to the right evaluation
of chapter three, are given in a sequence which is
entirely logical. In other words, the connective "and"
(*waw*) is not to be taken in the sense of "next" (e. g.
next God did thus and so) but rather in the sense of
a loose "also" without thought of time-sequence. The
stage is being set for the tragic drama of the next
chapter. The things enumerated by the author as
appearing on the stage, as it were, need not be listed
in the order in which they were placed there. The
logical sequence will, however, have to be explained
in detail as we proceed with our exposition *infra*.

5. To all this is added one of those farfetched
conclusions, which offsets by its boldness what it lacks
in substance and so manages to impress the unlearned,
the conclusion that even the different backgrounds of
the two authors involved can be definitely discerned.
For P, it is said, sees all the creative work of God
rise out of the primeval waters and therefore must
have been a man coming from a well-watered country;
whereas J sees the beginnings of God's creation in dry,
desert-like land (cf. 2:5 b) and so must himself have
been a desert-dweller. First of all, the conclusion

that because a man writes about a certain type of
land as having been the original, he himself must be
a native of that type of land is quite devoid of logic.
In the second place, the idea that the face of the
earth was for a time practically bone-dry, is the outgrowth of the misreading of 2:5 and utterly without
factual foundation.

An illustration of argument 2, above, on the
question of different vocabulary, so-called, may be
submitted. Skinner offers the following expressions,
characteristic of this document J: "to the east of,"
(2:14); "now" (*happa'am*, 2:23); "what is this?"
(*mah - zo'th* 3:13); "cursed" (*'arûr*, 3:14,17); "pain"
(*'itsabhon*, 3:16, 17); "for thy sake" (*ba'abhur*, 3:17).
There was no occasion to use these terms prior to
the time when they finally do appear in this concise
narrative.   Now the account actually demands them.
That does not make them stylistic peculiarities, nor
in the least indications of the hand of another writer.
This critical claim comes very close to being an absurdity. Yet with almost one voice critics keep
advancing it.

4 a. **This is the story of the heavens and the
earth at the time of their creation.**

This simple and very correct title, placed here by
the author himself, must be retained and defended as
being the most correct and appropriate. By disregarding its suggestion criticism has fallen short of
the right understanding of this portion, which extends
to the end of chapter four. This is, then, a story in
which heaven and earth share. Both are vitally in-
terested. It is, besides, a story that is enacted just
at the time of creation, or when the newly created
world in its pristine freshness was about to begin its
career. To overlook the interplay of the divine and
the human factors is one of the common shortcomings
of the treatment of this chapter.

Ignoring or deleting this heading, men have devised captions like the following, either for the chapter or for the section 2:4-4:26: "The Course of Creation and the First Relations of the Earth and Mankind" (Kœnig) ; "Paradise" (Procksch) ; "The Details Concerning the Creation of Man and Woman" (Delitzsch) ; "Creation — Second Account" (Knobel) ; and all these, strange to say, practically in opposition to the author's own title.

One method of dealing with this heading is to refer it to the preceding section, so that it is not a *super*scription but a kind of *sub*scription. In that event it is usually translated about as follows : "These are the origins of the heaven and the earth." Now it is a well-known fact that the book of Genesis is by its own author divided into ten sections, to each of which he gives the title "story" (*toledôth*) ; cf. 5:1; 6:9; 10:1; 11:10, 27; 25:12, 19; 36:1, (9) ; 37:2. This circumstance alone, plus the use of the round number ten, would definitely point to the fact that here the expression, "these are the *toledôth*" must also be a heading. In all other instances of its use in other books the same fact is observable; cf. Num. 3:1; Ruth 4:18; I Chron. 1:29; it is as always a heading.

Besides, though A. V. translates: "these are the generations," the term never means "generations" or "origins." It never tells how things or persons came into being. It tells what happened after such things or such persons had appeared on the scene. Another good rendering is "history." The plural form *toledôth* merely conveys the idea, so common in Hebrew, of the many individual items that go to make up a "history" or "story." B D B, limiting itself too closely to the idea of "begettings," interprets the expression to mean "account of heaven and earth and that which proceeded from them." It cannot mean "descendants" (Meek), for far more than a list of "descendants" is given in each *toledôth*; cf. especially 37:2 where the descendants are not given. B D B's error is practically the same.

Criticism makes a great problem for itself at this point. This first half of v. 4, being a "formal" expression, the critics must attribute to P. Now all evidence points to its being a heading over a J account. How did that come to pass? One answer is a mistranslation; Meek renders "origins," contrary to all usage. Others claim that 2:4 originally stood at the head of chapter one. They at once become responsible for an answer to the question: "How, then, did this portion slip into chapter two at this point?" Consult the critics for answers that are either naive or impossible. To others the activity of some later redactor suggests itself.

The expression "at the time of their creation" (*behibbare'am*) is rendered literally: "in their being created." Since it is a temporal phrase, we have rendered it: "at the time," etc. It marks the occurrences that are to follow as practically a part of the creation story (K. S. 401 k). The small Hebrew letter *heh* in the word has been fantastically explained, but never successfully. There is no call for textual alterations, (Kit.). The heading makes clear and very good sense.

Luther's rendering cannot be retained: *"Also ist Himmel und Erde geworden,"* "thus the heavens and the earth came into being." Kautzsch belongs to the same class: *"Das ist die Geschichte der Entstehung"* ("this is the story of the origin") — an attempt to combine the right and the wrong views.

4 b, 5. At the time when Yahweh God made earth and heaven, then no shrub of the field was as yet in the earth and no plant of the field was as yet sprouting forth; for Yahweh God had not caused rain to descend upon the earth, nor did man exist to till the ground.

Verse 4 a and 4 b are usually translated as a whole, with the result that two temporal clauses of nearly identical meaning appear within the sentence, calling forth artificial attempts at distinctions. By keeping 4 a separate as a title and by combining 4 b with 5, this trouble is removed, and a very natural rendering results. For the two initial clauses of v. 5, introduced by *waw*, may be correlative, as K. S. suggests: "when God made heaven and earth *neither* was there a shrub . . . nor had any plant sprouted" (K. S. 371 e). At the same time the complicated sentence structure which the critics make of v. 5-7 is shown to be quite unnecessary and quite cumbersome: v. 5 protasis; v. 6 rather parenthetical, or a concessive clause; v. 7 apodosis, (e. g. Dillmann) — all of which calls for a very artificial rendering (K. S. 416 a, 413 a). Nor is *térem* the conjunction "before," but the adverb "not yet" (K. S. 135, 357 r).

Verse 4 b takes us back into the time of the work of creation, more particularly to the time before the work of the third day began, and draws our attention to certain details, which, being details, could hardly have been inserted in chapter one: the fact that certain forms of plant life, namely the kinds that require the attentive care of man in greater measure, had not sprung up. Apparently, the whole work of the third day is in the mind of the writer. When verdure covered the earth, the sprouting of these types of vegetation was retarded, so that they might appear after man was already in full possession of his domain and in a position to give them their needed care. That is why it is remarked in the double causal clause 5 b: God had not yet caused rain to descend upon the earth; also, man did not exist as yet to till the ground. The fact that not the whole of vegetation is meant appears from the distinctive terms employed, neither of which had as yet appeared in the account. They are *sîach hassadheh*, well rendered by Meek

"field shrubs"; we render above: "shrub of the field";
and *'esebh hassadheh,* also well rendered by Meek,
"field plants"; our rendering: "plant of the field." For
the word *sadheh* means tillable ground, arable fields,
the ground "yielding plants and trees" (B D B). That
at least must be the meaning in this connection where
man's cultivation is referred to. It is not important
to the author to mark the point of time within the
creation week when this condition prevailed. Consequently, the opening phrase of 4 b, *beyôm,* is to
be rendered as it so often is "at the time" and not
"in the day." Apparently, too, though it is not specifically stated, types of vegetation are here under
consideration that grew up specifically in Paradise, for
the account centers around Paradise throughout the
rest of the chapter. Consequently, it will be very
difficult to determine just what is to be understood by
this finer type of vegetation here referred to as "field
shrubs" and "field plants."

From all this it appears sufficiently how absurd
the claim is that in this account (chapter 2:4 ff) man
is made first, then vegetation.

6. **So a mist kept rising from the earth and
kept watering all the surface of the ground.**

We render the opening conjunction *we* "so," in
order to show how closely this verse is tied up with
the preceding. This verse aims to show how the
deficiency of water mentioned in v. 5 was met. For
the same reason the noun begins the sentence (K. S.
339 e) : "mist" is in the first place for emphasis.
'Edh is not a wave, *Wasserschwall,* but may well
mean "mist," or "fog," according to an Arabic parallel
(K. W.). The Septuagint translators guessed at the
meaning of the difficult word, making it πηγή, "spring."
A regular and continuous mode of operation now begins, as the durative imperfect (*ya'aleh*) indicates,
(G. K. 107 b; K. S. 157; *yaktûl durans*). This may
refer to the continuous evaporation which began to

set in, or to the more or less frequent but periodic mists of evening or morning. In any case, since the lack of moisture has just been mentioned in v. 5, the likelihood is that in this concise account we are to think of the following threefold process: the rising of the mists, their condensation and the regular falling as rain; and are so to picture to ourselves the process of the "watering of all the surface of the ground." That this is the most likely sense appears from the fact that v. 7 at once proceeds to mention the removal of the second deficiency mentioned in v. 5; for v. 7 tells how man was put on the scene. The author is hastening onward in his report and cannot insert almost self-evident details (Strack).

Critics evidently make little effort to understand what is comparatively simple. Verses 5 and 6 are supposed to represent a "confusion of two points of view . . . there may be a Babylonian basis to the myth, it must have taken its present shape in some drier region, presumably in Palestine" (Skinner). Note the strange logic: only a native of a dry country can write v. 5 about the deficiency of water; only a native from a well-watered region is competent to write v. 6. In an effort to discover sources, criticism ends in absurdity. Unwilling to believe a simple reliable Scripture, criticism puts on it the stamp of "myth."

7. And Yahweh Elohim molded man out of the dust of the ground and breathed into his nostrils the breath of life, and man became a living being.

For the present, in direct connection with v. 5, it is stated how God provided for the deficiency that had to be removed before the special plants and shrubs mentioned could be allowed to spring forth. When then reporting that God did form man, the writer takes occasion to provide a few supplementary details, which will enable his readers to form a more adequate estimate of man. The title "Yahweh Elohim" suggests, as it does throughout the chapter, that this was a work of God that significantly displayed the faithful mercy of Yahweh as well as His awe-inspiring power. The verb employed here accords more with the "Yahweh" character of God; *yatsar* means to "mold" or "form." It is the word that specifically describes the activity of the potter (Jer. 18:2 ff). The idea to be emphasized is that with the particular care and personal attention that a potter gives to his task God gives tokens of His interest in man, His creature, by molding him as He does. No crude material notions of God need to be associated with this verb. Let them misunderstand who insist that they must! Nor can it justly be claimed that an author who previously spoke of this work as a "creating" and "making" must be so limited and circumscribed in point of style as to be utterly unable to describe such a work of the Almighty from any other point of view and say He "formed." Such an author must have an exceedingly cramped and wooden style.

Employing an accusative of material, the writer tells us that the material God employed in making man was "the dust of the ground." *'Aphar*, rendered "dust," does not refer to dry pulverized earth only. Here, without a doubt, a damp mass of the finest earth is under consideration. Luther's rendering is still unsurpassed, *Erdenkloss*, lit. "lump of earth." The term does not mean "mud," as the skeptics irreverently declare. Lest man form too high an estimate of the first man, it is here recorded that, in spite of the high station involved in being made in the image of God, man has a constituent part in his makeup, which forever forbids unseemly pride on his part — a thought frequently stressed in the devotional literature of the church from days of old. Without this fact to reckon with we could hardly have been in a position to understand how a temptation and fall were even possible. Practically everything written in chapter two definitely paves the way for chapter three.

Yet, in this strange mixture of dignity and lowliness, the story of man's creation definitely indicates how high above all other types of life man stands. The earth brings forth the others (v. 24). Man is formed out of the earth by God's personal activity. But more, a far more prominent distinguishing mark characterizes man's creation: God "breathed into his nostrils the breath of life." A personal, vitalizing act of the Creator imparts life to man — an honor bestowed upon none of the lesser creatures. This breathing on God's part must, as Keil rightly reminds us, be understood θεοπρεπῶς, i. e. in a manner befitting God. Nor can we for a moment hold that air or human breath was what God breathed into man's nostrils. It was His own vital breath. Nor will it do to associate a particular lapse of time or anything like toilsome effort with the whole process. This creative work may well have been the matter of a moment. In language such as man can grasp but which hardly can do justice to such noble divine works, the author depicts the singular grandeur of this work.

Much as we may be inclined to claim that the distinctive element in man's creation is the "breath of life" breathed into his nostrils, this is a supposition that cannot be maintained. For the expression involved, *nishmath chayyim*, is practically the same as that used in 7:22 with reference to all life that perished in the flood, the only exception being that the phrase is altered to "the breath of the spirit of life" (*nishmath rûach chayyim*). Not this breath itself but the manner of its impartation indicates man's dignity. So also the claim that man became "a living being," or literally, "a living soul," (A. V.) does not point to the distinguishing glory of man. For the same expression is used of other animate beings in 1:24.

It must be remembered that the author is at this point chiefly reporting the fact that this lifeless clay became animate by the breath of the Almighty. The fact that man is a superior being is indicated by the manner in which this is done, and this was already amply indicated before by the divine "image" (1:26). The expression "living being" employs the term *néphesh,* "soul," because the soul is the animate thing in man. God's Spirit animates the soul, though in a higher sense than is the case with the soul of beasts. Kœnig (T A T) correctly defines: "According to 2:7 the *soul* is that portion of the spirit which is breathed into man." The *neshamah* is "only the life-breath" (Keil); cf. I Kings 17:17.

8. **And Yahweh God planted a garden in Eden toward the east and put there the man whom He had molded.**

Here is a statement which more directly helps us to understand the things that follow and also furnishes further proof of the generous goodness of God toward man. The scene and the background of the third chapter are being supplied. God plants a garden. All that was written up to this point leads us to conceive of this activity as being also creative and divine. Yet the word that man would employ for such activity, "to plant," is appropriately used of God. The word "garden" (*gan*), an "enclosure" (B D B), or a sheltered, protected spot, corresponds to the Oriental conception of a garden. Paradise, the conception borrowed from the Persian by the Septuagint translators, is appropriate but suggests rather a royal park. A place of particular beauty and excellence best reflects God's favor toward His chief creature. From the author's point of view this garden lay "eastward." Though *miqqédhem* literally means "from the east" not "to the east," nevertheless our translation is correct. For the Hebrew point of view is gained by transporting oneself to the utmost limits in the direction indicated, then coming back: *from* the east (K. S. 318 a). This garden lay in a territory called *"Eden,"* a name used variously in later times in memory of the first Eden. *'Édhen* gains its name, no doubt, from the corresponding noun meaning "delight." In all instances following, the expression is less exact, and the garden is simply called "Eden"; it does not lie *"in* Eden."

In a summary way, moving ahead and including the outcome, the verse at once reports in newspaper-style that man was put into this garden. The fact of the matter is that a few other items must still be inserted in order that we may have a complete background of the events transpiring. When these have been recorded, the author will revert (v. 15) to the fact of man's being placed in the garden. No man will deny to an author the privilege of writing after this fashion. Practically all writers do something of the sort. This surely is no indication of so-called "doublets" — a term critics are so free to use — or proof of two parallel and not quite harmonious sources.

No doubt, the fact that man is created outside of the garden and then put into the garden serves the divine purpose of making man clearly aware at the very outset of the distinction between the garden and all the land that lay outside. In what manner man was taken and placed in the garden by his Creator cannot be determined. At the word of the Lord he may have been removed thither.

9. **And Yahweh God caused to spring forth all manner of trees pleasant to the sight and good for food, and in particular the tree of life in the midst of the garden and the tree of the knowing of good and evil.**

The focal point of the supplementary items that this chapter has supplied is being reached. Attention

centers upon two trees, more particularly upon one
of these two. The statement of v. 9 is an amplifica-
tion of the summary report in v. 8: "God planted
a garden in Eden." Overlooking this simple fact,
criticism shoots wide of the mark by drawing conclusions such as: according to J man's food originally
was only fruit of trees; only after the fall, according
to 3:18, does he eat of the herb of the field. Such
claims are merely attempts to bolster up a poorly substantiated theory of divergent sources and are at the
same time an unwarranted use of the argument
from silence.

Again, the fact of the matter is that God caused
an infinite variety of trees to spring up in the garden. The Hebrew expression used is the strongest
possible, *kol 'ets*, "the whole of trees," = every tree,
which is even stronger than our rendering above, "all
manner of trees" (B D B, and K. S. 78 b). Descriptive
phrases indicate how attractive they must have made
the garden, for they were "pleasant to the sight and
good for food." An epexegetical "and" (K. S. 375 c)
in the sense of "and in particular" now concentrates
our attention on two, rather on one, of these. To talk
of "the confusion regarding the two trees" (Skinner)
is proof of the critics' lack of understanding. The
whole issue is really very simple. Both trees are
mentioned because both were there and both were
destined for a very definite purpose. The tree of life,
as appears from 3:22, would have served its purpose
in the event of the victory of man in the first temptation. Its existence shows that God had made ample
provision for man's good. Since, however, it never
came to be used, it at once very properly recedes into
the background after the first mention of it and is
alluded to only after the Fall in 3:22. Its purpose
apparently was to confirm man in the possession of
physical life and to render physical death an impossibility. More of this in a moment.

The second tree is called "the tree of the knowing of good and evil." We have used "knowing" instead of "knowledge" because the infinitive *dá'ath* functions chiefly as a verb and takes a double object. For this reason, as in Jer. 22:16, the word "knowing," though in a sense in the construct state, takes the article rather than its objects, "good and evil." Besides, "knowing good and evil" is thus stamped as one complete idea. Naturally, this expression aims to cover the whole range of moral concepts in brief (K. S. 92 b), or, better still, the ethical contrast between good and evil. To try to make a distinction between these two trees, as though the idea of "the tree of knowledge is a more refined conception" than the tree of life, is to render a hasty verdict and to give proof of a misunderstanding of the whole situation.

This misunderstanding comes to the surface in the further claim in reference to the tree of knowledge that "its property of communicating knowledge of good and evil is, however, magical" (Skinner). Here, again, perfectly sound and entirely correct presentations of the case have long been offered by the church. But the critics completely ignore these explanations and offer instead a view derogatory to the dignity and inspiration of the inspired Word and drag it down to the level of the cheap magic of corrupt heathenism.

The church has always understood in reference to these trees that, in the nature of the case, eating of the fruit of one tree cannot impart life, just as little as partaking of the fruit of another cannot impart a sense of moral distinctions. However, we have an analogy to these cases in the matter of the sacraments. As in the sacraments by virtue of the divine Word the visible means become vehicles of divine grace, so here by virtue of the divine word, which designates the one tree as "the tree of life," "life" can in reality be imparted by its use when and under whatever circumstances God decrees. In like manner, the second tree, as its name implies, becomes an agency through which under certain circumstances, divinely appointed, man may come to an experimental knowledge of good and evil. He may through the presence of the tree be confronted with a choice, he may exercise his freedom to do God's will in the choice, or he may refuse to make use of his freedom. Had man persisted in his freedom, the experience as such would have wrought in him a knowledge of good and evil analogous to that of God, in this sense that, without having consented to evil, an awareness of its existence and its implications would have been aroused in him. The tree of the knowledge of good and evil would have effectively done its work. Then the *posse non peccare* would have resulted on man's part in the *non posse peccare*, and this state would have received fuller confirmation in his physical being by the use of the tree of life, the eating of whose fruit would have communicated to those using it in faith rare benefits even for the body. So the trees are rightly regarded as sacramental in a sense. Since the New Testament, by the analogy of the sacraments, presents so adequate a parallel and so satisfactory an explanation, criticism has gone sadly astray by drawing upon the analogy of magic from heathen sources.

The coarsest misconstruing of the purpose of the tree of knowledge is that of men like Ehrlich (K. C.), who says: "good and evil" here bear a physical, in fact an outright "sex connotation." All capacity of spiritual insight is lacking when commentators speak thus.

Unwilling to accept the high moral conceptions involved, Jeremias uses the common device of criticism of stamping the words "good and evil" as a later interpolation, using, however, the less obnoxious term "a theological interpretation" (*Theologumenon*).

When it is noticed that the trees stood "in the midst of the garden," though, to be exact, the expression occurs only in connection with the tree of life, the question is usually raised, whether there was not danger that man might have discovered and eaten of the tree of life before he even found occasion to eat of the tree of knowledge. However, on such purely speculative questions we may well trust that divine providence foresaw and regulated the affairs of man quite adequately. So also the other question, commonly asked here, may be rejected as merely curious and impossible to answer: "Did man know also the existence of the tree of life and did he know which it was?" To those demanding a suggestion, we offer one, as likely as any: Events may have begun to happen in such rapid succession from this point onward, that the very next issue confronting man was the Temptation.

10. **There was a river going forth from Eden to water the garden; leaving there it divided and became four branches.**

The report goes on to indicate how the fruitfulness and freshness of the vegetation in the garden was guaranteed, a thought that would appeal particularly to the Israelites, who, too, dwelt in a region where water was none too plentiful. So the impression of a perfect place is created in an all-sided way. Since the river is the important thing, the noun stands first. The participle (*yotse'*) emphasizes the continuousness of the act, but it is not to be translated as a present, "goes forth" (contra K. S. 237 c), because thus far the whole account lay entirely in the past, nor does the author at any time indicate that he still believed in the existence of the garden. The verb *yotse'* is repeatedly used in reference to the actual source of waters (Exod. 17:6; Num. 20:11; Judg. 15:19; Zech. 14:8). Therefore the stream originates in "Eden," whether within or just without the garden is not said.

"Leaving there" (so Meek), for *mishsham* = "from thence," it divided and became four chief branches (lit. "heads"). This is a very unusual situation. We know of no parallel to it. We know of streams uniting to form one major stream. Here the reverse is true: one major stream becomes four.

These four divisions are now enumerated. Criticism had not expected that they would be and therefore expresses its disapproval. Procksch calls the verses 10-14 "an erratic stone" built into the structure. Only prejudice can make such claims. What is more natural than to refer to the mighty garden stream that provided ample irrigation? What is more natural, if the truth concerning the mighty four resultant streams still was known, to make mention of them and briefly to indicate their course? By so doing the author intensifies the impression of a much different past and answers a number of questions as to how those streams may have run at that time. He who is in sympathy with the author's purpose finds all this very natural and easy to understand. Not so the critics. They also claim to be able distinctly to see the points where J glued together his sources.

Without going into needless detail — Delitzsch* offers that in his *Wo lag das Paradies?* — let us note at once that only the last two of the four rivers mentioned can still be identified, but whether they still flow as they once did is highly doubtful. They certainly no longer spring from one source, though their present sources in the Armenian highlands are said to lie only 2,000 paces apart.

As for the first two, Keil identifies them with the Cyrus, or Kur, and the Araxes, or Aras, which also flow together into one and flow into the Caspian Sea. To give greater likelihood to this interpretation he identifies the land of "Cush" with the old Koccaía,

---

* Friedrich Delitzsch, *Wo lag das Paradies?* (Leipzig, 1881.)

which is reputed to have reached to the Caucasus. The scriptural "Cush," however, lies south of Egypt and is Ethiopia. The old expositors, also Luther, report the tradition that the "Pishon" is the Ganges and the "Gihon" the Nile. Others, like Kœnig, then identify the Pishon with an arm of the Indus. But the problem of having the four come from a common source is thus made still more complicated. Delitzsch makes Pishon and Gihon two canals connecting the Tigris with the Euphrates. But canals are not rivers. Some, following the old tradition, say that these four famous rivers of antiquity are indeed meant, but that either the author's geography was quite faulty, or else he had in mind some oceanic river flowing about the whole ancient world.

The solution to the problem apparently lies in the fact that what the account pictures was once actually true, though we may never identify the first two rivers. But the extensive changes in the earth's geography caused by that vast catastrophe, the Flood, have entirely disarranged the old order.

The most fantastic interpretation is that of Gunkel, which Jeremias (p. 103) adopts: "The notion of the four rivers of Paradise will be a reflex from a heavenly picture. Gunkel assumes that the writer is thinking of the milky way with its four arms." We report this merely as a curiosity.

11, 12. The name of the first is Pishon. This is the one which encircles all the land of Havilah, where there is gold; and the gold of that land is good; there is bdellium and the onyx stone.

The "first" in Hebrew, according to common usage, is the "one" (K. S. 315 n). Encircling, (*sobhebh*) does not mean to flow entirely around; cf. Num. 21:4; Judg. 11:18. Havilah means sandy-land. Gold is often found in such sandy regions. The article before "gold" is the article of complete familiarity (K.

S. 297 a) ; others call it the generic article; see G. K. 126 m.

12) "Gold" stands first because it is the prominent noun. "Good" is used in the sense of "fine" or "excellent." The demonstrative "that" (written *hî'* with *waw* rather than *yodh* for the feminine) is the first instance of this so-called *Keri perpetuam* and is a stylistic peculiarity of the author of the Pentateuch (so still Kœnig) and not the result of redactional activity (so most critics). What could have prompted a redactor to make so trifling and yet so characteristic a change and make it so consistently? — "Bdellium" apparently was a precious gum of antiquity. Israel must have been thoroughly familiar with it, since in Num. 11:7 manna is likened to it in appearance. The *shóham* stone, rendered "onyx" above, may never be identified. Two other suggestions come down from antiquity, equally well substantiated: the beryl (Targum) and the chrysopras (Septuagint). To the original readers of the book all these terms were quite familiar, and the names involved suggested well-known localities.

The attempt to identify the Pishon with the Phasis, or present-day Rion, flowing into the Black Sea, is also futile.

13. **And the name of the second river is Gihon. This is the one that encircles all the land of Cush.**

The possibilities involved have been discussed above. Attempts to identify Cush with any land other than Ethiopia (like the Babylonian Cash or an Arabic land Cush) are farfetched.

14. **The name of the third river is Hiddekel. This is the one that goes eastward of Ashshur. And the fourth river is the Euphrates.**

All interpreters agree that Hiddekel stands for the river called in Assyrian: (H)idiqlat, and in old Persian: Tigrâ, i. e. Tigris. *Qidhmath* must mean "east-

ward." The Ashshur, or Assyria, referred to must be
the ancient city of that name which actually once lay
to the west of the Tigris, though the Assyrian kingdom later lay eastward of it. The excavations of the
German Oriental Society (1904) uncovered the site,
now named *Kal'at Schergat.*

Nothing is mentioned about the familiar
Euphrates except the name. The river required no
further identification.

All this would seem to indicate that the site of
the garden of Eden may have been in the Armenian
highlands, although no man would dare make any
positive claim. No man has ever discovered any trace
of its location. But how can men advance an unwarranted claim like that of Skinner: "a locality answering to the description of Eden exists and has existed
nowhere on the face of the earth."

15. **And Yahweh God took the man and put
him into the garden of Eden to till it and to look
after it.**

What was summarily reported in v. 8 is here
resumed in order to be amplified, for it is at once
stated why the Lord put man into the garden. This
natural explanation adequately explains everything.
The claim of two distinct accounts, not fully amalga-
mated, is quite unwarranted. Man's task in the garden is defined: he is "to till it and to look after it."
The ideal state of sinless man is not one of indolence
without responsibility. Work and duty belong to the
perfect state. "To serve," *'abhadh,* is here used
transitively in the sense of "to till." The second
verb *shamar,* usually meaning "to watch" or "to
guard," is here to be taken in the milder sense of
"keep." B D B very well suggests "have charge of."
Meek does even better: "to look after." For according to the nature of the whole account, which gives
the record of a creation, every part of which was
"very good," there can be no thought of an evil power

abroad in the world and trying to penetrate into the garden, as even Delitzsch and Whitelaw surmise. For in that case, we have the preposterous notion besides of man pacing along the border-lines of the garden at regular intervals during the day and at night doing sentinel duty — a very uneasy and disturbed existence. The more general sense of "have charge of" is otherwise substantiated in the Scriptures (see B D B). For even though the garden was in every sense good, yet care was necessary to keep it from growing in exuberant disorder.

Yannichéhû is a 2. *Hifil*, G. K. 72 ee.

16, 17. **And Yahweh God laid a charge upon the man, saying: From any tree of the garden thou mayest freely eat; but from the tree of the knowing of good and evil thou must not eat, for in the day of thy eating of it thou shalt certainly die.**

Everything preceding in this chapter has paved the way for this climax. The future of the race centers upon this single prohibition. Man is not to be confused by a multiplicity of issues. Only one divine ordinance must be kept in mind. By thus limiting the number of injunctions to *one*, Yahweh gives tokens of his mercy. Besides, to indicate that this one commandment is not grievous, the Lord sets it against the background of a broad permission: "from any tree of the garden thou mayest freely eat." We prefer to render *kol* "any" rather than "every," lest it appear as though the permission suggested to man to gorge himself; so also Meek. But this statement of the case in no wise conflicts with 1:29 where herbs are also mentioned, as though here, according to the construction of the critics, fruit of trees alone is allowed for man's food. This verse does not aim, like 1:29, to indicate the full scope of man's diet but has under consideration for the moment only of what trees man may eat fruit. The Hebrew construction puts the absolute infinitive by the side of the verb, something like: "eating thou mayest eat," in order to convey: "thou mayest *freely* eat." Of course, the imperfect is here permissive (K. S. 180).

17. However, the imperfect *to'khal* with the negative *lo'* involves the strongest form of prohibition, which we have sought to reproduce by "must." The *kî* that follows the negative clause does not in this instance mean "but," for the clause preceding was imperative not declarative. In this instance the expression *beyôm*, "in the day," is to be taken very literally and not in the sense "at the time," a meaning that would not fit here. For the thought actually to be expressed is the instantaneous occurrence of the penalty threatened, which is also again expressed in part by the imperfect with absolute infinitive, "dying thou shalt die" = "certainly die." This at once raises the question, "Why was this penalty not carried out as threatened?" We answer: "It was; if the Biblical concept of dying is kept in mind, as it unfolds itself ever more clearly from age to age." Dying is separation from God. That separation occurred the very moment when man by his disobedience broke the bond of love. If physical death ultimately closes the experience, that is not the most serious aspect of the whole affair. The more serious is the inner spiritual separation. Oehler (T A T p. 254) rightly maintains: "For a fact, after the commission of sin man at once stepped upon the road of death." The contention that the Old Testament does not know spiritual death, because it does not happen to use that very expression, is a rationalizing and shallow one, which misconstrues the whole tenor of the Old Testament. The common claim raised in this connection, e. g. by Skinner: "God, having regard to the circumstances of the temptation, changed His purpose and modified the penalty," makes of God a mutable being, who, like a rash parent, first speaks severe threats, then sees Himself compelled by developments to modify His purpose. The

explanation, "He shall be mortal," is based on the erroneous translation of the Septuagint.

Before leaving this verse it is a good thing to observe how definitely the account teaches that the first man was gifted with freedom of will. The moral sense must not first develope later; it is a part of the original heritage of man. It has been pointed out that in records such as these the Old Testament "veritably reechoes with imperatives," (Kœnig, T A T p. 233). A moral being standing on a very high plane of perfection at the time of his creation — such is the man of the creation account of Genesis.

18. **And Yahweh God said, It is not good for the man to be alone; I will make him a helper like him.**

The justifiable question, "How did woman originate?" has not yet been answered in an account dealing with all such basic origins. Besides, unless her status has been clearly defined, we are not ready for the narrative of chapter three. Therefore the account of the creation of woman follows. It is introduced by the basic assertion of God Himself: "It is not good for the man to be alone." Only quibbling can seek to find a discrepancy between this "not good" and the "very good" of 1:31. For in the latter instance the idea of moral perfection and perfect adaptation to its purpose is involved. In this instance, however, we have a "not good" of incompleteness, where the supplying of the deficiency lay in the original purpose of the Creator. Besides, to all intents and purposes, in point of time the work of the creation of woman falls within the sixth day, and so after all 1:31 comes later.

God did not create man an unsocial being. He, knowing better than man the social nature of man, voices it in a word spoken for man's guidance. In every way the normal thing for man is to go through life in fellowship with a wife. Man needs her. Her

position in reference to man is defined as first "a
helper," literally, "a help," *'ézer*, abstract for concrete
(K. S. 243 b). If a man is to achieve his objectives
in life, he needs the help of his mate in every way,
from the propagating of his kind down through the
scale of his varied activities. Her position is further
defined by the expression "like him," *keneghdô*,
literally, "as agreeing to him," or "his counterpart."
She is the kind of help man needs, agreeing with him
mentally, physically, spiritually. She is not an inferior
being.

19. **And Yahweh God molded out of the
ground all the wild beasts of the field and all the
birds of the heavens and brought them to the man
to see what he would call them; and whatever man
called each living creature, that was its name.**

Without any emphasis on the sequence of acts the
account here records the making of the various
creatures and the bringing of them to man. That
in reality they had been made prior to the creation
of man is so entirely apparent from chapter one as
not to require explanation. But the reminder that
God had "molded" them makes obvious His power to
bring them to man and so is quite appropriately
mentioned here. It would not, in our estimation, be
wrong to translate *yatsar* as a pluperfect in this instance: "He had molded." The insistence of the
critics upon a plain past is partly the result of the
attempt to make chapters one and two clash at as many
points as possible.

The bringing of these creatures before man to
have them named is a pedagogic device on God's part
to arouse man to the awareness of his not having a
mate as the other creatures had. Such an awareness
makes him appreciate God's gift the more. However,
that there is a limitation of the number of creatures
brought before man is made apparent by two things.
In the first place, the beasts are described as beasts

of the field (*hassadheh*) not beasts *of the earth*, as
in 1:24. Though there is difficulty about determining
the exact limits of the term "field" in this instance,
there is great likelihood (cf. also v. 5) that it may
refer to the garden only. In the second place, the
fish of the sea are left out, also in v. 20, as being
less near to man. To this we are inclined to add a
third consideration, the fact, namely, that the garden
could hardly have been a garden if all creatures could
have overrun it unimpeded. Since then, very likely,
only a limited number of creatures are named, the
other difficulty falls away, namely that man could
hardly have named all creatures in the course of
a day.

At once we are made aware of the high intelligence level of the father of the human race. For
the expression to give *names*, in the Hebrew usage of
the word "name," involves giving a designation expressive of the nature or character of the one named.
This was not a crude fable, where, according to a
Hebrew notion, the accidental ejaculations at the
sight of new and strange creatures were retained as
names for the future. Here was a man in deeper
sympathy with nature than any have been ever since.
That these names were appropriate and significant
names for the various creatures appears also from the
confirmatory statement of the author: "whatever man
called each living creature, that was its name." Such
a statement, imbedded in so marvelous an account,
could hardly be made, unless the names given had been
appropriate and worthy of man's intelligence.

Our translation of the close of the verse smoothes
out a certain difficulty in the original, where a literal
rendering reads: "whatever man called it, the living
creature, that was its name." That "living creature"
(*nephesh chayyah*) stands in apposition with "it"
(*lô*) is somewhat unusual. However, far from being
a stylistic defect, it deserves to be called entirely

appropriate. By it, as it seems, the writer is reminding us that each living creature was getting a name
in conformity with the type of life it lived. The critics,
always on the lookout for what might serve as proof
of their peculiar source theories, mostly see in this
phrase an addition by a redactor. But if the phrase
be unnecessary, as they claim, they impugn the intelligence of their redactor. However, if it serves a
good purpose, why cannot the original writer have
possessed sufficient intelligence to insert it? The chief
concern of a writer must not always be smoothness
of style. Intelligibility, clearness are of greater value.
Here smoothness is sacrificed to clearness.

The crudest misinterpretation of this giving of
names to the creatures is that rather common claim,
utterly without warrant in the text, that God was
experimenting to produce a mate for man, and when
it was found that of the existing beings none adequate
for him had been produced, then God proceeded to
make woman. Surely, the text never intended to convey that impression, as is also amply testified by
the fact that this erratic notion was reserved for the
invention of critics of a recent date. The more
reverent approach of olden times guarded men against
such crudities. Some go so far as to see a parallel
with the Gilgamesh epic, whose hero first consorts
promiscuously with the beasts and is beguiled by a
fair being to renounce their companionship. How
such filthy vaporings can be placed on a parallel with
the chaste and true scriptural account is beyond our
power to understand.

Yabhe' (brought) is without its object, because
it is readily supplied.

20. **So the man gave names to all the domestic
animals and to the birds of the heavens and to all
the wild beasts of the field; but a helper worthy of a
man was not found corresponding to him.**

Man carries out the appointed task. Queer
notions as to how man proceeded have been advanced,
based largely on the misconception that all creatures
upon the face of the whole earth had been supplied
with names. Whitelaw, quoting Willet, remarks:
"Nor did angels muster them, nor did the animals
come themselves, and, passing by, while he sat on
some elevation, bow their heads at his resplendent
appearance; nor were Adam's eyes so illuminate that
he beheld them all in their places, all which are but
men's conceits; but through the secret influence of
God upon their natures they were assembled round the
inmate of paradise, as afterward they were collected
in the ark."

In the enumeration of those creatures which were
given names, a third class appears at this point, "the
domestic animals" (*behemah*), showing that certainly
those nearest to man had not been overlooked. In
reality, then, these must have been included in the
term *chayyath hassadheh,* which could have been rendered (v. 19) "living creatures of the earth," although,
to preserve uniformity of expression, we did not use
that rendering. Let it also be observed that the *rémes,*
"the creeping things" of 1:24, are also passed by in
the matter of naming. Besides, no one will ever determine how diversified the species were already at the
time of their creation.

The fact that it is here remarked that "a helper
worthy of a man was not found corresponding to
him," does not argue for the fact that this review
of the beasts was an attempt to find a mate for man
among them, but rather that a realization of man's
loneliness was to be aroused in him. We consider the
text perfectly correct with its *le'adham.* Nor does
matsa' "one found" need to be changed to a passive
(Kit.) ; impersonal constructions are quite common.
The *le'adham,* without article, cannot here signify "for
Adam," as the noun without the article definitely does

after 4:25. Yet there is reason for using the generic "man" in this instance, because, as our rendering shows, the thought is a helper *for* a man, in the sense of *"worthy of* a man." He alone finds none of his kind.

21, 22. And Yahweh God caused a deep sleep to fall upon the man; and when he slept, He took one of his ribs and closed the place with flesh. And Yahweh God built the rib which He had taken from man into a woman and brought her unto the man.

We think the sequence of clauses as given above, following Meek, to be admirable. To say: "He caused a deep sleep to fall upon him and he slept" is too self-evident to have been intended by the writer. The Hebrew very readily allows for the above subordination, although it certainly did not follow from the Hebrew accents, which put the *Athnach* (something like a semicolon) *after*: "and he slept." *Tardemah* is indeed a "deep sleep," not a state of ecstasy, as the Greek translators render; nor a "hypnotic trance" (Skinner), for traces of hypnosis are not to be found in the Scriptures. A "trance" might be permissible. The root, however, is that of the verb used in reference to Jonah when he slept soundly during the storm. God causes such a deep sleep, because it surely would have been in part almost a horrid experience to live through to see a portion of yourself removed. A sleep like that caused by an anesthetic envelopes man's feelings and consciousness. The word *tsela'*, translated "rib," definitely bears this meaning, (contra v. Hofman), although it is not necessary to think only of the bare bone; for, without a doubt, bone and flesh will have been used for her of whom the man afterward says "bone of my bone and flesh of my flesh," (v. 23).

Though no definite reason for this type of procedure in creating woman is assigned, we are able to see the most eminent fitness in this much ridiculed act. For one thing, the absolute unity of the human race in its descent from one ancestor is established — a vital doctrine of the Scriptures (cf. Rom. 5:18 ff). Besides, at the same time the true dignity of womankind is guaranteed: woman is not of inferior substance. The truest of kinship with man is also established: she is of his bone and flesh. Even the very part of the body from which she is taken is of deepest moment: woman is neither of the foot nor of the head, for she is neither superior nor inferior to man; she is exactly on the same level with him as far as being a creature of God is concerned. If then, lastly, a part of the substance of man is to be used, none could be found that could be more conveniently dispensed with than a rib. Deeper thought on the subject throughout suggests a most excellent propriety in God's procedure in the whole matter of the creation of woman.

The preposition *min* replaces the more usual construct state in "from-ribs-his" (K. S. 278 a).

The activity of God in fashioning the rib taken from man is described as a building (*wayyi'bhen*). Rather than being an indication of the work of a different author, the verb grows out of the situation as being the most appropriate. It would not have been seemly to use *yatsar* "to mold," a verb applicable in the case of clay, not of flesh. "Build" applies to the fashioning of a structure of some importance; it involves constructive effort. Both of these factors are in evidence in the case of the creation of woman. When God brings her unto man, this act of his is the institution of marriage and stamps marriage as a divinely willed and approved state.

23. **And the man said: This now at length is bone of my bone and flesh of my flesh; she shall be called woman, because she was taken from man.**

There is a certain animation prominent in the first recorded word of the first man as he recognizes the purpose of this new gift to him — an animation which is made noticeable by the thrice repeated "this" (*zo'th*). The last two of these cannot well be made apparent in the translation of the second clause, which, translated literally would read: *this* one shall be called woman because from man was taken *this* one. Besides, that a being of this sort had been looked for with anticipation appears from the word *happa'am*, "now at length." Whether the article in this term really has demonstrative force in connection with a triple demonstrative already noted may in this instance well be questioned. The most complete physical congruity of this new person with himself is at once recognized by this first man. He gives expression to the thought in the words: she is "bone of my bone and flesh of my flesh."

He gives further expression to this idea by giving her a class name, which marks her as being far above all the other creatures upon whom names had been bestowed. By a clever play upon words he gives expression to this thought in a form that can at least be approximated by other languages, as also by the English: "called *woman* because she is taken from *man*," although all interpreters recognize that this is not the proper etymology of "woman." Luther does a bit better by coining a word: *Maennin vs. Mann*. The thought of the writer is only to give prominence to the most possible intimate kinship of these two beings and to express this by the kinship of sound. However, it must not be forgotten that the language used by the first man has, no doubt, been lost, so that the Hebrew must approximate the thought as nearly as its element allows. If, then, it be objected that the two words involved have, in reality, two different roots, we shall not be greatly disturbed. "Man," *'ish*, according to a parallel Arabic root, may have the basic idea of "exercising power." Similarly, "woman," *'ishshah*, must, because of the double consonant, be derived from a root with original *nun,* which according to an Arabic parallel, would mean "to be soft." But the writer is not studying etymology. He is expressing a fundamental similarity by the use of the best terms available.

The verb used for "she shall be called" is in reality the common impersonal: "it shall be called to her" (K. S. 324).

24. **(For this reason a man leaves his father and his mother, and they become one flesh).**

This verse might at first glance appear as the conclusion of Adam's first remark, and it is usually construed as such. However, the major difficulty in this interpretation is the fact that it must impute to the first man, in addition to all the other gifts that he possesses, also a kind of prophetic insight; for as yet man has had no experience of the fact of propagation whereby persons become father and mother. To attribute so much of foresight and insight to him is hardly feasible. But all of this difficulty is obviated if the explanation be adopted that here we have nothing other than a parenthetical remark of the author, who seeks to account for the deep and almost unaccountable attachment which man has for his wife. Several other parenthetical observations of the author are found in Genesis. See 10:9; 26:33; 32:32. The imperfect *ya'azobh* expresses the customary thing (G. K. 107 g): "man leaves." "Forsake" (A. V.) is too strong a verb. Meek renders *'al-ken* very well as "that is why." "Becoming one flesh" involves the complete identification of one personality with the other in a community of interests and pursuits, a union consummated in intercourse.

25. **And they were both naked, the man and his wife, but they felt no shame.**

In this brief statement one more feature is added to the picture of the primeval state of perfection:

nothing had transpired to rouse in man a sense of guilt. For to feel no shame is in a perfect state due to having no occasion to feel shame. Everything was at harmony, and man was in complete harmony with himself and with his God.

HOMILETICAL SUGGESTIONS

A number of good texts are found in this chapter. For expository treatment we should suggest the following: v. 1-3 deal with the subject of "Sabbath in Heaven," a good text for stressing the blessedness of rest after the divine example. Though v. 7 is somewhat short for a text, it yet presents adequate material for full treatment of the subject of "The Dignity and the Lowliness of Man." The divine creative act supplies the material for the first half of the subject; the substance employed, for the second half. The section v. 9, 15-17 suggests "the Place of Temptation in the Life of Man." Even for the perfect man tests, or at least a test, was essential for his proper moral development. A being so frail as not to be able to stand a test would have had little moral worth. There is sufficient material in the text to indicate that man had adequate proofs of God's will toward him and therefore was adequately equipped to ward off insinuations to the contrary. Then the section v. 18-25 provides occasion to develop the subject so little understood in our day, where thoughts of emancipation too largely have replaced the scriptural point of view—we mean the subject "Woman's Place in Life." It could be treated under the head of the "Institution of Matrimony." However, v. 28 of chapter 1 should really be added to round out the text, lest a neglected aspect of matrimony be passed by entirely.

CHAPTER III

The Temptation and the Fall

This is the most tragic chapter in the Bible. Perhaps no commentator has caught the sense of the full measure of tragic consequences entailed by the Fall more clearly than Luther in his detailed exposition of the chapter. This Scripture is an inspired account of how sin and all evil came into the world. From one point of view we may call it pure revelation, namely in the sense that man, left to his own devices, had forgotten this lamentable event of his early history, and so God had to renew the knowledge of it by revelation. For the very strange fact is to be observed that an actual parallel, which ties up the evils of the human race with the Fall and so with human sin, is not to be found in the traditions of the various races and peoples, who may yet have had a bit of truth concerning an earlier state of blessedness in a golden age of antiquity. Even those who persistently trace Biblical truth to Babylonian sources must admit: "The Babylonian version of the Fall of man (if any such existed) has not yet been discovered." Attempts to make certain dubious pictorial representations bear some resemblance to our chapter are based too much on forced meanings.

It cannot be denied that many things about the entire account may prove quite puzzling. We are provided with too few details concerning the exact measure of man's capacities in the original state; besides, the activities of the tempter may puzzle us.

But these and the many other problems about which we may vex ourselves are difficulties that lie rather in our limited understanding than in the account as we have it. Nor should we overlook the didactic skill of the writer who aims primarily to emphasize the fact that man fell by his own guilt and dragged down upon himself and his posterity a mass of miserable consequences. So the writer in a very satisfactory way informs us how evil originated in the world. The curious questions that we might desire to have answered beyond that are left aside, so as not to detract unduly from the major truth which is to be declared.

However, at least this one question must be touched upon in this connection: "Does this chapter present an actual narrative of facts, or have we here perhaps a skillful allegory, as many fathers of the church believed, or shall we label this 'merely a pictorial representation intended to convey some general impressions' (Dods) ?" Without a doubt, things are recorded as they actually transpired; this is a strictly historical account fully approved by the New Testament (II Cor. 11:3; II Tim. 2:13). Regarding the chapter from this angle does not impede our discernment of the deeper spiritual issues involved. In fact, the only safe interpretation of the Fall is that which accepts the record as unequivocally true and interprets it in the light of the rest of clearly revealed Scripture.

The claim of a few modern commentators that the chapter gives distinct evidences of meter (heptameter) has been demonstrated by K. C. as built on sand.

1. Now the serpent was the most clever of all the beasts of the field which Jahweh God had made, and she said unto the woman: And (is it really the case) that God has said ye shall not eat from every tree of the garden?

The serpent appears on the scene as the new and prominent factor in the discussion, and so *hannachash*

is placed first for emphasis (K. S. 339 h; G. K. 142 d).
This serpent actually spoke to Eve. This speaking is
not to be regarded as indirect, in the sense of speaking
by what she did, as for example perhaps eating of the
fruit herself (K. C.). She actually spoke. However,
when we go farther into the Scriptures, we find the
very definite fact, especially in the New Testament,
that the *devil* is regarded as the actual tempter. When
Christ says (John 8:44) that the devil is "a murderer
from the beginning" and that he is "a liar and the
father thereof," this word is a manifest allusion to the
event of this chapter. II Cor. 11:3 compared with
v. 14 of the same chapter suggests the same thought.
Rom. 16:20: "The God of peace shall bruise Satan
under your feet shortly," cannot be anything other
than an interpretative allusion to v. 15 of our chapter.
The words of Rev. 12:9, "the old serpent, he that is
called the Devil and Satan," harmonize only with our
interpretation of the passage. Cf. also Rev. 20:2. It
will hardly do to claim with modernists that the New
Testament writers saw the devil in the serpent, but
that on the level of the Old Testament men never
thought of the tempter as any other than only a serpent. For, as Lange has clearly demonstrated, the
truth concerning Satan emerged very clearly within
the limits of the Old Testament, and we surely have no
warrant to hold that the enlightened believers of the
old covenant never penetrated more deeply into truth
than to discern the mere letter. Even before the New
Testament revelation shines forth, the apocryphal book
of Wisdom (2:23 f.) ascribed the entrance of sin into
the world to the envy of Satan. These modern misconceptions disrupt the manifest unity and harmony
of revelation as given by the one Spirit of Truth. The
truth of the matter is, of course, as Luther already
clearly stated, that the third chapter as such states the
case in such a manner that we cannot but puzzle over
the speaking of a serpent, but the later revelation of

God has unfolded what still lay hidden in the first statements of revealed truth. So we are driven to the conclusion that Satan used the serpent as his tool or instrument and was in the final analysis the one who spoke through this creature. With his superior knowledge Adam ought at once to have sensed a grave irregularity in the serpent's speaking.

If, then, the further question be raised, why the devil used this means of addressing Eve, it must be admitted that such an approach successfully disguised the tempter. But if the more difficult question be raised, why the writer, who may have known about this Satanic agent, mentions only its visible tool, we have a twofold answer, in common with many other commentators: in the first place, the writer gives a faithful account of what actually transpired just as it transpired; in the second place, by describing the course of the temptation as directed by this visible agent he removes from the thoughts of his readers the possibility of the notion that since so dreadful a tempter assailed man, therefore man is not to be blamed for his fall — the mention of the devil might have led to the offering of excuses for man and so to a minimizing of man's guilt.

There can be no reasonable doubt as to the meaning of *nachash.* Scriptural usage, as well as all versions and an uninterrupted tradition through the centuries, vindicates the meaning "serpent."

The word we have rendered "clever" is *'arûm.* "Most clever" is the Hebrew superlative, which literally says "more clever than all beasts." (K. S. 308 b). We prefer "clever" to "subtle," because the word cannot imply a trace of evil in the animal world, for that would seriously conflict with 1:31. This was a purely harmless cleverness, after the pattern of Matt. 10:16. Such cleverness may well make this creature the most suitable vehicle of Satan's evil devices. From all this it dimly appears that the chief agent is a spirit of unusual power and cleverness and clearly, too, a fallen spirit. This again necessitates the assumption that the fall of the angels must have occurred prior to this temptation, yet not necessarily prior to the completion of the entire creative work. However, the other rather common assumption that evil had already penetrated into the world among the creatures, and that so the serpent herself was already tainted by evil, is clearly refuted by the modifying clause, "which Jahweh God had made," which clause applies indiscriminately to the whole creature world and describes it as good.

"The woman" is singled out to be tempted, because she is not naturally as strong as man, nor did she hear God's command from His own mouth but only, as it seems, mediately from Adam, and consequently she may have felt its weight less. The tempter's cunning is made manifest by this approach but much more so by the temptation which he presents and the adroit presentation of this temptation step by step.

The temptation opens with an *'aph ki,* i. e. "indeed that." The simplest explanation of this expression is that the verb "to be" is omitted, because it is so readily supplied. Therefore B D B is correct in rendering, "Indeed (is it) that?" So also K. C. Our translation above says practically the same thing. From the woman's answer it appears that the serpent's word was a question, although, as is often the case, it is not introduced by an interrogative particle. The Giver of the commandment is referred to by the serpent as "God," *'elohîm,* not as Yahweh; for the tempter could not with any measure of truth know anything of God's grace and fidelity. The most common term is employed.

The thought aimed at by this suggestive question is that there must be something about God's restraint of man that puts a very unwelcome curb and check upon man. The circumstance that God has permitted man to make use of all the rest of the trees is pushed aside as negligible. The fact that man is definitely barred from one tree is dragged into the forefront and magnified into a grievous and very unwelcome restraint that could hardly be thought of as imposed by God. A suspicion is cast upon God's goodness, and suspicion, as experience has amply demonstrated, most insidiously worms its way in where other sins often could not find entrance. In other words, man had had ample proof of God's love of and regard for him. To trust this loving Father was the normal attitude of this first man and the very soul of his proper relationship to God. The moment such trust begins to waver man has fallen.

To approach the question from another angle, as Luther rightly points out, the temptation involved directs itself against God's Word. More specifically, it seeks to make that Word doubtful to man. This Word was for Adam both law and gospel. Adam and Eve are to be led away from its truth according to the purposes of the tempter. In this respect the temptation is a type of all temptations which the evil foe presents.

By approaching the question as we have, we have eliminated the necessity of assuming that other words of the serpent had preceded and that here merely the continuation of that discussion is submitted. Rather, without preliminaries and with a subtle boldness a word is thrust at Eve, a word pregnant with evil and in substance a very dangerous temptation.

We must yet definitely reject the very common claim that *lo' mikkol* should be translated "not from any" (Meek). Though this use of the negative with *kol* ("all") is common enough, it can hardly be intended here. The exaggeration would be too gross and crude. The devil would have completely overshot his mark and roused a feeling of resentment at the coarse insinuation. Therefore A. V. is correct: "not from every." Cf. K. S. 352 s.

Some very strange modern interpretations must at least be referred to at this point. In the face of the plain meaning of this first key-verse, it is a willful misreading of the plain meaning of words when Haupt offers "the explanation of the Fall of man as the first connubial intercourse." Equally erroneous is Gunkel's claim that the chapter aims to overthrow "the then current opinion that agriculture was a blessing inaugurated by the deity," and to work this overthrow by "setting over against such an opinion the myth about God's curse upon the ground." Such views are entirely without a foundation and are shown forth as unwarranted by the simple fact that through the centuries no man ever even remotely discerned that such thoughts could be hidden in the narrative. Skinner finds difficulties in the chapter, chiefly in the temptation by the serpent, and offers as explanation the claim that the treatment of the story gives evidence of the "incomplete elimination of the mythological element under the influence of a monotheistic and ethical religion." What the critic finds hard to understand must have the source of its difficulty not in the critic but in the record. So a harmless and plain record is misinterpreted because the critic will not believe that "the function of the serpent" is as the text claims it to be.

Yet a word on the question often raised at this point: "Why must there be a temptation?" or "Why does God permit His chief creature on earth to be tempted? Does He not desire man's supreme happiness? Why, then, does He permit a temptation which leads to 'death and all our woe'?" The answer must always be that God will have only that count as moral behavior worthy of a being made in God's image, which is freely given and maintained even where the possibility of doing otherwise offers itself. To do what God desires merely because one cannot do otherwise, has no moral worth. It would be a morality like unto that

of beams which uphold the house because they have
been put in place and cannot but bear their load. To
do the right where there has never been an opportunity
of doing wrong is not moral behavior. The opportunity to do otherwise must present itself. This is temptation. A being who could not even suffer to be tempted
would be a poor specimen of God's handiwork. But the
true wisdom of God appears in this, that, though His
creature falls, God is still able to achieve His original
purpose through the redemption which is in Christ
Jesus, a redemption for which provisions are already
beginning to be made in this chapter.

2, 3. **And the woman said unto the serpent:
From the fruit of the trees of the garden we may
eat; but of the fruit of the tree which is in the midst
of the garden God has said: Ye may not eat of it,
neither touch it, lest ye die.**

In a way it may seem as though the unsuspicious
Eve, who has never been tempted, is at a grievous
disadvantage because of the very subtle nature of the
suspicion that the serpent seeks to engender in her
heart. But her advantages are sufficient amply to offset
the cleverness of the attack. There is, first of all, the
empirical knowledge of God's goodness and mercy
toward man. The whole of creation formed a strong
symphony of protest against any suspicions of God's
good will. Then, Eve had a very clear word from God,
simple and unencumbered by many details as to what
her moral duty was. Whether this word was heard
immediately from God or mediately from her husband
matters little and cannot impair the power of that
word upon her heart. And then, too, there was one
feature about the temptation that could well have
aroused instantaneous suspicion of the tempter: a mere
irrational creature spoke. The insight into the limitations of the being of the animal was sufficiently clear
to a creature like man, who had but recently been
entirely qualified to give names to all these beings and

discern their very nature. At this point Eve could easily have probed farther and divined the actual truth. Our first parents certainly had been adequately prepared for an emergency such as this.

At this point already we must begin to take issue with the claim that in the temptation as such the penalty resulting is quite out of proportion to the trifling nature of the misdeed. For those who raise such a claim liken the sin of our first parents to the taking of forbidden fruit by children and then claim: the mere taking of an apple certainly does not merit such dreadful consequences as are here pictured as resulting. Over against such misconceptions we strongly maintain that the taking of the fruit was not the fall into sin; that fall had occurred before this act; the taking of the fruit was an incidental bit of evidence of the fact that man had fallen. However, the Fall as such was nothing less in character than an entirely inexcusable piece of rebellion against a very gracious Father who not only had withheld nothing good from man but had even bestowed such an overwhelming wealth of good things that revolt against such a one must in the very nature of the case be a sin of the deepest hue, yes, even the one great sin in the history of the human race.

The beginning of this tragic and wretched fall is to be discerned in this section before us (v. 3). Eve's reply should have been an emphatic disavowal of the suspicion that God had been withholding good from man. Instead, it becomes a temporizing, a partial refutation, but at the same time a statement that allows room for the suspicion that perhaps God has not been as entirely good and gracious as they had hitherto supposed. But as soon as one does not wholeheartedly and unreservedly trust God, mistrust is gaining ground and sin has entered. Nothing of this appears definitely as yet in v. 2 where Eve restates what God has allowed them. Whereas the devil's charge pointed to unwel-

come restrictions, Eve emphasizes the fact that God
had allowed them to eat of the fruit of the trees of the
garden. But a significant omission in her statement of
the case must be noted. The original charter of privi-
leges under this head (2:16) had carried the word
"all"; then followed the one exception. Eve omits the
"all." She was beginning to lose sight of the boundless
goodness of God. Apparently, there sin took its beginning; God's mercies are lost sight of. Of course,
the imperfect *no'khal* is permissive, not merely a
present (K. S. 180). Therefore "we may eat," not
merely "we eat."

3)   Now follows a half-hearted defense consisting
in a restatement of the prohibition. During the course
of this restatement Eve veers from indirect discourse
to direct with the words: "God has said"; but unfortunately she mars a good case by sharpening and
thus altering God's original demand. Nowhere has it
been indicated that God said: "nor touch it." By this
insertion Eve betrays the course her thoughts have
taken. She feels that the prohibition was unduly sharp,
so unconsciously she sharpens it herself. But, again,
already the attitude of the heart to God is clearly seen
no longer to be one of perfect trust. The suspicion
which Satan so cleverly suggested was allowed to take
root. To have suspicions of God and His goodness is a
wicked insult of His majesty. All this, it is true, does
not at once appear in its most fully developed form.
The first steps on the road away from God have been
taken. Here the Fall took place. What follows is the
further unfolding of what lay in this first act and the
full evidence of it. A being that had been made holy,
just, and true and had been equipped with the strength
necessary for maintaining its moral integrity and
right relation to God, freely chose to ignore and to
despise His goodness and to mistrust Him, and so
severed its vital relation to Him.

On the ending of the form *temuthun* cf. G. K. 47 m.

Proksch shows the critical tendency to set harmonious things at variance with one another very significantly at this point. Because 2:9 mentions only the tree of life as having been "in the midst of the garden," but here, without doubt, it is the tree of knowledge which is said to be "in the midst of the garden," we are to class these two statements as being "divergent" from one another. The plain fact is that they are entirely *supplementary:* both were in the midst of the garden and perhaps even near one another.

Satan is not slow in discerning the advantage he has gained and promptly presses on to overthrow completely an opponent who has begun to waver, or, as Luther puts it, he observes that the wall has begun to totter and so braces himself against it, so as completely to crush Eve, as we now see.

4, 5. **And the serpent said to the woman: Ye shall certainly not die; for God knows that as soon as ye eat of it, your eyes will be opened and ye shall be like gods who know good and evil.**

After a careful approach, which tendered a mild suggestion, the devil boldly advances to a positive denial of the Word of God. It should not be lost sight of how in temptations the attack centers about God's Word. The very boldness of denial carries all before it. The denial, for that matter, is even a perversion of the word into its very opposite. God said: "You shall die." Satan replies: "Ye shall certainly not die." The father of lies is so saturated with lying that he even attempts to make God out to be a liar. Note the strength of the statement. A. V., "Ye shall not surely die," is not strong enough; rather, "Ye certainly shall not die." For the negative, which in cases where the absolute infinitive accompanies the finite verb usually stands between infinitive and verb, here emphatically stands first, yielding the emphasis we suggest by our translation. Cf. G. K. 113 v; K. S. 352 l.

Now follows the positive charge against God, that He "knew all along" (*yodhe 'a*, Kal participle, suggestive of continued action) that "as soon" (*beyôm*, here meaning "on the very day," that is to say, "at once") as they should venture to eat of this fruit, their eyes would be opened. Such a charge attributes envy to God and makes Him appear as one who withholds good from His creatures lest they mount to heights reserved for Himself. The heathen and the devil attribute envy to God. If Eve ventures to eat, it will mean on her part the complete disavowal of faith, and the Fall will be entirely consummated. The lead suggested by the Septuagint may be followed in the translation of the expression *ke'elohîm*. The Greek has ὡς θεοί, "as gods," plural. For the preceding verb *hayah* is more than just "to be," rather: "ye shall exist as gods" (K. S. 338 d), in other words: "you shall exist in the class of higher beings." This word of the devil's is calculated to beget an overbearing pride which aspires to wicked heights. Immediately preceding this lying promise is another which purposely savors of a certain vagueness: "your eyes will be opened." This must imply ability to discern and to penetrate into things not otherwise perceived, as the German expression has it, *hellsehend werden*. Just what advantage this involves is not further indicated, and so an attractive suggestiveness, more seductive than a specific promise, is achieved. However, the definition of what is involved in "existing as gods" savors of a similar elusiveness and vagueness. The devil gives assurance that that state will bring with it the knowing of good and evil. What advantages this entails is not stated. The good thing promised charms by its vagueness. But, surely, it was a bad bargain to accept such vague phantasmagories. True, "to know" (*yadha'*) implies more than intellectual apperception; "it is a function of the entire soul" (Procksch); it is *Empfindung*, perception. Here lies some of the diabolical cunning of the temptation: it seems to offer something very good — "ye shall be like gods."

Very clearly, as in all temptations, the devil's beguilements are an inextricable tangle of truth and falsehood. All the things promised were relatively true, as the sequel proved, but at the same time they were so far from offering the true realities that they could also be stamped as the most colossal falsehoods. However, their subtle cleverness cannot be denied.

6. **And the woman saw that the tree was good for food and that it was attractive to the eye and that it was a tree desirable for acquiring wisdom; she took of its fruit and ate and gave also to her husband who was with her, and he ate.**

This verse pictures not the genesis of sin but its full development and definite expression. The woman speaks not a single word. She is entirely engrossed in the contemplation of the things promised and in the hope of the realization of the spurious greatness suggested. By a natural law of progression the sin developes to the point where the one divine restriction is definitely cast off, and Eve stands forth in open defiance of her Maker. Sin always develops in this manner after foot has once been set on the downward path.

A closer contemplation of the tree in the light of the Satanic suggestion leads Eve to notice first something purely physical: "the tree was good for food." This is its appeal to the appetite. Here some commentators rightly sense that aspect of sin which (I John 2:16) is called "lust of the flesh." For, in reality, all aspects of sin lie embodied in this first transgression. Every part of the being of the first mother was drawn into the destructive vortex of the participation in sin. Then follows, introduced by a kind of polysyndeton (*wekhi* = "and that"), to make the separate parts of the temptation as they were felt one by one to stand out more prominently, the statement: "it was attractive to the eye." The æsthetic finds itself appealed to, or better, as again I John 2:16 has it, it was the "lust of the eyes" that here became operative. This was not a clean and holy perceiving but an unholy lusting. Note how every bodily function operates perniciously. Sin in all its enormity is most effectively portrayed as the monster that it really is. To this is added intellectual perversion: "it (was seen to be) a tree desirable for acquiring wisdom." This is what St. John describes as "the vainglory of life." *Haskîl* is intransitive, "to acquire wisdom," not, "to make wise." Meek offers the cumbersome and inaccurate "for its gift of wisdom."

So the picture is complete: every function of body and of soul is wrested from its original purpose and becomes embroiled in one vast confusion of its divine purpose. Nowhere is a more drastic picture offered of the horrible disturbance wrought by sin.

The actual evidence of full consent to the sin suggested, as far as man can see, lies in the taking of the fruit and the eating of it. Man cannot read the heart, but he can discern from the outward act what had transpired in the heart.

The man's consent to the same sin is reported with such brevity as to amaze us: "she gave to her husband who was with her and he ate." There must be a reason for this. This reason is primarily that through the woman, now already fallen, the same temptation was presented to Adam as had previously been presented through the serpent to Eve, and with the same result. Adam, then, must have fallen exactly as Eve had, with as little excuse, with as great a guilt. The only difference appears to be that, as Eve had eaten and apparently had suffered no ill effect, this constituted an additional argument why Adam need not hesitate to adopt the same course. Whatever stouter resistance Adam might have offered was completely overcome by this argument. The fact, however, that the prepositional phrase "with her" (*'immah*), which we rendered as a clause, is first found at this point, strongly suggests that at the outset, when the temptation began, Adam was not with Eve but had only joined her at this time. Here, too, Satanic ingenuity displays itself: to approach both while they were together would have found them in a position where they would mutually have supported one another. Such notions, then, as Milton's, that Adam sinned from a kind of sense of chivalry, not desiring to abandon Eve to her fate, have no support in the text. Nor has the opinion any value that Adam was too closely attached to Eve, a thought that would lead to a fall before the Fall, for it involves that he loved her more than he loved God.

Two scriptural points of view apply here. On the one hand, contrasting Adam and Eve, the Scripture may say: "Adam was not beguiled, but the woman being beguiled hath fallen into transgression" (I Tim. 2:14). Eve has a relatively greater guilt, if the comparative guilt of the two be mentioned. On the other hand, the sin of the two has so much in common that it is practically one sin, and Adam, as the head, may be referred to exclusively as the originator of sin and the Fall (Rom. 5:14; I Cor. 15:22): "as in Adam all die," etc.

Describing the whole scene as such, Delitzsch quite aptly points out how, after God had so bountifully offered proof of His goodness, our first parents behaved as though the devil intended only good and God intended only ill, and so he calls this "the devil's communion" (*Abendmahl*).

The *min* in the expression "of its fruit" is the *min* partitive.

7. Then the eyes of both of them were opened, and they perceived that they were naked; so they sewed fig leaves together and made girdles for themselves.

The act of sin having developed into a full-blown deed, which manifested itself outwardly, there now follows in v. 7-13 a description of the immediate effects of this sin upon man. The first noticeable effect is shame. Both are equally guilty; both experience the same result. Here is one of the saddest anticlimaxes of history: "they eat, they expect marvelous results, they wait — and there grows on them the sense of shame" (Procksch). They now have a knowledge of good and evil, but not as a result of having remained steadfast in the good but from the low level of sin, as it has been aptly put. The immediate gain of the experience of sin is so utterly sordid. How men like Driver can here find nothing more than the ordinary experience of transition "from the innocence of childhood into the knowledge which belongs to adult age," is more than we can understand. It is that too but much more. Here it is the direct reaction of a guilty conscience. The good Lord with definite purpose lets this effect be felt first in order that the baseness and the utter worthlessness of all of sin's achievements may be made apparent. To shield themselves from one another's gaze they fashion "girdles" for themselves from "fig leaves" (Hebrew: *te'enah* "fig," by metonomy for "fig tree"). No particular importance attaches to the fig tree in this connection. It is not that so-called fig tree of India which has leaves several feet in length. These leaves would not have required to be sewn together. Apparently, the leaves of the nearest available tree were seized, and this just happened to be a fig. That the sense of shame should concentrate itself around that portion of the body which is marked by the organs of generation, no doubt has its deeper reason in this that man instinctively feels that the very fountain and source of human life is contaminated by sin. The very act of generation is tainted by sin. If this scripturally portrayed origin of the sense of shame be accepted as true, then all contentions of anthropologists that shame is rather the outgrowth of inhibitions and custom fall away as secondary and incidental. The scriptural account goes to the root of the matter. The only gleam of light in the verse is the fact that where shame is felt, the evildoer's case is not hopeless. He is at least not past feeling in the matter of doing wrong. God's prevenient grace allows this feeling to arise.

Chaghoroth is not "aprons" (A. V.), for the root of the word means "to gird oneself"; primitive girdles is all that can be meant.

8. **And they heard the voice of Yahweh God walking about in the garden at the time of the breeze of the day, and the man and his wife hid themselves from Yahweh God in the midst of the trees of the garden.**

Yahweh God is represented as "walking about in the garden." The almost casual way in which this is remarked indicates that this did not occur for the first time just then. The assumption that God had repeatedly done this is quite feasible. Besides, there is extreme likelihood that the Almighty assumed some form analogous to the human form which was made in His image. Nor is there anything farfetched about the further supposition that previously our first parents had freely met with and conversed with their heavenly Father. In this instance they again hear His "voice." Though *qôl* does often mean "sound" (cf. II Sam. 5:24; I Kings 14:6) and now by almost common consent is quite regularly translated thus in this verse, yet v. 10 definitely points to the use of the word in the more common meaning of "voice," and this must be a reference to the word *qôl* used in our verse. This "walking about" (in the case of a man, we should have translated: "taking a walk") of Yahweh in the garden is said to have taken place "at the time of the breeze (*rû'ach* = 'wind') of the day." The *le* intro-

ducing this phrase is the *"le* temporal." Experience
has shown that in oriental countries the wind springs
up at the close of day. Consequently, all this transpired
in the evening. The article before "day" is the article
of absolute familiarity (K. S. 297 a), for this phenomenon occurred daily. Divine wisdom chooses the time of
day best suited for sober reflection and retrospection.
The waves of feeling that beat higher through the day
are beginning to subside, and the first parents see
things more nearly as they are. No other transporting
change or effect has been observed since the disturbing
sense of shame arose.

Upon hearing the voice of the Lord "the man and
his wife hid themselves." The second and the third
major results achieved by the misdeed are here portrayed. Mistrust and fear have, for one thing, taken
the place of the trust and the free communion with
Yahweh, that had previously prevailed. Instead of
running to Him they run from Him. Communion
with the heavenly Father is no longer their highest
delight. It is shunned as an evil and vexatious thing.
What damage and destruction sin is working from the
very moment of its appearance! The other grievous
hurt that has afflicted mankind is here set forth as one
that centered in the intellect, whereas the one just
mentioned had its seat in the affections. The intellect
is so disturbed that it fails to perceive for the present
— what would have been recognized at once on sober
second thought — that man cannot hide himself from
God, the omniscient and omnipresent. We have rendered *mippenê* "from" rather than "from the presence
of," because it really is only an expressive "from."
Either translation may be used.

Meek gives a ludicrously flat rendering when he
anthropomorphizes beyond what Scriptures allow and
offers the following example of quaint rendering:
"They heard the sound of the Lord God taking a walk
for His daily airing." Such a rendering is shockingly

irreverent. The inspired writers nowhere give evidence
of such low conceptions of God. Besides, the Hebrew
phrase cannot be rendered thus. Procksch offers a
similar unworthy interpretation when he calls the
conception of "God leaving His house at evening to
take a walk" "tremendously childlike" but yet "chaste
and noble." When the inspired Word shows God's
condescension by His consorting with men, instead of
catching the valuable truth, the critics try to degrade
the Word by imputing to it inferior motives. True
scholars glorify revealed truth; they do not belittle it.

9. **And Yahweh God called the man and said
unto him: Where art thou?**

But God's will to set man right and help him out
of his difficulty is so definitely fixed that it does not
desist as soon as an obstacle is encountered. If man
seeks to avoid God, God seeks out man. So the definite
searching question rings out through the garden:
"Where art thou?" God is not seeking information.
God's questions are pedagogic. Man is to be made to
realize that something must be radically wrong when
the creature, who hitherto had his chief delight in
associating with the good and loving Father, slinks
away in hiding under the trees deep in the garden.
Of course, there is the possibility that the *calling* and
the *saying* of this verse represent two separate acts
(K. S. 369 o), but the likelihood is that, as frequently,
the second verb is epexegetical to the first: "He called
and said" = He called saying.

10. **And he said: Thy voice did I hear in the
garden and I was afraid because I was naked and
so I hid myself.**

"Thy voice" stands first in the sentence by way of
emphasis. It would certainly be rather insipid in this
instance to render *qôlekha* "thy sound" or even "the
sound of you" (Meek). The first word of fallen man
lies before us. It is a revealing word. It is a compound

of half-truth, evasion and attempted deception. So dreadfully altered has man become. The admission that he was afraid at hearing God's voice is the only true thing about his statement. Fear grows out of sin and is its natural accompaniment, especially in man's relation to God. But man's explanation of what it was that caused such fear is not frank and honest. For while his conscience thunders in his breast that this fear is the outgrowth of his disobedience, his mouth utters the half-truth that it is because of his being naked. One cannot but marvel at what a wreck of his former good self man has become. The damage wrought by sin is almost incomprehensibly great. The tongue of man can hardly describe it, except where inspired utterances like those of this chapter lie before us. Here is one of the most telling indictments of the viciousness and supreme sinfulness of sin.

"I hid myself" *'echabhe'* is a *Nifal* form, used in the older reflexive sense.

11, 12. And He said: Who told thee that thou wast naked? Hast thou eaten of the tree of which I commanded thee not to eat? And the man answered: The woman whom thou didst set at my side, she gave me of the tree and I ate.

The rather prominent sense of shame on man's part still predominates over the more necessary sense of guilt. God's cross-examination continues in order to arouse the latter. How could God be conceived of as asking these questions out of ignorance, when His higher purpose is so clearly in evidence? The first question clears the ground by drawing attention to the fact that something must have occurred to make man aware of his nakedness: "Who told thee that thou wast naked?" Of course, since he found it out by himself, he himself must have done something which made him aware of this situation. As soon as his thoughts have been led to see that this admission is inevitable, the next question drives him still more inescapably to the admission of his guilt, namely the very direct question: "Hast thou eaten of the tree of which I commanded thee not to eat?" The inquest has been quite brief, but, like all the dealings of the allknowing God, successful in convicting the sinner. Adam sees that he has not eluded God. He that aspired to godlikeness now stands a shamefaced culprit without a word of defense left. The lame reply that he does make causes us to blush for him. It is a reply that offers further evidence of the complete corruption and contamination of all of man's nature by his sin. It is a reply that in cowardly fashion refuses to admit plain guilt and in an entirely loveless fashion lays the blame for it all first on his wife and then by a wicked charge upon God Himself in the words: "The woman whom Thou didst set at my side, she gave me of the tree and I ate." Her whom he first recognized as a great blessing from God he now describes as the cause of his fall, but chiefly he charges God, by imputation, by asserting that God set her at his side. Mutual recrimination as well as finding fault with God's works are some of the further fruits of the Fall. "Set at my side," literally, "give with me"; but "give" is frequently used almost as the verb "set" (B D B).

The preliminary purpose of the inquest has been achieved as far as man is concerned: he sees what he did, what is wrong with him, and what is the basic cause of his unfortunate state. His excuses and his charge against God are not worthy even of refutation or defense on God's part. So man is left at this point, and the inquest proceeds to the woman, with a like purpose.

13. **And Yahweh God said to the woman: What is this that thou hast done? And the woman said: It was the serpent that misled me, and so I ate.**

There is truth in the man's assertion that the woman gave to him. On this truth God's inquiry builds up, demanding of her in grave displeasure and with a note of reproach: "What is this that thou hast done?" The "this" points to the enormity of the misdeed and to the fact that it is almost impossible to believe that one who has seen such unnumbered tokens of love should cast off such love and the allegiance which it involves. Evasion characterizes also the woman's attitude. Truth no longer dwells in her breast. She knows that what she did was done of her own volition, yet she charges the serpent with it exclusively. "Serpent," standing first in the sentence, gains the peculiar emphasis that our translation seeks to express above by: "it was the serpent," etc. All true fear of God and love of Him has, of course, departed also from her heart, for by laying the blame upon the serpent she indirectly also charges the Creator for having let the creature cross her path. This charge and excuse does not merit an answer. The woman well feels what insufficient defense she has offered and feels it still more when God does not honor it as worthy of refutation. Man never can bring a good case into God's presence as long as his own works are being considered.

The Vulgate mistranslates when it offers a "why" for a "what" in the beginning of God's question.

14. **And Yahweh God said unto the serpent: Because thou hast done this, cursed art thou from out of the number of all the animals and of all the wild beasts; upon thy belly thou shalt go and dust shalt thou eat all the days of thy life.**

The serpent was the third active factor in the temptation. But because the agent behind her was a fallen spirit who was beyond the possibility of salvation, there is no attempt made to arouse a sense of guilt by a series of pedagogic questions. The divine

word at once becomes a sentence of condemnation.
The first part of this word definitely busies itself with
the serpent as a beast, but already toward the end of
this verse the Satanic agent behind the serpent is also
under consideration. Then in v. 15, though still speaking in terms applicable to the serpent, the word is
concerned almost exclusively with the evil power that
mastered the serpent in the temptation.

At the beginning of v. 14 the causal clause stands
first (K. S. 414 s). The sentence pronounced is a
divine curse (*'arûr* — Kal passive participle; no verb
form to express the voluntative, K. S. 355 l). The
use of the preposition *min* bears close watching. Although it may be used to express a comparative, and
so grammatically one might arrive at the meaning
"cursed *above* all animals" (A. V.), yet nothing indicates that all animals are cursed. The extent of the
curse should not be spread beyond what the circumstances actually warrant: for the present only the
serpent and the ground are cursed. Later (4:10) Cain
comes under the divine curse. Consequently, the *min*
partitive in the sense of "out of the number of" (G. K.
119 w; K. S. 278 b) is under consideration. This
particular or exclusive meaning of *min* is established
by cases such as Exod. 19:5; Deut. 14:2; 33:24. Therefore, this beast is singled out for a curse over against
"all the animals" (*behemah*) in general as well as over
against "the wild beasts" (*chayyath hassadheh*) in
particular. Kittel questions without good reason
whether "out of all animals" originally belonged to
the text. It makes excellent sense.

The fact that this beast still stands under a curse
is apparent from the peculiar revulsion that it still
rouses in most men. Its peculiarly sinuous movements,
its silent glide as a form of locomotion, its sinister,
dread and fascinating look, its vibrant tongue, its
peculiar rearing of the head: all contribute to remind

men of the peculiar history in which the serpent once shared.

Just what the curse, however, involves is also plainly stated in the verse. The first element is, "upon thy belly thou shalt go." This does not necessarily mean that a complete transformation of the serpent took place, so that "form and movements of the serpent were altered" (Keil). Some speak quite boldly at this point about a former erect posture, as though, for example, the serpent had strutted about proudly as a cock. It has been rightly pointed out that several parallels are available. Man worked before the Fall and still works since. Now work is in a measure a punishment. It seems likely that the rainbow existed before the Flood; but since that time it is a pledge of God's covenant. So for the serpent the going upon the belly becomes a badge of degradation; because for Israel the principle obtained that whatever crawled upon its belly was an abomination (Lev. 11:42). And, certainly, no man has ever seen anything noble or attractive about the serpent's gliding through the dust. Her type of movement reflects her humbler station. The second half of the curse involves a parallel thought: "dust shalt thou eat all the days of thy life." This is not a crude misconception like that of the Arabs who hold that certain types of spirits feed on dust. Serpents do not eat dust, and the Scriptures do not mean to say that they do. Parallel to the expression "eat dust" is the other more common one in the Scriptures, "lick dust," (Mic. 7:17; Isa. 49:23; Ps. 72:9) which in every case implies "to be humbled," "to suffer defeat." So in addition to a humiliating manner or mode of locomotion there will be a continual suffering of defeat "all the day" of her existence. The serpent will always be a creature that is worsted. But here already the words spoken reflect more upon the higher agent that employed the serpent, a thought that gets exclusive emphasis in the next verse.

But the question is bound to rise: "Why should an unmoral and therefore irresponsible agent be singled out for punishment?" Strictly speaking, this is not so much punishment as emphasis upon the defeat and humiliation of the old evil foe. To make his failure as apparent as possible he as well as the irresponsible agent that he employed will be crushed in a joint overthrow. Parallel run such instances of Holy Writ where a beast that kills a man is commanded to be destroyed (Gen. 9:5; Exod. 21:28), or where in the destruction of mankind the rest of the creature world must perish (Gen. 6:7; 7:21). This makes the seriousness of God's punishment more drastically apparent. Here may also be cited cases like that of Achan's destruction (Josh. 7:24). Since the rest of the creature world exists for man's sake, its destruction may serve a salutary purpose for man. Then, there also enters in the thought expressed by Chrysostom: God destroys the instrument that brought His creature to fall "just as a loving father, when punishing the murderer of his son, might snap in two the sword or dagger with which the murder had been committed."

15. **And enmity will I put between thee and the woman, between thy seed and her seed; he shall crush thee in respect to the head, thou shalt bruise him in respect to the heel.**

A marvelous text which Luther praises so highly as to say: "This text embraces and comprehends within itself everything noble and glorious that is to be found anywhere in the Scriptures." The same writer, however, indicates with equal emphasis that these glorious things are spoken in a form which for the present partly veils the full measure of truth, thus challenging the early believers to ponder deeply upon the word; but it is the New Testament that sheds a refulgence upon this word, so that it is seen to be a glorious compend of the Gospel and so rightly deserving the title long in use in reference to it, the *Protevangelium*, i. e. the first gospel proclamation. Lest this restriction, that we have made above, be pressed too strongly in the direction of making this appear as a very mysterious and veiled utterance, let us yet add that, since it was intended to furnish light for the first believers and for centuries was the only light that their faith had, it certainly must have furnished, as God's providence no doubt intended that it should, sufficient light for these patriarchs to enable them to walk by that light. In other words, we can and must subscribe to the statement that this word held up the Savior before their eyes, and so made it possible for them to believe on Him.   .

In the light of this fact, which we trust our exposition shall fully substantiate, we cannot but marvel at the rationalistic exegesis which says on every hand in our day: "it is doubtful if the passage can be regarded in any sense a Protevangel" (Skinner). Such interpreters see in the word before us nothing more than that "in the war between men and serpents the former will crush the head of the foe, while the latter can only wound the heel." Such a trite platitude would not have been worthy of recording. It stands about on the level of the astute observation that a man will slap at the mosquito that bites him. Such commonplace reflections are not worthy of the Scriptures. They are a type of exegesis like unto that which in connection with v. 5 attributes a deep sense for spiritual realities to serpents. But let us aim to gather in the fullness of meaning embodied in this verse.

The object, "enmity," stands first for emphasis (K. S. 339 m). Now enmity (*'êbhah*) is a term not applicable to dumb beasts. Its scriptural use limits it, like its verb root, to enmity between persons or morally responsible agents. This fact alone, as well as the sequel, rules out the idea of mere *hostility*, which is not enmity, between man and serpents. The personal tempter emerges ever more distinctly as the verse progresses. Besides, this statement emphasizes that it is God who will not suffer this enmity to die down: "I will put." God wants man to continue in undying opposition to this evil one and He rouses the enmity Himself. This He does first in the case of the enmity on the woman's part. We dare, however, not go so far as to attribute to God that He also rouses Satan to enmity. That would make God the author of evil. But true enmity on man's part against the evil foe is a virtue. The woman, as one factor in the enmity, is stressed to the exclusion of man because the woman was beguiled, but from her shall definite retribution arise for the serpent. There is an eminent propriety about having the one at whom the devil aimed his attack be the one from whom his downfall emanates. So the first step in the process is that the woman herself is brought to substitute enmity for the confidence that she shortly before displayed. The present of the verb (*'ashith*) is the type of present or future that is used in depicting a future scene in a more elevated rhetorical style (K. S. 132). The marvelous promises of God's achievements can be recounted by this type of form.

The promise expands. This enmity is to be of broader scope; it is to involve coming generations: "between thy (the devil's) seed and her (the woman's) seed." There would be something supremely trivial about this solemn utterance if it did no more in the expression, the serpent's "seed," than to think of generations of serpents as yet unhatched. There must be meant the children of the evil one who are of their father the devil and will do the lusts of their father (John 8:44). If "seed" must refer to a whole class and so is used in the collective sense in the one half of the statement, then "seed" (again *zéra'*) in the second half or parallel member of the statement must be used collectively for the descendants or posterity of woman. To take the word "seed of the woman" at this point at once in the sense of an individual and so as a definite and exclusive reference to Christ the Savior is wrong and grammatically impossible. Even Hengstenberg and Keil unreservedly admit that. So the second part of the verse points to an enmity established by God and involving on the one side the posterity or children of the evil one and on the other side the posterity or children of the woman, those who share her definite opposition to the evil one.

Now a peculiar thing happens in the course of the further unfolding of the clash between the forces listed thus far. First came: Satan (1) vs. Woman (2). Then came seed of the one (3) vs. the seed of the other (4). The seed of the woman (4) is now mentioned by "he" or "it" (*hû'*). Though the pronoun is singular, it refers back to *zéra'* (4) which we just proved to be used collectively. The peculiar thing that now happens is that the climax of the struggle is seen to be not between (4), a group, and (3), a group, but between (4), seemingly a group, and (1), an individual, "thee," and in this conflict between (4) and (1) the battle is fought out and won by (4). That the battle is actually fought to a decisive conclusion appears from the verb employed and from the manner in which it is employed. The verb *shûph* decidedly means "crush" (K. W.), a meaning which even Skinner finally decides it is "better to adhere to." Of course, as Luther clearly shows in his translation, we have a zeugma (K. W.) in the use of this word: the head is *crushed* but the heel is *bruised;* Luther: *zertreten* vs. *stechen.* This is too obvious to require lengthy defense; for when man steps on a serpent's head, a crushing results; but when the serpent strikes while the contest is on, only a sting on the heel or a bruising results. But at the same time a crushed head spells utter defeat. A bruised heel may be nursed till healed, and if the bite have been poisonous, the poison may be removed by sucking or cauterizing. (4) merely suffers; (1) is crushed. So in a very positive way the victory is guaranteed to the seed of the woman. The struggle is not to be interminable. It does end in complete defeat of the serpent, who is here, to cap the climax in establishing her identity, again addressed as "thou," a form of address involving, where moral issues are at stake as here, a being with moral sense and responsibility, i. e. Satan himself. But we cannot stop short at this point.

If (4) engaged with (1) in the decisive battle and (1) was an individual, there is, on the very face of it, great likelihood that (4) points *also* to an individual. This thought becomes clearer when we reflect on the term "seed of the woman." Within the broadest sense of the term would lie all mankind; they are all Eve's posterity or seed. But plainly the word cannot here be meant in that broadest possible sense, for only they are under consideration who hold enmity against (3), i. e. against all the children of the evil one. For that matter, they even constitute a minority of all of the woman's descendants; they are a "little flock," (Luke 12:32). So within the circle of the broadest possible meaning of *zéra'* must be drawn a circle quite a bit smaller. These represent the true seed of the woman. But even as those who constitute (3) find their cause represented most sturdily by and embodied in (1), an individual, so they who constitute (4) must find their cause represented most sturdily by and embodied in an individual in whom the idea "seed of the woman" finds most perfect expression. He is the very center of the circle above referred to. And since our thinking must naturally arrive at this conclusion, it seems that godly thought on the part of earnest believers in days of old must have arrived at the same conclusion. The victory would be concluded by one born of woman. Both the ultimate victory and its achievement by the seed of the woman are taught with unequivocal plainness by this word. Our interpretation, therefore, of the term "seed of the woman" sees in it perfectly natural concentric circles of meaning, even as such also is the case with the term "servant of Yahweh" in Isaiah. Israel as a whole bears that name; also the godly in Israel; Cyrus is honored by it; but in Isaiah 53 and elsewhere it is pre-eminently the designation of the Messiah. To such an interpretation of *zéra'* there ought to be still less objection when it is remembered that the word is also used in reference to an individual and not only in the collective sense; cf. Gen. 4:25; I Sam. 1:11; II Sam. 7:12.

When these contentions are attacked on the score that *zéra'*, when used of an individual child, "denotes the immediate offspring as the pledge of posterity, never a remote descendant," then an intentional feature of the whole prophecy is overlooked. There is a vagueness about the whole in point of time which invited men to trust God for whatever time He might be pleased to choose to bring it to fruition. Men had to be ready to settle down to a wait until it might please the sovereign Ruler to bring to pass what He here definitely had promised.

It should be clearly observed that this gracious promise is the opening of the sentence or doom that God pronounces. Even on the first pages of the Bible we are shown the face of a God "merciful and gracious, slow to anger and abundant in goodness and truth" (Exod. 34:6). He delights in showing mercy. "Where sin abounded, grace did the more abound" (Rom. 5:20). Grace, provocative of faith, precedes the sentence.

One point of view, usually overlooked but made plain already by Luther, deserves mention. By leaving open the question of just what woman the Savior was to be born, God mocks the tempter, always leaving him in uncertainty which one would ultimately overthrow him, so that the devil had to live in continual dread of every woman's son that was born.

But is the particular expression "seed of the woman" perhaps so phrased in reference to Mary and the virgin birth? Not primarily, but at least incidentally. The expression "seed of man" would not have been so directly motivated. As pointed out above, the one tempted and brought to fall is chosen by God to produce the one that is to bring Satan to fall, that Satan might in no wise boast himself against God. But at the same time, to show how completely God governs and controls all things as well as foreknows them, an expression is chosen that meets with literal fulfillment in Him who is virgin born and not of the seed of man. Yet we prefer to state the case thus: the expression used does not specifically prophesy the virgin birth, but it coincides and agrees with it under divine providence. For it is not to be forgotten that the expression "her seed" in its first meaning is a collective noun and includes all who are enrolled in the struggle against Satan, without being themselves virgin born.

After modernists have refused to let the Messianic import of the passage stand, which was of old accepted by the Jewish and by the Christian Church, it is interesting to observe what they substitute for it, for even for them the mere notion of enmity between men and snakes is rather a trite matter. Some hold that we have here "the protest of ethical religion against the unnatural fascination of snake-worship." Rather a farfetched substitute! Again, since the word does have a rather solemn sound, how account for that? It is suggested that here we have one of those strange words that like oft "recurring motives of the Genesis' narratives" explain "the more perplexing facts in the history of men and peoples" and "are the working out of a doom or 'weird' pronounced of old under divine inspiration." Similar instances are listed, as 4:15; 8:21 ff.; 9:25 ff.; 16:12; 27:27 ff.; 46:19 ff.; ch. 49. The thought is that mysterious things are to be explained as the working out of words of fate uttered long ago. But rather than think of some word of blind fate about snakes, this should be listed as a definite word of prophecy and promise. Procksch lets the word carry no more meaning than that man and serpent both perish in this weird contest: the fight ends in a kind of draw — a very hopeful (?) prospect outlined by the Lord! Even Koenig dares go no farther (*Die Mess. Weissagungen*) than to find in the word the sure promise of the defeat of the serpent but no reference to the Messiah.

Those who would charge our interpretation with being too deeply involved or to abstruse or too difficult for the Old Testament believer to discover, should remember that the Jewish Church, according to the *Targum,* regarded this passage as messianic from a very early day. If Irenaeus is mentioned as the first one of the Christian church fathers definitely to state this view, that does not materially alter the situation. Not every messianic passage is mentioned definitely in the New Testament, yet cf. Rom. 16:20. A significant New Testament fact, however, looms up very prominently and serves the same purpose: after Christ's public ministry is officially inaugurated by His baptism, He encounters the devil in a temptation, even as the first parents encountered him. This, first of all, confirms the fact that the first tempter was the devil, but it more distinctly displays the first crushing defeat that the seed of the woman administered to His opponent. On the cross this victory was sealed and brought to its perfect conclusion. The cry, "It is finished," marked the successful completion of the task.

Unfortunately, the Catholic church, following an error of the Vulgate, translates *hû'* as "she" (*ipsa*) instead of, as the Hebrew alone allows: "he" (*ipse*). So she refers the passage to the virgin Mary. Even the original translator of the Vulgate, Jerome, was aware that the retention of this form was an error.

16. To the woman He said: I will increase very greatly thy pain and thy conception; in pain thou shalt bring forth children; unto thy husband thou shalt be attracted, and he shall rule over thee.

Divine wisdom and justice dictate this sentence. Justice is made apparent in the fact that in the three elements embodied in the sentence each stands in direct relation to the misdeed of the woman, being a penalty commensurate with the wrong. In this way divine wisdom displays itself; for such punishment is calculated to keep awake in womankind a direct remembrance of the fateful deed of the first mother. The first part of the penalty is found in the words: "I will increase very greatly thy pain and thy conception." This does not imply that pain would have been the normal thing for womankind. Nor is this the pain connected primarily with childbearing; although that is included. What is done is that woman from this time onward has numerous forms of pain laid to her lot. Physical infirmities of a painful kind are in a great measure her portion. Because of her more delicate makeup many things besides cause her a greater measure of mental and spiritual pain. The just retaliation lies in this that she who sought sweet delights in the eating of the forbidden fruit, finds not delights but pain—not joy but sorrow. For *'itstsebhon* includes both "pain" and "sorrow," in fact, everything that is hard to bear. The conjunction before "conception" is to be taken in the sense of "and in particular," a meaning found e. g. in Ps. 18:1 (Heb.) ; Isa. 2:1. Nowhere shall the rich measure of "pain" be more in evidence than here. We have here more than what a hendiadys ("the pain of thy conception") allows for (cf. K. W.). "Conception" will be multiplied. When its painful character becomes apparent, woman will seek to have little of it, but her common lot according to this word will be a frequent recurrence of it, as, barring a few exceptions, the history of the race amply testifies. To allow for no misunderstanding of the word at this point, for frequent conceptions might in themselves at first glance not appear to be an evil, the explanatory sentence is appended without a connective (K. S. 338 p) : "In pain thou shalt bring forth children." This asserts that each conception shall culminate in the pains of parturition. This form of the word for "pain" is briefer than the preceding one, but since the same root appears in both, we used one word for both. "Misery" (*Beschwerde*) would also cover the term quite well.

The second part of the penalty is: "Unto thy husband thou shalt be attracted." *Teshûqah* might be rendered "desire" or even better "yearning." This yearning is morbid. It is not merely sexual yearning. It includes the attraction that woman experiences for man which she cannot root from her nature. Independent feminists may seek to banish it, but it persists in cropping out. It may be normal. It often is not but takes a perverted form, even to the point of nymphomania. It is a just penalty. She who sought to strive apart from man and to act independently of him in the temptation finds a continual attraction for him to be her unavoidable lot.

The third part of the penalty is: "he shall rule over thee." She sought to control him by taking control into her own hands (II Tim. 2:14) and even by leading him on in the temptation. As a result her penalty is that she shall be the one that is controlled. Man's position in reference to woman now is fixed: he bears the rule. When all is done in the spirit of Christ, such rule is not harsh or unnatural; nor is it cancelled. There it expresses itself in such a way that it is not to be felt as a burden. But where sin prevails, such rule may be degraded into a miserable domination, such as the East has particularly experienced. God did not ordain this harshness, but man transcended his rights, and sin poisoned a necessary restriction. This

word, then, does not reflect the narrowness of the East
but is a wholesome restraint and reminder for womankind.

The expression, "I will increase very greatly," is
the usual verb plus absolute infinitive. On the ending
of the infinitive see G. K. 75 ff. Verbs of ruling with
be; see K. S. 212 e.

17. **And unto the man He said: Because thou
hast hearkened unto the voice of thy wife and hast
eaten of the tree of which I commanded thee saying:
Thou shalt not eat of it, cursed be the ground on
thy account; in misery shalt thou eat of it all the
days of thy life.**

The penalty laid upon man is given at greater
length; but then it must be observed that a good part
of the word, especially the conclusion of v. 17 as well
as v. 18 and v. 19, apply to woman as well as to man.
In other words, the first word of v. 17 should be pointed
la'adham and rendered "unto the man" rather than
"unto Adam." Note also the contrast with v. 16,
"unto the woman." Observe also that at v. 20 the
proper name, Adam, has not yet emerged.

But man's punishment fits his particular misdeed.
Because he submitted to his wife, whereas he should
have ruled, therefore he shall experience insubordina-
tion on the part of the soil, whereas otherwise he would
have exercised complete control. This involves, first
of all, difficulty in the matter of securing his sustenance: "in misery shalt thou eat of it all the days of
thy life." It shall yield produce, but the winning of it
shall always be attended by *'itstsebhôn,* "misery,"
"toil," "sorrow." The former ease of tilling the soil
shall be a thing of the past. On no place of the earth's
surface can such toil be evaded. In some places there
may be more of it, in others less, but "toil" is the common lot of man. The immediate cause for this is the
fact that "the ground is cursed." A divine word

blighted its fruitfulness. There was a deep reason
and a necessity for that. It was no longer fitting that
an imperfect man dwell in the midst of a perfect
dwelling place. Divine pedagogy makes the outward
circumstances correspond to the inward state, so that
man might the more keenly feel his wretchedness.
Therefore the explanatory phrase says that it was done
"on thy account," not by accident, not because God
delights in blasting a perfect world, but for man's
sake: such a world would best tend to induce man to
be ready to accept God's salvation. Of course, the
expression, "thou shalt eat of it" (the ground) means
"to derive a living from it" (Meek). But the thing
that stands out as prominently as any in this verse is
that this, as well as the consequences yet to be enumerated, are directly traced to man's sin: "because thou
hast eaten," etc. There are not some mysterious words
of doom that trail man wherever he goes, but there is
an inescapable divine sentence, which man has fully
merited, which follows him wherever he goes through
life. Not blind fate but human guilt and consequent
divine punishment explain man's lot; and chief of
these is man's guilt. It may not be amiss to add that
a bit of gracious promise lies imbedded in this hard
word of punishment; viz., the expression, "thou shalt
eat of it," does give to man the assurance that as a
return for his hard labor he shall not lack the food
he needs.

18. **Thorns also and thistles shall it cause to
spring forth for thee and thou shalt eat the herb of
the field.**

While man is eating and is destined to eat the
"herb of the field" (*'ésebh hassadheh*—here for all the
food of man which was still vegetable in character),
the ground was of itself bringing forth thorns and
thistles. This seems to us to be the connection of the
two halves of this verse. So that not only is difficulty

and toil experienced while man is winning his food
(v. 17), but also that which he does procure is gotten
in meagre quantities only (v. 18), because undesirable
elements grow without receiving attention. This, too,
is one of the effects of the curse of the ground. God
is here not ordaining a different diet for man — "the
herb of the field," an expression erroneously translated
by some, "wild plants."

However, the disorders and irregularities observed
throughout the world are far more numerous than
those recorded in v. 17-19. Why should only those be
mentioned that accompany agricultural endeavor?
First of all, because in that particular direction they
are most readily observed, for all men must in a
measure engage in tilling the soil. But besides, no
doubt, we have one type of disorder mentioned here
as a sample of all the rest. As the soil and its culture
are disordered, so is every department of life and the
world. So Calvin interprets. Luther surmises that at
first only these few disabilities were laid upon man and
that they increased progressively as time went on —
a view that is less acceptable. In any case, the penalty
agreed with the simpler aspects of life that were in
evidence in the early history of mankind.

19. **In the sweat of thy face shalt thou eat
bread until thou return unto the ground, for from it
thou wast taken; for dust thou art and unto dust
thou must return.**

This part of the penalty emphasizes primarily
the lifelong continuance of the toil imposed on man —
till he returns unto the ground. Otherwise, the opening
words of the verse are nothing more than a paraphrase
of v. 17 d, "in misery shalt thou eat of it." But the
paraphrase is drastic in its coloring. It actually represents man as having such brief respite between
portions of his work that, as he sits down to meat, the
sweat still courses down his face as a result of his

previous hard toil. From this lot there is no deliverance until man's return to the ground. It is not here said that this return is man's death, for, in reality, "death" is used in a far more comprehensive sense in these chapters. But the fate of his body is foretold: being of dust, it must return to dust. Though this is stated as an inevitable consequence, it will not do to claim that such physical dissolution would have been man's lot anyhow. For this statement is part of the general penalty. This penalty now determines that man's lot after the body must be to return to the dust whence he came. This is a solemn word whose truth is felt with overwhelming force each time we see it fulfilled. "Dust thou art and unto dust thou shalt return" is not, we repeat, a general maxim, which holds good in any event.

It would be one-sided in v. 16-19 to speak only of penalty. Of course, the thing dwelt on is primarily penalty. But, at the same time, there are traces of mercy that shine through it all. It is not plain penalty but corrective penalty. There may be much pain and suffering on the woman's part, especially in childbearing, but the future of the race is guaranteed in such childbearing. At the same time this experience effectually reminds the woman of her grievous transgression — also a salutary effect. The same result is secured by the particular form of punishment that is laid upon man. So, on the whole, it must also be admitted that, though work may be a grievous burden, it is also a very definite and valuable blessing. Thus God stands revealed even in this, not only as a God of justice but also as a God of mercy.

Though spoken to Adam and Eve, these words are not addressed to them merely as individuals but as progenitors of the human race, as is amply indicated by experience. For all the children of Adam and Eve have found themselves suffering the same lot as that which our first parents were here told would be inevitable. Such Scriptures as II Tim. 1:14, 15 more particularly support this contention.

20. **And the man called his wife's name Eve (Life) because she was the mother of all living.**

God's wise pedagogy through it all has not been in vain, as now appears from Adam's reaction. The account still refers to him by the generic name "the man," as appears from the use of the article before *'adham*. This act of Adam's, whereby he gives his wife the name "Life," is proof of a faith that involves more than the idea that God is indeed speaking the truth when He indicates that Eve will bring forth off-spring and so be the mother of all the living. That would hardly be significant enough to mention, being quite self-evident and quite readily believed. But we do justice to this word when we see in it the conclusion on man's part, that, since all living beings shall come forth from her, therefore also life itself in that fulness of sense in which the word is often used in the Scriptures ("death" is also used in the fullest sense in these chapters). Consequently, by the significant nature of the name employed, as well as by the significant way in which the matter is reported at this important juncture, we are to understand that Adam refers to the things implied in the promise of the victory over the devil. In other words, he here gives evidence not only of believing that God spoke the truth but evidence of belief in the salvation which God had promised. This, then, was on Adam's part, as far as was possible under the circumstances, a true and living faith in Christ. This faith of his surely could not have all the clearness that marks the faith of New Testament believers. But the essentials of faith were in evidence. And since faith cannot come into being unless true repentance precedes, we are justified in saying that indirectly the repentance of Adam is here taught. Again everything has been done in perfect harmony with the rule that God follows of begetting faith by the means of grace. The words of the sentence spoken had prominent elements of the Law in them and so were calculated to work repentance. Equally prominent were the elements of Gospel which were calculated to work faith in the hearts of these first hearers. So the question is answered, whether after the Fall Adam repented and believed.

The proper name for Eve, *chawwah*, is by far not as uncertain in meaning as some would claim. Nor is there any evidence that the Hebrew root could yield the meaning "serpent" just because of a similar Arabic form. A parallel is found in the analogous verb *hayyah*, which also existed in the parallel form *hawwah* (Gen. 27:29) and survives in this form in the proper name *Jahweh*. So *chayyah*, meaning "to live," could easily have had the older form *chawwah* with the same meaning. "Life" is the well-established meaning of this proper name. The second half of the verse is the author's statement, not Adam's, as 2:24.

21. **And Yahweh God made garments of skin for the man and for his wife and so clothed them.**

Now God makes necessary provision for man's physical well-being. The covering that man had made for himself was inadequate, and so God showed him how to provide a more suitable and durable covering for himself. By so doing God gave His approval of the sense of shame which had led our first parents to cover their nakedness, and at the same time He furnished protection against the rigors of climate which would be encountered outside of the garden. The expression "and he made" (*wayyá'as*) is best understood not that He personally did the making, but that He gave such directions as man required to learn how to make appropriate skin garments. That God does provide for the proper clothing of man's body does suggest and does render reasonable the conclusion

that He will provide for the proper covering of man's
guilty soul. But this verse does not teach that, nor
is it an allegory conveying a lesson to that effect. The
meaning is what the letter of the statement says —
no more. God's reason for the choice of just such a
type of garment was that there was none simpler and
more readily prepared. That being the case, no deeper
meaning need be attached to the fact that these garments were of skin. Nevertheless, since the slaying of
beasts for man's needs was thus sanctioned, this may
have suggested to man the idea of sacrifice, yet not
of sacrificial meals, for man had as yet no divine warrant for the use of animal food. Further reflection
on this means of providing garments may have taught
man some useful lessons. One certainly was that there
must be some deepseated disorders in the world at
large since man's sin, if the giving up of the lives
of beasts was necessary to provide man with garments.
Death was present in various forms since man's lapse
into sin. It is difficult to say whether the slaying of
beasts for purposes of clothing in Adam's day already
involved sacrifice.

Kothnôth does generally mean "tunics," but here,
no doubt, it is used in the general sense of "garments"
(*Kleid* — K. W.) ; "coats" (A. V.) is too specific. The
pointing of the text should be slightly altered to
la'adham, "for man," instead of *le'adham,* "for Adam."
The generic use of the word is intended because "and
his wife" follows, also generic, not "Eve."

**22-24. And Yahweh God said: Behold, man
is become as one of us to know good and evil, and
now lest he reach forth his hand and take also of
the tree of life and eat and live forever — so Yahweh God expelled him from the garden of Eden to
till the soil whence he was taken; and He drove
the man forth and placed the cherubim eastward
of the garden of Eden and a revolving swordlike
flame to guard the way to the tree of life.**

Since the actual commission of sin the author has with very deliberate purpose been using the name "Yahweh God" for the deity. In the temptation the devil naturally could not want to refer to Him as such. But now, since v. 8, it has been the definite purpose of Moses to portray God as one who, though eternal and unchangeable, manifested the unchangeableness of His mercy toward even the fallen ones. The God of mercy has been portrayed since v. 8. So here too in v. 22 barring man from approach to the tree of life is mercy. Therefore *Yahweh* is used, as well as *'Elohim*.

Whereas in v. 8-21 we had the substance of what God spoke to man in mercy and in judgment, we have in v. 22 the persons of the Holy Trinity in divine counsel among themselves. As might well be expected, from the divine point of view man's act is not only trivial but sad. Man achieved in a relative sense a kind of parody of godlikeness. A divine and holy irony takes note of this. True, there is nothing in these remarks of God that could for a moment make it appear as though the Lord found fallen man a fit object for venting His amusement. Perhaps, since human terms but imperfectly describe the deity, words such as sarcasm or irony — over the relative propriety of which a vigorous debate is still being waged in reference to this passage — had better both be avoided, lest we create a conflict with the pure pity that, without a doubt, stamps his mercy as truly divine. We might, then, substitute the word "sadness" as descriptive of God's attitude. At the same time, the turn of the narrative practically requires that attention be drawn to the equivocal sense in which the promise was made: "Ye shall be as gods." What a sorry godlikeness, if we may use the paradox, and what a pitiable achievement on man's part!

The expression "like one of us" cannot be made to include the angels, as though God were saying that He and they constitute the class of higher beings.

For, in the first place, in any case such a levelling process that puts God and created beings in one class is precarious; and, in the second place, the like expression 1:26 stands too near to leave room for anything other than a reference to the persons of the Trinity. If, then, it be claimed that the revelation of Scripture is up to this point too meagre to allow for a clear understanding of this fact, we readily admit that in the earlier stages of revelation this word may not have been *fully* apprehended. But some of the revelation coming from God must be progressively apprehended. The Old Testament pointed in the way of the full truth. The New Testament sheds its light back upon this word too clearly to be ignored. But as Luther already rightly claimed, this word shows the unity of the divine being ("God said") and a plurality of person ("us"), this latter fact, however, primarily in the light of the New Testament.

At the same time, there is one very necessary step that must be taken before this episode of the Fall is completely adjusted, and that is, man must be completely shut off from access to "the tree of life." About the purpose of this tree we learn only from its name and from the remark here made in reference to it. It had the power to impart imperishable physical life — for the plain statement of the case is that had man eaten, he would have "lived forever." But since, to the best of our knowledge, no tree of itself can possess such virtue, it seems best again with Luther to assume that this remarkable power was characteristic of the tree not by its inherent natural qualities but by virtue of the power of the Word of God, who was pleased to ordain that such should be the effect of partaking of the fruit of this tree. For man in his fallen and sadly altered state the acquisition of the quality of imperishability for this sin-torn and sin-defaced body would have been a grievous calamity. He would never have been able to "shuffle off this mortal coil." Christ's work of restoration would have been precluded, where He "changes this body of humiliation that it may be fashioned like unto His glorious body, according to the working whereby He is able even to subdue all things unto Himself" (Phil. 3:21). Further speculation about the nature of this tree is useless. But this purpose is clearly revealed by this one word of divine revelation. The whole purpose of the narrative becomes distorted by the critics who claim to find in v. 22 a "crude form of the legend" besides "more of the characteristically pagan feeling of the envy of the Gods." There is nothing crude about divine pity. Nor, to tell the truth, can anything crude be extracted from this verse except it be first placed there by the critic.

The construction *ladhá'ath* offers that use of the preposition which is best rendered *"in respect of* knowing." For the whole, see G. K. 114 o. On the expression "as one from us" cf. G. K. 130 d on the construct state before a preposition; also K. S. 277 n. K. S. tangles up the situation by supplying words before "lest" (*pen*). This negative clause of purpose must be attached to what follows.

Of course, there is a bit of truth in what K. C. claims, that withholding man from the tree of life was punishment. But in the altered state of man the results of eating of the fruit of it would have been most disastrous.

Now with v. 23 the sentence structure is altered. Direct discourse merges over into the doing of the thing that lay in the divine intention — an effective way of saying that God carries out His purposes.

23) The act of God in putting man out of the garden is here described as He "expelled" him (*shillach*). Being the *Piel* stem of the verb to "send," "expel" (Meek) is a good rendering. That is, however, only the more general statement of the case. The more specific word, describing the manner of doing it, is

given in v. 24, and He "drove forth" the man. This
second verb *garash* pictures Him vividly as driving
man before Him. The first verb would be covered in
all its connotations if God had merely ordered man
to depart. Now according to v. 5 as well as v. 15 it
was already ordained that one of the duties of man
was to be to "till the soil." But now after his expulsion
from the garden this remains as his only work, and
there is the suggestion that there is something unwelcome and degrading about it all because the clause is
added, "from whence thou wast taken." All the other
noble prerogatives of man are largely cancelled, such
as "having dominion" and "ruling." Man now actually
stands in heavy bondage to the very soil that he was
first privileged to control. Some try to make this verse
a mere doublet of v. 24, whereas, in reality, both tell
two very different stories, even on the expulsion there
is no overlapping: the one describes the act in general
terms; the other is more specific.

24) There was something particularly shameful
about being driven forth from the garden. Divine
goodness aimed to make man feel his altered state very
keenly: first blessed fellowship, then harsh expulsion.
To make the severity of His judgments immediately
apparent and the removal of them humanly impossible,
a double guard is placed against any possible attempts
at re-entering the garden. Between man and the
garden, that is "to the east," "cherubim" are placed.
They are a type of being somewhat like angels. Because
they are elsewhere in the Scriptures definitely described
as "the living ones," *chayyoth* and ζῶα, we are well
justified in claiming that because of this distinctive
name they must represent the highest type of living
beings. They are particularly found in the Scriptures
as honored by the privilege to stand in the immediate
presence of the heavenly King, and they are specially
associated with Him in works of judgment, as here.
K. W. well defines that they are "representatives and

mediators of God's presence in the world" (Ps. 18:10), *Repraesentanten und Vermittler der Weltgegenwart Gottes.* The root from which the word may be derived would suggest that the word as such means "a brilliant appearance" (*Glanzerscheinung*). How these marvellous beings appeared was well remembered by the Israelites at least, for they seemed to require no further description when they were told to make two cherubim upon the mercy seat of the ark of the covenant and otherwise to use the figures of cherubim for ornamental purposes; cf. Exod. 25:18; 26:1.

Quite distinct from these cherubim was the "revolving swordlike flame," which is often represented erroneously as a sword in the hand of the cherubim. The only connection that the flame and the cherubim have is that they both effectually bar the way to the tree of life, and since God's wrath at man's misdeed is displayed by their presence, it is perfectly correct, as Keil does, to let the flame represent God's wrath. However, the literal expression is "the flame of the sword, the turning one." This is best taken as meaning a flame, swordlike in appearance and continually rotating or even, perhaps, moving zigzag like flashes of lightning; at any event, a sight effectually deterring man from attempting to enter, so effectually, no doubt, that he did not even venture to approach the garden from any other side.

All speculations as to how long the garden of Eden continued upon earth after the Fall are bound to be quite hopeless. Certainly, for at least a time after the expulsion the garden was still upon earth, and both the cherubim and the vibrant flame of fire continued in their God-appointed place. But to venture to say that the garden as such remained until it was destroyed by the Flood is an assertion that can be as little proved as the other claim that it was removed or "vanished from the earth with the expulsion of men from the garden of Eden" (Keil).

We leave this chapter with a sigh over the glory that was lost and with deep regret over the loss of man's original innocence. There is no chapter in the Scriptures that more effectively reveals the source of all evil that is in the world; and so it becomes a very helpful chapter for the man that is ready to accept its truth.

HOMILETICAL SUGGESTIONS

A few suggestions as to the homiletical use of this chapter. "The Fall into Sin" as such can be expounded on the basis of v. 1-8, though to an extent the basic elements of the narrative are fairly well known to most Christians from their childhood days. Yet many trivial conceptions have been carried over into maturity which may well be corrected. Since our day is particularly weak on the subject of sin and its pernicious effects, v. 9-19 presents a very suggestive portion for the treatment of "the Curse of Sin," or, "the Consequences of the Original Sin." Within this section is one verse that for all its brevity still contains enough material for a complete sermon, namely v. 15 which contains "the First Gospel." As we showed above, v. 20 gives indication of man's penitence and faith. Therefore it would be quite in order to treat v. 20-24 under a heading like "Tokens of God's Mercy to Penitent Man."

CHAPTER IV

The Early Development of the Sinful Human Race

The book of Genesis has thus far progressed in a very natural and logical sequence of thought. After the story of Creation was unfolded as an orderly work, displaying to the fullest extent the mighty power of Him who is its Creator, chapter two informed us more in detail in regard to the conditions of our first parents, enabling us to appreciate fully the situations that were soon to be encountered. Then in chapter three came the necessary test of man, resulting in his tragic Fall; at the same time we were informed in detail what far-reaching consequences grew out of this initial sin, consequences that burden the human race ever since and help us far more readily to understand what man's lot actually is and why it is as it is. Now, in the fourth chapter, we are shown what transpires as the human race embarks upon its career under the curse of sin but also with the promise of hope as a guiding star. Just what was the development of our race in its first steps toward fuller maturity?

Unfortunately, students of history and of anthropology too largely ignore this one chapter, which happens to be the only authentic record of this early development. Having cast off the only reliable account of man's first deeds and achievements, practically all writers of the present then proceed to draw very largely upon their imagination, which happens to be cast into the thought-patterns of evolutionistic conceptions. Then they misread the available archaeological hints — for actual archaeological evidence for earliest man is not available — and the result is a highly fantastic and entirely incorrect story of man's development from the cave-man stage, as it is claimed, to the point where the first higher cultural achievements are found and the historical period actually begins. At the same time the very reliable Biblical chronology of chapter five is distorted and generous insertions of long periods of time are made, and so the value of our chapter (4) is completely lost sight of. For man not only did not start on the low anthropoid or simian state that is usually assumed, but as a human being he at once stood on the high intellectual and physical level that the preceding chapters described. But, unfortunately, the actual degradation that sin brought is not reckoned with. Whereas man was not an inferior being on a lower level, such writing of history degrades him without warrant. Whereas he was brought low by the Fall, this pseudo-science ignores his true degradation. In both respects the chapter before us, being strictly historical and entirely correct, serves to set the student of the history of mankind right; and at the same time it gives to all men a clear account as to how man progressed and how sin grew.

The following is the natural division of our chapter: a) v. 1-16 give an individual instance of the early development of the now sinful human race, as significant an instance as skillful writing of history could have found; b) v. 17-24 give an account of the development of the family of those who were estranged from God; c) v. 25, 26 give an account of the development of the family of the godly. All this, of course, is done in the characteristic lapidary style of the Scriptures, where significant individual instances are made to display graphically what course was being pursued. Modern criticism, proud in its own conceit and refusing to accept instruction, fails to see all this and loses itself in a seemingly wise discussion about the various and inconsistent sources from which the author (J) drew

his material, but at the same time such criticism cannot
successfully hide the fact that in reality it too knows
nothing about these sources. Nobody does. At the
same time criticism seeks to undermine the credibility
of the record by disparaging remarks. We, however,
accept the chapter in its fullness of truth as an accurate
and correct account as to how the development of the
human race after the Fall progressed — a progress,
by the way, of which we cannot feel particularly proud.

1. **And the man knew Eve his wife, and she
conceived and bare Cain, and she said, I have gotten
a man-child with Yahweh.**

The relative completeness of the Biblical record
appears from this that the first descendants of the first
parents are reported in it. Adam, here still called by
the generic title "the man," begets a son, Cain. With a
significant delicacy and a very proper euphemism it is
said he "knew" his wife. This common expression,
used only in reference to connubial intercourse, signifies, as usual, a deeper knowing, an understanding of
the divine purpose, in this instance the purpose which
lay behind the forming of woman. As a protest
against any notion of promiscuity on the part of the
first man the account significantly adds to the proper
name Eve, "his wife," as though to indicate that he
knew and instinctively felt that the marital relation
was intended to be monogamous: it would not have
occurred to our first parent to "know" any other than
"his wife." Apparently, the statement coming at this
point, aims to indicate that Adam did not know Eve
during the time of their stay in the garden. Whether
this was largely due to circumstances, or to the brevity
of the stay in the garden, or was providentially regulated, will, perhaps, never be fully determined, although it will be practically impossible to rule out the
providential factor. With a certain measure of fullness of expression, characteristic of Hebrew style at

times, it is reported that "she conceived and bare Cain." The giving of this name is at the same time accounted for by the remark that she made at the time he was born. She said, "I have *gotten* a man-child." The Hebrew verb for this is *qanah;* the Hebrew proper name is *qa'yin.* The similarity of the two is sufficiently apparent for practical purposes. It matters little if it be objected that as to form the noun can hardly come from the verb root *qanah.* Eve was not at the time of her remark aiming to establish an exact etymology as philologists might. She could well be satisfied with a kind of alliteration between the two; as long as the name only served to recall her significant utterance, and that it adequately did. Though now modern philology guesses about at various meanings of the word, from "smith" to "lament," it is sufficient to hold that to the first mother the name served to recall her hopeful utterance. *Qanah,* by almost universal consent, must here mean "acquire" or "get." To us it still seems that in spite of the philologists' protests she wanted after she had said "gotten" to give a name like "Got," if we may be permitted to coin an English parallel. Such a name would continually recall how she "got."

However, the significant part of her remark is that she got this son "with Yahweh." The experience of birth with its travail having been successfully terminated, she ascribes what she acquired to Jehovah's help. In this phrase lie both thankfulness and praise: thankfulness at deliverance from pain and danger, praise that Jehovah is manifesting His grace and faithfulness in giving a son. So the use of the name "Yahweh" should be observed. Apparently, then, since the name stresses His gracious faithfulness, Eve praises God that He who promised victory to the seed of the woman actually lets "seed of the woman" be born. Nothing indicates whether Eve did or did not anticipate that this very seed, Cain, should personally

crush the serpent's head. But, in any case, she had a
token of Yahweh's fidelity. That she expresses it as
she does also affords proof that the mother of our race
had not remained in her sin but had come to repentance
and faith in God's promises. Consequently, her utterance is also to be regarded as a word of faith.

This translation of the expression *'eth Yahweh*
is sanctioned by almost all versions: the Targum has
"from"; the Greek has διὰ τοῦ Θεοῦ; the Vulgate has
per deum. The preposition *'eth* has the meaning "with"
or "with the help of" also in Gen. 49:25 a; Judg. 8:7 b;
Esther 9:29. Luther translated: "I have the man, the
Lord," making *'eth* the regular sign of the accusative.
However, grammatically we must object to this original rendering on the score that *'eth*, being the sign of
the definite object, sets the definite object *Yahweh*
by the side of the very indefinite object *'ish*, "a man."
In the second place, nothing had as yet indicated to
Eve the divine character of the seed of the woman.
To claim that she could quite naturally have anticipated
that fact, would practically make revelation unnecessary: man could adequately surmise the most vital of
truths. Thirdly, Luther himself wavered on this point.
In his commentary stands *den Mann des Herrn,* "the
man *of* the Lord."

That the word *'ish* in that case must then mean
"a human being" (*Mensch*) is not unusual. It has the
same meaning in Num. 23:19. We believe we have
caught the spirit of the word in rendering "man-
child." Eve in spirit sees the child already grown to
full manhood.

It is necessary to observe that this remark of Eve s
demonstrates clearly how our first parents put all their
hope and trust in God's Word. They had but few
words from the Lord. Outstanding was the word of
gospel concerning the ultimate victory of the woman's
seed. This furnished the ground for a true hope, for a

distinct, though as yet not fully developed, faith in the Christ.

An interesting argument for the unity of Genesis and its composition by one author may briefly be inserted here. Popular etymologies, like that of the name "Cain," are found repeatedly in Genesis, and, strange to say, in all the chief so-called sources, J, P, and E. This constitutes one of the many strong arguments for the composition by one author, although criticism refuses to use this valid argument. Here are the facts (according to Strack): J has 2:23; 4:25; 5:29; 9:27; 10:25; 11:9; 50:11 etc.; P offers 17:5; E gives 41:51, 52; cf. also chapters 29 and 30; 35:18; Exod. 2:10, 22 etc.

On *watta'har* see G. K. 75 r.

The fact that Eve, the mother, is the one that supplies the name is no indication that the Bible teaches that the matriarchate existed from days of old. Naturally, on occasion the mother will desire and fix a certain name upon a child. Occasionally the father's wish will prevail. Note that among the instances to be cited on v. 25 both sides of the matter stand out clearly.

Meek's rendering is poor exegesis: "I have won back my husband; the Lord is with me." It requires several highly improbable things: a serious quarrel between the first parents and several grave deficiencies in the text. To alter texts when the desired meaning is not readily forthcoming is poor scholarship.

2. **After that she bore his brother Abel, and Abel was a keeper of sheep and Cain was a tiller of the soil.**

The scriptural record definitely knows who the second one of the sons of Adam was. The fact that it is not again reported that Adam "knew his wife and she conceived," but merely, "she bore," does not in any way indicate, as has been frequently maintained, that

Abel was of the same birth and Cain's twin brother. The following cases of the omission of the mention of conception without the suggestion of twin births may be listed: 4:20, 22, 25; 6:4; 22:20, 24; 25:2; 30:10, 12, 21; 35:16; 36:4; 38:5 etc. (K. C.).

The name Abel is significant. *Hébhel* means "breath," "vapor," "vanity." Somehow the vanity of human existence had impressed itself on our first parents. The exact occasion for this realization cannot be determined. It may have been due to the fact that man was barred from access to the tree of life. Those that argue that Eve thought Cain to be the Messiah see in Abel's name proof of her disillusionment. Even more likely is the supposition that the sum total of human existence marred by sin had impressed man with the emptiness of it all.

The expression, "after that she bore," in Hebrew offers the idiomatic statement: "she added to bear," the main verb being used almost as an adverb (G. K. 114 m). On *lalédheth* cf. K. S. 399 b.

The condensed account at once advances to the point where the two sons have each their own occupation. Abel was a shepherd of sheep, i. e. of *tso'n*, i. e. of smaller cattle like sheep and goats. Cain is a "server of the ground," the more realistic Hebrew expression for "tiller of the soil." Nowhere does the account intimate that any one of these two occupations was inferior to the other. In fact, the great likelihood is that both were already followed by our first parent. He had warrant for the first both in his original destiny to tend the garden (2:15) as well as in the burden laid upon him in 3:17, 18, 23. He had warrant for the second in God's clothing him with skins (3:21). The word spoken in 1:29 no doubt excluded the use of cattle for food; whether for milk will have to remain an open question. Each son assumed one phase of his father's double activity, and so each had a life's task

well-pleasing to God. There is no need for man, as the
Bible knows him, to wander through mazes of development because of his crude state before he can arrive
at agriculture. In flat contradiction to evolution the
first man was an agriculturalist and a shepherd — at
least, these two occupations were followed by his
children.

**3-5. And it came to pass after a time that Cain
brought some of the fruits of the field as an offering
to Yahweh; and Abel on his part also brought some
of the firstborn of his flock, namely, some of the fat
pieces. And Yahweh regarded Abel and his sacrifice; but Cain and his sacrifice He did not regard.
Then Cain became exceedingly angry and his glance
fell.**

With rapid strides the narration progresses and
takes us to the point where on one occasion the two
brothers bring a sacrifice. Nothing indicates that this
episode marks the inauguration of sacrifice by mankind. It may not even have been the first time that
these brothers offered sacrifices. The casual way of
reporting the fact that they brought sacrifices would
rather lead us to believe that something was being done
which was not of a character to challenge attention
because of its newness. There is no ground for the
claim: "The whole manner of the narration suggests
rather that the incident is conceived as the initiation
of sacrifice." More nearly true is the supposition that
sacrifices were originated by their father, Adam. And
since no commandment is recorded authorizing or
requesting sacrifice from man as a thing divinely
sought, we are, no doubt, nearer the truth when we
let sacrifices originate spontaneously on man's part as
a natural expression of a devout spirit and of gratitude
toward the omnipotent Giver of all good things. Sacrifice meets a deep need of the human heart. If sacrifice had originated in a commandment of God, it

might well be thought of as a thing of sufficient importance to be permanently recorded in divine Scriptures. The later Mosaic regulations merely take the sacrificial customs prevalent at the time and regulate and sanction them.

Consequently, we dare not construe the terminology of our account after the analogy of Mosaic sacrificial terminology of the period of the wilderness wanderings. The word for offering, *minchah,* is used in its broadest sense, covering any type of gift man may bring. Nor do the later connotations of sacrifice apply at this time. Neither of the two sacrifices is made specifically for sin. Nothing in the account points in this direction. Consequently, the merit of the one over against the other does not lie in the fact that it was a bloody offering. The nature of the sacrifice as to its material is determined entirely by the occupation of him who brings it.

In fact, throughout the narrative one should carefully guard against imputing to these sacrifices things that we cannot prove to have been part of them. We are not even sure that an altar was built for the purpose. The first altar is mentioned after the Flood. We cannot prove that fire was employed to consume the sacrifice. That the animal sacrifice was killed is made apparent by the use of the term "fat pieces."

But to follow the account step for step — these sacrifices are brought "after a time," literally translated: "after the end of days." The expression is intentionally vague. It seems to suggest nothing as to the lapse of time since the birth of the brothers. Since sacrifices would most naturally be brought after the termination of the agricultural year, we may incline to think of the fall of the year. But the time element is entirely unimportant and therefore left indefinite.

We can only surmise why Cain is mentioned first as bringing a sacrifice. It may be because he was the first-born. It is more likely that it is so reported because he actually brought his offering first. There is even the possibility that this particular incident occurred after the brothers had many times before brought their sacrifices after the example of what they had seen their father do. Though the first to bring his offering, Cain does not thereby prove himself the more devout in his religious observances.

What he brings is described as "some of the fruits of the field." *Min* before *peri* is the *"min* partitive." These constitute an "offering to Yahweh." *Minchah* may be merely a "gift" or "tribute." But when brought to Yahweh, it constitutes an actual offering. "Fruits of the field" are the natural offering of the agriculturalist and are as acceptable as any kind, if brought in the right spirit. The law of Moses specifies many different kinds of vegetable or meal offerings as the natural offering of a grateful people. One of the most unwarranted claims made is that of Gunkel: "This myth indicates that God loves the shepherd and the offering of flesh, but as far as the farmer and the fruits of the field are concerned, He will have none of them." Apparently, this offering is described as brought *"to Yahweh"* because hitherto when sacrifices had been brought, it was because God was being thought of as the faithful and gracious Lord. To the Yahweh to whom sacrifice had regularly been brought Cain assayed to bring his sacrifice.

It should not be overlooked that v. 3 begins with an idiomatic expression frequently used when details are to be introduced, the expression, namely, "and it came to pass" (*wayhi*). Instead of: "after a time he brought" the Hebrew prefers to say: "And it came to pass after a year and he brought," co-ordinating rather than subordinating clauses (K. S. 341 s; 369 i).

4) In order to make the contrast of Abel's offering more apparent, the construction of the sentence

begins, not after the rule of the verb first, but with the subject "Abel," emphasized by a *gam hû'* = "even he" or "on his part." Since the contrast is so marked, there can be no doubt that the significant words "of the first-born" and "some of the fat pieces" in addition to "of his flock" aim to show a distinguishing feature of this sacrifice. Since one merely gave of what he had acquired, but the other gave "firstlings" and "fat pieces" of what he had acquired, it is evident that the one gave because it was time and custom to give — pure formalism; whereas the other gave the best — pure, devout worship. *Chélebh* means "fat." The plural of the noun cannot mean "fatlings" nor only "fat" (A. V.) but must be the "fat pieces." The "and" before this word is used, as often (cf. Exod. 24:12), in the sense of "namely" (*waw* explicative). Those that see the merit of Abel's sacrifice in the fact that it was bloody certainly do so without the least warrant from the text. Nothing anywhere indicates that that particular aspect of sacrifices had as yet been developed or considered at such an early age.

5) With characteristic spiritual discernment the Scripture goes to the heart of things. Formalistic worship is of no value in God's eyes; it is an abomination in the sight of the Lord. Our narrative gives expression to this thought by stating that "Yahweh regarded Abel and his offering; but Cain and his sacrifice He did not regard." The meaning of the verb *sha'ah* is "to gaze," but when it is used with *'el* in a connection such as this, it means "regard with favor." But the significant thing, noticed by Luther and most commentators since, is that this regarding with favor directs itself first to the person, then to the offering; so in the case of both the brothers. This fact very significantly shows that the determining factor in worship is the attitude of the individual. Him, or his heart, God weighs. If he is not found wanting, the gift is acceptable. If he fails to please the Almighty, his

gift is reprobate. This fact is so important that it
alone is stated. The writer regards it as quite unimportant to record how the divine favor or disfavor was
expressed.

Since this fact will never be determined, we may
at least mention what has been suggested. An old
Greek translation rendered the word *sha'ah* ἐνεπύρισεν,
"He kindled." Evidently the translator had in mind
that God on various occasions did kindle an acceptable
sacrifice (Judg. 6:21; 13:19, 20). However, the double
object *"Abel* and his sacrifice" makes this view untenable. Others think of some visible token such as the
rising of the smoke of the one sacrifice as proof of its
acceptance and the falling of the smoke of the other as
proof of its rejection. This, however, is a pure guess.
To suppose that God's favor was displayed in the
ensuing prosperity of Abel and His displeasure in
Cain's failure to prosper as time went on, seems the
most reasonable of all but lies open to the criticism that
such gradual unfolding of favor or disfavor would
have come to light sooner or later anyhow, whereas
our account centers attention on a particular sacrifice
and what apparently were the immediate results. But,
then, there is still a possibility which dare not be
rejected. If the garden still remained on earth and
was, as many suppose, the place of God's manifestation
to men — for cherubim are the mediators of His presence to the world — then He will have conversed with
these sons of Adam somewhat after the pattern of His
conversing with Adam and Eve in the garden. In that
event they who brought their sacrifices would have
brought them to Him whose presence was manifest in
the garden, and they could have discerned from His
attitude whether their offering was accepted or not.
But all this raises the difficult question: "Was God's
presence actually manifested in some visible way from
the garden up to the time of the Flood?" Our answer
must be, "No man knows." Enough that both brothers

recognized how God felt about their offerings. The rest actually does not matter.

Cain's reaction to God's disapproval is twofold: he "becomes exceedingly angry and his glance falls." God's displeasure had revealed to Cain a reprehensible state of heart. That such was his attitude should have duly alarmed Cain. God's not looking with favor was also a gracious divine warning (N. B. "Yahweh"). Cain adds a second sin to the first by his anger, and a very serious sin at that, by his excessive anger. The Hebrew uses the expression *wayyíchar leqáyin* = "and it burned for Cain," the verb omitting the natural subject *'aph,* "anger," and using an impersonal expression. With true psychological insight the author narrates how this strong anger displayed itself outwardly. This was done by the falling of the glance, literally of "the face" (*paním*). Here, without a doubt, "the glance" is meant K. W. — *Blick*). For anger that does not break out into violence seeks to hide itself by not looking freely into the eye of the one at whom it is directed. Since the glance thus feels checked, it naturally falls. So there was the inward passion and the visible outward indication of its presence. Even if commentators insist on translating *paním* "face," they scarcely have anything different from our explanation above, for the falling of the countenance still centers in the expression of the eye.

6, 7. And Yahweh said unto Cain: Why art thou angry and why has thy glance fallen? Is it not so, if thou doest right, there is acceptance; and if thou dost not do right, then at the door there is sin, a crouching beast, striving to get at thee, but thou shouldest rule over it?

The *wayyó'mer,* "and He said," requires attention. It expressly forbids making this whole experience one that plays entirely in the heart of Cain as an inner struggle with the clash of conscience and the evil desire.

The author does not play fast and loose with the expression "Yahweh said." Equally incorrect is the attempt to get around the problem as to how God may have spoken by assigning the words to Adam, the father, who, as an enlightened personality, admonishes his son with words that may be called God's words because they were suggested by His Spirit. But there is really nothing in the text to indicate Adam's participation in the admonition. The fact, then, remains that in some objective way God actually transmits this warning to the man Cain who stands on the verge of a very grievous sin. God's mercy to fallen mankind is amply displayed in this warning; therefore again "Yahweh."

The first part of the warning is a question calculated to arouse Cain to a realization of some grievous disorder in his conduct. If he analyzes "why" he did begin to be angry and drop his glance, he will realize that what caused him to act thus — God's acceptance of one offering and the rejecting of the other — should rather have made him feel that the one who was justified in becoming angry was the Almighty Himself. Cain should have displayed sorrow over his sin rather than anger over the God who graciously warned him. This initial searching question is followed by another double question (v. 7) both parts of which are controlled by the initial interrogative particle *halo'*, a particle suggesting an affirmative answer (K. S. 353 e; 353 k; 318 l). The second question more definitely constitutes a warning, since Yahweh discerns that the initial suggestion is not being heeded. Note that all this is ascribed to "Yahweh" who displays His grace in what He does.

Now the double question as such, though it has manifest difficulties, is not as perplexing as the critics stamp it, who either make it "the most difficult verse in the chapter, yea, in all Genesis" (Procksch), or else assail Scripture by asserting: "Every attempt to extract a meaning from the verse is more or less a *tour de force.*" The first major difficulty is the rendering of the infinitive *se'eth,* from *nasa'.* This verb has as primary meaning the idea of "lifting," "lifting up," and "taking," and so occurs in a wide variety of meanings. However, several of these, though legitimate meanings, reject themselves as ill-suited to the connection. So the attempted improvement of the A. R. V. "shall it not be lifted up." This rendering supplies as object *panîm,* "countenance," considering the expression to stand in contrast with v. 6, the *falling* of the countenance. Luther objects: "Is such a remark not just a little too trite and obvious? Of course, if you do right, you wear a cheerful countenance and a free and happy glance; but is that of sufficient importance for a divine utterance to Cain?" So, in the second place, all attempts to supply the otherwise proper object "sin" or "guilt," and following the basic sense of "take away" for *se'eth,* and so causing the expression to be equivalent to "forgive" — all such attempts, we say, naturally shatter on the fact that Scriptures nowhere teach that forgiveness is achieved by our doing right: we simply do not merit forgiveness. Why impute such a saying to the Lord here? However, if we supply the *panîm* of v. 6 as object, the resultant expression "take or accept the face" means "to receive graciously," a meaning found also 32:21. This meaning is covered by our translation "acceptance." A. V., therefore, was perfectly correct: "shalt thou not be accepted." Luther has the same thought: *so bist du angenehm.* The meaning of the whole statement, then, is this: As long as you do right you are acceptable to God, not in the sense of meriting such acceptance, but rather in the sense, warranted by the connection, of a warning and a searching question: Have you forfeited your acceptability by doing ill? This thought is also implied in the form of the verb *têtîbh,* a *Hifil,* and therefore causative, emphasizing the moral respon-

sibility. For if a man does not make his doings right,
for that he is personally responsible.

Now the warning becomes still more pointed, applying directly to Cain's case, showing what the situation is if a man does "not do right," or (*Hifil*) "cause
his doing to be good." In that event "sin" (*chatta'th*,
here mentioned for the first time in Scripture, a word
bearing the basic meaning of "missing the mark")
has become a very definite possibility, even a menacing
threat. It is to be likened to a wild beast (therefore
robhets, masculine, not feminine agreeing with "sin")
crouching at the door. And as promptly as such a
beast immediately at hand would seize a man going out
at the door, so promptly will sin leap upon one and hurt
him. This figure is appropriate also from this point of
view: the hurt is inevitable, the ultimate escape possible but problematic. Completing the picture, there
is the expression "striving to get at thee," which A. V.
rendered: "unto thee shall be its desire." Literally the
preposition and the noun must be rendered: "toward
thee its striving." We believe we catch the meaning
well in this connection by rendering: "striving to get
at thee." The added thought is that this "crouching
beast" is not a mild, passive thing, a tame leopard or
some harmless pet. Rather, it thirsts after your blood.
So the threatening character of the danger is made
fully apparent to Cain, and the warning is complete.

Now follows the clear suggestion, what course to
take: "thou shouldest rule over it." Such a statement
at this point does not imply that a sinful man of himself is readily capable of mastering sin that threatens.
But we have here a statement in full conformity with
the tenor of revealed truth: in the strength, which the
Word of God here offers to man as a means of grace,
supplies for man, he is to rule over and master the
threatening danger. We believe that in this sense the
imperfect *timshol* expresses obligation: "thou shouldest
rule." If some of these words happen to occur in 3:16

in reference to the woman (there rendered: "unto your husband you shall be attracted (striving) and he shall rule over you"), we see nothing more than an accidental similarity in this. To hint at textual corruption because of this similarity is presumption.

When Jamieson and others suggest that *chattath* should be translated "sin-offering," that imports a rare and technical meaning, of whose use we have no evidence until at a much later date, and necessitates as Jamieson himself suggests "previous instruction in the mode of worship." On the improbability of the divine institution of sacrifices we suggest the consideration that had this outward act been divinely ordained, man, too much inclined to purely outward acts in religion, might quite readily have overemphasized the importance of the external. Consequently, the Scriptures do not represent sacrifices as originating at God's command. When the practice, natural enough in itself, requires regulation and purification, God supplies such regulations in the days of Moses.

There is something ominous about Cain's silence. He is not reported to have thanked for the warning, or to have repented of his jealousy, or to have mended his ways. A stubborn silence seems to have been all he had to offer.

It should be pointed out more directly that Cain's sin in reference to his brother was primarily jealousy culminating in hatred, a sin that seems comparatively weak and insignificant but which carries possibilities of great development within itself.

Now the account proceeds in a drastic manner to show what possibilities for development lay in the sin which had by this time fastened itself strongly upon man. Possibilities for evil that no man would have suspected lay hidden in sin. Of a sudden it breaks forth and displays to the full its vicious nature and terrible curse. There is no book that so emphatically reveals what a cursed thing sin is as the Bible. Man should know what an octopus fastened its tentacles upon the race when sin took hold of it. With terrible realism the narrative continues.

8. **And Cain said unto Abel his brother — and it came to pass when they were out in the field, Cain attacked Abel his brother and slew him.**

There has been much needless speculation as to what Cain said to Abel. There are also unnecessary attempts to supply what some deem an accidental omission. A. R. V. acts on a wrong assumption when it translates *wayyó'mer* "told." There is a different verb for "telling." *Wayyó'mer* actually means "and he said." This verb is almost always followed by direct discourse. The few instances where it is used in the sense "and he spoke" (like II Chron. 32:34; Exod. 19:25) might allow us to translate "spoke" in this instance; but the result is practically the same if we assume that the obvious object of the verb is omitted, as in 2:19 a; 3:21 b; 4:9 b. This object, as quite naturally follows from the ensuing context, is, "Let us go out into the field," as the Greek and the Latin translations, as well as the Samaritan translation suggest. But this merely supplies what is obviously meant. The text (contra Kittel) needs no correction. Therefore all the other suggestions fall away, such as: He told Abel what God had said; or, He feigned friendliness; or, He discoursed on God's providence, and the like. But if the object that we suggest be supplied, then, apparently, Cain, far from heeding the divine warning, has even gone to the point of planning to remove his brother from the scene of action. He induces him to go "out in the field," or "out in the country" (Meek), where both will be "safe from observation" (II Kings 11:29).

When they are out there, Cain "attacks his brother." The Hebrew says: "he rose up against him."

But in such connections that verb rise (*qûm*) does not mean the literal rising from a sitting posture but, in a more general sense, "to undertake something"; therefore "attack," in this case. We could call this *"arise in a hostile sense"* (B D B). To make the horrid and wicked nature of the deed doubly apparent, the appositive noun, "his brother," is appended to the object "Abel." His attack is so successful that it results in actual murder: "and he slew him." So the first murder was fratricide. Sin could hardly have displayed more drastically the potentialities that lie in it. In the second generation it has already grown to the proportions of murder. Clearly, the term "seed of the woman" (3:15) must suffer modification. Here already is a clear instance how "the seed of the woman had already (in part) become the seed of the serpent" (Keil).

Even more effective than the account of the nature and horribleness of sin is the account of God's mercy shown to the sinner, as v. 9-15 records it. For though this mercy has to be tempered by justice, it, nevertheless, looms up large as being entirely undeserved by a murderer like Cain. This mercy first takes the sinner to account, trying to rouse him to repentance (v. 9). Note: *Yahweh* is the subject.

9. **And Yahweh said unto Cain: Where is Abel, thy brother? And he said: I do not know; am I my brother's keeper?**

As always, God does not ask in order to secure information. The question is pedagogic, in order to remind Cain that God knows where Abel is. To ascribe those words to Adam as a spokesman for God is farfetched. Here is the second cross-examination found in the Scriptures. The contrast with the first is apparent. The first found Adam and Eve humble, though given to evasion and excuses. The second finds Cain impudent and hardened, at least at the beginning of the interview. Yet the first question had effectually

presented to Cain the startling reminder of the slain
man lying inert in his own blood out in the field. The
heartless lie and bold rejoinder on Cain's part is: "I
do not know; am I my brother's keeper?" The question
gains a slightly different force in the Hebrew, where
the predicate stands first for emphasis: "Am keeper
of my brother I?" like: "Am I supposed to *watch*
him all the while?" He feels too guilty to draw attention to himself by way of contrast and to say:
"Am *I* my brother's keeper?" The interrogative *ha*
anticipates a negative answer.

10. **And He said: What hast thou done?
The voice of the spilt blood of thy brother is crying
out to Me from the ground.**

First the divine word attempts to waken in the
man a realization of the enormity of his misdeed. The
"what" naturally implies: "What horrible thing?"
On the form *meh* see G. K. 37 d. Then the word proceeds to a direct charge which completely startles the
sinner out of his security.

God reveals that He knows of the blood that has
been spilt, He refers to it as *damîm*, plural, vividly
suggesting the many drops shed, a shade of meaning
that we have tried to convey by the rendering "spilt
blood." This is represented as crying out persistently
and continually; for the participle expresses what continues in the present or keeps repeating itself (K. S.
236 a; 238 a). Here the participle involves the idea
of a certain insistence. That a voice should be attributed to blood is not strange inasmuch as the soul is
regarded as lodged in the blood of man (Lev. 17:11),
and the death of God's saints is precious in His sight
(Ps. 116:15). That God requires blood, that is, seeks
out and avenges all instances of unjust shedding of
blood, appears from Job 16:18; Gen. 9:5; Ezek. 3:18;
24:7, 8; 33:6; and Ps. 9:12. Men may esteem souls
or blood lightly. Not so God.

The tendency to render *qôl*, "voice," as "hark," supported also by G. K. 146 b, should be restricted. The far better and more vivid rendering here is "voice."

Now with v. 11 the word of *Yahweh* reveals Cain's punishment. Behind this punishment and the revelation of its scope, no doubt, also lies divine mercy; for Cain's hard lot is to drive him to repentance.

11, 12. And now cursed shalt thou be, driven away from the ground which has opened its mouth to receive thy brother's blood from thy hand. When thou tillest the soil, it shall not in the future yield its produce to thee; thou shalt be shifting and straying about in the earth.

Hitherto the ground had been cursed (3:17) and the serpent (3:14), certainly not humankind. Now for the first time the divine curse is laid upon a mortal. This fact alone stresses, as perhaps nothing else could, God's earnestness over against sin. However, this curse is carefully defined as to what it includes, for it is not a curse that bars Cain from the possibility of salvation. This curse is not the sentence of damnation. It merely involves two things: a) being driven away from the cultivated and arable portion of the land and winning his sustenance under the greatest of difficulties; and b) being compelled to shift and stray about in the earth.

There is something very proper about the first part of this curse. The precious human blood was spilled upon the *'adhamah*, the tillable soil. That soil opened its mouth and greedily drank in the blood. This was a profaning of blood and a staining of the soil. Mankind must at once be taught that such precious things as blood, or life, are not to be wasted so lightly. This lesson can be taught in the fate of the first murderer. To make that fate stand out Cain is cursed *min-ha'adhamah*, "away from the ground." The construction is pregnant. The preposition *min* practically presents a condensed negative result clause, and the phrase means "so that there is no ground for you" (K. C.) or, as we have rendered somewhat more concisely: "driven away from the ground." Cain is not to be permitted to settle down where cultivated areas (*Kulturland*) offer themselves. Of course, he will have to do some work by way of raising fruits of the earth; he will till the soil. But from this time on (this is practically the force of *lo'-thoseph*; see G. K. 109 d. h) the ground will not give of its strength (*kóach* cf. Job 31:38, here, of course, means "produce") to Cain as readily as it does to others. Only with the hardest of struggles will Cain be able to gain a bare pittance.

The second part of the curse may also quite properly be regarded as involved in the first, or as producing the first. For if a man be continually "shifting and straying about in the earth," it will not be possible for him to settle down to any fixed occupation like agriculture. So God lays on Cain the second part of the curse in order to gain the result, namely, the first part. *Na' wanadh* was rendered by the King James' translators as "a fugitive and a vagabond." This was a good rendering; not quite as apropos, however, as Luther's *unstaet und fluechtig*. "Vagabond," from the Latin *vagare*, "to stray about," has, however, come to mean "tramp" or "hobo." Therefore A. R. V. substituted "wanderer" quite appropriately. We have rendered "shifting and straying about" in an effort to recapture the telling alliteration of the original. *Na'* from the root *núa'*, is allied to the Arabic root meaning to sway like a branch. *Nadh* (root: *núdh*) basically means "to nod," "to stray about." Behind all this lay an added purpose: to impress the sanctity of human life and the enormity of the sin of murder upon mankind. Cain was not only known by report to these early generations of men, but he, the fugitive, had no

doubt been seen by most of them, unhappy wretch that
he was, straying about from place to place without
peace or rest. Quite inaccurately and with a shallow
interpretation Procksch sums up the case with the
remark: "Thus Cain ceases to be a farmer and becomes
a bedouin."

13, 14. **And Cain said unto Yahweh: My
punishment is greater than I can bear. Behold,
Thou hast this day driven me forth off the ground
and I must stay hidden from Thee, and I must be
shifting and straying about in the earth, and it will
happen that whoever finds me will slay me.**

The bold impudence of Cain's first answer to
Yahweh now yields to a hopeless despair. Note that
throughout the account God is designated as Yahweh,
to remind the reader of the gracious faithfulness which
characterizes His dealings with sinners. Cain's answer, however, gives no indication of a repentant
spirit. There is no grief over sin in the word, "My
punishment is greater than I can bear." Cain is very
sorry to have gotten into such a mess. He does deplore
the set of miserable consequences that he has brought
down upon his head. All he speaks about is the punishment that has fallen to his lot. Therefore, the word
'awon must be rendered "punishment." It might mean
"guilt," or just "sin." But here the context demands
the common enough meaning "punishment for sin."
Therefore, it is not the enormity of his guilt that
strikes heavily into his conscience, as Luther's translation suggests: "My sin is too great to be forgiven."
Cain merely cringes at the thought of what he must
bear. This is a rather common experience in the
psychology of sinners: bold impudence becomes a
whining fear and complaint. This thought is elaborated in v. 14. *Gadhol* as comparative, see G. K. 133 c,
K. S. 308 b. *Min* introduces a negative result clause:
K. S. 406 h.

14) The "behold" (*hen*), used with perfects, only marks a measure of vivacity or agitation in the expression (*Lebhaftigkeit:* K. S. 131) and is akin to our "look," or "see." There is complaint in the words: "Look, you have this day driven me off the ground." Cain recognizes that the fruitful portion of the earth, "the ground," is barred from him. He feels that in such favored portions of the earth God can be thought of as being present in a more intimate sense. To be barred from this portion of the earth is, therefore, to him synonymous with being hidden from God. So he exclaims, still by way of complaint, "I must stay hidden from Thee." For though the sinner has no personal desire for communion with God, he may yet recognize, as a result of training and earlier experience, that to be kept from approaching God is a grievous punishment. An analogy to this view of the superior blessedess of the *'adhamah* is found in 27:27 where Isaac speaks of "the field which God has blessed" as a particularly favored spot. Similarly, Israel and David later considered the land of promise as a place of the very special manifestation of God's favor and felt that it was not a light thing to be separated from it, for there God had vouchsafed to manifest His goodness in richer measure; cf. Gen. 46:3, 4; I Sam. 26:19. Yet this way of looking at the situation does not imply wrong views about God's person, as though He were not omnipresent, for, as K. C. has pointed out, at once God is viewed in v. 15 as a God whose power reaches everywhere and is able to avenge wrong no matter where it be done. The earliest writers, like Moses, had an adequate and correct conception of God, as the spirit of inspiration speaking through them gave it to them. So, too, according to the Scriptures man is not a being, who is by slow degrees penetrating through the mists of unenlightenment. From the very outset God has granted to him a true and correct conception of Himself. No trace of evolution here. We have tried to cap-

ture the imperfect, or present idea in *'esather* by rendering it *"stay* hidden." Besides, the imperfect here rather expresses necessity ("must") than futurity (K. S. 181: *soll und muss*). The article in *hayyôm*, being the article of what is customary, comes to mean "today" or "this day" (K. S. 299 a).

Two more items of bitter complaint are voiced by Cain. First: "I must be shifting and straying about." He has heard his doom and knows it is inescapable. Gone is the boldness with which he first faced God. His complaint reaches its climax in the last item, expressing his gravest fear: "It will happen that whoever finds me will slay me." The psychology of the reaction is characteristic. Murderers fear that they in turn will be slain by others. The coward Cain did not hesitate to slay Abel, but he is dreadfully afraid lest another slay him. In fact, he is so apprehensive that he anticipates that everyone whom he meets will be inclined to wreak vengeance upon him. The Bible records all this in order to make it very apparent that "the way of the transgressor is hard."

Critics try to prove the unhistorical, if not mythical, character of the whole narrative by the oft repeated charge that Cain speaks as if he were living in a world quite full of people. Such an assumption is quite unnecessary. There is no flaw or inaccuracy in the record. The sequel proves that other children of Adam were already living at this time or shortly thereafter. These, as well as others who may yet arrive at years of maturity, the conscience-stricken, guilty murderer fears. Such an assumption squares with all facts and is perfectly natural. Such simple and satisfactory explanations, however, do not satisfy the critics. Procksch claims that the only satisfactory explanation of the statement is to be found in the assumption that Cain was not an individual but a clan (*Stamm*), and so the origin of a clan feud is here being described. A natural explanation is thereby rejected for an unproved and unprovable hypothesis.

15. **And Yahweh said to him: Wherefore, if anyone slays Cain, vengeance shall be exacted sevenfold. And Yahweh gave Cain a sign that whoever found him would not murder him.**

Because Cain pleaded so earnestly "therefore" (*lakhen*) Yahweh (who is merciful) appointed that "vengeance was to be exacted" (*yuqqam — Hofal* of *naqam*) from such a one "sevenfold." This "sevenfold" apparently means "seven times as heavy a punishment as Cain had merited" (Delitzsch). The statement as such gives assurance to Cain. This divine word will become known. Men will not soon dare to fly in the face of it. The Jewish fables, reported by Luther, telling how Cain was later slain by Lamech, though accidentally, are not worth recording. For the presumption is very strong that Cain was not slain. In fact, the merciful Lord ("Yahweh" again) made assurance doubly sure by even giving Cain a sign.

Now when the question is raised, "wherein did this 'sign' consist?" it is usually regarded as a "mark" (A. V.) set upon him (so also Luther). But this assumption overlooks the fact that the text does not say that God set a mark *in* or *on* Cain (Hebrew, *be*) but *for* Cain (Hebrew *le*), marking a dative of interest or advantage. Consequently, we are rather to think of some sign that God allowed to appear for Cain's reassurance, "a sign of guaranty" (K. W.) or a "pledge or token" (B D B). As parallels might be cited the signs vouchsafed to certain men to whom God promised unusual things: Gideon (Judges 6:36-40); Elisha (II Kings 2:9-12). God let this sign appear, therefore, for Cain, and he felt reassured. There is, therefore, no ground for supposing that Cain went about as a marked man all the rest of his life. Anyhow, *'ôth* does not mean "mark."

Yet in the face of later developments, especially 9:6 where the principle of the need of execution of murderers is laid down without exceptions, it seems strange that the first murderer should have been spared. A multitude of reasons can, however, be adduced why God should have spared Cain. Among those that have been offered the following stand out. The presence of this tragic figure, the "fugitive and the vagabond" among men, served as a more potent warning to men as to the enormity of the curse of murder by the very misery of his existence. In addition, it must be admitted that banishment from God's presence was the heaviest punishment of all, heavier than the loss of life, and this heavier punishment Cain knows he has suffered. Then, too, there was a salutary lesson in this that God reserved for Himself the right to determine which life was to be terminated and which not; so God's supremacy as the Judge of all flesh was guarded, and a premium put on the value of human life. Then we may also consider the validity of the principle enuntiated later, that it pleases the Almighty to let tares and wheat both grow together till the harvest. Closely allied to this is the other argument that God allows sin to run a free course and to develop to the full the potentialities that lie in it, so that the nature of evil as evil may be fully revealed in the historical development of mankind. To all these may yet be added the argument that the more rapid development of the human race, which had to be guaranteed in the days when men were few upon the earth, would certainly have been seriously checked if the first one of the sons of Adam had been put to death. However, it appears that one other argument perhaps ought not to be pressed, namely that God lengthened Cain s days that he might repent. True, God's mercy is displayed richly in His dealings with Cain as Yahweh, but it also has become very much apparent by this time that each successive advance of mercy resulted in a more rigid shutting of Cain's heart. Mercy apparently had done its work before this last provision was made by God. The ultimate impenitence of Cain seems to be suggested by the nature of his descendants, who are described in the following words.

The participle *horegh* is rendered as a conditional sentence in this particular verse; see G. K. 116 w.

16. And Cain went forth from the presence of the Lord and dwelt in the land of wandering east of Eden.

The expressions: "driven forth from the ground" (v. 11), and "driven forth from the ground and I must be hidden from Thee" (v. 14), and that of this verse, he "went forth from the presence of the Lord," all refer to the same thing. Where God had hitherto by preference revealed Himself, there Cain can no longer stay; he is shut off from God. It is somewhat precarious to assume that the revelation of God took place in a special sense from the site of the old garden of Eden, where here by various statements the text associates it with the region where "the ground" was. The land which A. V. calls "the land of Nod," *'érets nodh,* signifies "the land of wandering or straying," and it will, therefore, hardly signify any special land or country. Because of the nature of the curse upon him Cain was simply condemned to ceaseless wanderings. To these he now went forth, the text says. However, one general region alone saw him; that was the region "east of Eden," the region where mankind as a whole dwelt at first (3:24). No "land of Nod," furthermore, has ever been identified.

Not without reason the fathers saw in these first sons of Adam prototypes of the two divisions into which the human race is divided ever since: the church and the world. The antagonism between the two began at this point and is characteristic of all human history

ever since. This is a point of view clearly maintained
by the New Testament. There the opposition of Cain
to Abel is traced to the fact that "his works were evil
and his brother's were righteous" (I John 3:12) ; and
at the same time it is stated that "Cain was of the evil
one." It was more than a momentary flash of anger
that revealed itself in Cain's deed. A basic change
of heart had taken place in him, a shift of allegiance
to "the evil one." Since such opposition is fundamental,
it is the beginning of the tragic division of the race
that is in reality the explanation of a good bit of the
history of the world.

Confirming our interpretation of the relative
merits of the two sacrifices, comes the other New Testament passage Heb. 11:4, which with characteristic
depth traces the ultimate source of every good work
to "faith": "By faith Abel offered unto God a more
excellent sacrifice." The same author (12:24) makes
excellent use of the thought of Abel's blood crying for
vengeance when he contrasts the efficacy of Christ's
blood that, pleading for mercy for them that are
sprinkled by it, will surely "speak better than that of
Abel."

b)   17-24: **The Development of the family of the
Cainites**

17. **And Cain knew his wife and she conceived and bare Enoch, and he (Cain) was engaged
in bulding a city and he called the name of the city
after the name of his son Enoch.**

Though this portion may rightly be said to sketch
the development of the family of the Cainites, it would
not be incorrect to regard it as an account of the beginnings of civilization or culture. For, strange to
say, civilization did make far greater strides among
those alienated from God than among those who were
devoted to Him. Yet this is not very strange, if closely

considered, for they, being addicted and devoted to the
things of the world and not satisfied with the world's
treasures — for who can be? — they, we say, do all in
their power to make an empty existence attractive by
the cultivation of the natural resources of the world.
Besides, the children of this world are in their generation wiser than the children of light.

First, however, the development and growth of
this family as such is sketched through several generations, with such brief historical events inserted as are
of moment in this history.

Cain is first disposed of. For that matter, a
characteristic feature of the author of Genesis may
well be noted at this point. He regularly disposes of
the less relevant but necessary by taking it first and
sketching it briefly. Then the heavier emphasis can
be laid on what is of particular moment in the development of the kingdom of God. So here after the Cainites
come the Sethites from 4:25 practically to 9:28. Then
the families of Ham and Japheth are briefly disposed
of, as well as that of Shem (ch. 10-11:26), to make
room for that of Terah, or Abraham 11:27-25:11.
Ishmael is treated briefly (25:12-18) to prepare for
Isaac 25:19-35:29. Again Esau's development is
sketched 36:1-37:1; then follows the story of Jacob at
length from 37:2 to the end of the book.

Cain's wife must have been his sister who followed
him into exile; for Adam had sons and daughters according to 5:4. Nor can marriage to a sister at this
early stage of the development of the human race be
considered wrong or unnatural. If according to divine
purpose the human race is to develop from one pair,
then the marriage of brothers and sisters as well as
of other close relatives will for a time be a necessity.
Later on the nations may see fit to classify such unions
as incestuous and seek to keep the human race from
running its shoots back to the parent stem; and so they
further its natural spread. But in the earlier history

of mankind the union of those closely related was not abhorred. Abraham's wife was his half-sister (20:12) ; cf. also 24:4 and 28:2.

On the expression "knew his wife" see 4:1. The name Enoch, Hebrew *chanôkh*, signifies, "dedication," and so by metonomy may come to mean "commencement" or more concretely "beginner"; K. W. *Anfaenger*. It appears that Cain promises himself a new beginning in life through this son; Enoch is to initiate a new start. At the time, however, when the son was born, the father was building a city, and with the pride characteristic of the children of the world sought to perpetuate his son's name by applying it to the city.

Cain's building of a city does not conflict with and remove his curse (v. 12) which involved inability to settle permanently anywhere. It may have been on Cain's part a kind of titanic attempt to fly in the face of Heaven's decree. But the very nature of the statement implies that he did not complete what he undertook; for we read: "he was building," *wayhi boneh*, progressive, which we have rendered "he was engaged in building," to make the inceptive nature of the undertaking more prominent. The city may have been finished, but not by Cain. Others may have lived there, not he. Nothing points to an amelioration of the original divine sentence. On the participle *boneh* as expressing this idea of progression see K. S. 239 b. Consequently, the text correctly treats the participle as a verb with a direct object, as is indicated by the *seghol;* the treatment of it as a noun making him an actual builder would have necessitated the construct state of the participle and consequently a *tsere.*

The critical objections to the idea of the building of a city at so early a date in history fall away as soon as we remember that, of necessity, nothing more could be meant than a walled enclosure with a few houses. The primitive city need have been no more.

Besides, this well accords with the accursed timorousness that marked Cain. In spite of promise and sign he never felt safe. He felt a city might afford a feeling of safety, but he was never able to complete his city. The Hebrew word for city agrees with our explanation. For *'ir* is most likely derived from the root *'ûr*, "to rouse" or "to raise an alarm." Consequently, the city was the place of refuge when an alarm was raised: K. W. succinctly: *Alarmplatz*.

It is very interesting to note how early cities in reality appear on the scene. During the lifetime of the second generation of mortals the first one is built. Evolutionistic thinking, of course, grievously distorts the picture and tells fanciful tales about many many earlier stages through which human development had to run.

We append a double list of names of Cainites and Sethites in order to make the similarity of the names as apparent as possible. It will be observed that Enoch and Lamech appear in both. All the rest bear strange resemblances each to some one of the other group.

Adam	Adam
Cain	Seth
Enoch	Enosh
Irad	Kenan
Mehujael	Mahalalel
Methushael	Jared
Lamech	Enoch
Jabal—Jubal—Tubal Cain	Methuselah
	Lamech
	Noah
	Shem—Ham—Japheth.

It is quite reasonable to assume that the identity or similarity of names is traceable to the contact, more or less close, that the two branches of the human family had with one another. No one will be able definitely to say which group did the borrowing. Both may have done it in a measure. Nor does the fact that one group runs through seven generations before it branches out into three prominent characters, and the other through ten before it does the same prove these to be artificially constructed genealogies. The God of history may well have guided things according to a definite pattern of numbers even as He does in the field of botany or chemistry. Unfortunately, we cannot be very sure about the meaning of many of these names, a difficulty which is increased by the fact that these are Hebrew equivalents of the original language of the race.

If one critic remarks about this section that "it involves a series of anachronisms and is not historical," and goes so far as to claim that this is so self-evident that it "requires no proof," we regard such bold assertions unwarranted; for the truth has often been explained, but some people fail to see it. If, then, another critic praises Buttmann for having been the first to recognize that the two genealogical tables, 4:17-24 and chapter 5, are but *two* variant forms of *one* tradition concerning the genealogy of the human race, we can do no more than marvel at the unproven claims that men will make when they seek to discredit the Scriptures.

18. **And to Enoch was born Irad; and Irad begat Mehujael; and Mehijael begat Methushael; and Methushael begat Lamech.**

No one will ever satisfactorily explain, as far as we are able to discern, how the two variant forms of the one name crept into this verse: Mehujael and Mehijael. That the subject '*Iradh* is counted as a kind of retained object with the passive is discussed K. S. 108; G. K. 121 b. Irad may mean "townsman" (Keil). Mehujael may mean "God is the giver of life" (K. W.). Mehijael seems to mean "God is the fountain of life" (K. W.). Methushael perhaps means "man of God," the *sh* being a kind of relative. The meaning of "Lamech" is extremely doubtful. It seems strange to find at least three of these names compounded with the divine name *'el* = God. However, that may indicate that occasionally a Cainite was devout or at least had better aspirations, or it may be traceable to the borrowing of names by the Cainites from the Sethites. Many a man has a name of the noblest meaning without even being aware of it. At least the great antiquity of the name *'el* is indicated by these compounds (K. T. A. T. p. 143).

19. **And Lamech took unto himself two wives; the name of the one was Adah, the name of the other Zillah.**

In this simple statement is recounted the origin of bigamy. Note well that the practice originated among those who had become estranged from God. Up till this age the original purpose of God in creating one man and one wife and uniting them in marriage had apparently been understood as sanctioning only monogamous marriage. In the seventh generation from Adam comes a man in the line of the Cainites who dares to fly in the face of this divine institution. The names of these two wives, if they be at all indicative of their character, as names in these early days often were, suggest that physical attractiveness may have been a governing motive in Lamech's choice. For Adah means either "ornament" or "morning"; whereas Zillah may signify "shade" or "shelter." Nevertheless, the ungoverned lust of the flesh will, as usual, have played a large part in inducing the man to take a second wife. It should also be noted that the expression "take a wife" (*laqach 'ishshah*) is the one that signifies "to marry." The dative of the personal pronoun *lô* is used as a reflexive (K. S. 28).

20-22. **Adah bore Jabal. He was the ancestor of those who live in tents and have cattle. And the name of his brother was Jubal. He was the ancestor**

**of all who play the lyre and the pipe. Zillah on her
part bore Tubal Cain, a hammerer (smith) who
devised all manner of things of bronze and iron.
Tubal Cain's sister was Naamah.**

Here we have the record of the most important
cultural achievements of early days. Strange to say,
they are traceable to the gifted sons of the bigamist.
Of these sons Adah bore two and Zillah one.

Jabal perhaps means "wanderer," a name indicative of the later nomadic habits of the man. It appears that many of the names of these early days may
not originally have been given to their bearers, but
may have originated in the course of time as descriptive of the outstanding characteristic of the person. The notable thing about Jabal is that he hit upon
and developed the idea of having a movable domicile,
a tent, to use while traveling about with his flocks in
search of pasturage. This new departure, of course,
describes nomadism. The noun *'abh*, "father," is used
to describe him as the "originator" of the idea or as
the "ancestor" of all such — one of the many and
varied uses of the word *'abh*. A still more elastic use
is found when *miqueh*, "cattle" (more than *tso'n*, including even camels and asses [Exod. 9:3]) is attached,
thus: "father of cattle." This may also be explained
by the figure zeugma, where one verb takes two objects,
the second of which ought more properly to be joined
to a second verb. The participle *yoshebh* is used collectively and is used with the accusative, as in our
English phrase, "inhabiting a tent"; cf. G. K. 117 bb.

"Jubal" may mean "sound" (*Hall* — K. W.) because the man originated sweet sounds. He had inventive genius along another less practical line. He
was the originator (*'abh*) of all who "catch" *(tophes)*
the strings of the "lyre and pipe." *Kinnôr* is more of
a zither than a harp; therefore we render the word
lyre, because only as lyres developed did harps result.

The *'ûghabh* was by far not as elaborate as an "organ"
(A. V.) but merely a combination of a few reed pipes.
However primitive they may have been, these two
instruments laid the foundation of musical development; for both stringed instruments and wind instruments owe their origin to this invention.

22) Zillah's son was an inventive genius too.
"She too" *(gam hî')* or, as we translated above, "on
her part," shared in producing famous men. Her son's
name, "Tubal Cain," is sometimes explained as meaning "Tubal the smith," or again *Eisenspan von Schmie-
derei* (K. W.), "the splinter of iron resulting from
pounding the iron." The words that follow are variously translated: either as above, or as "the hammerer of every cutting device of bronze and iron."
This latter construction puts four successive words in
the construct relation to one another — rather unusual.
Therefore we take *kol* in the sense of "all kinds of
things" and construe it as the object of *choresh* and
make "bronze and iron" accusative of material. In
both cases the meaning is much the same, with this
major difference: the one lets the man devise only
cutting instruments, the other, all kinds of instruments
and utensils. Observe, though, that bronze precedes
iron.

Na'amah's name means "pleasant." This is significant. This family knew by various devices to make
life pleasant for itself. Though these inventions bring
a kind of taint with them, being originated by the godless, yet two things must be remembered. Music, for
example, carries many elements in itself that can dis-
tract the soul unduly; so can other worldly productions
unduly absorb the soul. On the other hand, all such
achievements may be taken in hand and sanctified by
injecting in them a spirit from on high. Such is again
especially the case with music, which has thus been
taken in hand and has experienced its noblest development in sanctified use.

> 23, 24.   **And Lamech said unto his wives:**
> **Adah and Zillah, hear my voice,**
> **Ye wives of Lamech, give ear unto my speech.**
> **I slay a man for wounding me**
> **And a youth for giving me a stripe.**
> **For, if Cain is to be avenged sevenfold**
> **Then Lamech seventy-seven fold.**

This portion caused commentators in days of old untold difficulties. Jamieson reports that Origen devoted two whole books of his Genesis commentary to these verses, and finally rendered the verdict that they were inexplicable. Other commentators were misled by the Jewish fable of the accidental slaying by Lamech of old Cain and a youth who guided him through the forest, and so for a long while they went off on a false scent.

Yet, on the whole, the present-day approach, which classifies this as "Lamech's Sword Song," is correct. Incidentally, here is the first piece of poetry of which we have a record, not so noble an origin, it is true, but under such circumstances did it take its rise. We claim that approach, then, to be correct which pictures Lamech as handling one of the weapons just manufactured by his son Tubal Cain and as sensing the possibilities that lie in possessing such a weapon. For the waw conversive which binds the opening *wayy'o-mer* to the preceding section, bears just this connotation; as a result of his son's invention of weapons, Lamech, seeing what possibilities lay in such weapons, "said." This poem does not hang suspended on thin air. That it is a poem is apparent from the very manifest parallelism of the members; the characteristic feature, at least, of Hebrew poetry. From one point of view, of course, this poem is a glorification of the sword. But penetrating deeper into its character, we find it to be a glorification of the spirit of personal revenge. So the poem has an unholy savor and reflects

admirably the spirit of those who have grown estranged from God and His Word. So all human culture
and the achievement of civilization degenerate apart
from God.

It need not surprise us that this word was spoken
to Lamech's wives. They are an audience that needs
must listen, and boasting is most safely done at home
before their ears. Whether Lamech really was the
dangerous fellow that his words make him out to be
we have no means of knowing. The elevated tone of
the poem is made apparent by the sonorous and dignified double address. "Adah and Zillah" and "ye wives
of Lamech." Again, the poetic character of the piece
is reflected in the use of a poetic shortened form for
the imperative, *shema'an* (G. K. 46 f), as well as by a
term used largely in poetic diction, *'imrah,* "utterance,
speech "

The perfect tenses that follow have been the
source of much difficulty. Some, taking them as simple
historical perfects, read them as a record of a deed
done. But in that event it strikes us as most peculiar
that Lamech should have slain both a man and a young
man. Murderers very rarely proceed to wholesale
slaughter, all the more not when, as in Lamech's case,
they have reason to recall what befell a notorious
ancestor of theirs when he committed murder. Then,
since apparently the preceding verses had just recorded
an invention, the next and more natural step in the
narrative would be to canvass the possibilities latent
in the invention. So it would be far more plausible to
picture Lamech as handling a newly forged sword or
swinging it boldly about his head and uttering this
sonorous bit of poetry as he does so. In this event,
the perfects would have to be regarded as expressing
complete assurance, or definite certainty, or promise.
Some compare 1:29 and 4:14 a. They are, of course,
then analogous to prophetic perfects and refer definitely to the future. What Lamech threatens is: if

any man wounds me, or if any young man bruises me,
I shall kill the offender. "Man" and "young man"
constitutes a more picturesque way of saying: "anyone." "Wound" (*pits'i,* a cut wound, introduced by *le*
of norm) and "bruise" (*chabburathi,* a stripe caused
by a blow) include all forms of hurt, the more grievous
and the less grievous. Consequently, the threat covers
every case where a painful wrong is inflicted, no matter
who does it. Lamech tries to give his threat a veneer
of just retribution by making the distinction: for a
real wound, I shall take a man's life; for a bruise, the
life of a youth. *Yéledh* here hardly means "child," as
its first meaning might lead us to suppose. The suffix
on "wound" and "stripe" is called by Strack the suffix
expressing the eventual. Not: the "wound," etc., that
I have received, but: the wound I may receive. We
have sought to indicate this by: "for wounding
me," etc.

Now comes the climax of this ungodly song of
hate. The "for" introducing it introduces as reason
not what immediately follows but "the second part of
the sentence." Lamech remembers the sentence and
the divine promise to his ancestor. On this he builds
up. If God will see to it that the one who harms Cain
will have a sevenfold measure of punishment, Lamech,
not needing or even despising God's avenging justice,
will provide for himself by the strength of his own
arm, re-enforced by his son's weapon, a far more
heavy punishment than God would have allowed —
seventy-seven fold. The arrogance and presumption
are unbelievable. The spirit of self-sufficiency here
expressing itself overleaps all bounds. This, then,
coupled with its hate and revengefulness, makes it one
of the most ungodly pieces ever written. Such are the
achievements of human culture divorced from God.
"My fist shall do more for me than God's vengeance
for Cain," Strack paraphrases. An allusion, by way
of contrast to this wicked utterance, apparently lies in

Matt. 18:21 f., where such a high measure of forgiveness, "seventy and seven," is laid upon Christ's followers. They are not only to be free of the spirit of retaliation but are to possess instead a rare spirit of forgiveness.

c. **An account of the Development of the Family
of the Godly** (v. 25, 26)

Without lengthy introduction, without the use of
explanatory phrases, the writer sets another group
that was developing in those days into sharp contrast
with the development of the group just described.
This makes for very effective writing. Such contrasts
by their very sharpness give evidence of comsummate
literary skill. The critics, somehow, cannot understand such skill and see merely what they claim to be
evidence of a different document. So they speak with
great erudition on a subject about which no man knows
anything. Incidentally, they hardly notice that the two
branches of mankind are as widely different from one
another as they possibly can be. Simplicity of life and
devotedness to their God characterize this second
group, the Sethites.

25. **And Adam again knew his wife and she
begat a son and called his name Sheth, for God
hath set for me other seed in place of Abel; for Cain
slew him.**

When the expression is a bit more detailed, there
is not always a special significance attached to it. Here
we are hardly justified in supposing that the author is
trying to say that sexual communion was interrupted
for a time because of Abel's death but was now again
resumed. The fact is a son was born. How thoroughly different the spirit of this family is from that
which we have just studied appears from the fact that
in the birth of their children already these parents see
the gracious hand of God. This son is "set" *(shath)*

by God in place of Abel. The mother wishes this fact to be continually in evidence and so gives her son a name indicative of this fact: *sheth,* A. V.: "Seth." The play on words is thus made apparent in English. Since "set in place of" means "to substitute" we may adequately interpret the name Seth to mean "substitute," *Ersatzmann* (K. W.). Procksch, without good reason, questions the propriety of this very obvious interpretation. The explanatory remark "for Cain slew him" is not inserted by Moses as his own explanation, the fact being too evident to require explanation. But as a word of Eve it definitely connects the two acts and states that *God* meant Seth to be a substitute for the slain Abel; or, because Cain slew the one, God gave the other — an explanation which amounts to the same thing as the first.

In this verse we have the first undoubtedly clear use of *'adham* as a proper noun. Apparently, from this point onward, Adam is under consideration as an individual more than as the first "man," as his name signifies (K. S. 295 b). Besides, it may be well to append a list of the instances where the father or the mother give the names to their children and so to show the futility of the contention that the matriarchate prevailed of old according to the Scriptures. The mother gives the name in 19:37 f.; 29:32 f., 35; 30:6, 8, 11, 13, 18, 20 f., 24; 35:18; 38.4 f. The father gives the name in 4:26; 5:29; 16:15; 21:3; 38:3; 41:51 f. The impersonal subject "one" is found in 25:25 f.; 38:29 f. in the matter of giving names.

26. **Also unto Sheth there was a son born, and he called his name Enosh. At that time a beginning was made of calling upon the name of the Lord.**

For the present there is no need of tracing this family through many generations. The spirit that animates becomes evident at once. When Sheth, or Seth, who has the godly spirit of Adam begets a son, he gives to him the name *'enôsh,* a word which we still believe bears the basic meaning of "frailty." For though the lexicographers unanimously (Buhl, B D B, K. W.) derive it from a root "to be intimate with" in the sense of social familiarity, we yet feel that that derivation fails to do justice to those instances of the use of *'enôsh* as a common noun, where it is used in contrast with God, as B D B lists these passages. In fact, this gets to be so distinctive a use of the term that it stands out. Cf. especially in Job the passages: 4:17; 7:17; 9:2; 10:4, 5; 15:14; 25:4; 33:12. Other significant instances are II Chron. 14:10 (Eng. v. 11) ; Ps. 8:5; 9:20, 21; 90:3; 103:15 etc. Since this third root *'anash,* according to Arabic parallels, is quite possible, we strongly cast our vote for this meaning: *'enôsh* = the "frail one," "the mortal." Seth was so impressed with the weakness of mortals that he gave his son a name indicative of this truth. Such a name, however, does not reflect pessimism or discouragement. It is expressive of truth, deep unvarnished truth. But the very next statement now goes on to show what this family did when their own frailty became clearly apparent to them: they turned all the more eagerly to their God and sought him, making a regular and public practice of it in worship. For by common consent the lexicons interpret the expression *qara' beshem yahweh* to mean: to "use the name of Yahweh in worship" (B D B). The preposition *be* before Yahweh expresses a kind of means: to call out by the use of the name. K. S. makes it a Beth of interest (212 c). The adverb *'az,* "at that time," distinctly binds such public worship back to the time when Seth called his son Enosh. The "name" here, as usual, means the whole truth that God had revealed about Himself. Since the name "Yahweh" is attached to "name," this means that from days of old God was known in the capacity of *Yahweh,* or in the character of *Yahweh,* whether that word as such was known at this early

date or not. The thing that the name stood for was
known. Men do not first in the age of Abraham or
Moses begin to comprehend God's faithfulness, unchangeableness, and mercy. Since this calling out by
the use of the name definitely implies public worship,
we have here the first record of *regular public* worship.
Private worship is presupposed as preceding. The
great importance of public worship, both as a matter
of personal necessity as well as a matter of public
confession, is beautifully set forth by this brief record.
This act bears eloquent testimony to the courage of
this group, who wanted to be known as such whose
hope was placed only in Yahweh. It is not enough to
say that "Yahweh's religion began with Enoch." It
began with Adam and developed into regular public
worship in three generations.

HOMILETICAL SUGGESTIONS

The first fifteen verses of this chapter may be used as a
unit. In that event they may be treated under the head of "the
First Murder," or "the Rapid Development of Sin," or even
"the Horrible Possibilities Latent in Sin." Verses 9-15 lend
themselves to the treatment of the subject of "Impenitence" or
"the Despair of the Impenitent."

The second half of the chapter offers a topic that is always
helpful and perhaps more timely now than ever. In v. 16-24
one may find "the Beginnings of Civilization." Here, of course,
a certain caution is in order. Though it was the Cainite group
that devised these beginnings, and though this was a typical
instance of worldly-mindedness, yet over against these undeniable facts it should be clearly stated that attempts made by godly
men to "subdue" the world and the created things in it are in
conformity with God's original purpose (1:28). If worldly-
minded men make inventions and discoveries because they know
no higher goal, godly men should make endeavors along the
same line in order to fulfill their God-given destiny and to
please their Father in heaven. If the entire section v. 16-26
is treated, in some way the contrast between the spirit of the
world and the spirit of God's children should be the dominant
thought.

CHAPTER V

III. The "History" of Adam (5:1-6:8)

We may find subdivisions in Genesis and append to them our own titles. Moses has taken care of the major divisions by inserting them himself as "histories" *(toledôth)*. On the meaning of the term *toledôth* and the instances of its occurrence see 2:4.

As it was necessary at 2:4 to determine with what propriety the section there beginning could be called the "history of heaven and earth," so here there is necessity to discern how very appropriate it is to term this portion "the history of Adam." Had the choice of title been left to us, we should perhaps have felt inclined to term this a genealogy of the patriarchs, which it also certainly is. But with greater propriety Moses speaks of the "history" or "story" of Adam. For this whole period of development of the line of godly men was Adam's history working itself out; the age was dominated by the spirit and the influence of Adam. This group, not the other described in 4:16-24, had the spirit of Adam. So we notice at the same time that only the group described in chapter 5 carries along with it the promise of the seed of the woman. The men here described are for the present the woman's seed, and in this line the Seed of the woman is ultimately to develop. The writer saw this, for he knew the promise given to Abraham and Israel and observed that only this one line terminated in Abraham. We may further say that in another sense Adam dominated this age and this group. For what he taught as truth or as God's Word concerning the original state, concerning the Fall and God's promises after the Fall, as well as his attitude in faith toward all these promises of God dominated more than one half of the

entire period, namely Adam's lifetime, and continued
to be the controlling influence during the rest of it.
For this whole group walked in his footsteps.　True,
in the concluding section 6:1-8 the definite departure
from what he taught and exemplified is recorded, but
just that prepares for the definite conclusion of this
era.　It certainly was in a prominent sense the Story
of Adam.

On the whole, these patriarchs, it appears, may
well be regarded as men deserving of an unusual measure of renown.　If during a millennium and a half
these are the only names worthy of being handed down
in the inspired record, we may well conclude with Luther that they "were the very greatest heroes who ever
came upon earth barring Christ and John the Baptist."
Besides, since this point of view is supported even by
the fact that in point of longevity their strength and
natural vigor far excelled that of later generations, it
would seem quite proper to conclude that in other
respects also they represented a less decayed stage of
human life.

a)　The Separate Development of the Godly
(5:1-32)

**1, 2.　This is the book of the history of Adam.
At the time when God created Adam He made him
in the likeness of God.　Male and female He created
them and He blessed them, and He called their name
man at the time of their being created.**

In this instance the demonstrative "this" points
forward: what follows is Adam's history.　The heading is unusual: instead of the usual expression, as in
2:4 and in all other headings of this character in
Genesis, "this is the story," we read: "this is *the book
of the story.*"　"Book" *(sépher)* refers to any document, long or short, as long as it is complete in itself.
In Deut. 24:1 the term is applied to a bill of divorce;
in Jer. 32:12 to a deed.　Here 5:1-6:8 is the "book."

Does this seem to indicate a written document from antiquity which Moses incorporated in his book? Who can say? At least, such a possibility cannot be ruled out. Since we have no means of knowing who was the one that penned the document, we are hardly safe in following Whitelaw, when he ascribes the writing to antediluvians and so arrives at conclusions concerning the culture and the degree of advancement of these early peoples. Yet the possibility of what he contends for cannot be denied. The first Adam, *'adham* in v. 1, is certainly a proper name, according to the analogy of all the other headings of this nature in Genesis, in all of which, with the necessary exception of 2:4, proper names occur. The next *'adham* in v. 1 seems to hover on the border-line between the proper noun and the generic word "man." The *'adham* of v. 2 is quite likely the generic. Then v. 3 ff. the word again is to be regarded as the proper noun. Such seeming vacillation is due to the process of gradual crystallization of the generic noun into a proper noun (K. C.).

The rest of v. 1, plus v. 2, is not to be combined into a very complex sentence, a thing foreign to the simple style of Genesis here (K. S. 416 a). But why repeat things previously stated? Why recall the God-likeness, the two sexes, God's blessing and the naming of the race? This brief recapitulation serves to recall the first chapter and the glorious original state of the first man as well as his glorious destiny. After the things recorded in chapters 3 and 4 man, destined to such high things as the opening chapters indicate, achieves a record no higher than that of this fifth chapter. All things in these opening chapters belong together in a most intimate sense. Here is not a more or less clumsy combining of various sources, P dominating the scene (except in v. 29) for the first time since 1:1-2:3. The whole is poured into one mold by one author, and part balances and supplements part in the most skillful style of writing possible.

Verse 1 b and 2 recall the following to our mind: "At the time (*beyôm* "in the day" in the broader sense) when *'elohîm* (the Creator who is to be feared) did create man He made him in the likeness (not *"after* the likeness" as in 1:26, for the two prepositions are often used interchangeably) of God" (not merely *His* likeness — emphatic repetition) ; besides, even as in 1:26; 2:5, 2:18 ff. man is first referred to generically and then follows the definite indication that man had a woman at his side, so here v. 2 supplies "male and female He created them" — the separate mention of woman's being created as well as man's being quite necessary for the Orient in days of old already. That these persons enjoyed God's blessing is recalled as a matter still calling for grateful remembrance. A fact not previously mentioned is supplied here, that the naming of man, which might have been inferred from 1:26, was attended to by God at the time when He created man. After such a beginning of man's history what a marvelous future could not have been expected! Instead, what a poor and meagre history — as the chapter now proceeds to unfold!

3-5. **And Adam lived one hundred and thirty years and begat (a son) in his likeness, according to his image, and he called his name Seth. And the days of Adam after his begetting Seth were eight hundred years, and he begat sons and daughters. And all the days of Adam which he lived were nine hundred and thirty years; and he died.**

This gives the brief record of the first of the patriarchs in the form which is stereotyped after this pattern with a few exceptions, such as the more elaborate form of v. 3; v. 22 and v. 24; the words after "saying" in v. 29; v. 32; *wayhi* v. 31 for *wayyihyû* in the preceding instances. Of course, the critical assertion is now almost universal, that so precisely formal a style is one of the outstanding characteristics of P. But the simpler and more obvious explanation is that Moses, the inspired writer, possessed the capacity of employing a great variety of styles as the circumstances suggested. What is more concise than such a formal style when a broad area of time is to be covered rapidly in a condensed account that emphasizes the chronological aspect of history? Yet, even so, the author is complete master of the situation. Outstanding matters like 3 a, v. 22 and 24, as well as v. 29 are preserved, and the iron fetters of routine form are broken. Criticism ascribes v. 29 to another author J, so postulating for P a binding rigidity of style. This priestly author appears to them to have been so tightly manacled by his style that, after he once had cast the mold, it was impossible for him to extricate himself. But by the solemn repetition of the concluding phrase, "and he died," Moses was able to emphasize besides the sad mortality of man. There is something appalling about the dread finality of this phrase. Bonar is said to have described this as "the solemn toll of the patriarchal funeral bell." When discussing the style of the chapter, critics should extol the merits of it and laud that capable flexibility of it which Moses, like other great masters of style, displays — although this is a matter that has to do purely with externals.

At once we are struck by the longevity of these patriarchs; all except three lived in excess of nine hundred years. It is useless to attempt to evade this fact. The attempt to let the personal names represent tribes shatters on the clear statement of how old each father was when he begot a son. A complete generation is not thus brought forth within a tribe. Equally abortive is the attempt to claim that numerous links in the chain may have been omitted. Again the precise measuring of each forward step in reference to successive individuals peremptorily rules out such a claim. The most common suggestion by way of escape from the difficulty is to make "year" mean a shorter period, either one month or two, etc. Unfortunately, the term "year" knows of no such usage, and the suggestion must be treated as a mere surmise. He, however, who is duly impressed by the excellence of man's original estate, will have no difficulty in accepting the common explanation that even under the curse of sin man's constitution displayed such vitality that it did not at first submit to the ravages of time until after many centuries had passed. Besides — a fact established by fossil finds — there are ample indications of a more salubrious climate in the antediluvian days. Nor should we forget that here is the race of godly men who lived temperately and sanely.

If Adam was one hundred and thirty years old when Seth was born, and if, on the other hand, it seems extremely likely that Cain and Abel had been born quite a while before that, we may well wonder at the great lapse of time between the birth of the first two and the birth of Seth. The common explanation is not without merit, that the grief over Abel weighed very heavily upon the first parents. On the other hand, there is a very strong possibility that, as in many instances, a century or more passed before the son was born that carried on the line, so in the more deliberate course of events of these early days Adam may have been nearly a hundred years old before Cain and Abel were born. But we do observe distinctly that all life was marked by a certain leisureliness and temperate self-control that makes it stand out over against the hectic present.

The outstanding thing to be remarked about Seth is that he was in the likeness and according to the image of his father. First, note that the order of nouns and of prepositions is reversed from 1:26; for here we read, "in his likeness, according to his image." This, of course, proves nothing more than that the distinction between "image" and "likeness," as well as the distinction between the two prepositions "in" *(be)* and "according to " *(ke)*, is not very pronounced.

Yet this use of both phrases here emphatically asserts what it asserted when it was said of man that he was to be made in God's image and according to His likeness, namely: he was made in a very distinct resemblance with, and correspondence to, the original Pattern. Here now with emphasis: Seth was a being essentially like *Adam*. Now, as stands out as clearly as it can, between 1:26 and 5:3 the Fall intervened. The pristine likeness is God. It may yet be said with far less emphasis than in 1:26 that man is "according to the likeness of God," but after all that chapter three told that implies, as our dogmaticians so aptly have stated the case, that the formal side of the divine image alone remains; the material side has been lost. Therefore Scriptures do in a modified sense assert that man has something of the divine image left; cf. I Cor. 11:7; Jas. 3:9. This verse, then, by contrast actually may be read thus: "Adam begat a son in *his* image according to *his* likeness."

Criticism, treating Genesis as a book made up of composite elements that have not been fused into a unified and harmonious whole, gets into somewhat of a tangle at this point, a tangle that works out to the sad discredit of Genesis. Since this is ascribed to P, and P did not write chapters three and four, P knows nothing of a Fall (argument purely from silence). Therefore, if 5:1 says God made man in His image, and v. 3 says Seth was in *man's* image, *ergo:* Seth must be in God's image as Adam originally was. Then, concludes criticism, the Bible does not rate the Fall half as seriously as do our dogmaticians. But notice what this says about the Scriptures. The author of chapter three (J) knows of a Fall extremely serious in its consequences. Chapter five (P) knows of no such Fall: contradiction within the Scriptures. So, while forfeiting the reliability of the Scriptures, the natural powers of man are exalted and man is praised and flattered. What a sorry denial of truth!

Seth is mentioned as the one who carried on the line of promise. Cain belongs to another group, see 4:16 ff. Abel is dead. Criticism again makes the assertion: P knew nothing of Cain and Abel.

After the birth of Seth other sons and daughters are born. How many, we are not told. The emphasis lies on the chronology and on setting forth the prominent links of the chain. Adam came to be among the oldest of mankind. His total age was 930 years.

The solemn "and he died" is offset by the fact that in spite of death God's promise prevailed in the more abundant seed of the woman. God's justice and wrath against sin as well as His mercy are thus strongly emphasized in this chapter. These two facts are held in clear balance over against one another. "Death reigned" indeed "from Adam" (Rom. 5:14) onward; so by emphasizing the mortal consequences of sin the scriptural record lets no man esteem lightly the transgressing of the commandments of God. But where sin prevails, grace does the more prevail. This the Scriptures never minimize. Man is not to be left comfortless.

For convenience' sake we tabulate at this point what the record offers, as well as a few suggestive computations based on the figures of this chapter.

Chronological Table — Adam to Noah

	Age at birth of first son	Year of birth	Years after birth of son	Total age	Year of death
Adam	130	1	800	930	930
Seth	105	130	807	912	1042
Enos	90	235	815	905	1140
Kenan	70	325	840	910	1235
Mahalalel	65	395	830	895	1290
Jared	162	460	800	962	1422
Enoch	65	622	300	365	(987)
Methuselah	187	687	782	969	1656
Lamech	182	874	595	777	1651
Noah	(500)	1056	450	950	2006

N. B. We have included two of the above numbers in parenthesis. The 987 stands under the caption, "Year of death," but Enoch did not die; consequently marks of parenthesis. In the case of Noah the same mark enclosing the 500 indicates a mere possibility: nowhere does the account indicate that the above, mentioned after Adam, are really the first-born. Seth definitely was not. The likelihood is very strong that the three sons of Noah, born when he was 500 years old, will not have been his eldest children.

Other suggestive points to be discerned from this Table are that Enoch's translation (987) occurred about midway between Creation and the Flood (1656). Again, Adam was still living when Lamech, Noah's father, was born (874). Any tradition that Adam desired to hand down was only in the second generation at the time the Flood came: Adam to Lamech. Methuselah died in the year of the Flood (1656), yet he need not have perished in the Flood. It is facetiousness to let him perish in the Flood and then to remark that he died "of an accident." Apparently, the Flood did not sweep a single one of the Sethites, the true "seed of the woman," away. There is a fine propriety of divine grace in that fact. Besides, it may be remarked that Noah barely missed knowing Adam and Seth; Lamech did know Adam. What a power for godliness that should have been to see so many staunch believers living simultaneously and encouraging one another in steadfastness!

There is no reason for doubting the correctness of the chronology submitted by the Hebrew Masoretic text. This is and is intended to be a complete chronology, complete as far as marking the actual lapse of time is concerned. No other nation has anything to compare with it. Yet, strange to say, the only reliable chronology which we have, which actually purports to be an adequate chronology dating back to Creation, is continually being questioned, corrected, amended and condemned in favor of fallible documents which are historically but poorly attested and marked by many a gap. The claim that the Scriptures do not give a complete and accurate chronology for the whole period of the Old Testament that they cover is utterly wrong, dangerous and mischievous. At the slightest objection men are ready to cast aside as inadequate the only adequate chronology mankind possesses.

The variations offered both by the Septuagint and by the Samaritan Pentateuch are so manifestly altered according to a particular principle as to be useless, especially when we consider that both groups were ready to alter the text to suit their convenience, a charge that cannot be laid against the Jewish scribes. So, for example, the Greek version lengthens almost all the figures in the first column, usually by adding one hundred years, so that their first column would read 230, 205, 190, 170, 165, 162 (!), 165, 167 (!), 188 (!), 500. Then they are able later on to give a total for the age of the postdiluvians until Abraham that is more nearly like the age limit of Moses' time, i. e., seventy to eighty years. Again, the Samaritans have diminished a few of the totals of the first column to make it appear that the decrease in age from Adam on was more regular. The numbers of the first column, if taken from the Samaritan Pentateuch, would run thus: 130, 105, 90, 70, 65, 62, 65, 67, 53, 500. Such artificial regularity does not mar the Hebrew numbers. Volumes have been written on this question, and most of the present-day treatment is entirely without value, because the reliable figures of the Hebrew text are, without valid reason, treated as undependable. If a man wants the only correct chronology reaching back to the beginning, here it is — Chapter Five.

The famous list of the first ten Babylonian kings, as given by the Babylonian priest Berossus, quoted by Eusebius, has nothing in common with our chapter, except the number ten and perhaps a few very minor points of similarity on the meaning of certain names. But these points of correspondence become the merest trifles if held over against the glaring dissimilarities of the two lists, which Strack has successfully emphasized. Chief among the dissimilarities is the fantastic age limit of these Babylonian kings: Alorus begins with 36,000; Megalorus, Euedorachus, and Xisouthrous each achieve 64,800 years. This whole fantastic record may have retained a few traces of the original tradition which the Bible gives with unimpaired correctness. N. B. "begat" (v. 3) has no object; the object is easily supplied.

Verse 3 says: *"he* called"; 4:25 says: *"she* called his name Seth." No contradiction. Both concurred in calling him Seth; Eve may have first suggested the name.

6-8. And Seth lived one hundred and five years and begat Enosh. And Seth lived after his begetting Enosh eight hundred and seven years, and he begat sons and daughters, and all the days of Seth were nine hundred and twelve years; and he died.

The meaning of the names Seth and Enosh has been discussed; see 4:25 and 26.

9-11. And Enosh lived ninety years and begat Kenan. And Enosh lived after his begetting Kenan eight hundred and fifteen years and begat sons and daughters. And all the days of Enosh were nine hundred and five years; and he died.

"Kenan" perhaps means "smith." As might have been remarked above on v. 5, the expression "all the days of" is idiomatic for "the whole length of his life."

12-14. And Kenan was seventy years old and begat Mahalalel. And Kenan lived after his begetting Mahalalel eight hundred and forty years and begat sons and daughters. And all the days of Kenan were nine hundred and ten years; and he died.

The name Mahalalel may be interpreted to mean "Praiseworthy is God."

15-17. And Mahalalel lived sixty-five years and begat Jared (or Heb. **Jeredh**). **And Mahalalel lived after his begetting Jared eight hundred and thirty years and begat sons and daughters. And all the days of Mahalalel were eight hundred and ninety-five years; and he died.**

Jared means "descent." It may indicate the decline in longevity which has been in evidence in each successive case, Jared being the first man to fall under the total of nine hundred. This explanation acts on the assumption that Jared may not have been the name originally given at birth, because he was born in the year 460 from Creation. The name surely has nothing to do with the chimerical Jewish notion that the name was given in remembrance of the fact that in his day angels began to "descend" to earth in order to commingle with men.

18-20. And Jared lived one hundred and sixty-two years and begat Enoch. And Jared lived after his begetting Enoch eight hundred years and begat sons and daughters. And all the days of Jared were nine hundred and sixty-two years; and he died.

Enoch (Heb. *chanôkh*) means, as in 4:17, "beginner." This name and that of Lamech are identical in the Cainite and the Sethite line.

21-24. And Enoch lived sixty-five years and begat Methuselah. And Enoch walked with God after his begetting Methuselah three hundred years and begat sons and daughters. And all the days of Enoch were three hundred and sixty-five years. And Enoch walked with God; and he was not, for God took him.

Methuselah seems to mean "man of the weapon" or spear (*Mann mit Wurfgeschoss* — K. W.). Why

he should be so called is hard to determine, except that
he may have excelled in the use of the spear, but surely
not for murderous purposes like Lamech the Cainite.
Then also not for the purpose of hunting, unless it be
for securing the pelts of animals for clothing.

But this man Enoch, who represents the seventh
generation in his line, even as Lamech the Cainite did
in his, commands attention. If seven be the number
of divine operation, then Enoch's case would exemplify
what divine grace can accomplish by way of complete
consecration. We do not believe that the seven is
secured in this instance by manipulation of the genealogy or by skipping intervening grades. Enoch actually
was the seventh from Adam.

Now the significant thing reported concerning him
is that he "walked with God" *(hithhallekh 'eth ha-
'elohîm)*. The *Hithpael* stem signifies "to walk about"
= "to live." The particular preposition used, *'eth*,
denotes "intimacy, fellowship" (B D B). Here it is
customary to collate the other prepositions that are
used in connection with the same stem. *"Before* God"
(Heb. *liphne*) is found in 17:1; 24:40; or "after"
('acharey) in Deut. 13:5(4); I Kings 14:8. Now it is
true that *'eth* in reference to God appears only in
reference to Enoch and Noah (6:9) and so gains the
meaning in Mal. 2:6 of the most intimate communion
with God as exemplified by the most godly of men.
But true as all this is, the expression as such is not
sufficiently analyzed when this fact is determined.
Does "to walk with God" actually mean a physical,
outward meeting as the expression of closest fellowship? So some maintain, citing the following supposition as proof: God still had the place of his manifestation on earth at the Garden; there Enoch met with
Him and walked with Him. But several valid objections rise at this point. Was Enoch not a sinner
also? If so, was not he, as well as all his fellow-sinners,
to be kept from the garden by the cherubim and the

swords of fire? Besides, was not the general rule of Moses' day, applicable in this instance as well as in all others: "man shall not see me and live" (Exod. 33:20)? This maxim was not a human opinion but spoken by God Himself.

We are thus driven to take the expression, "to walk with God," figuratively, in the sense of inner communion, as living one's life in such a way that in faith one remains uninterruptedly conscious of the nearness of the almighty God and so walks as the thought of that presence determines. Life was lived to please God, so far as this was humanly possible. This involved, in complete conformity with what the New Testament teaches, a life of prayer and of watchful use of the means of grace, that is, in this instance, holding fast and feeding upon the promise of victory through the Seed of the woman. To interpret "to walk with God" in this sense is further recommended by certain grammatical considerations. Certainly, the parallel expressions are to be taken figuratively and not literally: 17:1 cannot be taken in any other sense than this; Deut. 13:5(4) plainly refers to fidelity in following after Jehovah in the sense of the explanatory expressions following: "fear Him, and keep His commandments, and obey His voice, and . . . serve Him and cleave unto Him." In other words, the type of walking with God which is still possible is the type that Enoch exemplified. Even the article *ha'elohim,* i. e., "the true God," points in this direction. Any other type of communion with the true God is visionary and the dreamer's choice. The versions, finally, fully confirm this interpretation. For the Septuagint says: εὐ ἠρέστησεν τῷ Θεῷ = "he was well-pleasing to God." The Targum has: "He walked in the fear of Yahweh." See also Heb. 11:5.

One side of such walking with God is very fortunately stressed by Luther on good scriptural grounds over against the purely mystical and contemplative

aspect of it that we might be inclined to overstress.
Developing the thought expressed in Jude v. 14, 15,
Luther rightly contends that Enoch's communion with
God was coupled with aggressive testimony to the
unbelievers of his generation, and, therefore, he is to
be regarded as a man who manifested "great boldness
in testifying for the Lord and His church against
Satan's church and that of the Cainites." To this must
be added another factor clearly contained in the text.
Such communion with God went hand in hand with
raising a family and begetting children: "Enoch
walked with God and . . . begat sons and daughters."
Celibacy is not requisite for a holy life.

When the statement occurs a second time (v. 24),
"and Enoch walked with God," it is for the purpose
of binding it up closely with what follows: "and he
was not, for God took him." These two so combine
that their meaning is designed to be: the reason why
God did this unusual thing in Enoch's case was because
Enoch walked with God. The expression "he was not"
('ênénnû) means he was translated. See Heb. 11:5.
It could not mean: he died, because of the double
preceding emphasis on his communion with God, and
because "God *took* him" *(laqach)* involves the same
word as that used in the translation of Elijah (II Kings
2:3, 5). In a chapter where every other life (except
that of Noah and his sons for the present) closed
with: "and he died," the omission of that phrase is
too significant to allow for the conclusion that he
did die.

Standing thus halfway between Adam and the
Flood, this translation of Enoch constitutes a most
welcome testimony to the prospect of life eternal, both
to the older generation as well as to all those who were
to follow as his younger contemporaries. For a group
of believing men, such as the Sethites were, would not
have failed to see the purpose of his being taken away.
Skinner must have ranked the spiritual capacity of

godly men like these patriarchs very low to advance the claim: "it is hardly correct to speak of it (the use of "He took") as containing a presentment of the idea of immortality." It was the first definite indication of immortality offered in the Scripture when God took Enoch.

Some take grave exception to the thought apparently involved in this translation of Enoch if it be claimed that this translation involves immediate glorification. This, they say, is impossible, because "the first-fruits" of the resurrection must be Christ (I Cor. 15:20). Correct as is this claim in reference to Christ, it should be particularly noted that this involves only being the first-fruits in the *resurrection*. However, in Enoch's case *glorification* only is involved. Not having died, Enoch could not be resurrected. But since Enoch was of the Sethite line, where faith in the Savior to come prevailed, he having lived in such faith, after his removal shares the glory that is theirs who believed on the Savior. He is glorified as believers in Christ are, and that, of course, at once. They who here invent an intermediate state, a receptacle where the Old Testament saints abode till Christ came, are building up an unscriptural speculation. This modern view of Sheol is wrong and very mischievous. Such an interpretation runs afoul of the verb here used: God "*took*" him. What manner of *taking* would that be where the individual taken is *left* in Sheol to wait in a shadow existence for long centuries? Besides, the Bible teaches nothing about a *Totenreich* with various compartments.

The total age of Enoch, 365 years, presents an accidental correspondence with the number of the days of the year. No further significance is to be attached to the fact.

On the forms and the use of *'ênénnû* see G. K. 152 m. Though the term means "he *is* not," yet in connection with a past tense in the narrative it comes to mean: "he *was* not" (K. S. 140 b).

25-27.   **And Methuselah lived one hundred and eighty-seven years and begat Lamech.   And Methuselah lived after his begetting Lamech seven hundred and eighty-two years and begat sons and daughters.   And all the days of Methuselah were nine hundred and sixty-nine years; and he died.**

"Lamech" may mean "warrior or conqueror." Methuselah was that one of the patriarchs who lived the greatest number of years.

28-31.   **And Lamech lived one hundred and eighty-two years and begat a son.   And he called his name Noah, saying: This one will bring us comfort in the face of our work and (more particularly) in the face of the toil of our hands (arising) from the soil which Yahweh has cursed.   And Lamech lived after his begetting Noah five hundred and ninety-five years and begat sons and daughters. And all the days of Lamech were seven hundred and seventy-seven years; and he died.**

"Noah" means "rest." The birth of this son is recorded in such a way as at once to make it evident that he stands out in connection with a critical juncture in the history of the race. For, first of all, departing from the stereotyped expression used in the chapter, Moses says: "Lamech begat" — not Noah — but "a son" and called his name, etc. Then, in the second place, with a measure of formality he adds, "and he called his name," an expression not used since v. 3. Thirdly, the reason for the giving of this name is mentioned: "He will bring us comfort." He is called *Noach* for *yenach(ch)am*. The author is not giving etymological derivatives. *Noach* as such comes from an entirely different word, viz. *nûach*, "to rest." But the two verbs *nuach* and *nacham* have a kind of assonance, they sound somewhat alike, and Lamech played upon this similarity in a perfectly permissible pun. The name *Noach* was to remind of the comfort this man would bring. By the spirit of prophecy

Lamech, like other godly patriarchs, sensed that in an unusual way this one would bring comfort to the troubled race. In reality Noah did this by preserving the small godly remnant in the ark. This unusual form of the comfort Lamech may never have dreamed of. Yet his prophecy is a valid one. No doubt, in expressing it he had hoped for much more. His prophecy, however, may meet its highest fulfillment in the removal of the curse from the earth, which removal came after the Flood, 8:21 f.

This comfort was to come in the face of (*min*, like 4:11, = "over against," *gegenueber*—K. W.) "our work," "and in particular (*waw augmentativum*, K. S. 375d) in the face of the toil of our hands." Apparently, the misery of work in the sweat of the face as "toil of the hands" was beginning to weigh heavily upon men. Life in the externals was a ceaseless round of toil. Men longed for deliverance or at least for comfort under the burden. They knew definitely the whole situation that had made human existence so wretched; they traced their wretchedness back to the curse pronounced upon the ground because of man (3:17). Here Lamech says of their misery that it is "(arising) from the soil which Yahweh has cursed." The particular emphasis on "which he has cursed" is secured by putting in the clause after the sentence seems to run to a conclusion (K. S. 375 d). In reality, according to 9:8 ff., Noah does become the mediator of a new and definite relationship between God and mankind, a relationship guaranteed by a covenant with a particular sign, the bow in the heavens. In the face of all this it is not good to claim that Lamech prophesied but missed the mark, as even Luther suggests.

On the other hand, the favorite modernistic interpretation of the comfort brought by Noah is both shallow and unscriptural. The wine, (9:20 ff.) which Noah discovered, was, it is claimed, the comfort of which Lamech prophesied. In the face of the much greater things that came from God through Noah, as indicated above, such an interpretation is quite trivial. Besides, also 9:20 ff. makes it more than doubtful whether the author regards wine as a great comfort of the human race, not to mention the many warnings against abuse of this divine gift recorded here and there in the Scriptures. Meek must have been trying to incorporate this misconception when, misconstruing and misplacing phrases, he arrives at the rendering: "This is the one, after the work and the labor of our hands, to bring us consolation from the very soil which God cursed."

Interpreters misconstrue the passage and the spirit it breathes if they lay into it the idea that some personal, purely human achievement of Noah's is the ultimate source of the comfort that is to be brought to mankind. Prophecy does not thus glorify human prowess and capacity. The basic thought of the prophecy is that *God* has destined this son to be the channel or mediator of great comfort to the human race. The divine agency in the blessing is the big factor.

32. **And Noah was five hundred years old, and Noah begat Shem, Ham, and Japheth.**

At this point important developments in the history of the race appear, developments in which the *three* sons of Noah figure. Therefore, the line of descent has to supply more than one name. The Hebrew idiom uses the noun ("son of") for the adjective ("old"), see K. S. 306 h. Certain details that might satisfy our curiosity but are otherwise unimportant are not definitely decided by the brief statement of this verse; such as: Were other sons begotten of Noah before these three? (Most likely not!) or, Were these three triplets? (most likely not; for begat here has the looser meaning, "began to beget," as in 11:26).

The meaning of these three names involves etymological difficulties. "Shem" may mean "renown."

Ham, Hebrew *cham*, may be derived from the root *chamam*, "to be hot," and may thus involve a reference to the fact that most Hamites live in hot, southern countries. Therefore, perhaps, "Southlanders" (K. W.). Its resemblance to the original Egyptian for Egypt is etymologically doubtful (Buhl). "Japheth" might mean "beauty" (K. W.) ; but compare 9:27.

But this "History" (*toledôth*) involves more than the genealogical table of the Sethites: it includes 6:1-8.

HOMILETICAL SUGGESTIONS

Not every man would venture to use this chapter as a text. We should hardly favor that method of treatment which picks out a few verses at random and uses them separately or jointly, like v. 3, 24 and 29. But if it is borne in mind that the chapter tells how the race of godly men developed in the days before the Flood, we certainly have a unity in the text, and certain items of this development are true as long as the world stands. The factors that stand out call for a rearrangement in homiletical treatment. To give due prominence to the hope characteristic of such lives the truth expressed in v. 29 should be given the strongest emphasis: Men of God had hope, hope to come of one born of woman; their life was not aimless; God-promised deliverance made life worth living. Then it may well be pointed out how such hope influenced the lives of godly men: in Enoch's case this was particularly apparent; he lived a godly life and received a gracious reward. But the stern realities of life are also reckoned with by godly men: they know how sin has mutilated man—now each man begets children "in his own image" (v. 3) no longer in God's image (v. 1) ; now every man must reckon with the closing chapter that reads: "and he died." The longevity referred to in this chapter shows the high original estate from which we have fallen and to which we shall be renewed.

CHAPTER VI

b)   The Commingling of the Two Races (6:1-8)

We have just emphasized the fact that this is the closing portion of this particular history. Since this appears as plainly as possible, if the headings of the parts of the book are accepted on their face value as natural marks of division, and if the literary unity of the book is adhered to, we should do foolishly to lose sight of the fact. Here now is the natural sequence of thought: after the Cainites were observed to be going in one definite direction in their development, and the Sethites, too, were seen to be going in an entirely different direction, and these two streams of mankind were strictly keeping apart because they were so utterly divergent in character, now (ch. 6) the two streams begin to commingle, and as a result moral distinctions are obliterated and the Sethites, too, become so badly contaminated that the existing world order must be definitely terminated.

With this natural sequence of thought growing out of the text and supported by a correct interpretation, criticism fails to see the obvious and introduces elements of thought entirely foreign to the connection and makes a mythical tale out of a simple and practical lesson, as we shall indicate presently. The best refutation of this erroneous view is first of all the unfolding of the natural meaning of the passage.

1, 2.   **And it came to pass when mankind began to multiply upon the face of the earth and daughters were born to them, that the sons of God saw the daughters of men that they were fair and they took to themselves wives, whichever they liked best.**

In point of time, as will appear in connection with v. 3, we are shortly before the birth of Noah's sons (5:32). Men have become quite numerous upon the face of the earth. No man will ever determine how many they were. But where mankind comes to be of great numbers, somehow the places where they congregate together thickly become the scenes of the development of evil on a greater scale. So here. However, when it is remarked that "daughters were born unto them," that certainly cannot mean to describe something new: daughters had been born right along. However, this fact is mentioned as having a bearing upon the situation about to be described. Mark well that the bringing forth of daughters is being considered as taking place throughout all "mankind" *(ha'adham)*, for the *lahem*, "to them," refers to the collective singular "mankind."

Now "the sons of God" are found looking indiscriminately at this group and observing only the fact that "fair" ones *(tobhoth)* were to be seen in the whole group. That is all that they observe. They ask or care nothing about anything else. Whether these fair ones are Sethite or Cainite means nothing to them. That is the sad moral indifference that the author emphasizes.

But who are these "sons of God"? Without a shadow of doubt, the Sethites — the ones just described in chapter five as having in their midst men who walked with God, like Enoch (v. 22), men who looked to higher comfort in the midst of life's miseries, like Lamech (v. 29), men who publicly worshipped God and confessed His name (4:26). Such men merit to be called the "sons of God" *(benê 'elohîm)*, a title applied to true followers of God elsewhere in the Old Testament Scriptures. When the psalmist refers to such (Ps. 73:15) as "the generation of thy children," he uses the same word "sons," describing them as belonging to God. Deut. 32:5 uses the same word

"sons" ("children," A. V.) in reference to Israel. Hos.
1:10 is, if anything, a still stronger passage, saying
specifically to Israel, "Ye are sons of the living God"
(Heb. *benê 'el chay*). Ps. 80:17 also belongs here.
Criticism resorts to a technicality at this point. If God
said to me: "Thou art my Son," criticism's claim would
be: "You have not been called 'God's son,' but 'my
son,' " — a mere technicality. So in the face of the
passages we have just cited criticism claims the Scriptures do not use the expression "sons of God" for the
godly, because "thy children" is used in three instances
and in the fourth another name is used for God, *'el
chay*. We might word the case thus: strictly speaking,
"sons of God" is a title applied to the godly; grammatically, the very expression "sons of God" does not
happen to be used in reference to them in that very
form.

Over against this usage that we have cited criticism arrays another, the substance of which is: The
title "sons of God" is used in reference to the angels.
This claim cannot be denied; see Job 1:6; 2:1; 38:7,
and Dan. 3:25; also *benê 'elîm*, "sons of the Mighty,"
Ps. 29:1 and 89:7. But this claim becomes erroneous
when it is thus worded: The title "sons of God" is
used *only* in reference to the angels.

But of these two uses of the title, which shall we
choose in this instance? We have had no mention made
of angels thus far in Genesis. We have met with other
sons of the true God, in fact, the whole preceding
chapter, even 4:25-5:32, has been concerned with
them. Who will, then, be referred to here? Answer,
the Sethites, without a doubt.

At this point criticism leads forth its strongest
argument, saying that the contrast between "sons of
God" and "daughters of *men*" demands that the former
be *divine* and the latter *human*. We answer: Not at
all; least of all in the face of the very natural approach
we have just established, namely, that the sons of God

of 4:25-5:32 are still under consideration. We have shown above how "daughters of men" refers indiscriminately to all "the daughters of mankind," which were unfortunately lumped together by the sons of God without regard to their classification, whether Sethite or Cainite. When God's children lose sight of such basic distinctions and look about only for the pretty faces and the shapely forms, then, surely, degeneracy has set in.

If the objection be raised, that in the preceding section the title "sons of God" had not been used in reference to the Sethites, we answer: It was reserved for use by Moses until this point to make the high standards that the Sethites should have observed in this matter all the more prominent. Or if it be objected: "sons of God" or "sons" is used of Israel *as a people*, not of individuals, this objection matters little. Here the Sethites are also being referred to as a separate group or *people*, and not as individuals.

The reference to heathen legends about the promiscuous mingling of gods and men in mythological adventures certainly can have no bearing upon our case. Such mythological tales about racy escapades on the part of the old gods would hardly be matter by which Biblical material is to be judged or with which it is to be compared. Critics, however, have waxed so bold in this instance that Procksch simply offers the superscription "The Marriages with Angels" *(Die Engelehen)*, for this section. Besides, they are so sure that the section is of mythological import that they claim the original account did not read "sons of God" but "gods," striking out "sons of." So Meek translates, "the gods noticed that the daughters of men were attractive; so they married those whom they liked best."

Such an approach introduces the mythological element as well as polytheism into the Scriptures and makes the Bible a record of strange and fantastic tales and contradicts the passage Matt. 22:30: "For in the resurrection they neither marry nor are given in marriage but are as angels in heaven." For the expression used here (v. 2), "they took to themselves wives" (*wayyiqechû nashîm*), is the standing expression for marital union. This verse does not refer to adulterous irregularities but to permanent union. Critics nowadays readily admit this, but usually wind up by wondering, not at their interpretation, which speaks of actual marital union with angels who took up a settled habitation on earth, but by wondering at the fact that J, as they say, should have written such strange tales, which they themselves do not believe possible. On this use of *laqach* cf. Gen. 24:4; 21:21; 11:29; 12:19 etc.

The closing words, "whichever they liked best," help to clinch our interpretation, for they indicate that the controlling factor was the chance fancy of the moment rather than sound judgment which weighs the moral character and the suitability of the one chosen. Literally translated this expression would be: "from all whom they chose." The *min* here used is the "*min* of explanation," which does not mean selecting some from "all" but carries the force of "whichsoever" (K. S. 83).

Those who wish to find a New Testament reference to these angel marriages point to II Pet. 2:4 and to Jude 6, but neither of these passages refer to anything other than the original fall of the angels, as Keil has adequately shown. The marriages of angels have to be injected into these New Testament passages. Besides, then there would be a twofold fall of angels: the original and this, the second.

There is another harsh dissonance resulting from this strange critical construction as one tries to reason out the connection of v. 3 with what precedes. For v. 3, as we shall see at once, speaks of sharp restrictions laid upon *man* for his misdeeds. Here, then, would be

the very queer sequence of thought: v. 2, *angels* sin;
v. 3, *men* are punished. In vain the critics urge that,
of course, the punishment of angels is presupposed
but only that of man is mentioned. But if the angels
really acted with the bold presumption the text indicates ("whichever they liked best they took"), then
the women taken were practically innocent. Besides,
what none of these commentators seems to have realized: if all mankind is punished as a result of what
happened, these irregularities must have been quite
common, well-nigh the rule, in fact. Is any critic ready
to admit that? In a parallel case the evil angel has his
punishment meted out first (3:14, 15); it is not simply
taken for granted. Feeling all this, some critics charge
the section with lacking logical progression of thought,
failing to detect that the lack of logic lies in their
erroneous interpretation. Procksch even charges J
with creating intentional obscurities and blurring the
connection of parts, an almost unbelievable course of
procedure. But when critical hypotheses fail, it cannot be the critics who are wrong, but the original
writers were guilty of absurdities.

3. **And Yahweh said: My spirit shall not
judge among mankind forever, because they also
are flesh. Yet shall their days be one hundred and
twenty years.**

This verse is a veritable *crux interpretum*. The
critics magnify the difficulty to the point where they
render the verse: "My spirit shall not [. . . . in?]
man forever; [. . . . ?] he is flesh." Our rendering
above, which is in reality the substance of Luther's,
except that Luther preferred a passive for the sake
of better idiomatic German, we believe can be sus-
tained by good arguments, makes good sense, and
fits well into the context.

In the first place, we have rendered the verb
yadhôn "judge." In support of this rendering observe

that Symmachus and Luther rendered it thus. Besides, the fact that *dîn* means "judge" cannot be questioned. But in how many instances verbs like *dîn* run parallel forms like *dôn* or *dûn!* K. W. admits this meaning. With the Hebrew meaning so readily available, it seems quite unnecessary to seek out Assyrian or Arabic parallels. Now the meaning that results is simple and most appropriate. A measure of the truth had been available for these antediluvians. This divinely revealed truth counted as God's Word for them. God's Word, according to the consistent and the uniform teaching of the Scriptures, is the means of grace. Through it *God's Holy Spirit (rûchî)* operates, instructing or also reproving and judging men. This work of His had gone on until this point, aiming to correct and to check the strong propensity toward evil during the days of progressive degeneration. In spite of all the Spirit's corrective efforts "mankind" *('adham)* had persisted in abandoning the way of truth and life. Men had finally, as the one suggestive illustration showed, no longer cared about having their homes centers of godly instruction where divine truth prevailed, being taught by father and by mother, but instead chose any woman whatsoever, as the fancy of the moment moved them, to rear their offspring. At that point God determines that He will let His Spirit no longer do His work of reproving and restraining *(yadhôn)*, because man has degenerated. Man is no longer simply sinful, as he has been right along since the Fall; the race has also as a whole practically sunk to the level of being "flesh" *(basar)*, just plain, ordinary, weak and sinful stock, abandoned to a life of sin. Man has forfeited all hope of further efforts of God's grace. So the expression: "because they also are flesh" fits into the picture. "Also" refers to something in addition to what had been in evidence till now, the ordinary sinful state prevalent since the Fall. This additional something is: they have degenerated to the point of being mere "flesh" — the word having the ethical connotation as in the New Testament. See the same use in 6:12, 13 and Job 10:4.

Of course, we are reading *beshaggăm* (with short *a*) on good textual grounds (see Kittel), and as the Septuagint translators read: διὰ τὸ εἶναι αὐτοὺς σάρκας. Unfortunately, they, like Luther, omitted the "also." We render *beshaggam*: "because that also."

On first thought we seem to concur with B D B that the rendering of *yadhon* as "strive with" (A. V., A. R. V.) "is hardly justified." Yet, on second thought, is not the judging activity of the Spirit at the same time a striving with men to restrain them from their evil ways? The King James translators apparently were thinking of the same thing as Luther, and their rendering must be classed as quite satisfactory. We can well leave the welter of confusion and conjecture offered by criticism off at one side. It boots nothing of value.

Entirely in harmony with our rendering is the concluding statement of the verse, which marks the setting of the time limit of divine grace. For these words, "yet shall their days be one hundred and twenty years," are to be taken in the sense of the traditional interpretation: one last period of grace is fixed by God for the repentance of mankind. The previous word indicated (3 a) that God might well have cut off all further opportunities of grace. This word (3 b) shows that grace always does more than could be expected. Before disposing of the guilty ones a time of grace of no less than one hundred and twenty years is allowed for their repentance. This use of "days" (v. 3) is established by the use of the same word (v. 4) "those days." Consequently, the modern interpretation that takes this word to mean that God here decreed that in the future the span of man's life was not to exceed one hundred twenty years is quite unfounded. This view is proved untenable by the fact that quite a few after the Flood lived in excess of this limit: 11:11, 13, 15, 17, 19, 21, 23, 25; 25:7; 35:28; 47:9. The evasions of the critics in meeting this argument need not be mentioned, being too palpable.

On the use of the divine names notice the expression "sons of *God*" (*'elohîm*) v. 2, because theirs is a general relation to God, not a specifically theocratic one (Lange). On the other hand, v. 3 brings "Yahweh" because it offers a special display of God's mercy in providing for years of grace.

We append, as worthy of note, the traditional Jewish interpretation which makes "the sons of God" of v. 2 to be persons of rank — an impossible thought — and "the daughters of men" to be women of low rank — equally unlikely.

4. **The Nephilim were in the earth in those days and also afterwards when the sons of God went in unto the daughters of men and they bore unto them. They were the heroes, which in olden days were renowed men.**

Really quite a simple verse, unless one proceeds from the misinterpretation of the preceding verses and tries to link it up with the idea of angel marriages, a misconstruction prevalent since the days of the Septuagint translation. The basic rules of interpretation merely have to be observed: the presupposition, namely, that the Scriptures make good sense, develop their thoughts logically and naturally, and that simple grammatical rules still are in force. Says Skinner: "It was precisely this perspicuity of narration which the editor wishes to avoid." But why charge a Biblical writer with trying to write something not clear! Procksch assumes that the author J had quite a different original account, which he doctored up but left in a "wrecked state" (*truemmerhafte Gestalt*), which, of course, rather perplexes us. So men speak when they cannot find their meaning in the text.

Note now the simple fact that v. 4 does not follow v. 2. Note also that it does not attach itself by the expressive Hebrew "and" to what precedes. Verse 4 begins without a conjunction. It does not try to show what manner of persons the children of the misalliance of v. 2 were. Anybody can figure that thing out for himself. If fathers do not care to choose God-fearing wives to rear their children, the result will be that the children are not taught the fear of God, and so the godly ways of the patriarchs are abandoned. That's the result, nothing more. But v. 4 speaks of another class of ungodly men of olden times, setting the noun *"nephilim"* first by way of emphasis to make the new more prominent. But who were the *Nephilim?* Apparently, a type of men who were the climax of all such who inspired fear, as the only other passage where the term is used indicates, Num. 13:33. For there the spies first call all Canaanites "men of stature," and then they mention that even "Nephilim," sons of Anak, were there. Consequently, we are driven to seek some meaning for the word which makes them awe-inspiring. Following the Hebrew root *naphal* is by far the simplest. One meaning of this verb is to "fall upon = attack" (B D B): see Jer. 48:32; Josh. 11:7; and without any preposition, Job 1:15. This verb could readily yield this noun in the sense of "attackers," "robbers," "bandits." So we have the thought: the descendants of the godly patriarchs abandoned their spiritual heritage (v. 1, 2) so that God was moved to determine upon their destruction ('v. 3); and there were also violent attackers and robbers abroad in those days (v. 4). There was a negative breakdown of some, positive aggressive wickedness of others. Such an interpretation makes good sense. Besides, the very clause that follows makes it clear that these Nephilim, whom Luther describes quite aptly as "tyrants," were on the earth already at the time when the Sethites commingled with the Cainites,

but also that they continued after that sad confusion.
The time clause, "when the sons of God went in,"
makes this sad confusion stand out as a major calamity, so important that one could actually reckon time
from it. Then the text adds that these Nephilim were
the "heroes" of antiquity, the men of renown (Heb.
"men of the name"). They achieved a reputation the
world over by their violence, but a reputation better
deserving of the term notoriety. The world certainly
did not in those days, even as it does not now, esteem
godly men highly. Only the wicked were renowned
or had a name *(shem)*.

The translation "giants" (A. V.) is most unfortunate. It originated with the Septuagint (γίγαντες).
It does not follow from Num. 13:33, even if there the
"attackers" should also happen to have been giants.
For "sons of Anak" means "sons of the long-necked
one," and this *may* refer to gigantic stature. The unfortunate thing about this mistranslation is that it
directs attention away from the moral issue (wicked
bandits) to a physical one (tall stature). Besides, then,
with a show of propriety modern interpreters combine
the idea of giants with the misinterpretation about
angel marriages and claim that the giants were the
result of this union. But, in reality, nothing of the
sort is found in the text. It is the result of a clever
combination or of a mistranslation. Meek renders:
"There were giants in the earth who were born to the
gods whenever they had intercourse with the daughters
of men." This amounts to an unwarranted alteration
of the text in the interest of a dogmatic preconception.
Note well, too, that if there were a notice about giants
inserted here it would not at all fit into the connection.
Several critics are compelled to admit that they do not
know why v. 4 does not follow v. 2. Certain older
translators were nearer the truth than the Septuagint.
Aquila, who like Symmachus wrote to correct the
Greek version, rendered *Nephilim* ἐπιπίπτοντες = "they

who fall upon." Symmachus, in a similar strain, βίαιοι
= "powerful."

The article before *Nephilim* is categorical (K. C.).
Yabho'û, imperfect, expresses continuance: "they kept
going in" (K. S. 157; G. K. 107 e). *Bô'* is euphemistic.
Hemah is a characteristic sudden change of subject
(K. S. 399 B).

5. **And Yahweh saw that the wickedness of
mankind was great upon the earth, and that every
imagination of the thoughts of his heart was only
evil continually.**

The verses 5-8 represent the divine reaction to the
wickedness of man. Therefore v. 5 looks back directly
upon what preceded. Two significant instances have
told the whole story: the Sethites had grown indif-
ferent to their heritage; the Cainites had developed
high-handed violence. When Yahweh regards this, he
sees that it constitutes *"great* wickedness." Aside from
these outward manifestations, He discerns the inner
trend of men's thoughts: they have put no restraint
upon their natural inclinations, consequently their
thoughts are only evil continually. It is true that the
antediluvian generation is being described — God is
not here discovering the innate human depravity —
yet since the description shows man as simply having
let himself go, this still must rank as a *locus classicus*
for the natural depravity of the human heart, as Luther so staunchly contends. Yet the mode of expression
is very suggestive: The heart is the place of the activity of man's thoughts, "the thought-workshop" *(Denk-
werkstaette,* K. C.). These thoughts produce *yétser,*
"formings," "imaginings," "thought combinations,"
Dichten und Trachten, (Luther). But what a sweeping condemnation: "only evil continually." A striking
alliteration and assonance makes the statement unique
and most expressive in Hebrew: *raq ra'.* This natural
trend would have been checked, and among the growth

of weeds would have sprung up plants delightful to
God and to man, if men had accepted the judging and
correcting work of God's Holy Spirit (v. 3). But that
work was being consistently refused.

On the heart as primarily the place of thought,
see Ps. 33:11; Prov. 19:21; I Chron. 29:18.

6-8. **And it repented Yahweh that He had
made mankind upon the earth and it grieved Him
at His heart. And Yahweh said: I will wipe out
mankind which I have created from the face of the
ground, from man to animals, to creepers, and to
the birds of the heaven; for it repenteth me that
I made them. But Noah found grace in the eyes of
Yahweh.**

When God's repentance is mentioned, it should be
noted that we are using an inadequate human term for
a perfect and entirely good divine action. Luther
especially stresses that such expressions are found in
the Scriptures so that we mortals with our feeble
understanding might be helped to catch hold on divine
truth according to the measure of our poor human
ability. Procksch well defines this repentance on God's
part not as a change of purpose but of feeling out of
which a new course of action developes. Scriptures
frequently use the phrase "God repented" (see Exod.
32:14; Jer. 18:7, 8; 26:3; 13, 19; Jonah 3:10; I Sam.
15:11); but sometimes in the same breath repentance
in the sense of alteration in God is denied (Num.
23:19; I Sam. 15:29). This repentance is the proper
divine reaction to man's sin. The parallel expression
well defines it: "it grieved Him at His heart," Hebrew
even stronger: "into His heart," *'el-libbo.*

7. The gravity of the situation is made apparent
by the severity of the divine resolution: "I will wipe
out mankind." Sin has become so predominant and
crass that the extremest measures alone can cope with
it. There can have been no prospect of the reform of

the corrupt mass of mankind. The ease with which God's greatest works are done is revealed in the word "wipe out," which, by the way, contains a significant allusion to God's mode of procedure in this instance. Strange to say, this word is ascribed to *Yahweh*, the God of fidelity and grace; for the destruction of mankind at this time was for the purpose of making possible the development of the seed of the woman destined to crush the serpent's head. Yahweh's right thus to destroy the major part of mankind is indicated by the adjective clause: "which I have created." The Giver of life is the Supreme Lord over life and death. The thoroughness with which He is about to do His work is indicated by the enumeration of all other forms of life that are to perish with man: "animals" (*behemah*, here including wild as well as domesticated animals, as in v. 20; 7:23; 8:17), "creepers" and "birds of the heavens." Fish naturally are not mentioned because of the mode of the destruction in this instance. The universality of the judgment thus serves to impress upon man how serious the issues really are. Beasts and other creatures, which were originally created for man's sake, may well perish if a purpose salutary to man is served.

8. Evidence of the fact that it is *Yahweh* that does this work lies also in the preservation of Noah. In the midst of God's judgments His "grace" *(chen)* also shines forth. Though the word is often used of the favor one man enjoys in the sight of another, such favor, when it flows forth from God, is that unmerited, rich favor we are wont to call "grace." In spite of A. R. V. the richer connotation of "grace" (A. V.) should be preserved. This closing statement prepares a transition for the following story of the Flood.

An instance of the purely mechanical method of procedure of the critics is given in their labelling the two expressions "which I created" and "from man to . . . heavens" (v. 7) as glosses because they are claimed to be in the style of P. Such criticism of style, purely arbitrary as it is, makes it impossible for J to enumerate the classes that must perish. P carries a monopoly on enumerations as well as on these particular words.

IV. The History of Noah (6:9-9:29)

If any measure of competence can be ascribed to the author, then there is no need of providing a heading for this section by the use of our own ingenuity, for Moses has inserted a very accurate and usable one: "the history *(toledôth)* of Noah." This is not the story of the Flood. It is Noah's story. As Keil has rightly pointed out, three elements of Noah's story are presented. First, an indication of Noah's piety (very brief); then, the story of his preservation; lastly, an account of God's covenant with Noah as the father of a new race. Everything has to do with Noah. No one can deny that such a treatment of the subject matter is perfectly permissible.

The critics assign this portion of chapter six (v. 9-22) to P. In fact, throughout the Flood story they claim to be able to separate the two documents P and J in a very clear-cut fashion and point to this unraveling as proof of the brilliance of their achievements. So Skinner claims: "The resolution of the compound narrative into its constituent elements in this case is justly reckoned amongst the most brilliant achievements of purely literary criticism." In fact, critics know the very pattern after which the compiler worked. They tell us that he "instead of excerpting the entire account from a single source, has interwoven it out of excerpts taken alternately from J and P, preserving in the process many duplicates, as well as leaving unaltered many striking differences of representation and phraseology." Such positive claims have unduly impressed many. They have struck terror into the hearts of those who believed otherwise. Yet there

have perhaps never been such misleading and unfounded claims as just these in reference to so-called
sources. Aside from some incidental refutation which
may be made as we proceed, we shall offer a detailed
examination of the critical position and its major
arguments at the close of our treatment of chapter six.

a) Two verses cover the report concerning
Noah's piety, v. 9, 10. Yet v. 9-12 may be regarded
as forming the entire section, because v. 11, 12 fit in
the dark background to the bright picture of v. 9
and 10.

9. **This is the history of Noah. Noah was a
righteous-perfect man among his contemporaries.
With God Noah did walk.**

Since so much depends in this instance on the
personal character of Noah, nothing is more natural
than to indicate very plainly just what manner of man
he was. If out of all his contemporaries he alone with
his family is saved, then he must have been most
unusual. To stand one's ground and to remain unin-
fluenced by the attitude and conduct of all men to the
contrary, gives indication of a strength of character
almost without parallel in history. All the world said
he was wrong in holding fast to his piety; he knew
they were wrong and he was right. Few as the words
are that describe this character, they have unusual
weight. First of all he was "righteous-perfect." By
hyphenating these two adjectives we really do not
intend to express a compound but rather to indicate
that we have here two words that constitute a phrase
or a double expression. The same combination appears
in Job 12:4. There as well as here there is no conjunction connecting the two. Together, then, these two
words constitute an expression that covers a state
approximating perfection as nearly as man can.
"Righteous" *(tsaddîq)* is a word commonly used in
reference to men. It means that they conform to a

standard. Since Noah conformed to the divine standard, he met with God's approval. However, the term
is basically forensic. Therefore, though there be divine
approval, that does not imply perfection on Noah's part.
It merely implies that those things that God sought
in man were present in Noah. Primarily, God desired
man to believe Him and His promise of help through
the seed of the woman. This basic requirement Noah
met, and his conduct showed it. Because of such faith
Noah is justified. The complementary expression is
"perfect" *(tamîm)*. Since the Hebrew root involves
the idea of "complete," we are justified in concluding
only that there was an all-sided life, well rounded out
in all its parts, with no essential quality missing. This
term, too, does not connote moral perfection. But both
together describe a life of true faith and sincere consecration. It is not quite accurate to let "righteous"
refer only to Noah's relation to the first table of the
law; the word reaches farther. Nor is it quite correct
to limit "perfect" to the second table. But rightness
and completeness are stressed. They who see in the
word "righteous" the idea of righteousness by faith
interpret soundly, even though the fullest New Testament connotation dare not yet be laid into the expression.

The modifying phrase "among his contemporaries" involves a contrast. Noah stood out over
against his contemporaries, for they lacked these
qualities. *Doroth,* which we have rendered "contemporaries," is generally a very expressive term here.
It does mean "generations" and pictures for us the
successive generations that have come and gone during the five hundred years of Noah's life. Over against
them all he stood out as "righteous-perfect."

The deepest source of Noah's godliness is revealed
in the words: "with God did Noah walk." The inversion, different from 5:22, puts "with God" first for
emphasis. Though living among successive, mostly

wicked generations, his walk was with God. Cf. 5:22 for the very same expression. Personal communion with God was the taproot of this outstandingly good life. The marvel of this whole description is that it says so much about Noah in so very few words. One would expect a man to whom this description applies to stand firm in the face of a world gone to seed, and would also expect that God would make an exception in his case when He came to destroy the world.

10. And Noah begat three sons: Shem, Ham and Japheth.

The purpose of this verse is not usually discerned. True, 5:32 is almost identical. But whereas the first statement concerning Noah's three sons naturally served to round out the Sethite genealogy, here, by following directly upon the statement of Noah's piety, the object must be to remind the readers of the effect that that piety must have had on his sons. If a man like the one described in v. 9 might well be spared by God, so might the sons who were deeply influenced by the father's example.

11, 12. But the earth was corrupt before God and the earth was filled with violence; and God beheld the earth and behold it was corrupt, for all flesh had corrupted its way upon the earth.

Since the *waw conversive* ("and") introduces this verse, it binds it closely to the preceding. In this instance, however, a definite contrast is involved to the bright clear example of Noah. Therefore we translate the conjunction "but." Besides, we are here now definitely informed of the universality of the corruption of mankind. Outstanding examples of wickedness had been mentioned in the beginning of the chapter. In v. 1-8 we were informed how deep sin had penetrated. Now we are shown how far it had spread. Since a judgment of moral values lies before us, "earth" must be used by synecdoche for the "inhab-

itants of the earth." "Before God" means "in the
judgment of God." Here is, therefore, not a merely
pessimistic utterance of some disgruntled individual.
The emphasis of the verb lies primarily on the fact
that in God's esteem devastation had been wrought
Man had received the earth at God's hands and had
sadly ruined his heritage. The second half of v. 11
marks a climax: "the earth was filled with violence."
Chamaṣ is highhanded dealing; violating the rights
of others. This term most correctly describes the
form of moral corruption prevalent in the earth.
Men's rights were being trampled upon. Nor were
these cases isolated: the earth was filled with deeds
of this sort. *Chamaṣ* is accusative of the thing wherewith another is filled (K. S. 112).

12. The form and the nature of the opening
statement of this verse remind very definitely by way
of contrast with 1:31. As then a divine inspection
resulted in a verdict of approval, now just as positively
the fact that was revealed was that the earth was
corrupt. The expressive "behold" points to the unex-
pected: it would hardly be believed that the earth
would so soon and so completely have degenerated.
The expression "all flesh" can here refer only to mankind because of the qualifying nature of the object
"its way." "Way" is the course man is to follow. Only
a moral being can corrupt its way. Therefore "all
flesh" refers to the totality of mankind in so far as it
is not submitting to the Spirit's guidance, as in 6:3.

Critics have difficulties with these two verses.
Ascribing them to P, they miss entirely in P an indication of where the world went wrong. Consequently,
they try to make v. 12 present the case as strongly as
possible and draw in the beasts as well under those
who had corrupted their way in "commencing to prey
upon each other and to attack man." B D B is right
when it refers the word "way" of v. 12 to "moral

action and character." Moral issues exclusively are under consideration here.

The word "earth" is taken proleptically, and its clause really follows, as in 1:4 (K. S. 414 b.).

Of course, the point of view of v. 12 is purely anthropomorphic. Its purpose is not to state that now God first discovered that the earth had really grown quite corrupt. God had been thoroughly aware of every increase of wickedness. But the verse does indicate that in the esteem of God, the perfect and righteous Judge, the measure of the world's iniquity was full.

b) The second portion of Noah's story now follows in 6:13-8:22, telling how he was preserved in the universal destruction.

13. And God said to Noah: The end of all flesh is come before me, for the earth is filled with violence through them; and behold, I am about to destroy them together with the earth.

In God's judgment the destruction of the world is determined. His purpose is here communicated to Noah. The 120 years of grace must have been concluded. The "end" *(qets)* is here used, of course, in the sense of "destruction." "All flesh" here, as in v. 12, describes all mankind in so far as it has rejected the Spirit's guidance. "Before me" is used exactly as in v. 11 in the sense of "according to my judgment." The whole statement cannot mean: "has come to my knowledge" (as Esther 9: 11) but "has entered my purpose" (Skinner). Meek renders quite acceptably: "I have resolved on the extermination of all mortals," but, unfortunately, he introduces a tone of arbitrariness which is just the thing that is not involved in the phrase "before me."

There come times in the events of this world when God's gracious dealings with men are definitely terminated. Such times come only when grace has been

offered in richest measure. But when the end is resolved upon, there is no recall. Such a case is marked
by the "end" that God here determines. His reason
for His steps shows this course to be entirely just:
"the earth is filled with violence through them."
"Through them" *(mippénêhem)* is really: "from their
faces" or "from before them." But that clearly means
that the violence has gone out from them. The phrase
could also be translated "because of them." Man has
no one to blame but himself. But this end is not coming
on like a blind fate. God indicates His initiative in
the work of destruction, in fact, vividly points to His
participation by a "behold." Works of retribution are
as much holy and good works and worthy of God as
any other. The participle after *hinneh* indicates an act
as imminent: "I am about to destroy" (K. S. 237 g.).
But in order to make the sweeping nature and the
dread earnestness of this destruction most clearly apparent, it is His purpose to destroy men "together with
the earth." Thus, when man is wiped away and his
habitation with him, men realize more fully how serious
the nature of their misdeeds is. The critics did not
expect the phrase "with the earth" and so subject it to
severe criticism. It makes too good sense to call for
criticism.

The suffix in *mippenêhem* refers back to the collective *basar*.

14, 15. **Make thyself an ark of gopher-wood;
make the ark with cells; and smear it with pitch
within and without. And this is how thou shalt
make it: three hundred cubits is to be the length of
the ark, fifty cubits its width, and thirty cubits its
height.**

The means by which God will destroy mankind
and the earth has not yet been revealed to Noah. For
the present only the device by which Noah is to be
saved is revealed to him, but the nature of the device

is such that it is comparatively easy for Noah to draw conclusions as to the impending catastrophe, which will be mentioned in v. 17. This entire revelation to Noah proceeds in a very orderly fashion. He is first given the essential directions about the ark. It is called *tebhah.* Since the same word is used only in reference to Moses' ark of bulrushes besides, it appears quite likely to be akin to an Egyptian word, *ṭeb(t),* although it will not do to be too positive about such things, as this word may be carried over from the original language of mankind. No one knows what type of tree is meant by the name "gopher." It may contain the root of the Greek word "cyprus." The translators have been puzzled by it from days of old. The Greek rendered it "square," the Latin "smoothed," etc. The word for "cells" *(qinnîm)* is used also for "nests." Consequently, such rooms are meant as may suit the needs of various beasts. Since rooms on shipboard are "cabins," the word may also be rendered thus. But as the description proceeds, we discover that it is rather inaccurate to speak of a ship. This was not a ship but a huge floating *box* with dimensions quite nearly proportionate to those of a ship. This vessel was not intended for sailing or navigating of any sort. It was designed to float. It is rendered watertight by a generous coating inside and out with "pitch" *(kópher).* The Assyrian word for "pitch" *kuprun,* as well as the Arabic parallel guarantee this meaning. From this noun, perhaps, the verb *kaphar* is derived, yielding the expression here used "to pitch with pitch." The definite article with *kópher* is the article of conformity *(der Zugehoerigkeit* — K. C.). "Cells" is a kind of accusative of product: "make it cells" (G. K. 117 ii.; K. S. 327 w.).

15. Reckoning the cubit at eighteen inches, we have the following dimensions: length, 300 cubits = 450 feet; width, fifty cubits = seventy-five feet; height, thirty cubits = forty-five feet.

The introductory *zeh* illustrates the neuter use of the demonstratives (K. S. 45).

Efforts to find an allegorical meaning in the ark such as that it represents Christ's body, that is the church, and that its one door represents Baptism are perhaps best described by the adjectives Luther employs in reference to them when he labels them as "harmless" and "not so very skillful." No one can deny the propriety of the thought, as long as it is used only as an illustration and not offered as a deeper meaning of the text as such.

16. **An opening for light shalt thou make for the ark and to a cubit shalt thou make it complete toward the top; the door of the ark thou shalt put in its side; with lower, second, and third stories thou shalt make it.**

This verse concludes the description as to how the ark is to be made. A *tsóhar* is to be "toward the top." Since the word for "noonday" comes from this root, the meaning "an opening for light" *(Lichtoeffnung)* is the more appropriate, not roof. It seems just a bit too obvious to specify that a "roof" should be built, and then to suggest that it is to be "toward the top." This direction would border on the ridiculous. But an "opening for light" certainly was a necessity. This means more than a window. It means an opening of a cubit from the top or "toward the top" *(milma'lah)* to be made entirely around the structure. This is implied in the verb from "make it complete" *(tekhallénnah)* which, being in the *Piel* stem, signifies, as we might say, "run it completely around" toward the top. Of course, certain details are not mentioned in this connection. We shall never know whether other openings, aside from "the window" (8:6), were provided. We shall never be sure whether the eaves projected out sufficiently over the "opening for light" to guard against the rain. But persons who were capable

of constructing so vast a structure may well be credited
with the requisite intelligence to provide for such
details. We are at least informed that light and ventila-
tion were taken care of and may dismiss all minor
questions as irrelevant. The author selects a few significant factors and at the hand of these lets us form
a general conception. Though no attempt at completeness is made, such as a set of full specifications for
a building to be erected by a contractor would provide,
we realize that such a thing cannot lie in the purpose
of the author. The situation by no means calls for
criticisms such as: "The details here are very confused
and mostly obscure" (Skinner).

Besides, it is quite clear what Moses means when
he says: "the door of the ark shalt thou put in its
side." Again it matters little for present purposes
whether this door was in the first or second story.
But we know that a door was provided. We translate
"the door," since the definite noun "the ark" makes the
noun in the construct state definite. The article here
signifies the *customary* or *usual* door that you might
expect. The last major direction provides for three
"stories." "Decks" would be a good word if this were
a ship. The Hebrew happens to be unusually brief but
not obscure, saying: "with lower, seconds and thirds
thou shalt make it."

For those inclined to be too critical it may yet be
added that surely God's direction to Noah may have
been far more detailed. Any writer recording the story
may abbreviate at any point and give merely the substance, if the details be no longer relevant to his
purpose.

A Dutchman, Peter Janson, in 1609-21 made a
novel experiment in building a vessel thus proportioned
and thus satisfying himself both of its seaworthiness
as well of its relatively high storage capacity. But a
bit of reflection might have satisfied almost any man
of the seaworthiness of such a box. Furthermore, the

enormity of the project harmonizes well with other
huge enterprises carried through by men of antiquity
and argues well for the high intelligence and the wonderful capabilities of antediluvian man — a fact,
which clashes rather roughly with the conceptions of
evolution.

Dagesh forte omitted in *l* of *milma'lah;* see G. K.
20 m.

There follows in very good order first the definite
revelation of the coming of a universal flood (v. 17),
but for Noah's comfort it is at once said that he and
his family are to be spared (v. 18). Then the beings
that are to be housed in the ark during the time of the
Flood are listed (v. 19, 20), and Noah is bidden also
to provide food for all that are to be in the ark (21).
Noah's compliance with all these demands is recorded
as an apt close for this section (v. 22).

17. **For behold, I for my part am about to
bring the Flood, waters, upon the earth to destroy
all flesh, that has in it the breath of life, from under
heaven; everything in the earth shall expire.**

The initial "and" is explanatory, therefore "for"
(G. K. 158 a.). The expressed personal pronoun "I"
provides a contrast with the closing word of v. 16,
"*thou* shalt make," "but *I*," etc. (K. S. 360 e.). The
particularly noteworthy fact here announced (therefore "behold") is that which would almost have passed
belief: a universal flood is about to be brought by Him.
The pronoun with the participle expresses something
as impending (G. K. 116 p). The word for "flood,"
mabbûl, does not seem to be derived from any Hebrew
root but to be allied with the Assyrian *nabâlu,* "to
destroy." Therefore the author inserted an appositional *mayîm,* "waters," to indicate at once what manner of destruction was meant. *Mabbûl* occurs only in
the Flood story and in Ps. 29:10 and is the technical
expression for this particular Flood. Here the ex-

pression "all flesh" must refer to man and beast because of the modifying clause, "that has in it the breath of life." Yet, according to 7:22, even here the obvious restriction has to be made of creatures living on the dry land. Aquatic animals do not perish because of waters of a flood. *Rûach,* which in other passages also means "breath," is here described as "the breath of life" because this breath is the essential condition of life. The expression is not identical with 2:7 *(nishmath chayyim)* but practically of the same meaning. In order to emphasize that "all flesh" is actually to be taken in its broadest sense, by way of repetition of the thought, the clause is appended: "everything in the earth shall expire."

The disagreement in case of *'anî* (nominative) and *hinnî,* (accusative) is not disturbing (K. S. 343 a).

18. **And I will establish my covenant with thee, and thou shalt come into the ark, thou and thy sons and thy wife and thy sons' wives with thee.**

The "covenant" *(berith)* is somewhat puzzling from one point of view. Does the term refer to a particular guaranty of preservation in the impending Flood, or does it refer to some covenant previously made with Noah but not mentioned here; or does it refer to the covenant whose details are to be made known 9:9 ff.? The first possibility is not very likely, because nothing more of the covenant is mentioned in this connection, and it would, indeed, seem strange that a covenant be made without specific mention of its terms, or at least just as strange if one covenant be made one year and a new one about a few years later. God's covenants are never thus multiplied. The second possibility has still less to recommend it. Why should some mysterious previous covenant be implied, and why should no distinct mention of it have been made? But the third possibility has much to support it. God promises that He will make a covenant with Noah. Nothing is said of the making of this covenant at this time, for other issues clamor for more immediate attention. But Noah is made aware of the fact that he shall live to experience the making of a covenant with God. Since such a covenant is actually made after the Flood (9:9 ff.), the simplest conclusion is: That is the covenant that God referred to when these words were spoken. Since its terms are there fully revealed, we need not infer with Luther that the covenant referred to the promised seed. The promise of the fact that such a Flood is never to take place again has, no doubt, in the providence of God direct bearing upon the preparation for the victory of the seed of the woman.

So, then, Noah has the prospect before him of yet being honored to experience the establishment of a covenant. The usual expression for entering upon a covenant *(karath)* is not here used but the verb *heqîm*, "to set up," (used also in 17:19, 21; Exod. 6:4), which must mean "make" not "keep," for the covenant is not yet made.

Now Noah receives instruction that it is only he and his immediate family who are to be privileged to enter the ark. The word is very specific. Noah is to know very exactly how many are to share in this privilege. Besides, God, the Almighty Judge, is the only one competent to decide so important a matter. To impress this fact duly upon Noah this detailed enumeration "thou and thy sons and thy wife and thy sons' wives" is found again in 7:13 and in 8:16. However, 8:18 merely repeats the same words in order to emphasize that so specific a command was carried out to the letter. This is the simple explanation as to why these very words recur several times. The claim that this is one of the linguistic peculiarities of P is beside the point. Compare on the admission of the critics, however, 8:1. Then 7:1, usually assigned to J, says nothing different, and so even on the ground of style the differentiation between sources fades out.

19, 20. Of all living things, of all flesh, two of each thou shalt bring into the ark to keep them alive with thee; male and female shall they be. Of the birds after their kind, and of the animals after their kind, of all creeping things after their kind, two of each shall come to thee, to be kept alive.

In this very orderly set of directions for Noah there now comes a specification of what creatures and how many of each are to be brought into the ark. "Living things" only *(chay)* are to be considered. For the preservation of plant life divine providence will take care. In apposition with "living things" stands "of all flesh," an expression which must here refer to animals, as the sequel shows. "Flesh" still means that which is weak and perishable, and so implies that particular care must be taken in its preservation: it cannot provide for itself in such an emergency. Criticism cannot see why here only *"two* of each" are mentioned, whereas in 7:2, in the case of clean beasts, *seven* of each are to be taken. Criticism falls back upon its favorite mechanical explanation: different sources, allowing, of course, that J and P actually disagreed on this point. The simple explanation is this: here in chapter six summary directions are being given. The rule is to be: two of each. When these general directions are amplified in regard to the clean beast just before the Flood occurs (7:1 ff.), that certainly does not clash with the first specifications; it merely amplifies the original directions. On the question of how all these creatures could be secured, the verbs used offer an excellent solution. The nineteenth verse says: *"thou* shalt bring" (*tabhî'*—Hifil = "cause to come in") ; v. 20 says: *"they* shall come" (*yabhó'û* —Kal, active) as in 7:9, 15. Two thoughts are here combined. Each sets forth one side of the truth. On the one hand, the creatures come voluntarily, as even the wildest of beasts have been known to seek the nearness of man when calamities impend. The creatures, rendered docile by the apprehension they felt of coming danger, are then without difficulty brought into the ark by Noah. Consequently, all thoughts about elaborate trapping expeditions may readily be dismissed. The difficulty Noah is said to have had on this score is thus readily seen to have been quite negligible. The explanatory clause, "male and female shall they be," quite naturally looks to the mating and propagating of the various species. On the article before *chay* see G. K. 35 f.

20. To leave nothing for Noah to guess at the classes to be considered are enumerated: "birds, animals, creeping things." "Animals" *(behemah)* employs the Hebrew original in a broader sense than 1:24, where it means "cattle" and excludes wild animals. But this broader use of the term is not uncommon nor inconsistent with the root meaning of the word. Of these major classes the various species *(mîn)* are to be brought in.

This raises the difficult question: "How could room for such a diversified lot of creatures be found in this one ark?" No one happens to know how widely diversified the species were at the time the Flood occurred. Since no one can prove anything on this question either pro or con, the question may well be left to rest. Untenable claims have been made by those who seek to invalidate Scripture testimony but without proof. This happens to be a point on which no data may ever be available. Why question the possibility or the consistency of this matter in an account where everything else is so simple and consistent? Had we actually seen how this matter was adjusted, we might marvel at the stupidity of our question.

The last infinitive Hifil, *lehachayôth*, is used absolutely without an object in the sense of "for the preservation of life," literally: "to cause to live."

21. **And do thou for thy part take for thyself from all manner of eatable things, which are wont to be eaten, and store it by thee, to serve as food for thee and for them.**

Sustenance is not going to be provided miraculously. *Noah* must see to that, as an emphatic pronominal "thou" points out to him. *Kol* in this instance must have its common meaning: "all manner of." *Ma'akhal* refers rather to that which is edible than simply to "food." The imperfect *ye'akhel* implies the idea of the customary: "which are *wont to* be eaten" (G. K. 107 g). A big additional task is thus laid upon Noah. One must marvel at the completeness and the plainness of the divine directions for Noah, as well as at their compact brevity.

The problem of providing food for so many creatures for somewhat more than a year is simplified by the very proper consideration that beasts are very shrewd about adapting their food supply to their needs. When they have no physical exercise, like brooding hens, they cut down promptly on the amount of food consumed. Likewise during the time of hibernating. A kind of winter sleep may providentially have taken possession of all inmates of the ark, materially cutting down their needs and reducing them to a very small minimum.

Again one must marvel at the excellent divine wisdom, which laid the care of the inmates of the ark upon man and thus provided ample activity for man, guarding him against morbid and dismal brooding over the fate of mankind, which might have resulted from a state of inaction and proved very trying, if not dangerous, to man.

22. **And Noah did so; exactly as God commanded him, so he did.**

This part of the narrative closes with the report
that Noah did as he was bidden, in fact, carried the
divine orders out to the letter. We should have expected that on Noah's part. A man who walked with
God would be expected to take such an attitude. The
enormity of the task did not overwhelm him. The
dismal nature of the impending catastrophe did not
rouse undue questionings. Noah obeyed orders as
Heb. 11:7 rightly says: "by faith."

It is usually assumed that during all this time
Noah preached to his generation. Correctly so, inasmuch as II Pet. 2:5 terms him "a preacher of righteousness." Even if his words had not been many, the
building of the ark as such was thundering testimony
to a godless age, as Hebrews also says (11:7):
"through which (building of the ark) he condemned
the world."

Criticism, as usual, detracts from the major issues
by inapropos remarks, in this case on the pleonastic,
"He did so . . . so he did." For it does happen that
this very form of statement recurs, as K. C. has observed, thirteen times and always in passages ascribed
to P (See Exod. 7:6, 12; 28:50; 39:32, 42 f.; Num.
1:54 etc.). For a moment it almost seems as though
for once we had discovered an actual stylistic peculiarity: always in P passages. Besides, thirteen times
seems a heavy array of evidence. However, the problem is quite simple. Wherever detailed formal directions are given, such a passage is on that score already
assigned to P. How natural for a man like Moses to
have a peculiarity of style, which leads him, each time
he makes a list of detailed divine orders to be executed
by man, to indicate that godly men did as they were
bidden and to use a set formula, characteristically his
own, for this purpose. Nothing here at all in conflict

with the idea of Mosaic authorship. Such human traits as fixed word patterns for analogous situations are not suppressed by the Spirit of inspiration. Moses too had such habits of writing, without a doubt.

Since we are on the subject of literary criticism, let us go a step farther and refute some of the major contentions on which criticism bases its much vaunted distinction of sources, which is so greatly stressed especially in connection with the Flood story.

On the matter of the use of the divine names in this story observe how much is to be said in support of our position. The whole critical world, of course, cries these arguments of ours down as futile. But note the very good sense that pervades the whole situation when these basic facts are kept in mind: when God's *gracious* dealings with Noah and with mankind are to be considered, then the name *Yahweh* is used; but when God is thought of as the *Almighty Ruler* of heaven and earth, whose particular province it is to judge men and to determine their fate, this God whom men should reverently fear is called *Elohîm*.

We have just demonstrated the propriety of the use of Yahweh for 6:1-8. By the way, "God" in 6:5 (A. V.) is a mistake. The Hebrew reads "Yahweh."

But in 6:9-22 Elohîm is used throughout. Is it not appropriate to speak of Elohîm at this point? *He*, great and awe-inspiring in His being, lets a man like Noah walk with Him (v. 9). In the sight of Him, the Judge, the earth is corrupt (v. 11). *He*, in His sovereign right, determines to destroy (v. 13). What He who has authority to command thus ordains (v. 22), Noah feels obliged to carry out.

Chapter 7:1-7 records how *graciously* God deals with Noah to preserve his life; therefore "Yahweh," (v. 1, 5). In v. 9 appears "Elohîm" because the obedience of the creature world to its Sovereign Ruler is under consideration. So also in v. 16 a. But 16 b brings "Yahweh" because this was a kindly deed on the Lord's part.

God's sovereign control is under consideration in 8:1; therefore "Elohîm": the Almighty is about to terminate this vast catastrophe. This same great God ordains (v. 15) what things Noah must do. But Noah is considering God's gracious providence when (v. 20) he brings his grateful sacrifice to "Yahweh." "Yahweh" regards this sacrifice (v. 21).

The common response of the critics to such an interpretation of the divine names leaves the strength of our argument unimpaired. They usually contend that if we dwell on the meaning involved in these names of the deity, one name could be substituted for the other and the whole would still make very good sense. We do not deny that, but we do claim that there is a definite viewpoint from which the author approached the individual divine acts, and this viewpoint is reflected in his choice of the various possible names. And we further claim that the particular divine name under consideration can be shown to make very good sense and to be eminently reasonable in every case. Moses used the divine names according to the actual meaning, and the result is a point of view in regard to individual divine acts which is most instructive. Deeper thought, not a mechanical use of one only known name, lies behind the choice of divine names.

But the claim that the two major documents involved can be so clearly distinguished that the individual vocabulary of each can be discerned, seems in the eyes of many to carry convincing weight. But upon closer examination it too collapses and shows forth most startling weaknesses. We shall trace down the so-called distinctive features of vocabulary as Skinner lists them.

1. J is said to use the expression *'ish we'ishto* (7:2) "man and his wife," whereas P uses *zakhar*

ûneqebhah ("male and female") 6:19; 7:9, 16. But on the difficult matter of style who would venture to pronounce a single use of an expression (7:2) as indicative of a linguistic peculiarity? When we take that particular verse in hand, we shall show why in that connection the somewhat unusual expression was well motivated.

2. Again, the following so-called stylistic peculiarities are referred to: J used *machah* ("wipe out") in 6:7; 7:4, 23; P uses *shachath* and *hishchîth* ("go to ruin" and "ruin") 6:13, 17; 9:11, 15. This, however, represents nothing more than a natural variation of expression by one and the same author. 6:7 describes God's resolve and the ease with which it is to be carried out. 6:13, 17 are used in God's conversation with Noah, first this particular verb *(hishchîth)* in the announcement of the destruction; then follows the announcement of that destruction by a flood. The circumstances demand the use of the same word. 7:4 *machah* comes at the very beginning of the Flood and again is descriptive of the ease with which God will do the work. But what appears as the resolve of God, first mentioned in 6:7 before the ark is built and in 7:4 just before the Flood begins, is most naturally referred to by the same verb in 7:23 when it is to be reported that God actually did what He had resolved to do. In 9:11 and 15, the water being mentioned, it is but natural that a verb be employed which records the destructive effect of the water *(shachath)* and be repeated for emphasis. All this can quite readily be accounted for on the supposition that there is but one author.

3. J used *mûth* ("die") in 7:22 whereas P is said to use *gawaʻ* ("expire") in 6:17; 7:21. Note that 6:17 says that the creatures *will* expire, but 7:21 gives the fulfillment of the threat: they *did* expire. Since 7:22 after 7:21 distinctly aims to make the preceding expression more emphatic and general, it

provides a synonymous subject and a synonymous predicate. This situation is thus easily accounted for as proceeding from the pen of *one* author. Besides, if 7:22 is the only passage available for J, is that *one* example proof of a linguistic peculiarity?

4. Critics call *kol hayqûm* ("all existence") 7:4, 23, a mark of J, whereas P is said to prefer the expression *kol basar* ("all flesh") 6:12, 13; 7:21. Yet in 6:12 and 13 a very specific thing is under consideration: man, who is *flesh,* is corrupt; therefore, man, who is *flesh,* shall perish. 7:4 tells of God's resolve to destroy all that lives, all existence (*yeqûm*). 7:23 reports how this resolve is carried out. But since 7:21, 22 and 23 summarize the great extent of the destruction by the use of every possible synonym, noun and verb, it need not surprise us to find *kol basar* here again. Again the expressions employed are readily accounted for as the work of *one* author.

5. J is said to use *qal* ("be light") 8:8, 11 but P, *shûbh* ("return") 8:3 and *chaṣer* ("fail") 8:5. Between 8:3 and 8:5 the critics create an artificial distinction. Since 8:3 uses a different verb ("returned") to express more fully the thought of the subsiding of the waters, whereas 8:5 uses "decreased," on the strength of the supposition that one author would not do thus, 8:3 is asigned to J. But by the time the narrative reaches the point of 8:3 Noah is neither concerned about whether the waters are "returning" (*shûbh*) or whether they are "decreased" (*chaṣer*). He knows both these things are so. He wants to know whether they are very low, i. e., whether they "were abated" (*qal*). So he sends forth the dove, and when she returns with an olive leaf, he knows they *were* abated (*qal*). Why cannot one author write thus?

6. Again J's *charabh* ("be dry") 8:13 b is said to be distinct from P's *yabhash* ("be dry") 8:14. One single use of a verb is supposed to constitute a proved stylistic peculiarity. The only evidence on which

8:13 b is assigned to J is because the verb is different. Note well the procedure. First it is assigned to J because it is a different verb. Then after assigning it to J, the critic uses the verb thus assigned as *proof* that J uses a different vocabulary than P. We simply call this an argument in a circle.

7. Again J: *nishmath chayyîm* ("breath of life") 7:22 vs. P: *rûach chayyîm* ("spirit of life") 6:17. In the first place 7:22, 23 are assigned to J because they repeat with amplifications what 7:21 (P) said. An author apparently dare never amplify and use synonymous expressions. But why cannot an author in 6:17 speak of the perishing of everything wherein is "the spirit of life" and then later in amplifying the expression say: "the breath of the spirit of life" (7:22)? The appearance of the phrase *rûach chayyîm* in both expressions argues just as stoutly for *one* author.

8. J: *lechayyoth* (7:3) vs. *lehachayoth* (6:19, 20). Both verbs mean "to keep alive." The first is Piel, the second Hifil. In 6:19, 20 *all manner of creatures* are to be kept alive. In 7:3 *seed* is to be preserved or kept alive. Since the expression changes, why should not the author also vary the stem from a Hifil to a Piel to express the shade of difference involved? For *one* author to do thus is most natural.

9. J: *kol bêthekha* ("all thy house") 7:1 vs. a specific enumeration of P in 6:18; 7:(7), 13; 8:16, 18. This argument collapses as soon as one discovers that 7:7 is really found in a passage usually assigned to J. Consequently, J gives a specific enumeration as well as P.

To all this add another very strange fact. The difficulties of the critics are not all solved by the mere assumption that two practically complete Flood stories were fused into one. R, the Redactor, is credited with a certain measure of independent activity in discharging his fusion duties. Sometimes portions of the one or the other document are omitted when a confusing or disturbing repetition would result. So portions of J are said to be omitted in favor of the fuller account of P, for without this assumption J would appear to have had no record of the building of the ark, a very serious shortcoming. Here is Strack's statement of the case: "Since J must very evidently have had a complete Flood story, R must have stricken out what J said in order to avoid disturbing repetitions." But a Redactor who so carefully avoids disturbing repetitions lets manifest contradictions stand. So, as almost all critics admit after their separation of the sources is complete, according to J the Flood lasted forty days (some say: sixty-one), but according to P 150 days. Again, P speaks of two animals of every kind; J of seven of the clean beasts.

Not only is there a flaw in the critical constructions put upon the so-called sources; the whole setup is scientifically and critically absurd and impossible. The above represents only a partial refutation indicating what lines have been followed and what more could be said. Rupprecht and Moeller have covered the ground in a more exhaustive manner.

HOMILETICAL SUGGESTIONS

We suggest the following three sections in this chapter as best suited to separate treatment. First the section v. 1-8 which constitutes a unit in itself. This may be treated from the broader point of view, resulting from the general connection, and then some such topic as "The Ripening of the Flower of Sin" would be in order. Again, it would be very much in order to treat these verses from the point of view that they record how the two branches of the human race at this point merged into one another, due to the inconsiderate marriages of the "sons of God." That suggests some such subject as "Mixed Marriages." Then, there is the section v. 9-12, which treats primarily of Noah's piety. Noah does rank exceptionally high for piety, and from this point of view his character deserves to be studied. In the third place, we have the group of verses v. 13-22 constituting a unit. Everything centers about the Ark, of course. Yet to use "the Ark" as a subject would be altogether too superficial. If God's kindness in devising such a means of escape is considered, a preacher may operate with a theme such as: "The Ark—a Testimony of Divine Grace." Heb. 11:7 suggests very appropriately the theme—"Noah's Faith." Appropriate as the thought is that the Ark symbolizes the Christian church, is such treatment of the passage not too purely that which falls under the censure of being allegorizing? Perhaps the section v. 13—7:5 had best be used as a unit, for 7:1-5 alone in less suitable for use as a text.

CHAPTER VII

Entrance of Noah Into the Ark; The Coming of the Flood

Even though we set a caption for this chapter, we are still considering the History of Noah (6:9), and more particularly the second part of it which treats of his preservation. In point of time this chapter sets in seven days before the Flood. The building of the ark is finished. The supplies are stored. The living cargo alone remains to be housed.

1. **And Yahweh said unto Noah: Enter into the ark, thou and all thy house, for thee have I seen to be righteous before me in this generation.**

Of God's mode of speaking to Noah we know nothing. Noah knew that God spoke.

In a way the reader might argue that all that was needed at this point of the narrative was the direct command to enter the ark because the Flood was about to come. Yet such cold logical reasoning overlooks the human factor, namely, how a detailed statement with personal reassurance was an imperative necessity for a man who had to stand practically alone over against the generation of his day. What reassurance for Noah to know that he was not acting on his own initiative or on the strength of some supposition that now the time had come actually to enter the ark. Since 6:18 had definitely listed those who were to be permitted by God to share this haven of refuge, it is sufficient here to use the summary expression for them, "all thy house." A check-up on chapter five will show that none of the Sethite line outlived the Flood year. Consequently, we need not assume that a single one

who was a true Sethite perished in the Flood. Nor can
we in any way prove that this last communication
made to Noah concerning the coming of the Flood in
seven days, made sufficient of an impression on his
contemporaries to induce at least some to turn to
repentance, even though entrance into the ark was
denied them. Matt. 24:38 seems to eliminate such
a possibility.

When Noah's righteousness (see on 6:9) is referred to as a reason for the sparing both of himself and
of his house, the case is hardly covered by the reflection
that the "members (of the family) are saved for the
righteousness of its head." There is an element of
that in it all. The blessing that may grow out of the
godly conduct of a consecrated individual may, indeed,
redound to the good of others who are associated with
him and be much greater than what these persons
would have received apart from their associations with
such an individual. See how Israel is blessed both for
Abraham's and for David's sake. However, prominent
as such blessings are, we have every reason to assume
that the father's influence affected the personal attitude
of the members of his household to Yahweh, so that
of their own volition they chose to walk in the godly
patriarch's footsteps. Yet had Noah not stood firm,
they themselves might soon have wavered. Therefore
Yahweh ascribes righteousness to Noah alone in this
his generation. Note how the forensic idea definitely
appears in the word *tsaddiq* in this connection. Nor is
the conclusion right that the sole approval of Noah
involved the positive disapproval of all others (Lange).

A double accusative follows the verb "see" (K. S.
327 s).

2, 3. **Of all clean animals take to thyself seven
of each, a male and his mate; but of all animals
which are not clean, two each, a male and his mate;
also of the birds of the heavens, seven each, male**

and female, to preserve seed alive upon the face of all the earth.

In 6:19 a general direction had been given to Noah to the effect that two of every kind of beasts were to be taken into the ark. There was then no occasion for giving all details. Now that the entrance into the ark is imminent, these last details are added. In spite of the simple naturalness of this explanation which meets all needs and adequately solves the problem, critics, for the most part not even mentioning this obvious solution, keep referring to the two accounts J and P and the discrepancies between them. No doubt, from the earliest days the natural explanation advanced above has readily occurred to the simplest Bible reader, and for him no difficulty existed.

Here we are suddenly confronted with the notion of unclean and clean animals. There is no indication in Scripture as to how this distinction arose. The Mosaic law sanctions and defines it. But we are left to our own devices for an explanation as to how it originated. Since the Mosaic law under this head sanctioned what apparently had long been in existence, there is no ground for tracing the origin of the distinction to a divine ordinance. The more satisfactory explanation is that which claims that in an earlier age, when man's insight was less blurred by being absorbed in purely worldly matters, it became quite apparent to man that certain forms of animal life were in reality rather striking pictures of sin and its uncleanness. So a natural abhorrence against such creatures arose, and it was thought to be good pedagogic training for a man to remember such a distinction and to draw practical conclusions from it in the use of beasts particularly for food. Whether this practical application of the idea in reference to foods was made already in the days before the Flood cannot be determined. But the distinction as such is referred to as current and well known.

The Hebrew expression "take seven seven" means "seven each" (K. S. 85; 316 b; G. K. 134 q). Hebrew parallels support this explanation. In any case, it would be a most clumsy method of trying to say "fourteen." Three pairs and one supernumerary make the "seven." As has often been suggested, the supernumerary beast was the one Noah could conveniently offer for sacrifice after the termination of the Flood. In v. 3 the idea of "the birds of the heavens" must, of course, be supplemented by the adjective "clean," according to the principle laid down in v. 2. The birds are separately mentioned so that Noah might not be left to his own devices in fixing the limits of what v. 2 included.

The expression found twice in v. 2, "a male and his mate," is rather unusual from our point of view in that a literal translation would read in reference to these clean beasts, "a man and his wife." The expression is the same as that used in 2:25 in reference to Adam and Eve. However, the strangeness of the expression disappears as soon as we notice that both terms "man" and "wife" have a greater latitude of meaning by far in Hebrew. So "wife" may be used in reference to all manner of beasts to express the distributive and reciprocal idea, "each" (B D B 61, a). If, then, here the expression takes the place of "male and female," which is actually used of the clean birds in v. 3, no particular significance is to be attached to it. Of two available expressions the one involving the greater dignity ("man and wife") is twice used in reference to clean beasts.

The object of gathering all these clean beasts together in the ark is said to be "to preserve seed alive." The expression "seed" *(zéra‘)* is here used quite appropriately, because these creatures naturally come under the point of view of such from which all others are again to spring. At the same time the

thought is expressed that these apparently few creatures will under divine providence be adequate again
to cover "the face of all the earth." There is a promise
latent in this expression of purpose.

The criticism that calls this distinction of clean
and unclean on the part of the writer "a proof of the
naïvité of his religious conceptions" is proof that the
author of the criticism has not apprehended the deeper
scriptural truth involved.

4. **For yet seven days and I am going to
make it rain upon the earth for forty days and forty
nights and I will blot out all existence which I have
made from upon the face of the earth.**

There is nothing vague about this last direction
which is imparted to Noah. God speaks with authority
as one who has absolute and perfect control of all
issues involved. Noah will have seven days in which
to complete his preparations. Then there will break
forth a rain whose exact duration divine providence
has fixed and foreknows, a rain of forty days and
nights. The number "forty" cannot be merely accidental. According to the scriptural use of numbers
forty regularly describes a period of trial terminating
in the victory of good and the overthrow of evil; see
Num. 14:33; Exod. 24:18; I Kings 19:8; Jonah 3:4;
Matt. 4:2; Acts 1:3. Since the rule of evil has in this
case become well-nigh universal, God determines to
"wipe out all existence" *(kol yeqûm)*, that is, everything that stands up *(allen Bestand)*. In the adjective
clause "which I have made" lies both a sorrow at the
thought that His own creatures should have degenerated thus, as well as the assertion of His right to
destroy thus. What He has made, He may destroy.
Again the descriptive word "wipe out" is met. The
participle *mamṭir* expresses duration: I am going to
cause rain for a long time. The *le* before "days" is
the *le* temporal (K. S. 331 f).

5. **And Noah did just as the Lord commanded him.**

One of the remarkable features of this Flood story is its entirely objective character. Noah's subjective feelings or reactions are not even indicated by a single word. It is as though human emotions were but trivial things in the face of the vastness of the disaster that befalls the earth. Enough to know the implicit obedience of this man of God. He received orders. He obeyed them to the letter. *Kekhol,* "according to all" must equal "just as." The sum of what he did is reported in v. 7-9. But before that is reported, it is thought essential to stress his complete obedience.

6. **And Noah was six hundred years old when the Flood came, waters upon the earth.**

The entrance into the ark is about to be reported. This certainly constitutes an important juncture in Noah's life. This was practically the moment when the rest of mankind ceased to be, and when Noah virtually became the sole head of the race. At important junctures such as these authors love to pause for reflections. One common reflection of biographers in particular is to mention the age of the hero at the time of an outstanding event. Moses here quite naturally does the same thing in reference to Noah. This fact, which is so simple that it lies on the very surface, is not observed by criticism. For a simple obvious fact a devious and complicated theory is substituted. Because P is supposed to supply exact data, this verse is assigned to him, and this is supported by the claim that v. 5 is really continued by v. 7 (Dillmann, etc.). However, v. 5 in a summary way reported Noah's obedience and so closed the paragraph. Now v. 6 marks the beginning, as above shown, of a new era, as it were, and offers an exact date for this era.

As in 6:17, the word *mabbûl,* "catastrophe," is modified by the apposition "water" to show what kind

of a catastrophe this was. *Ḥayah* does not here mean
"to be" but goes back to the original meaning "to
come to pass." The Hebrew idiom expressing age is
covered by the very flexible *ben* ("son"), "a son of
six hundred years." The number 600 has nothing
whatever to do with the Babylonian *ner*, or period of
that length. The correspondence is purely accidental.
The two coordinated clauses, "Noah was six hundred
years old" and "and the Flood came, etc.," are to be
combined as in our translation: "and" is the equivalent
of "when." K. S. 362 n makes an artificial separation
of the two clauses in the interest of the source theory.

7-9. **And Noah and his sons and his wife and
his sons' wives with him came into the ark from the
face of the waters of the Flood. Of all clean beasts
and of all beasts which were not clean and of the
birds and of everything that creepeth upon the
ground, two by two came unto Noah to the ark,
male and female, just as God had commanded
Noah.**

The enumeration of those who entered the ark is
not a purely formal repetition of 6:18. A summary
like 7:1 might have been in order ("all thy house"),
but this simple repetition makes the fact very prominent that the original provision (6:18) had been meant
literally and that no additional features were to be
added, as actually, however, was the case in reference
to the beasts, where first all are mentioned and the
fact that they shall enter two by two (6:19), and then
the modification of this order in reference to the clean
beasts appears (7:2, 3). Strange to say, there actually
was not one single person outside of the family of
Noah whom divine grace could save. The expression
"from the face of the waters of the Flood" is the
equivalent of our statement "to escape the waters,"
etc. (Meek).

In this instance the readiness of the beasts to
come in is stressed; *ba'û* = "they came" v. 9. Again,

since by far the majority of the beasts naturally belonged in the category of the unclean, the provisions
just reported in reference to the clean may be taken
for granted.   The report, therefore, merely contains
what held true in regard to all: they came in "two by
two." Such a statement is said to be made *a parte
potiori,* i. e., according to the portion that predominates.   Besides, this cannot be said to clash with v. 2
and 3 because two of all clean beasts certainly did go
in.   The "creepers" (*romes*) are added at this point in
order to show how broad Noah conceived the term
"all beasts" to be.   This is quite logical, because
creepers certainly could not keep alive in a Flood such
as this.

One outstanding instance of the lengths to which
criticism ventures to go is supplied by the reconstruction of original documents which, it is claimed, can be
restored by the skill of the critic.   J's narrative is said
originally to have run thus in sequence of verses:
10, 7, 16 b, 12, 17 b, 22, 23.   Even aside from all the
flaws that we have pointed out as inherent in the
critical assumption, it requires a faith far greater
than the faith in verbal inspiration to accept contentions such as these.

In v. 10 the Creator's authority is the dominant
viewpoint; therefore *Elohîm* is used.

**10, 11.   And it came to pass after the seven
days that the waters of the Flood came upon the
earth.   In the six hundredth year of the life of Noah,
in the second month, on the seventeenth day of the
month, on that very day all the fountains of the great
deep were broken open, and the windows of the
heavens were opened.**

Since "seven days" were mentioned in v. 4, these
must elapse before the Flood can come.   So, apparently,
the expression "at the seven of the days," with *le*
temporal, is best taken in the sense: "after the seven

days," than "on the seventh day." Luther and A. V.
also agree to this. The Hebrew with its preference
for co-ordination of clauses says: "*and* the waters
came" after "it came to pass." We naturally would
say after such a beginning: "*that* the waters came."
See K. S. 370a; G. K. 164 a. Besides, the second clause
is not introduced by the verb because the noun
"waters" is the emphatic thing.

11. Now the date is fixed more exactly as befits
the importance of the event. In the memory of the
survivors it was a day never to be forgotten. As above
indicated, it was the six hundredth year of Noah's
life. The saints of the Lord, whom He hides before
the storm breaks (Isa. 26:20), are so important in His
eyes that time is reckoned according to their life. But
as far as the year itself is concerned, it was the seventeenth day of the second month. But does the author
mean the ordinary civil or agricultural year, which
takes its beginning with fall when the agricultural
tasks begin anew; or has he the ecclesiatical year in
mind which began with April? From Exod. 12:2; 13:4
it appears that this ecclesiastical year first came into
being with the Exodus. Besides, the heavy rain mentioned v. 12 as *géshem* applies primarily to the autumn
rains. All this makes the month corresponding roughly
to our October the more likely.

The source of the waters was twofold. Though it
was indicated above (v. 4) that the source of the
waters of the Flood would be what would normally be
expected, namely the rain from above, which was in
reality the chief source, now the auxiliary source is
mentioned and put first in order, because it was the
thing that attracted notice first because of its unusual
character. This auxiliary source is "the fountains of
the great deep." The "great deep" must be subterranean water of which there is still much and of which
there may have been more in early days. It seems to
be an established fact that "outbursts of subterranean

water are a frequent accompaniment of seismic disturbances in the alluvial districts of great rivers." *Tehôm* is similarly used for subterranean waters in Gen. 49:25 and Deut. 33:13. Consequently there must have been vast upheavals on every hand, for these fountains of the great deep "were broken open" (*nibhqe'û* — from *baqa'*, "to cleave"). To make plain the fact that the heavens poured down torrential rains, the figurative expression is used: "the windows of the heavens were opened," an expression still employed because of its aptness. As little as we go on record by the use of this expression as believing that there are actual windows in the heavens, so little need such a conception, pressed out of the literal understanding of figurative language, be attributed to Biblical writers. As in connection with 1:7 the idea of a kind of sidereal ocean had to be rejected as a purely fanciful notion of commentators, so here.

However, at this point note should be taken of the tremendous geological possibilities that lie behind the breaking open of the fountains of the great deep. The vastness of these eruptions must be in proportion to the actual depth of the Flood. For as the Flood was of astounding power and magnitude, so must have been each of the causes mentioned, the upper and the lower waters. Such eruptions from subterranean sources must have caused a rush of waters upon the earth comparable to the highest tidal wave. Such waves in turn must have been capable of producing effects of almost incalculable magnitude. So, then, the effects caused by the waters of the great deep (1:2), as they surged about on the earth in process of formation, together with the effects brought about by this great Flood, seem to us an entirely adequate explanation for geological formations of every kind, as they are now to be observed.

On the peculiar repetition of *shanah* ("year") in v. 11 see K. S. 337 i and G. K. 134 o. K. S. renders the phrase literally: "In the year (which coincides with) the six hundredth year," making it an appositional genitive. To prevent too long an accumulation of construct relationships the substitute of the dative with *le* is used before "the life of Noah" (K. S. 281 f).

12. **And the rain was upon the earth forty days and forty nights.**

To remind at once of the tremendous rainfall that resulted the duration of the fall is added to the idea of the torrential downpour. This verse, therefore, does not break the thought-connection, except for critics, who are operating with the double source idea and so fail to see the legitimate value of a repetition. In fact, in point of thought v. 12 may be considered as so closely attached to v. 11 as to be separated from it only by a comma. After v. 4 had promised that a forty days' rain would come, the writer is under obligation to report the fulfillment, a thing which may be done as readily here as anywhere. Besides, the author for the present uses the expression in this connection only to impress us with the amount of the resultant water. In v. 17 the similar statement aims to lead us to the end of this period.

13-16. **On this very day Noah and Shem and Ham and Japheth, the sons of Noah, together with the wife of Noah and the wives of his sons with them came into the ark. They and every sort of wild beast according to its kind, and every sort of domestic animal according to its kind, and every sort of creeper creeping upon the earth according to its kind, and every sort of bird according to its kind, everything with feathers and wings; of every sort of flesh which had in it the breath of life two by two came unto Noah into the ark. And those that came — male and female of all sorts of flesh came, just as God had commanded him. And Yahweh closed the door after him.**

With a solemn repetition, characteristic of all
epic poetry of days of old, this solemn epic aims to
produce upon the reader's imagination the effect of
the tremendous numbers that had to be housed in
the ark and what a scene it presented as they were
being brought in during the course of that last fateful
week. The attentive reader catches all this, and the
effect is well-nigh overpowering, but the critic sees
only idle repetition and two original sources, assigning
this portion to P. The solemnity of the event calls for
such a solemn rehearsal of names as we find in v. 13.
Incidentally, the phrase "on this very day" indicates
the fearlessness of faith manifest in these godly men.
There was no timid fleeing to the refuge of the ark
before the Flood actually set in. The word we have
rendered "very" is the Hebrew *'étsem* ("bone") ; by
a natural idiom in the *bone* of a thing is in the *very*
thing itself. "Three" is feminine by attraction with a
feminine noun; the masculine would be the normal
form (K. S. 312 a; 349 a; G. K. 97 c). *Ba'*, the perfect
"came," points to the moment when their entering
was an accomplished fact: "had come" is a permissible
rendering.

14. *Kol*, in this and the next two verses, regularly
signifies not "all," for not *"all* beasts," etc., entered,
but rather "of every sort." *Chayyah* (collective)
"wild beasts" are here mentioned for the first time as
entering the ark. Previously the generic word "animals" *(behemah)* included them. Here now *behemah*
must mean the "domestic animals," as in chapter one.
We have rendered *rémes* "creeper," as in v. 8. In 1:24
we had rendered the same word "reptiles," pointing
out the relative inadequacy of either translation. In
any case, land creepers or reptiles only are meant
here, because no provision needed to be made for the
various forms of aquatic creatures.

After the general expression, "every sort of bird
according to its kind," comes an apposition which in

Hebrew reads: "every little bird of every wing," or even better: "every sort of little bird of every sort of wing." Meek has found a very happy rendering for the phrase by the expression: "everything with feathers and wings." That is practically what is meant. Insects are manifestly included under this head.

15. This verse generalizes very broadly: those that had "the breath of life" in them "came" to Noah. Again their voluntary approach, seeking refuge from an impending calamity whose nearness was sensed, is emphasized. Even their appearing in pairs seems to have been providentially arranged. When critics draw the phrase "on this very" day down through v. 14 and 15 and make the author say that Noah's family as well as all beasts entered in *one* day, and then speak of the man J, supposedly the author of the section, as here "furnishing an example of his love of the marvelous," we may well dispose of the matter by calling it an example of critical captiousness.

16. This verse really presents an anacoluthon because of the absolute nominative which stands first: *habba'îm*, "those that came." Then "male and female" step in to become the regular subject of *ba'û*, "they came in." However, the anacoluthon makes very smooth reading and not only presents no difficulty but stresses with particular clearness the voluntary approach of those whom Noah was bidden to gather. So a solution presented itself in very simple fashion to what must at first have appeared to Noah as an insuperable difficulty.

God, the awe-inspiring Ruler of all, *Elohîm*, laid all these commandments upon Noah by virtue of His supreme authority. In the same breath, with skillful use of the proper divine name, the author asserts that it was *Yahweh*, the always gracious and faithful, who "closed the door after him," so guarding him against possible assaults of the wicked, as well as preventing him from attempting to show ill-timed mercy to last-minute penitents.

17.   **And the Flood came upon the earth forty days, and the waters mounted and lifted up the ark and it went along high above the earth.**

Since v. 24 is about to speak of the prevailing of the Flood for 150 days, it would place this verse needlessly at variance with this later statement to make it read: "the Flood *was* upon the earth forty days," (A. V.). Rather, the original meaning of *hayah* prevails here: "it became" or, as we rendered, it "came.' This is the first statement in reference to the increase of the waters, and it asserts that forty days the waters were in process of rising — as long as the rain continued its heavy downpour. Naturally: "the waters mounted" (*rabbah* = "grew great"). It was not long before sufficient water was displaced to "lift up" *(nasa')* the ark. So it "went high" *(rûm =* "be high") above the earth.

Now follows what rhetoric might call an account abounding in tautologies. But these are not idle, verbose repetitions. As Delitzsch well puts it: "These tautologies paint the dreadful monotony of the endless and vast expanse of the waters which covered the earth." This must, therefore, be described as a very effective adaptation of style to subject matter, as the reverent Bible reader has always felt it to be, and as the child in its day already sensed when it listened to the telling narrative.

18-20.   **The waters grew mighty and mounted greatly over the earth and the ark floated along upon the face of the waters. But the waters grew extremely mighty upon the earth, and all the high mountains which are under all the heavens were covered. Fifteen cubits and upwards did the waters grow mighty so that the mountains were covered.**

The first verb *gabhar* recurs in each of these three verses. Its root meaning is "to be strong." Here it could be rendered "prevail" (A. V.) ; Luther: *ueberhand nehmen.* Our own rendering "grew mighty" merely retains the basic meaning but is not to be preferred to "prevail." Our reason for rendering thus is that thus one shade of meaning is at least not lost sight of, namely that these mighty waters did actually prove themselves "mighty." What power behind raging, surging waters! On the one hand, how God's power in keeping the ark amid such dangers stands out the more distinctly! On the other hand, what opportunity for working vast geologic changes lie dormant in these "mighty" waters! The native force of *gabhar* is enhanced by one *me'odh,* "exceedingly" in v. 18 and by the doubling of the same adverb — a Hebrew superlative — in v. 19. When will geologists begin to notice these basic facts? It will be noticed that we are letting *me'odh* of v. 18 modify two verbs; for in the light of v. 19 it may well be construed thus. *Rabhah,* the second verb, means "to become much." Of necessity, under the circumstances the ark could not remain stationary. Therefore, the next verb, *halakh,* it "went," that is to say, it "floated" upon the face of the waters.

19. A measure of the waters is now made by comparison with the only available standard for such waters — the mountains. They are said to have been "covered." Not a few merely but "all the high mountains under all the heavens." One of these expressions alone would almost necessitate the impression that the author intends to convey the idea of the absolute uni-versality of the Flood, e. g., "all the high mountains." Yet since "all" is known to be used in a relative sense, the writer removes all possible ambiguity by adding the phrase "under all the heavens." A double "all" *(kol)* cannot allow for so relative a sense. It almost constitutes a Hebrew superlative. So we believe that

the text disposes of the question of the universality of the Flood.

By way of objection to this interpretation those who believe in a limited flood, which extended perhaps as far as mankind may have penetrated at that time, urge the fact that *kol* is used in a relative sense, as is clearly the case in passages such as 41:57; Exod. 9:25; 10:15; Deut. 2:25; I Kings 10:24. However, we still insist that this fact could overthrow a single *kol*, never a double *kol*, as our verse has it.

If in this connection the fact be urged that the fifteen cubits — half the height of the ark — mentioned v. 20 as the distance which the waters rose above the mountains, must represent roughly the draught of the ark, or the depth to which it sank into the waters, and must have been calculated according to the height of Mt. Ararat upon which the ark finally rested, we can accept this interpretation as reasonable. But the objection continues: Mt. Ararat (or Mt. Masis) has an altitude of 16,916 feet, whereas peaks in the Himalayas rise about 29,000, and others, too, surpass Mt. Ararat; how can the fact that Mt. Ararat was submerged point to the submersion of these peaks? We hold that the solution lies in this that those few peaks that rise above Mt. Ararat were unknown both to the people of the days of the Flood as well as to the contemporaries of Moses. All the mountains they knew of were covered. In any case, as Keil indicates, such mountain peaks in relation to the whole earth would amount to no more than a few pinpoints on a globe, and are disregarded because of the limited horizon of the ancients.

For here is a consideration that weighs very strongly in this connection: a flood of more than 16,000 feet, that is to say, of more than three miles in depth could not be confined to any portion of the earth but must necessarily spread itself out over the entire earth's surface. The counterclaim that such a mass

of water would have wrought the complete destruction
of the earth by its tremendous weight is offset by the
fact that in proportion to the earth as a whole such
a Flood would mean no more than a profuse sweat on
the human body.

However, other considerations are urged against
the universality of the Flood, such as the physical impossibility of transporting certain animals which are
distinctive for the country of Australia, such as the
kangaroo, and having them cross vast oceans and
lands to find Noah and then to return by an equally
difficult route to their remote habitation after the
Flood. By way of answer we point to two difficulties
which lie in the way of maintaining this argument
consistently. The one, there is absolutely no way of
telling how the various continents were formed and
shaped in days of old and whether they were more
intimately connected with one another prior to the
Flood and immediately thereafter. To assume that
Australia lay isolated in days of old as it does now is
merely an assumption. The other consideration is
that we cannot even tell how the fauna of Australia
came to take foothold there in any case. The same
argument that would not allow creatures to find their
way to Australia after the Flood apparently would not
allow creatures to find their way there in any case
unless these creatures be autochthonous.

But still it is maintained that when the Scriptures
refer to the Flood they speak only of the universal
destruction of mankind and not of its universal extent.
The passages employed are Isa. 54:9; Matt. 24:39;
II Pet. 2:5 and 3:6 and the apocryphal passage Wisd.
10:4. However, if these passages be scanned closely,
it will be seen that in none of them is there occasion
to refer to other than the human beings as objects of
destruction. But silence on the subject of the destruction of the rest of the physical world is by no means
proof that the physical world was not included as a

whole. Besides, no one actually knows to what extent men had spread abroad upon the face of the earth. The general assumption still seems to be that in seventeen centuries men had gotten but little beyond the region of the Tigris and the Euphrates, and this when the known longevity of at least some men gave the human race opportunity for more rapid expansion. Men may have colonized the Western Hemisphere before the Flood, for all we know.

21-23. All flesh that moved upon the earth expired, including birds and domestic animals and wild beasts and all swarms that swarmed upon the earth, as well as all mankind. Everything that had the breath of the spirit of life in its nostrils, of everything that was on the dry land died. And He blotted out everything that existed upon the face of the ground, from man to beast and creeping thing and to the bird of the heavens, and they were wiped out from the earth. And there was left only Noah and those that were with him in the ark.

The words used in v. 21 and 22 are chosen as reminders of God's threat spoken in 6:17. For there God spoke of "all flesh," of its "expiring," of "the spirit of life." So the phraseology aims to chronicle the literal fulfillment of what God had foretold. Besides, wherever terms of classification reminiscent of the Creation Story are used, the similarity of terms is designed and by no means accidental. As these broad class terms (domestic animals, wild animals, reptiles, birds) cover all that God created, except, of course, the fish, so the Flood is to be portrayed as a disaster equally broad in its scope, affecting all animal life that was created, with the exception of what was in the ark. "Flesh" *(basar)* here refers to all forms of life as perishable. *Ramas,* usually rendered "to creep," must here bear the broader meaning "to move," as in 1:21 and 8:19. Verse 21 comes to a climax in the assertion that "all mankind" also perished.

22. This verse dwells upon the fact that "all
that had the breath of the spirit of life died," because
the waters of the Flood naturally stifled the breath
of all being. Still, the expression used, though it includes mankind, is not the same as that used in 2:7
in reference to mankind only, where God is said to
have breathed into man's nostrils "the breath of life,"
nishmath chayyim. Here in v. 22 the expression used
is "the breath of the spirit of life," not the distinctive
breath that animates man but the breath by which
the Spirit of life, God's Holy Spirit, animated living
beings. A fine distinction of terms is observed. At the
same time it is clearly pointed out that all created
life retains its life only by the animating, sustaining
power of God's Spirit. The frequent recurrence of
the word "all" emphasizes the completeness of the
destructive work of the Flood.

The *be* of v. 21 is called the *Beth sphaerae,* that
is to say, the *be* that marks the sphere within which
things were done, and it is the equivalent of a partitive
genitive (K. S. 279 a). Our translation renders it:
"including" (Meek). Criticism, unwilling often to
penetrate into the meaning of unusual terms, renders
the strange verdict on the expression "the breath of
the spirit of life" that it "is an unexampled combination arising from a confusion of a phrase of J *nishmath chayyim* with one of P *rûach chayyim*" (Skinner). This amounts to the statement: if the author
or redactor had known his Hebrew as the critic does,
he would not have written thus.

23. As the Hebrew text stands, and it need not
be corrected, it suddenly introduces the great Author
of this catastrophe without specific mention of Him
by any name, merely as "He." Therefore *wayyimach*
may well be read as apopopated Kal imperfect, as the
Masoretes intended it to be. *Yeqûm* (from *qûm*)
signifies all that "has existence," or literally, "all that
stands up" (*Bestand,* K. W.). With one more solemn,

if not intentionally dreary, repetition of the classes that perished this part of the account closes, exempting specifically Noah and those with him in the ark from the universal destruction.

24. And the waters prevailed upon the earth one hundred and fifty days.

To impress the reader, in a measure at least, with the great length of time during which the waters maintained their maximum height, the writer lets the statement concerning the 150 days conclude this portion of the Flood story. What a dreary and monotonous, if not dreadful, sight to behold nothing other than the blank expanse of water for so great a length of time! From the idea of *gabhar*, "be mighty," "conquer," we derive the thought at this point that the conquering, dominating force over all the earth was the mighty mass of water. Since the verb *gabhar* is used (v. 18) of the time before the waters reached their maximum height and not only to mark this maximum, we feel sure that the 150 days must include the forty days of rain mentioned v. 12.

A flaw in the critical method is apparent in reference to v. 22 and 23. Formal statistical enumerations are a characteristic mark of P. Then according to all tokens especially v. 23, like v. 14 and v. 21, ought to be assigned to P. Instead it is given to J. Reason? Otherwise J would have no statement to the effect that all creatures were destroyed. All we can say in reference to such a mode of dealing with sources is that it is a clever manipulation; but it should not be called scientific procedure.

HOMILETICAL SUGGESTIONS

In connection with the preceding chapter we already pointed out that the first five verses of this chapter fit in best with the third section of chapter six. It seems to us that the rest of this chapter, namely v. 6-24, should again be used as a unit.

Whatever treatment of these verses one may use, the thought of judgment must predominate, a judgment so solemn and awful that perhaps no other Scripture is quite as strong from this point of view. We suggest as themes: "Whatsoever a man soweth that shall be also reap," or still more pointed: "Be not deceived, God is not mocked." Then one may take as starting-point the thought of II Pet. 3:5-7 and treat the Flood as a type of the Final Judgment, a thought also suggested by the Savior's Word: "As were the days of Noah, so shall be the coming of the Son of man" (Matt. 24:37).

CHAPTER VIII

The Abatement of the Flood; Noah's Exit
from the Ark

The Flood story proceeds with a simple narration utterly devoid of all extraneous matter and of all ornamentation — a type of epic simplicity which in itself is a guarantee of absolute veracity and historical fidelity.

1-3a. And God remembered Noah and all the wild animals and domestic animals which were with him in the ark, and God caused a wind to pass over the earth and the waters abated. Also the fountains of the deep were stopped and the windows of the heavens; and the pouring rain from heaven was restrained. And the waters subsided from upon the earth more and more.

Behind the working of nature, according to the Scriptures, stands God. In perfect harmony with this principle the subsiding of the Flood is attributed to God's remembering Noah. In this expressive sense "remember" *(zakhar)* is often used (9:15, 16; Exod. 2:24; 6:15; Gen. 30:22; I Sam. 1:11), implying a "remembering with kindness, granting requests, protecting, delivering" (B D B). It would never occur to one familiar with Hebrew to draw the conclusion from this statement that for a time God had forgotten Noah. Nor is the expression so distinctly a characteristic of the portions assigned to P, as Strack intimates, for its use is also attributed to E (Gen. 30:22) to JE (Exod. 32:13) or to H (Lev. 26:42). This activity, though often ascribed to Yahweh, is here attributed to Elohim, for, as the sequel goes on to show, "wild and domestic animals" are also remembered, and God's work under this head is in reality analogous to His creative work, for it involves the preservation and the multiplying of all manner of life upon the earth. "Elohim" more appropriately describes God in His creative and sustaining capacity. So, again, we have here not a stereotyped use of divine names but rather a discriminating use according to their basic meaning. Incidentally, there is a tender touch in the account that describes the Almighty God as having concern for all His creatures (cf. Ps. 147:9 and Jonah 4:11).

As God employed natural agencies, operating with unusual potency, to bring about the Flood, so similar agencies are brought into use to remove the Flood waters. However, since it was necessary on the one hand to have the power of these agencies increased or accentuated to produce results as vast as those here recorded, it follows without further specific statement that the causes at work to remove the waters will have been more highly potentialized. Procksch, therefore, has no need of making the criticism: "that the wind should have made the whole earth dry in about five months is a very childlike conception." The least bit of readiness to interpret the verse in harmony with all the facts recorded would have checked his uncalled-for criticism. Besides, as we are at once told, other agencies co-operated to secure the desired result. But, we are sure, as an element of the miraculous entered into the matter of the coming of the Flood, so a similar element contributed to its abatement. So eager is the writer to draw the result achieved to our attention that he at once begins to speak of the fact that "the waters abated."

2. Then he proceeds to fit into place the other auxiliary agencies: a) "the fountains of the deep were stopped" and b) "the windows of the heavens." Since 7:11 had told us of the opening of these sources of water, the author owes us a statement as to whether these continued open. But since the closing of these two cannot subtract from the waters but merely prevents further increase, the mention of these two

is brought in as an afterthought, even as is the third contributory agency, the "pouring rain" *(géshem)* mentioned previously 7:12. These three together, then, may be regarded as causes contributing only negatively to the abatement of the waters. The critics, bent on discerning various documents and a measure of conflict between these documents, fail to discern the simple analysis of the relation of v. 1 and 2 and claim to have a clear indication of various sources that were not sufficiently harmonized at this point. In fact, the critical analysis assigns to J (1 b?) 2 b, 3 a, (4 b?) 6-12, 13 b. To P: 1, 2 a, 3 b-5, 13 a. 14. Criticism claims the possible original sequence in J to have been: 6 a, 2 b, 1 b, 3 a, 4.

The opening verb *yissakherû*, "were stopped," is quite naturally masculine since the first subject "fountains" is masculine, even though a feminine follows ("windows"). See K. S. 349 m.

3. The fact that the waters subsided with marked rapidity and not as an ordinary wind could make them do, is indicated by a strong form of expression in the Hebrew which our rendering ("more and more") reproduces very imperfectly. The double infinitive absolute *(halôkh washôbh)* appended to the finite verb would yield a connection which might be rendered: "they subsided going and returning," which amounts to: "they subsided with a very pronounced fall." See G. K. 113 r on these absolute infinitives. Strack misses the force of the double infinitive when he renders it *allmaehlich* = "gradually." Meek does better, but has too weak an expression in "steadily."

3b, 4. **The waters declined after the expiration of one hundred and fifty days, so that the ark came to rest upon the mountains of Ararat in the seventh month, on the seventeenth day of the month.**

Comparing 7:24, we discern that the one hundred and fifty days here mentioned are the same here and

there. The total length of time that the waters dominated the earth without suffering abatement is here
under consideration. About the first thing to happen
when the abatement began must have been the grounding of the ark (*wattánach* = "and she came to rest").
It could well have been on the first day of the abatement
because, according to 7:20 a drop of only fifteen cubits
was necessary, and, surely, the waters must have fallen
more rapidly than that. But if we assume that the
first day of abatement brought with it the grounding
of the ark, we must assume that the highest peak of
the entire vicinity is the one under consideration, according to 7:20. The only difficulty encountered by
this assumption is that this highest peak, Masis, commonly called Ararat, is the most inaccessible of all, and
the problem of bringing all the animals down from
this height must have been not inconsiderable, yet
within the realm of the possible. Divine providence,
of course, displays itself gloriously in all that befalls
Noah and the ark — in the mere fact that the ark
came to rest on *terra firma;* but primarily also in the
fact that so huge a structure came to rest on an even
keel, as it were, where a pronounced tilt in the course
of its settling might have resulted in the perishing
of all.

However, some confusion has grown out of the
customary interpretation put upon the expression "the
mountains of Ararat." This is usually interpreted as
though it read "upon Mount Ararat." However, the
Hebrew has "mountains" *(harey)*, the plural of in-
definiteness as in Judg. 12:7 b, where naturally the
translation runs: "in *one of* the cities of Gilead" but
the original has "in the cities of Gilead," (cf. K. S.
265 c). Likewise, in Biblical usage Ararat is a country; see II Kings 19:37 = Isa. 37:38; Jer. 51:27. He
that feels he cannot accept the idea that the ark landed
on the magnificent peak Masis, may take the other
traditional view, offered by the Targum, that it was

the "Kardu mountains," i. e., the mountains in Kurdistan, southwest of Lake Van, "commanding a view of the Mesopotamian plain." The island of Ceylon, as some hold, cannot even be considered. But whichever of the two views offered above one may accept, in either case a providential factor can clearly be observed in this location. For it marks the spot from which the human race was to spread abroad. From several points of view this location is central. Access to the Mesopotamian plain is easy. Asia Minor presents itself on the other hand. Syria, Arabia and Africa lie conveniently to the south and southwest. Asia is accessible to the north and northeast. Europe is approachable through Asia Minor; India through Mesopotamia. Here is the scriptural center from which the nations went abroad over the face of the earth.

On the short "a," in the Kal of *yachserû* (v. 3) see G. K. 63 f. On the form *wattánach* (v. 4), G. K. 72 t.

5, 6. And the waters remained, decreasing continually, until the tenth month, and in the tenth month, on the first day of the month, the mountain tops came into view. And it came to pass after forty (more) days Noah opened the window that he had made in the ark.

Even as expressions were multiplied in chapter seven to give an impression of the marvelous increase of the waters until the waters prevailed over all, so expressions are multiplied to help us grasp the magnitude and the rapidity of the decrease. The abatement of the waters may not be classed as merely normal, brought about by ordinary processes of evaporation. The expression here used is: "the waters remained, decreasing continually." The *hayû* cannot have the two following absolute infinitives joined with it and be treated as mere auxiliary, thus: "they were decreasing." Absolute infinitives are not used thus, nor is the verb *hayah* (cf. K. S. 402 b). *Hayah* must here have a meaning like "exist" or "remain." But as "the waters remained," the decrease went on rapidly: *halôkh wechasôr* literally: "going and decreasing" — an emphatic combination.

The chronology of the Flood is complete for all practical purposes. The major items discovered by the occupants of the ark are listed. So on the first day of the tenth month "the mountain tops came into view," literally: "the heads of the mountain were seen." We prefer not to render "were seen," for that might imply that they were visible before but just did not happen to be seen, which certainly was not what the writer meant.

6. Forty days after the appearance of the mountain peaks "Noah opened the window that he had made in the ark." We can conjecture little that is satisfactory about the nature, size, and location of this window. The name *challôn* must be from the root *challal* meaning "to pierce." It must have been cut in the side wall. It must have been of such a kind that it could be opened. We wonder chiefly at the fact that Noah did not remove it sooner. Our lack of knowledge of details makes it impossible to furnish an answer. We prefer to render as above, making the clause "which he had made" clearly modify the noun "window," as without doubt it is designed to, even though it follows the word ark in Hebrew. There would, however, be no point in asserting here that Noah had made the *ark*. A. V. is ambiguous.

7-12. **And he sent forth a raven, which went flying back and forth until the waters were dried up from upon the earth. Then he sent forth a dove from him to see if the waters had abated from upon the face of the ground. But the dove found no resting-place for the sole of her foot, and so she returned to him to the ark, for water was upon the surface of all the earth, and he put out his hand and**

took her and brought her to him into the ark.   Then
he waited again another seven days and again sent
forth a dove from the ark; and the dove came back
to him at evening, and, lo, there was a fresh olive
leaf in her beak.   So Noah knew that the waters
were abated from off the earth.   Then he waited
again another seven days and sent forth a dove, but
she did not again return to him.

The open window must have been of a kind that
did not afford a very wide view.   In fact, Noah was
unable to determine to what extent the waters had
abated.   The only solution for the difficulty occurring
to us is the possibility of a window high under the
eaves, but the eaves projecting rather far so that a
bit of ground, perhaps a nearby ledge of the mountain,
was all that could be seen, and this ledge prevented
the view into the valley or out into the plain.   So Noah,
thoroughly conversant with the ways and habits of
birds, uses them for securing additional information.
First he sends forth a raven — the article *ha'orebh*
is the generic article (K. S. 300 a) ; we say "a raven."
Should the bird fail to return — for the impulse to get
free from the ark may have stirred strongly in all
occupants — Noah knows the bird can subsist; for,
being a scavenger bird, it will find carcases here and
there.   Its failure to return tells him that at least there
is no more a blank waste of water, and that the waters
have subsided materially.   One can hardly conceive
how painful the suspense in the ark was growing at
this time.   The actions of the raven are described as:
he "went flying back and forth," literally: "he went
forth, going forth and coming back."   This might mean
that he occasionally perched on the ark, but how could
Noah have known that?   More likely it means, since
yatsa' is used with the absolute infinitive, that it merely
flew back and forth.   The occupants of the ark may
have heard its cawing, now on one side, now on another.   Since this bird is not particular as to where it

perches, the slimy surface available here or there will not have repelled it.

8. Another bird is chosen for a similar purpose to convey further information. For the dove (*yônah* with generic article, as in v. 7) is a more cleanly bird, which will not alight in places that are not clean. That seven days had elapsed since the sending of the raven appears from the use of the words "again" and "another" in v. 10. That such comparatively long periods elapsed between successive sendings shows that, in the face of all natural desire to be informed as to how far the abatement had progressed, Noah had possessed his soul in patience, the patience of faith. When this cleanly bird "found no resting-place for the sole of her foot," she returned to Noah before evening, strong-winged bird though she was. This conveyed the information to Noah that water was still upon the surface of all the earth. With the insertion of details, for it was a memorable deed and indicative of the kindly relationship existing between this man of God and the lesser creature, the narrative tells us how "he put out his hand and took her and brought her to him into the ark." Above, the dove (v. 8) had been sent forth *me'ittô*, "from with him," a phrase not used in reference to the raven, apparently because the tame friendly dove stood closer to him than the raven. Now the dove is said to return "to him." These are niceties about the narrative which commentators scarcely seem to notice. The verb for "he put out his hand" is *shalach* in the *Piel*. It is the same verb in the Hebrew idiom "to send forth" (v. 7), where Meek renders, very appropriately, "release."

10. Each venture at sending forth a bird has yielded some definite information. The dove is still the most suitable messenger to send forth. Whether the article before the word now designates the same dove that was sent first or is still the generic article is somewhat difficult to determine. We incline to the

opinion that it points to the same dove. But that the intervals of time are in each case seven days suggests, on the one hand, that in antediluvian days time was apparently reckoned by weeks. On the other, there seems great likelihood that so godly a man as Noah will on each occasion have accompanied the sending forth of the bird by prayer. But that does not yet warrant the conclusion of T. Lewis that this necessitates that the days involved were "days held sacred for prayers and religious rest," that is to say, antediluvian Sabbaths. But that Noah waits no longer than seven days in each instance indicates that he was also aware of the exceptionally rapid decline of the waters. He expected that seven days might materially alter the situation.

11. In this case he was correct in his anticipation. The dove stayed away all day. She had found rest for the sole of her foot, for she would hardly remain on the wing for an entire day. She might perhaps have stayed away but for the urge to return to those of her kind and for something she was driven to do by the guidance of God to give Noah a further token of life returning to the earth. Doves are not considerate birds who bring men tokens of the state of affairs upon the earth. That this dove brought a leaf in its beak is to be attributed alone to an impulse divinely directed. The "fresh olive leaf" may be used by synecdoche for a small twig, although that is not essential. A single leaf could be identified and would serve its purpose. "Fresh" *(taraph)* indicates that it had just been plucked and was not an old one swimming in the waters. So, being fresh, it pointed to an olive tree then in foliage. Though these trees will grow in water, yet they are found only below certain levels. So Noah could conjecture about how far the water level must at least have gone down into the valleys. Whatever could lead Procksch to claim because of the olive leaf that "we again have a Palestinian landscape before us" is more than appears to our understanding. Olive

trees are found in many oriental countries and also, according to the authority of ancient writers, in the land of Armenia. The touch added to the narrative by the phrase "at evening" is suggestive. Just as the hope for the return of the dove has about died down, the bird puts in its appearance.

12. Each time the experiment yielded some result. It practically was a barometer for those immured in the ark; a barometer indicating the fall of the waters. It was therefore worthy to be repeated once more. The dove's failure to return testifies eloquently to the practically complete subsidence of the waters.

On v. 7-12 note the following grammatical facts. Verse 7 *yebhosheth* is an irregular segolate infinitive used as object of the preposition *'adh* (K. S. 228). In v. 9 the negative *lo'* creeping in between the "and" and the verb results in the abandoning of the use of the imperfect with *waw conversive.* "Another," *'acherîm,* may refer to the idea of doubling as well as to the idea of "different." (K. S. 315 p).

13, 14. **And it came to pass by the first day of the first month of the six hundred and first year of Noah's life that the waters were dried up from off the earth; so Noah removed the covering of the ark and looked abroad and, lo, the face of the ground was dry. But by the twenty-seventh day of the second month the earth was dry.**

As much as is needed of a Flood chronology, relatively complete, is given in this account. Here are the last items of it. By the time the first day of the year comes about, this being now the six hundred and first year of Noah's life, it is quite in order to take stock again as to how things stand. It could practically be said that the earth was dry. This new juncture in the narrative is introduced, as so often in Hebrew, by a *wayhi,* "and it came to pass." Noah, who had been extremely cautious to do nothing that might in the least conflict with the divine purpose, now felt that circumstances permitted the removal of the roof of the ark, here called "covering," *mikhseh* from kasah, "to cover." The fact that the tabernacle had a covering of skin, which is also designated by this word, should not induce interpreters to conclude that the ark had a covering of skin — altogether too frail a substance to withstand the downpour of rain that this vast structure was exposed to. When the covering was removed, Noah discerned that at least the surface, i. e., "face," of the ground was dry — a fact so significant after its being long covered by waters as to warrant its being stressed by the emphatic "lo." But, of course, ordinary common sense told Noah that after a Flood that had continued so long and wrought such vast upheavals the ground could not yet be dry enough to allow the occupants of the ark to leave. Instead of an object clause after "he saw" we find a *hinneh* ("behold") clause (K. S. 361 g). On the Hifil form *wayyásar* see G. K. 72 t.

14. Now the statement follows that the earth itself as a whole *(ha'árets)* actually was dry by the twenty-seventh day of the second month. A comparison with 7:11 nets the result that the total duration of the Flood was one year and ten days, at least that was the length of time that Noah was confined in the ark.

Among the various difficulties encountered by the critics after they have the account separated into parts according to the sources J and E, are some that can with difficulty be accounted for even by the explanation that they are the work of the so-called Redactor. So on v. 13 they confess to be puzzled as to why J should not in his account have had a statement to the effect that the ark grounded. Apparently, according to J Noah leaves the ark without its ever having settled on *terra firma!* The definite findings of criticism apparently are far from being as satisfactory and as unimpeachable as the critics would have us believe.

15-17. **And God spake to Noah saying: Go
forth from the ark, thou and thy wife and thy sons
and thy sons' wives with thee.** **Bring forth with
thee every animal of all flesh that is with thee including birds and cattle and all creeping things that
move upon the earth, and let them spread abroad
on the earth and be fruitful and multiply upon the
earth.**

Throughout this whole account Noah appears as
a man who walked with God. He did not venture to
do things according to his own thinking. He entered
the ark when he was bidden; he left it when God told
him to. The future of the whole race was tied up
with what he did, and he knew it. If now this speaking
(v. 15) is ascribed to *Elohîm* = God, and not to Yahweh, the point of view of the writer is very plain.
The things that God ordains are like a new creation
after the devastation of the Flood. As then the basic
command went out, "Be fruitful and multiply and fill
the earth" (1:22), so now (v. 17). As God, the Almighty Creator, who is to be feared, is the one to whom
such basic creative activity is ascribed, so now. We
see no reason for the different order in which the
persons in the ark are listed v. 15: Noah and his wife
first, then the sons and their wives, where previously
6:18 and 7:7 the sequence was: Noah, sons, his wife,
their wives — no reason, we say, except such natural
variation in relating things as all authors employ. A
weakness of the critical position: on this point 6:18
and 7:7 are identical; yet 6:18 is ascribed to P and
7:7 to J.

17. The opening word *kol-ha(ch)chayyah*, of
course, is the broadest term, "every animal." The
"beth of enumeration" that follows we have rendered
"including." God gives specific and detailed orders so
as to prevent misunderstanding. Besides, all creatures
are not simply to be liberated to trot forth from the
ark in wild confusion, which confusion might have

resulted in the death of the weaker creatures. They are to be "brought forth." (The suggestion of the Masoretes that the regular Hifil imperative *hôtse'* we read *haytse'* is not quite clear.) Then, as for·the first creatures that God created, the basic ordinance is given: "Be fruitful and multiply upon the earth." Contrasting this word again with 1:22, we notice that "fill the earth" is not a part of it. This seems to point to the fact that creatures originally multiplied to the point where they were more numerous — schools of fish, droves of wild beasts — as also seems to be indicated by the vast quantities of fish and trilobites that are found imbedded as fossil remains in many such deposits, as well as by the huge number of mammoths and ivory tusks found in North Siberian deposits.

18, 19. And Noah went forth, also his sons and his wife and his sons' wives with him. Also all the animals, every creeping thing and every bird, in fact, everything that moveth upon the earth went forth from the ark according to their species.

With great circumstantiality all details are faithfully recorded, because every step is of great importance to the future of the race and of all creatures. It must be admitted that such a mode of presentation sets forth the record of these events with fine dignity. Again, merely to speak of a different source, blurs this fine point. Cf. the remarks on v. 15.

19. In spite of the dignified precision of his statements the writer is not coldly stereotyped in his expressions. The same ground is covered as in v. 17 but with expressions slightly different. Here the participle *rômes* bears the general meaning found already in 1:28 and in 7:21. The added phrase "according to their species," though modifying the verb "went forth," is not to be pressed too closely, as though in the narrower sense it described the very manner of going forth, as though they went forth strictly only by species. We

rather believe that what is meant is to remind us that the great variety of species all went forth intact. None had been lost. God's purpose to save them all by the ark had been successful. The *le* before "species" is the *le normae* (K. S. 332 q).

20. **And Noah built an altar to Yahweh, and he took of all clean cattle and of all clean birds and offered a burnt offering upon the altar.**

Taking only the expressions of v. 21, some regard the purpose of this sacrifice to be only propitiation. In view of the whole preceding situation and the natural feeling of gratitude that must have possessed the heart of any one, or any group, that find they alone have been spared in a universal catastrophe, we find the ruling out of the idea of thanksgiving in connection with this sacrifice to be preposterous. The purposes of thanksgiving and of propitiation blend in this sacrifice. It is, indeed, the first altar of which the Scriptures tell. That Gen. 4 does not mention an altar may signify nothing: the sons may have been using their father's altar, and so none needed to be built. To deduce from this first mention of an altar that prior to the Flood altars to raise up offerings to heaven were not thought of because God's presence was still manifest in the Garden, as the place of revelation, is building up too much conjecture on the mere silence of Scripture. We do not know whether the Garden continued to be God's place of manifestation after the Fall. We do not know whether altars originated now or in Adam's time. *Mizbéach* strictly means "the place of slaughter." This altar is raised to *Yahweh,* because Noah is mindful of the gracious fidelity which God in the person of Yahweh so mercifully displayed. This is an added argument for the fact that the offering was one of thanksgiving. The expression "he took of" could here very well be rendered: "he took *one of*" — as K. C. actually renders it; cf. 3:6. Under the circumstances the seventh one (7:8) of the original seven, the unmated one, could best serve the purpose. If the definition of what was clean or unclean corresponded roughly to what the Mosaic law defined later, as we have every reason to believe, cf. Lev. 11 and Deut. 14, this must have been a generous sacrifice and in proportion to the number of creatures extant the most liberal sacrifice ever offered. But, of a certainty, never was there a man who had greater occasion to render hearty thanks to God. *Wayyá'al* (G. K. 72 t), "and he offered," from *'alah,* "to go up," in the *Hifil* must mean, "to cause to go up." The object to be supplied in thought is not the beast which is brought up upon the altar but the smoke of the sacrifice, as the use of the verb *'alah* in Judg. 20:40; Jer. 48:15 and Amos 4:10 indicates. Consequently, the derived noun *'olah* signifies "a burnt offering going up in smoke" (K. C.).

The true piety of the man Noah would be expected to give some true token as in this sacrifice. This sacrifice presents one of the most solemn scenes of all history: round about, the earth which is rapidly rejuvenating; the background, the most awful catastrophe in the annals of mankind; above, the true and faithful Yahweh, who is man's only Hope.

21. **When Yahweh smelled the tranquillizing odor, He said within His heart: Never again will I curse the ground for man's sake, because the imagination of man's heart is evil from his youth; never again will I smite all living things as I have done.**

The Hifil *wayyárach* is explained G. K. 72 t. *Nîchóach* comes from the root *nûach,* "to rest." It, therefore, means "restful," "soothing." Though we have used the synonym "tranquillizing" above (B D B), it appears to us as a bit too strong. "Pleasant" should cover the case: *angenehm* (K. W.). He viewed the sentiments behind the sacrifice with satisfaction. For in addition to the thoughts expressed above, that

namely the burnt offering set forth the idea of gratitude and of propitiation, it must be borne in mind that
the chief thought behind an *'olah* was to typify the
idea of complete self-consecration, even as the offering
in its entirety ascended to God in the fire. "Within
his heart" is a more expressive way of stating the
reflexive, "to himself," cf. 24:45. The substance of
what He said is revealed more fully in the following
chapter. For the present the Spirit of revelation makes
it known that this resolve was made by God as an
answer to the prayer embodied in the sacrifice. Here
again in this sacrifice or prayer the word was fulfilled,
where it is written: "The effectual fervent prayer of
the righteous man availeth much." Such blessings for
the race were secured by the prayers of godly Noah.

First Yahweh promises in mercy, as His name
indicates, that there is never to be a recurrence of the
Flood. This is described in the words: "Never again
will I curse." Spoken directly after the Flood, this
statement must refer to the Flood as in a sense a
divine curse. The fact that the account has not
hitherto called the Flood a "curse" does not alter the
situation. Nothing worse ever befell the earth. To
think of the curse of 3:17 as removed at this point lies
entirely outside of the connection. Besides, we should
have difficulty in determining wherein the post-diluvian
earth actually possesses an advantage over the antediluvian. The reason advanced for sparing the earth
is much like that given in 6:5 for destroying the earth.
The difference, that this verse says "from his youth,"
is little different from that of 6:5 "only evil continually." That can hardly be the point here (contra
Keil). Rather, man's iniquity may at one time be ample
cause for destroying the earth. That catastrophic
destruction may be done with such emphasis as to
constitute a lesson for all times. From that point
onward man's total depravity, which is also his pitiable
weakness, may also serve as good ground for not

repeating the punishment. The seeming contradiction, which already puzzled the fathers, solves itself by the simple fact that one and the same truth may, according to varying circumstances, be regarded from different viewpoints. Of course, here again in its earliest pages the Bible gives indubitable proof of the natural depravity of the human heart. "Youth" *(ne'urîm)* is the Hebrew plural expressing a state or condition. We feel that the Hebrew expression, "I will not add again to curse," is covered quite adequately by our idiom: "Never again will I curse." The second statement substitutes "smite" *(nakhah)* or "strike" for curse. All such visitations are strokes from the hand of the Almighty. This blessed promise amply demonstrates the Yahweh character of God.

22. **As long as the earth shall stand, seed-time and harvest, cold and heat, summer and winter, day and night shall not cease.**

With the initial promise of v. 21 God ties up several more, all in the spirit of the first and displaying in generous measure the same grace that prompted the first. The first takes away the dread fear of a recurrence of the great tragedy. But for that promise man, seeing the evidences of the Flood round about, would long have lived in continual apprehension of a repetition of it. There are other regular features of life on this earth that man can also depend upon as recurring as long as the earth stands, the knowledge of which will impart a stability to life and make for peace of mind more than almost any other temporal gift can. The regular variation of times and seasons here promised is not to be regarded as merely natural, fixed by nature's ordinance, but as an outgrowth of God's specific promise. The first phrase runs thus, according to the Hebrew: "still all the days of the earth." Our rendering or A. V. makes idiomatic English. The basic guarantee covers the regular alternation of "seedtime and harvest." *Zéra'* ("seed") must hear mean "seedtime" as the contrast with "harvest" indicates. Then are mentioned those two elements which primarily contribute to the proper maturing of the grain, "cold and heat." These two, by their regular alternation, delightfully relieve one another and make life more bearable. Then are mentioned those two periods in which cold and heat specifically reign, namely "summer and winter." Over against these seasons again stand those smaller divisions of time, "day and night," which in the very nature of man's constitution are essential to his well-being. So, then, everything between the wide limits of food and sleep and all that makes both possible is fixed by unalterable divine ordinance. However, the opening word implies, since these things continue all the days the earth stands, that the earth is not eternal. It would lead into fruitless speculation to attempt to determine whether this word indicates a radical change of seasons or climate upon the earth after the Flood. If it be argued that "cold and heat" implies something new, for before the Flood a tropical or semi-tropical climate prevailed upon the whole earth, we must admit that we cannot determine what is new and what not among the four pairs mentioned.

On *wacham* (long "a" with the conjunction) see G. K. 104 g.

HOMILETICAL SUGGESTIONS

Attractive as some portions of this chapter are in themselves, like v. 6-12, and of perennial interest for children, yet we do not believe that they lend themselves to separate homiletical treatment. Perhaps it is best to take a larger portion like v. 1-19 and to treat it under a general heading like "God's Faithfulness." They that concentrate on smaller sections may find themselves running into an unseemly trifling or an unwarranted allegorizing. Separate from this first section is the last part of the chapter, either v. 20-22 or 19b-22. Different viewpoints may prevail in the treatment of this last portion.

Either we lay the emphasis on "Noah's sacrifice" of gratitude and reconsecration and let the last two verses constitute the divine reaction to Noah's attitude; or else we may stress such a thing as "God's Promise that there shall never again be a Flood" and all the auxiliary promises that go with it. Then Noah's sacrifice will still be a motivating cause of this promise.

CHAPTER IX

a) The Basic Ordinances Governing the Postdiluvian World (v. 1-7)

Certain things follow as a direct sequel to the Flood. Our chapter supplies the needed facts. First, basic ordinances are set forth by God. These ordinances are more nearly adapted to the altered conditions that prevail since the Flood, or at least they govern situations that are the outgrowth of sin and definitely require regulation. None of the regulations that follow is temporary or ever to be abrogated as long as the present world era continues.

1. And God blessed Noah and his sons and he said to them: Be fruitful, multiply and fill the earth.

The previous chapter closed with a word whereby a fixed sequence of times and seasons was guaranteed for the time of the duration of the world. Now a blessing is laid upon man to make such work to prosper as he shall undertake to do within the times and seasons appointed. First comes what God gives to man (v. 1-3); then follows what God asks of man (v. 4-6). Mercy again takes precedence over justice, even as in 3:15. When God "blesses," He not merely wishes well but imparts good. This blessing is imparted by God, *Elohîm*, inasmuch as it involves His relation to the creature world in His capacity as its Ruler and Sustainer, as in chapter one. It is imparted to the father and his sons, inasmuch as they are the representative heads of the human family. Of course, womankind thus shares in this blessing. The substance of the blessing is the word spoken: "Be fruitful, multiply and fill the earth." In part, like the original creation blessing (1:28) it involves a gift, namely the gift of fruitfulness. That man cannot impart to himself. The second term, "multiply," involves both a gift, viz., the capacity for multiplying, as well as a duty. All things being equal, man is under obligation to propagate his kind. Coupled with this is the divine command to "fill the earth." Mankind is not to concentrate in some few spots but is to spread out so that the earth presents no unoccupied and uncultivated areas. But since this is a part of the blessings, it involves the imparting of such gifts as man needs for the successful carrying out also of this duty. It has been remarked that after the Flood the marching orders under which mankind is advancing no longer include the original "subdue" the earth. For this the explanation seems to be that fallen man no longer has the capacity for subduing the world adequately and well. Sin has marred his makeup. But here men have suggested that the rest of the truth is that the perfect man, Christ Jesus, is He for whom so high a prerogative is now reserved (cf. Eph. 1:22; Heb. 2:8, 9).

Luther rightly dwells on the fact that all these words of God bring encouragement to man in one way or another; for after the Flood the great grief of the survivors at the sad lot of their contemporaries tended to weigh too heavily on their souls. That man might now have assurance of success in his enterprises and so work joyfully God speaks kindly encouragement.

2. **The fear of you and the terror of you shall be upon all the beasts of the earth and upon all the birds of the heavens. All of what creeps upon the ground and all the fish of the sea, into your hand is it given.**

The difference between the tenor of this verse and the beautiful harmony of the original creation is immediately apparent. Now "fear" and "terror" dominate

all creatures. "Terror" is the stronger of the two
words. "Dread" (A. V.) is hardly strong enough. The
pronominal suffixes are like objective genitives (K. S.
37; 336 a). The same two words occur in Deut. 11:25.
There was really need of some such regulation. The
beasts, by their great numbers, as well as because of
their more rapid propagation, and in many instances
also because of their superior strength would soon have
gotten the upper hand over man and exterminated him.
God, therefore, makes a natural "fear," even a "terror,"
to dwell in their hearts. Even the birds, at least the
stronger among them, need such restraint. "Cattle"
are not mentioned, for by nature the domesticated
animals stand sufficiently under the control of man.
Distinct from this is the second thought that mankind
shall have control of all the smaller forms of animal
life as well as of the fish, to do with them as may seem
good to it. For the expression "to be given in anyone's
hand" signifies to be delivered into absolute control
to be dealt with as the other may determine. Cf. the use
of the phrase in Lev. 26:25 and Deut. 19:12. The *beth*
before *kol* denotes the sphere and really introduces the
double subject of the verb. The Septuagint translators
were only making an unnecessary attempt at improvement when they added to the first half of the verse the
third object "upon all the cattle" (Kit.). "Cattle" are
not to flee from man. The truth of the fulfillment of
this word lies in the fact that wild beasts consistently
shun the haunts of men, except when driven by hunger.
No matter how strong they may be, they dread man's
presence, yes, are for the most part actually filled with
"terror" at the approach of man.

3, 4. **Everything that moves and is alive may
be food for you. As I once gave you every green
plant, so now I have given you everything. Only
flesh with its life, that is its blood, ye shall not eat.**

Now man's power over the animal world is enlarged
in another direction: animal diet is made permissible.

If men before the Flood ever ate the meat of beasts,
they did so without divine sanction. The reason for
man's receiving this permission can only be surmised.
Some claim that man's strength, waning more per-
ceptibly after the Flood, required more solid nutriment.
That is not impossible. For the full impact of the
deteriorating effects of sin became progressively more
apparent as time went on. Others hold that among
the tokens of God's goodness there was also this, that He
enlarged the scope of man's diet in order to show man
His varied and manifold mercy. In any case, if a
"thing" moves (*rémes* in the broader sense) and is
"alive," man may eat it. Of course, the manifest thing
need not here be said: if the creature in question does
not appeal to him, he may refrain from eating it.
Consequently, no distinction is here to be made between
clean or unclean. For such distinctions are largely
relative. What one man or one group abhors, may be
freely eaten by others. All such details need not be
incorporated in a broad statement of permission such
as this.

Here is appended a distinct reference to the previous permission in reference to vegetable diet (1:29,
30). The first phrase "as the green plant" is really a
contracted clause, which we have, therefore, expanded
into a clause.

The pronoun *hû'*, which here serves as a copula,
occupies a position between subject and predicate adjective (cf. also G. K. 138 b). The concluding *kol*,
though without an article, still has the sign of the definite
object, because, in the nature of the case, it may be
regarded as in itself definite (K. S. 288 e).

4. One restriction is attached to this broad permission. This restriction, however, has to do only with
the manner of eating animal food: it may not be eaten
"with its life, that is its blood." The word for life is
here *néphesh*, elsewhere commonly rendered "soul,"
see B D B 659, No. 1. The rendering "life" is, however,

more common. The *be* here used is the *"beth* comitative," the flesh accompanied by its "life." In apposition with "its life" stands "its blood." (K. S. 402 s). The deeper issue involved becomes apparent when we notice the scriptural truth that life or the soul resides in the blood (Lev. 17:11). The blood is, therefore, deserving of very considerate treatment. Not exactly that the blood must be poured out, and the soul thus restored to its Maker before man eats the flesh. That view is never recorded in Scripture; although it is stated that the blood must first be drained (Lev. 7:27; 17:10, 14). Nor is there danger that the eating or the drinking of blood lets the beast's soul find entrance into man's soul, and that so man would become more brutish. Such commingling of souls is indicated by nothing. Our explanation briefly advanced above covers this aspect of the case, viz., because even a beast's soul is a thing divinely created, the medium in which it lives and has its being is almost indentical with it and should be respectfully treated, not devoured. Besides, Keil no doubt is correct when he claims these restrictions are given in view of the ordinances that are later to govern the use of blood in sacrifices. This provision, then, of Noah's time prepares for the sacrificial use of blood, and that which is to be sacred in sacrifice, in fact, is the heart and essence of the sacrifice, should hardly be employed that a man may glut his appetite with it. In fact, it is not an overstatement of the case to remark that ultimately this restriction is made in view of the sanctity of the blood of our Great High Priest, who is both priest and sacrifice. Apparently, this prohibition demands primarily that all blood be properly drained from animals slain for food. Naturally, this provision would rule out all such cruel practices as those of the Abyssinians, who gouge out portions of meat from the shanks of living animals, fill up the cavity with dung, and then eat the warm bloody meat. Such brutality, however, will hardly have been reflected upon as the more common likelihood. Luther erroneously reflects only this thought in his translation.

5. **But also for your blood, as being related to your souls, I shall demand an account; from every beast I shall demand it; also from man, that is from one another, will I demand the soul of man.**

As now one restriction is promulgated in reference to the blood of beasts, so another more essential one must be established in reference to the blood of man. The more frequent killing of beasts is not to beget a general indifference to the shedding of any and every blood, including man's. Where man's blood is shed ruthlessly, without warrant and authority, there God Himself shall demand an account. He may do this by prompting human agents to punish the evildoer, or He may achieve His ends by ultimately exacting vengeance upon the murderer who has not been brought to the bar of justice by man. Though *darash* primarily means "seek" or "require," this latter thought is "often joined with the collative thought of 'avenging'" (B D B). Therefore we render: "demand an account." The explanatory phrase is in the spirit of v. 4, when it says: "as being related to your souls," *lenaphshote-khem.* The introductory *le* signifies a dative of relation. Blood as such could hardly claim such importance. But since this blood stands related to souls, vengeance must be exacted for it. Blood, souls, life rank even higher in importance than man is inclined to grant. Furthermore, it is not indicated in what way God shall demand an account of every *beast.* The publishing of this word is to induce man to act. If a beast, having been made for man's sake, should in some way or other kill man, men should avenge this grievous irregularity by putting the beast to death. Exod. 21:28 furnishes an example under this head. Vilmar points out how in times of old men, especially certain Germanic tribes, rightly felt the enormity of the calamity of having a man slain by a beast. We seem largely to have lost this point of view. This same consideration, namely that the beast exists solely for man's sake, is reflected also in words such as 3:14 and Lev. 20:15 f.

There is a measure of difficulty about translating the second half of this verse, especially the phrase *miyyadh 'ish 'achiw*, literally, "from the hand of a man his brother." The phrase is the equivalent of the reciprocal pronoun "from one another." At the same time it goes a bit farther than the mere reciprocal pronoun, in actually pronouncing a man every other man's brother.

6. **Whoso sheddeth man's blood, by man shall his blood be shed; for in the image of God made He man.**

This verse attaches itself directly to the preceding, particularly to that part which says: "from man will I demand the soul of man." This verse now shows how God does this demanding: He lets man be the avenger. As Luther already very clearly saw, by this word government is instituted, this basic institution for the welfare of man. For if man receives power over other men's lives under certain circumstances, then by virtue of having received power over the highest good that man has, power over the lesser things is naturally included, such as power over property to the extent of being able to exact taxes, over our persons to the extent of being able to demand various types of work and service, as need may arise. Government, then, being grounded on this word, is not by human contract, or by surrender of certain powers, or by encroachment of priestcraft. It is a divine institution. Besides, this power of life and of death is bestowed upon man only in an official capacity, insofar as the governmental power is centered in him. It has remained for the shortsightedness of our day to claim that this verse is in conflict with the basic word of the Decalogue, "Thou shalt not kill." In reality, the Decalogue lays down principles of *personal* morality; this word, however, lays down principles of *official* conduct. Of coure, it is rightly claimed that in the last analysis no man has a right to take life, unless he be properly authorized by God to do so. But the reasonableness of the word as a whole is immediately apparent. Man's life is so valuable a thing, or, in other words, his blood is so valuable a thing, since man is made in God's image. He that kills a man destroys God's image and lays profane hands on that which is divine. The crime is so great that such a one actually forfeits his own right to life. There is a just retaliation about having life paid for life. No man can question the justice of the price demanded. Besides, we surely would not catch the purpose of the word if we were to take the imperfect *yishshaphek* as merely permissive or suggestive; it must be rendered as a strict imperative. Consequently, capital punishment is divinely ordained. For the proper safeguarding of the human race this basic ordinance is laid down. When lawgivers attempt to tamper with this regulation, they are trying to be wiser than the Divine Lawgiver and overthrow the pillars of safety that He Himself provided for the welfare of mankind.

It is true that this fundamental ordinance does not specify details as to how it is to be carried out, except that the work is to be done "by man" (*be'adham,* the preposition being a *beth instrumentalis,* K. S. 106). In other words, the ordinance is made elastic enough to cover all conditions. When at first no formally constituted government is at hand to be the agent, then individuals will be authorized to act. Under certain circumstances, on the frontiers of civilization, such a situation may arise even at this late date. Later on when governments came into being, they were the logical agency to act. Strictly speaking, K. C. is correct when he claims that the custom of blood revenge (*Blutrache*) is not ordained in the Scriptures. For blood revenge, unfortunately, substitutes revenge for the purposes of fair justice, and frequently it degenerated into the most cruel of feuds. When, therefore, the Scriptures do speak of blood revenge, it is merely for the purpose of mitigating its cruelty, Exod. 21:13; Deut. 4:41 f.; 19:2-10; Num. 35:6ff. However, words like Deut. 19:12 are in entire harmony with our passage.

The article with *'adham* is generic.

7. **But as for you, be fruitful and multiply; bring forth abundantly in the earth and multiply in it.**

Though this seems practically like a repetition of v. 1, in this connection it is more. It sets off strongly by contrast with v. 6 that man is not only not to be slain, but that it very definitely is the Lord's purpose to have man be fruitful and multiply and have numerous offspring in the earth, for *shirtsû* literally means: "swarm ye." It must be regarded as a basic ordinance actually binding upon man for all time as long as the earth shall stand, to multiply upon the earth.

That a contrast with v. 6 is actually intended in the above verse is indicated by the emphatic personal pronoun, *'attem*, which we have rendered, "as for you" (K. S. 17).

b) **The Covenant of the Rainbow** (v. 8-17)

As the section v. 1-7 abounded in tokens of God's mercy toward the family of Noah, so our section (v. 8-17) gives an added token by way of a visible external proof and guarantee.

8-10. **And God spake unto Noah and unto his sons with him as follows: As for me, I shall carry out my covenant with you and with your descendants after you, and with every living creature which is with you, birds, domestic animals, and wild animals of the earth that are with you, as many as go forth from the ark of all the wild animals of the earth.**

Since this is a merciful act, it might have been ascribed to Yahweh. The author with equal propriety prefers to have it regarded as the work of the mighty Creator (*Elohîm*), for it establishes permanent future conditions for all God's creatures. Again Noah and his sons in their representative capacity are addressed. The covenant which was promised 6:18 before the Flood, here goes into effect. A covenant *(berîth)* is the most solemn and binding form of divine promise, given for man's double assurance and because of man's carnal weakness, but quite unnecessary when God's part of the agreement is concerned. Therefore, such covenants are not to be put on a parallel with human covenants in which two contracting parties meet on the same level and make mutual pledges. Divine covenants emanate from God — therefore the emphatic initial *'anî*, "as for me" — He makes them, He fixes the terms and the conditions, He in sovereign freedom binds Himself. The emphatic *'anî* is completely misunderstood when it is set in contrast with the *"you" (attem)* of v. 7, for this pronoun belongs into a different situation that deals with basic ordinances. Yet in the very nature of the case a contrast is implied in such covenants. Here the verb used for the setting up of the covenant is not *karath*, which signifies strictly the entering upon a covenant, but the Hifil *heqîm*, "to cause to stand," used like Lev. 26:9; Deut. 8:18, in the sense of "keeping" or "carrying out." For when 6:18 promised a covenant as future, this word reckons with the covenant as practically existent and concerns itself merely with "carrying into effect" (B D B) its provisions.

Consequently, the discussion runs quite beside the point when it asks whether v. 1-7 are preliminary to this section in the sense of laying down the terms to which man must obligate himself in order to meet his part of the covenant. The section v. 1-7 does lay down basic ordinances with such finality that Noah and his sons most naturally accepted them. But these divine regulations stand quite apart from what attitude man might take in reference to them. Therefore nothing is reported about the attitude taken by man. Procksch, in the fashion characteristic of critics when they purpose to correct what to them seems a very unreliable text, sets the section v. 8-17 first and lets v. 1-7 follow, though not even a single other critic has ventured upon such a step. Such efforts confirm critics in the erroneous thoughts they read into the text.

Now, with marked fullness of expression, the ones whom the present covenant includes are listed. This fullness of expression is to be accounted for, as Luther above all others rightly contends, by the fact that Noah and those with him must have "lived in great trembling, fear and sorrow, and so it was absolutely necessary to repeat and reimpress continually one set form of speech." So, then, the beneficiaries under this covenant are the eight persons then living ("you") and their "descendants" after them (here the Biblical term "seed" is used) as well as all "living creatures," which may as yet quite properly be said to be "with" Noah, because either they had just come forth from the ark and were in the immediate vicinity, or else they were still in process of coming forth. Even the subdivisions under the head of the term "living creatures" are mentioned, being introduced by a *beth of enumeration, (beth sphaerae)*, which we have covered in the translation by a simple apposition. The reason for such detail is to make the divine concern for even the least of the creatures strongly apparent to Noah. "The wild animals," *chayath ha'árets*, are for that matter even mentioned twice (v. 10) for the same reason, for they of all beings might seem to need divine favor least. Though the *min* in *mikkol* is a *min partitive*, there can be no objection to translating it, as many do: "as many as," for the partitive idea here actually merges into the appositional.

A peculiar difficulty arises in v. 10 for those who hold that the Flood was partial and not universal. They must support the strange supposition that God made a covenant with those creatures only which went forth from the ark. Others that never entered the ark must do without the benefits of such a covenant.

The participle *yotse'ey* is here treated rather as a noun and so stands in the construct state. In v. 18 the same participle is regarded more as a verb and is construed with a prepositional phrase to express the same idea (K. S. 241 d, 336 f). *Lekhol* is used instead of the construct relationship, because a noun has crept in between *yotse'ey* and *kol* (K. S. 281 g).

11. And I shall carry out my covenant with you, that never again shall all flesh be destroyed by the waters of the flood; and never again shall there be a flood to lay waste the earth.

Summing up all classes of living beings by the expression "all flesh," the promise reassures man that the preservation of all these shall be made as a result of God's covenant. All flesh shall never again "be destroyed," *yikkareth*, i. e., "cut off" from life, neither shall a flood "lay waste" *sha(ch)cheth*, i. e., "ruin" the earth. Floods on a smaller scale may destroy much flesh; a universal flood shall never occur. It seems the article before *mabbûl* ("flood") in the first case has not been sufficiently considered. Its use signifies first that this particular flood which has just about receded is not going to cut off all flesh again. The second use of the word without the article signifies that not any such flood will ever recur (*mabbûl* = "a flood").

12, 13. And God said: This is the sign of the covenant which I am establishing between myself and you and every living creature which is with you for all future generations: I have put my bow in the clouds and it shall serve for a covenant sign between me and and the earth.

The connection does not so much aim to express strict sequence of acts in the expression *wayyó'mer*, but rather is used in the frequent rather loose sense "further." Surely, man must have been much disturbed and greatly in need of assurance, if, in addition to a promise of future safety, which promise was guaranteed by a covenant, God gave a visible outward sign to make assurance doubly sure. Since God was in reality just then establishing this covenant, the durative participe is used *nothen*, i. e., "I am in process of giving." The verb *nathan* for establishing a covenant occurs also in 17:2 and Num. 25:12. The ones involved in this covenant are again distinctly named: on the one side God, on the other, man and every living creature. God dwells with emphasis on the fact that He is good even to the animal world. But, in reality, the animals are preserved for man's sake, as the expression "with you" indicates. That the covenant is to hold as long as the earth stands is indicated by the expression "to generations of eternity," *ledhoroth 'ôlam*. Of course, *'ôlam* signifies the hidden future, so "to all future generations" is a good rendering.

13. With emphasis this verse sets the word *qashtî*, "my bow," first in the verse. Literally, the verse says God "has *given*" *(nathátti)* his bow in the cloud. The perfect most likely is the perfect of solemn assurance or promise, like that found in 1:29; 4:14, 23; yet cf. G. K. 106 i, m, n. Now in itself this determines nothing on the question of the previous existence of the rainbow, for the perfect might mean, "I have just given," as well as, "I gave long ago." Still we hold that the preponderance of evidence points to the fact that the rainbow in the clouds now first came into being. For, though it is possible that a phenomenon which existed previously might now serve a new purpose, still the effect would be comparatively weak, and the effectiveness of the sign would be much impaired. It would be a case much like that where two by mutual agreement

arrive at the conclusion to let something serve as a reminder. But how much more effective would be a sign that appears for the first time, especially so solemn and awe-inspiring a sign as the rainbow with its ethereal beauty and vast span! There would, furthermore, be a splendid propriety to have a promise, which brings into being a relationship which did not exist before, attested by a sign which did not exist before. As the sign by its newness is a token of God's vast power, so the covenant, though promising a new situation, will be effective by the same vast power. It might be that the same physical laws prevailed on earth prior to this time, so that light falling on a spray of water against a dark background produced a miniature rainbow. But the text says: "My bow do I give *in the clouds,*" (*'anan,* "cloud" used collectively). It is not impossible that with the Flood came altered atmospheric and cloud conditions, for geologic evidence points to an earlier age when a climate uniformly tropical prevailed also in the arctic region.

So now when the marvelous and beautiful rainbow puts in its appearance, all believers in revelation recall with joy its higher significance as outlined in this chapter. Delitzsch has perhaps interpreted the deeper propriety of the various elements involved more adequately than any other interpreter. He writes: "As it (the rainbow) shines forth against a dark background which but shortly before flashed with lightnings, it symbolizes the victory of bright, gentle love over the darkly luminous wrath; growing as it does out of the interaction of sun and dark clouds, it symbolizes the readiness of the heavenly to interpenetrate the earthly; extending from heaven to earth, it proclaims peace between God and man; reaching, as it does, beyond the range of vision, it declares that God's covenant of grace is all-embracing." Our fathers did well to teach their children to pray at least the Lord's Prayer whenever the rainbow appeared.

We may also dismiss as utterly ungrounded and
entirely worthless the notion that the sign in reality
stands for Yahweh's warbow, which He used to shoot
His lightnings but now hangs up in the clouds as no
longer destined for such cruel purposes. Legends of
India, Arabia and Greece, which the critics are wont
to draw upon at this point, certainly do not prove that
such opinions were also held by Israel in days of old.
Certainly, the passages adduced do not apply except by
injecting the desired opinion: see Hab. 3:9-11 and Ps.
7:13. When critics then themselves admit that no traces
of this peculiar interpretation of the bow are any longer
discernible in Hebrew literature (Procksch), how can
they venture to prove that these traces once were discernible? But this much is true: "The bow in the hands
of man was an instrument of battle, the bow bent by
the hand of God has become a symbol of peace" (Words-
worth, cited by Whitelaw).

14-16. **And it shall come to pass whenever I
mass together clouds over the earth and the bow
appears in the clouds, then will I remember my
covenant terms which stand between me and you
and every living soul of all flesh, and there shall
never again be waters of a flood to lay waste all
flesh. And the bow shall stand in the clouds and
I shall see it to remember the everlasting covenant
terms between God and all living creatures of all
flesh which are upon the earth.**

One may disregard the situation and man's need
of definite assurance and regard the whole promise as
exceedingly verbose; or else one may rightly claim, with
Delitzsch, that these words are like blows of the hammer, which make the whole more firm and impress it
more deeply.

After an infinitive governed by a preposition ("in
my clouding together clouds" — cognate object after
Piel infinitive with suffix) the construction proceeds

with a converted perfect to complete the protasis ("and the bow appears in the clouds") ; v. 15 follows with the apodosis. Cf. G. K. 52 d and 117 r; also 114 r; also K. S. 413 a.

15. God's remembering is not to be thought of as over against the possibility of forgetting, as would be the case with man; but rather as a divine activity whereby His "covenant terms" (*berîth* here by metonomy signifying "covenant terms" rather than "covenant," K. C.) will be vividly before Him, and man may take joy from the fact that God thus thinks upon what He promised. The ones for whose good the covenant was made are again listed in terms used previously. *Hammáyin lemabbûl* furnishes an example of the use of *le* in place of the construct relationship. That *yikyeh* before *máyim* is singular is due to the fact that the verb frequently begins with the masculine singular when the number of the subject is not yet determined (K. S. 348 b).

16. The combination *berîth 'ôlam* without the article literally would yield the translation "to remember an everlasting covenant," which is the equivalent of: "to remember that there is an everlasting covenant." When God speaks and says the covenant is "between *God* and," etc., this is merely a more formal type of expression appropriate for a covenant.

17. **And God said to Noah: This is the sign of the covenant which I shall carry out between me and all flesh which is upon the earth.**

With this formal summary statement God's pronouncement closes. God could hardly have done more for man than to set forth with such simplicity and emphasis promises calculated to rouse new courage in the heart of the few survivors. Critics speak of material compounded laboriously from various sources. The devout mind sees God's adaptation to man's special need.

c) **The Future of the Races of Mankind Foretold**
(v. 18-29)

The episode that follows serves only as an occasion
for the patriarchal prediction that follows. It has so
little importance comparatively that it would certainly
be an ill-balanced judgment to give to this portion the
heading, "Noah the Vinegrower."

18, 19. **The sons of Noah that came forth from
the ark were Shem and Ham and Japheth, and
Ham was the father of Canaan. These three were
the sons of Noah, and from them were spread abroad
all the inhabitants of the earth.**

Since now the sons of Noah are going to be dealt
with, especially in chapter ten, as the founders of the
three great branches of the human family, they are
formally mentioned, and their going forth from the ark
is connected with their names, inasmuch as their going
forth was really epoch-making and an actual new departure made by these notable three branches. There
can hardly be any doubt about it that these are
mentioned in the order of their age, Shem being the
oldest. For the same order is observed each time that
all three are mentioned; see 5:32; 6:10; 7:13; 9:18;
10:1; I Chron. 1:4. This fact must be borne in mind
for the understanding of v. 24. Preparatory to the tale
about to be related the fact is inserted that Ham was
the father of Canaan. That is not a statement that is
to be ascribed, here and v. 22, to some later redactional
activity, but a fact absolutely essential to the understanding of the whole episode. Only previous misconception of the facts of the case would deny this.

19. Nor should the opening of this verse be regarded as superfluous, or merely as a somewhat verbose
statement. One might well suppose that Noah had begotten more sons after the Flood, for he was yet to live
more than 300 years (v. 28). So this statement, that
"these three were the sons of Noah," disposes satis-

factorily of that matter; and the concluding statement prepares for the elaborate table of the nations given in chapter ten.

In v. 18 the participle *yotse'im*, appearing in a connection which has reference to the past, must represent an adjective clause in the past tense, "who went forth" (K. S. 237 a; 411 a). In v. 19 *naphetsa* is best derived from a Kal *naphats*, used in a passive sense (See K. W.).

20, 21. **Now Noah began as farmer to plant a vineyard. And he drank some of the wine and became drunk and he uncovered himself in the midst of the tent.**

We have advanced quite a time from the Flood; at least, Noah's son Ham already has children, and even his youngest Canaan (see 10:6) is born already. Several decades may well have passed. Men have begun to rehabilitate themselves. Noah apparently took to agriculture at once, even as we already found the second man Cain engaged in this pursuit (4:2). The notion that mankind took a long time to advance to the point of becoming agriculturalists does not agree with the Biblical evidence. Nor is our contention invalidated by the article in *'ish ha'adhamah*, which does not need to be translated "*the* farmer" and so drive us to the translation: "Now Noah was the first farmer to plant a vineyard" (Meek). For Noah as a proper noun may impart of its definiteness to the noun in apposition with it (K. S. 333 z); or we may have the generic or categorical article (K. C.). Besides, it would seem strange indeed if the uses of wine were now first being discovered by man, whose earliest works, wherever we find them, give evidence of great ability. Besides, in the case of Noah's being the first wine-grower, Noah's drunkenness is entirely excusable; and yet the nature of this record seems to imply guilt on Noah's part. Consequently, we are rather led to the conclusion that Noah began to cultivate a plant of whose cultivation and uses he had previously known. Nor should we regard wine as a gift of God, given to refresh the soul *(nephesh)* of man, even as animal food was to help invigorate man's body (Vilmar). Such thoughts are pure surmises. *Yachel* is a converted Hifil of *chalal.* "He began and planted" = "He began to plant," (K. S. 369 m).

21. The having of grapes led to the making of wine. The having of wine leads to the drinking of it. In all this, taken by itself, there is no wrong. We have every reason to believe, however, that Noah was not ignorant of the potency of the drink he had prepared. But he neglected caution. He who maintained his ground over against a wicked and godless world, neglecting watchfulness and prayer in a time of comparative safety, fell prey to a comparatively simple temptation, which should have been easy to meet. It is not the young and untried Noah who sins. It is the seasoned man of God, ripe in experience, who is here brought low. The sober tone of the detailed narrative points strongly to Noah's guilt. Noah drinks to excess and actually "becomes drunk" *(shakhar).* The heat of wine leads the aged patriarch involuntarily to thrust back his garment, wherewith he had been covered or had from force of habit covered himself as he lay down in his tent. *Yithgal* as Hithpael should be rendered as a reflexive, "he uncovered himself." "He was uncovered" (A. V.) substitutes the actual result for this.

Criticism quite fails to recognize the unimpeachable impartiality of the Scriptures, which record the faults as well as the virtues of God's saints. So criticism calls this quite a different "cycle of tradition" than that which told about "the blameless patriarch, who is the hero of the Flood." Besides, in its attempt to create variations and contradictions criticism makes Noah's sons in our account appear as minors still

dwelling in the tent with their father — of which the
text surely reveals nothing; whereas in P they are
already married. Such an approach leads men to abandon a safe and easy road and to become mired in the
morass of fruitless speculation.

Min ("from") before "wine" is one of the Hebrew
modes of expressing the indefinite pronoun "some"
(K. S. 81).

22. **And Ham, the father of Canaan, looked at
the nakedness of his father and told his two brethren
outside.**

For the right understanding of what follows we
are again reminded, as in v. 18, that Ham is the father
of Canaan. At the same time, the repetition of the
statement in this connection seems to point more
definitely to a kinship of mind between the two. The
trait of inclination to the unclean is shared by father
and son alike, in fact, it even appears that the trait
manifested by the father has reached a higher measure
of intensity in the son. But as far as Ham himself is
concerned, the expression *wayyar'* is not a mere harmless and accidental "and he saw," but "he looked at"
(B D B) or "he gazed with satisfaction." What ordinary filial reverence should have restrained is given
free rein. The unclean imagination feeds itself by
gazing. But at the same time a measure of departure
from the faith is also revealed by Ham. That the son
should have treated with such levity a father eminent
for true piety, the one man whom God spared in the
destruction of the world, indicates that this son no
longer esteemed such true godliness as he ought to
have done. Similarly, *wayyaggedh* is not a mere "and
he told," though we know of no other way of translating it. The circumstances suggest that it means:
"and he told with delight." No object need be expressed
grammatically either in Hebrew or in English. In a
modified sense this event may be named a second fall

into sin, or the fall of the postdiluvians, yet with this proviso that, of course, since Adam's fall all men were born sinners. But the event does most assuredly show how soon the salutary warnings conveyed by the Flood were forgotten, and mankind began to incline toward a downward course.

23. **And Shem and Japheth took the robe and laid it upon the shoulder of both of them and they, walking backward, covered the nakedness of their father, their faces being turned backward so as not to see their father's nakedness.**

The conduct of these two brethren stands forth in strong contrast to that of Ham. They were men of pure mind and wholly given to the religion of their father. They are truly grieved at what befell their father — not amused. They seek promptly to veil their father's weakness with the mantle of charity. They promptly take *"the* robe," *(hassimlah),* the robe that was pushed back and so had very likely fallen off his couch to the ground. For in days of old the robe worn through the day was a man's covering by night (Exod. 22:26, 27). See K. S. 299 b rather than G. K. 126 r. This robe they take upon the shoulders of them both, and then, "walking backward they covered the nakedness of their father." To all this, practically clear enough in itself, is added the very explicit statement that "their faces were turned backward, so as not to see their father's nakedness." This was all, no doubt, done before Ham's eyes. No words are recorded as having been spoken by these two, apparently for the reason that none were spoken. The excess of restraint thus self-imposed spoke quite loudly for itself. If Ham could feel a rebuke, he would feel it sufficiently if no words were spoken, in fact, the finer tact of the two brothers discerns that a spoken rebuke often rouses opposition. So with silent sorrow they go about their task.

Wayyiqqach begins as singular, though a double subject follows, since the masculine singular frequently begins a statement when number and gender of the subject are as yet undetermined (K. S. 349 u). The author does not aim to distinguish Shem as the prime factor in this act (contra Hengstenberg).

24. And Noah awoke from his wine-stupor and learned what his younger son had done to him.

Yáyin, of course, is the word for "wine," but in a connection such as this it must mean the stupor, or state of drunkenness caused by wine (metonomy). *Wayyeda'* usually would mean "and he knew," but here it implies "knowing as a result of inquiry," i. e., "he learned," or "found out." Something struck the man as unusual at his awakening — perhaps the manner in which the robe was placed upon him. Surely, no one will have volunteered information. Certainly, the verb can hardly indicate that he perceived by prophetic inspiration. Ham is here called "his younger son." True, the adjective with the article may indicate the superlative. But such is not necessarily the case; cf. 1:16 *haggadhol* = "the greater," and *haqqaton* = "the lesser." Besides, on that score, according to 10:21, Japheth would then be "the oldest" (*haggadhol*), and the customary order (cf. our comments on v. 18): Shem, Ham, Japheth would be entirely meaningless, and a reasonable explanation for this sequence would be impossible. Yet some, who insist on making this verse offer a superlative, make 10:21 offer only a comparative (Meek). Apparently, critical commentators take delight in making Scripture seem to contradict Scripture.

25. And he said: Cursed is Canaan; servant of servants shall he be to his brethren.

Altogether too much emphasis has been placed upon the idea of the *curse* at this point. Meek represents one-sidedness when he provides the caption "The

Curse of Canaan" for v. 18-28. In this section the
curse is the subordinate element. Besides, without
trying to eliminate the idea of the curse, for it manifestly lies in the text, all who associate personal resentment or any form of ill will with this utterance of
Noah, do the godly man a gross injustice. Furthermore, to hold that this word broods like a dark and
inescapable fate over the future of a race, is to hold
to a very grievous misunderstanding. True, the feelings of a good man have been outraged. Equally true,
he gives vent to righteous indignation. But, for the
most part, being a man who has the Holy Spirit, he
speaks a *word of prophecy.* This prophetic word is
to serve as a guide for the human race as well as for a
solemn warning for all times to come. Blessings and
curses of parents may be more than idle words, but
a parent who stands in the fear of God would hardly
venture to lay grievous disabilities upon great portions
of the human race, nor would God grant their wish
if they attempted it. Being so accurate a delineation
of the future of the three branches of the human family
as we shall find this word to be, it approves itself to
the thinking man as a truly prophetic utterance.

Much serious misunderstanding has grown out of
a refusal to take this word at its actual face value, especially the word "Canaan." *Ham* is not cursed, no matter
how freely proslavery men may have employed this
text. Canaan is the fourth son of Ham (10:6) and so
may roughly be said to represent one fourth of the
Hamitic race. He alone is under consideration here.
The rest of the Hamitic stock, apparently, does not
come under consideration because it is neither directly
blessed nor cursed. Its influence on the development
of the rest of the human race is practically nil and,
therefore, need not be mentioned here.

Now the descendants of Canaan, according to
10:15-20, are the peoples that afterward dwelt in
Phoenicia and in the so-called land of Canaan, Pales-

tine. That they became races accursed in their moral
impurity is apparent from passages such as 15:16;
19:5; Lev. 18 and 20; Deut. 12:31.   In Abraham's
day the measure of their iniquity was already almost
full. By the time of the entrance of Israel into Canaan
under Joshua the Canaanites, collectively also called
Amorites, were ripe for divine judgment through
Israel, His scourge. Sodom left its name for the unnatural vice its inhabitants practiced. The Phœnicians
and the colony of Carthage surprised the Romans by
the depth of their depravity. Verily cursed was
Canaan!

But how about the justice of this development of
history? From our point of view most of the difficulties
are already cleared away. We render "Cursed *is* Canaan" not "be" (A. V.) ; and "servant of servants
shall he be," not in an optative sense *may he be.* The
evil trait, displayed by Ham in this story, had, no
doubt, been discerned by Noah as marking Canaan, the
son, more distinctly. Canaan's whole race will display
it more than any of the races of the earth. To foretell
that involves no injustice. The son is not punished
for the iniquity of the father. His own unfortunate
moral depravity, which he himself developes and retains, is foretold. Therefore, such unfortunate explanations as: Ham, Noah's *youngest* son, is punished
in his own *youngest* son, are rendered quite unnecessary. For this explanation is wrong already from
its first assertion that Ham is the youngest son of Noah.

Of course, "servant of servants" is a Hebrew
superlative, implying something like "lowest of slaves."
In reality, Carthage became slave to Rome, and what
was left of Canaan became slave to Israel. Therefore
"brethren" is here used in its broadest sense.

26.   **He also said: Blessed be Yahweh the God
of Shem and Canaan be his servant.**

Looking upon the oldest son next, Noah is moved
to a lively statement of praise of Yahweh because of
the magnitude of the blessings that He will bestow
upon Shem. Mark well, it is *Yahweh* who is called
Shem's God. This implies that the Eternal Unchangeable One is fulfilling promises of mercy to Shem. Only
in relation to Shem does God manifest His Yahweh
qualities. But what are these great blessings that
move Noah to break out in benedictions? Shall we
answer in general terms, the blessings of religion as
offered by Shem; or, the knowledge of the One God
which Shem transmitted to the world? Why be so
vague when more definite facts are available? The
answers just given will suit all those whose conception
of history and religion is evolutionistic. But then
Shem's heritage is largely the achievement of his own
religious genius, and then Shem ought rather to have
been praised, not Yahweh. However, if a promise of
definite victory through the seed of the woman is the
substance of Gospel as man knows it, it seems almost
impossible at this important juncture to have so
weightly an utterance as this, which is to guide humankind for some time to come, fail to tie itself up with
the Protevangel and fail to tell from which branch
of the human family "the seed of the woman" in
particular is to be expected. Modern commentators
can still learn from Luther on this verse, for he says:
"Noah here speaks not of bodily or temporal blessing
but of the blessing through the future promised seed,
which blessing he recognizes to be so great and rich
that words cannot fully express it nor do justice to it."
But Luther, too, recognizes that such a hope, though
seen to be so marvelous as to stir a man to praise, is
for the present but dimly apprehended. Men could not
discern such truths as yet with the New Testament
clearness.

Canaan's relation to Shem is specifically defined as a dismal echo of v. 25 running into v. 26. *Lamô*, though usually plural, "to *them*," must here be taken as a singular, even as is the case in Isa. 44:15. Therefore, a literal rendering would be: "and let Canaan be servant to him." Note that we have rendered *wîhî* "and let be." This does not overthrow our conception of the whole word of Noah because it is optative ("let") rather than pure future. The word is still prophetic rather than damnatory. Indeed, we should not venture to claim that Noah could not wish personally that these things might actually come to pass. The prophecy foretells what God will bring to pass. Why should not a godly man wish that God's will be done? Noah himself could discern that a position of servitude might serve a wholesome pedagogic purpose of restraint upon lascivious Canaan. Therefore, he might well wish that this befall Canaan for his own good.

27. May God grant ample territory to Japheth, and may he dwell in the tents of Shem, and may Canaan be his servant.

There is a manifold propriety about the words of this blessing. Canaan, *kená'an*, has analogy with the root *kana'*, "to be humbled." Ham, as interpreters have remarked, not too ready to submit to his own father, seems to have expected ready submission from his son and named him accordingly. In any case, Canaan finds his lot to be humiliation. So *Shem* means "name" also in the sense of "fame." Shem has the most prominent fame among the brethren. Similarly, Japheth is in the blessing by an equally apt paronomasia, associated with the analogous root *pathah*, "be open"; Hifil imperfect jussive *yapht*, "cause to be open" = "grant ample territory." It is foretold and hoped for that Japheth will be what his name implies. For, in reality, his descendants, the Indo-Europeans or Aryans, do spread out over vast stretches of territory from India across all Europe and of a later date over the Western Hemisphere. With surprising accuracy this feature of his history is foretold. But since Shem is the central figure, both of the brothers are shown in their relation to him, which is here said to be: Japheth is to "dwell in the tents of Shem." Such a sudden change of subject is not unusual in Hebrew (K. S. 399 B). To try to make God the subject would render Japheth even more richly blessed than Shem, a situation which would have called for a "blessed" upon Japheth's lot rather than upon Shem's. "To dwell in the tents of one" implies friendly sharing of his hospitality and so of his blessings. It cannot mean "displace" or "conquer," for that would conflict with the pure blessedness pronounced upon Shem. But the fulfillment bears out what this means. The Japhethites have now very largely come in to share Shem's blessings, for as Gentiles they have been grafted on the good olive tree. Shem's spiritual heritage is ours. Abraham is become our father in faith and we are his true children. The same somber echo closes this verse: "May Canaan be his servant."

28, 29. **After the Flood Noah lived three hundred and fifty years, so that all the days of Noah were nine hundred and fifty years; and he died.**

With an appropriate summary, cast after the pattern of chapter five, the total age of Noah is recorded, so that we are enabled to compare his age with the rest of the antediluvian patriarchs. To our surprise we find that he lived twenty years more than Adam. On the other hand, a bit of computation based on chapter eleven will reveal that thus Noah lived quite far into the life of Abraham. So the "history of Noah," which began with 6:9, appropriately closes with the length of Noah's life and with his death.

HOMILETICAL SUGGESTIONS

In this chapter v. 1-7 constitute a distinct unit. Each preacher may word the theme as he sees fit; but in the last analysis it will have to concern itself with "The Basic Divine Provisions Governing the World since the Flood." These provisions are still in force and are living issues, with the exception that where v. 4 prepared the mind of men to realize the importance of blood, particularly in the matter of sacrifices, now at least this verse helps us to recall the supreme importance of the blood atonement, a truth sadly neglected and but little understood. Then vv. 8-17 are seen to deal quite naturally with "God's Covenant of the Rainbow." Lastly, the section v. 20-27 concerns itself with the "Development of the Three Branches of our Race." The emphasis lies on Noah's drunkenness only in an incidental way, in so far namely, as it illustrates the propriety of Canaan's "curse." This section affords an excellent opportunity to preach Christ the Savior who even in these early days stirred the hearts of godly men to deep-felt praise; for faith has always been faith in the Christ.

CHAPTER X

IV. The History of the Sons of Noah

Quite naturally we ask after the story of the Flood, "How did the human race develop?" It is not the purpose of the author of Genesis to trace out this development. But there may be important facts in this connection that should be transmitted to the human race, facts that have not been preserved elsewhere and that form a part of the revealed truth which God deigns essential for man's well-being. These facts will be covered very briefly in chapters ten and eleven (in part). Then we shall be ready to proceed with the history of the chosen people.

First, then, we are to be shown what peoples or races came from the three sons of Noah. It would seem quite natural that before the earth again became densely populated men still preserved an accurate tradition of how the various races had derived their ancestry from the three sons of Noah. Since this "Table of Nations" is inserted just prior to the story of Abraham, it seems most reasonable to conclude that the table represents the state of the nations of that time. This assumption has far more in favor of it than have the suggestions of the critics who first divide the chapter into two parts, assigned to P and J respectively, and then with great hesitation, or else with unwarranted confidence, assign to P some time like the eighth century, or the time of Solomon (eleventh century B. C.), and to J, about the seventh century. When the eighth century is suggested, it is because Cimmerians (Gomer) then first appeared south of the Caucasus and so came to Israel's notice. Solomon's time is suggested because certain Semitic tribes of Arabia would not appear to have been met with by Israel before this king's trade ventures were undertaken. Or again, the mention of certain of the nations of the Table by later writers like Jeremiah and Ezekiel is treated as an indication of the time of the composition of this document. Behind all such late dates lies the assumption that Israel (or Moses) could not have a valid tradition about any people, except such a people had recently forged to the forefront, or unless Israel had established definite contact with them. It may be of interest to submit a sample of critical dissection: Verses 1-7, 20, 22, 23, 31, 32 are assigned to P (Procksch); J receives 8 b-19, 21, 25, 26, 27-30; the rest are glosses.

Apart from all this the list is severely criticized for not being more complete; for actually asserting that the three sons of Noah were the fathers of all races; for actually assuming that whole nations sprang from one forefather — a course of development for which, it is asserted, no parallel is historically known; and, lastly, for advancing certain claims which are not supported by any other historical documents.

However, each of these criticisms could rather constitute a distinct merit of this Table. So its incompleteness. For it transmits no more than its author or its time actually knew. Such fidelity in transmission of tradition, as Herder already indicated, is the mark of veracity. Then, where Noah's three sons are classed as the only fathers of the race and by implication, of course, Noah as the one father, that preserves for us the knowledge of the unity of the human race, as Israel alone of all nations had preserved this most essential truth. Whatever narrowness may have marked the later Israel, the Israelites of olden times had a distinct consciousness of the unity of the race. No nation had such a universalistic point of view. All nations had lost the sense of the solidarity of the human race except Israel. But as for the third objection, it must simply be noted that where other nations had largely lost the record of their beginnings, Israel had preserved its own record as well as those of others. When, then, one ancestor is assigned to a people, that fact need not exclude the gradual assimilation of other ethnic groups or tribes. But on the fourth objection we can only say that critics should prove grateful for this additional information derived from Israel's sacred writings. None of the additional information offered has ever been disproved, and, besides, secular writers are not at once rejected if they happen to stand alone in a claim that they make. Consequently, we must regard this document as a true and reliable testimony to the unity of the human race as well as of the development of the race from the three sons of Noah, and must be thankful for this indication of the breadth of view and universalistic standpoint of the Scriptures.

At certain points in the Table it will be impossible for us to determine whether the actual ancestor's name is preserved or only the name of the tribe (cf. v. 16, Jebusite, Amorite, Girgashite, etc.) or the name of the people (cf. v. 13, Ludim, Anamim, Lehabim, etc., all plural nouns). But even the tribal or national name may be derived from the actual ancestor. But if names like Sheba appear v. 7 under Ham's descendants as well as v. 28 under Shem's descendants, then we must allow either for two persons of the same name, or else for the possibility of intermarriage, whereby two different racial groups blended. Cf. also Havilah v. 7 and Havilah v. 28.

It would seem most reasonable to expect that the possibility of identifying all these peoples must needs be very slight. Nevertheless, since Samuel Borchart (1681) and Knobel (1850) made extensive investigations on the subject, a fair measure of certainty attaches to the study of the subject. Inscriptions on monuments have contributed substantiation.

The claim that these names are eponymous, that is to say, that fabled ancestors are assigned to various nations, as Rome was wont to consider Romulus and Remus its founders — this claim, we say, is merely an attempt to measure the sound tradition of Israel by the legends of classical nations. As a sound testimony to the unity of the human race and as a strong bulwark against foolish racial prejudice, this chapter serves a most excellent purpose.

No nation of antiquity has anything to offer that presents an actual parallel to this Table of Nations. Babylonian and Egyptian lists that seem to parallel this are merely a record of nations conquered in war. Consequently, the spirit that prompted the making of such lists is the very opposite of the spirit that the Biblical list breathes.

1. This is the history of the sons of Noah — Shem, Ham and Japheth — and (in fact) sons were born unto them (only) after the Flood.

On the word for "history" (*toledôth*) see 2:4. It is quite proper to call this tenth chapter plus the first part of the eleventh (v. 1-9) "the history" of the sons of Noah, inasmuch as in brief form this account tells at least how these sons of Noah in their progeny spread abroad upon the face of the earth. History condensed is still history.

The names of the three sons of Noah are again appended so that we may be sure that only these three actually were the sons of Noah also after the Flood. For the possibility of the birth of other sons of Noah after the Flood might occur to us. This concise way of putting the matter indicates that none were born to Noah after the Flood. However, on the other hand, to the sons of Noah children were born only after the Flood. This fact may seem strange, but it was apparently so ordered by Providence. This is the mean-

ing of the last clause, and therefore we have inserted
an interpretative "only." The "and" connecting the
two halves of the verse is one of the many instances
where it bears the meaning "and in fact" *(und zwar)*.

a) The Sons of Japheth (v. 2-5)

2. **The sons of Japheth: Gomer and Magog
and Madai and Javan and Tubal and Meshech and
Tiras.**

We shall identify these various nations briefly
without going into lengthy detail, for commentaries
offer a fair measure of unanimity, especially since
monumental inscriptions serve to confirm the historical
character of many of the earlier names in the list.
For details on identification Skinner presents much
valuable material. Most reliable is Koenig (K. C.).

Now the Japhethites are the ones we are wont
to identify with the Indo-Europeans. Just how the
table of the Japhethites arranges itself is. made
apparent by the following outline.

Japheth						
Gomer	Magog	Madai	Javan	Tubal	Meshech	Tiras
Ashkenaz	Riphath	Togarmah	Elishah	Tarshish	Kittim	Dodanim

At once it becomes apparent, as a comparison with
the outlines for Shem and for Ham will suggest, that
the author seems to know least about Japheth, or else
there was no more about Japheth to report. This
latter possibility is not so very remote. It is well known
how certain families just keep subdividing to a certain
point. So no further divisions are reported for Magog,
Madai, Tubal, Meshech and Tiras. Three descendants
of Gomer are listed and four of Javan.

"Gomer" is identified with the Cimmerians of the
Greeks (Κιμμέριοι). They came from the Caucasus into

Asia Minor settling south of the Black Sea. In the reign of Sargon they are mentioned as *Gimirrai*.

"Magog," according to Josephus, represents the ancient Scythian hordes, found originally southeast of the Black Sea. Perhaps they are the *Massagetes* who defeated Cyrus. Ezekiel mentions them 38:2; 39:6.

"Madai" are the Medes, found southeast of Magog and southwest of the Caspian Sea. This name appears rather frequently in the Scriptures, as any concordance will indicate. The Assyrian has *Madai* too.

"Javan," distinctly related to the Greek Ἰωύαν, are the Ionians, which name, after Alexander the Great, was applied to all Greeks. It is found repeatedly in the Old Testament, being translated "Javan" in the parallel passage of I Chron. 1:5, 7, as also in Isa. 66:19; Ezek. 27:13, 19, but translated as "Greece" or "Greecia" in Dan. 8:21; 10:20; 11:2; Zech. 9:13; and Joel 3:6 (plural). Western Asia Minor is the original seat of Javan.

"Tubal" is to be assigned to the eastern part of Asia Minor. The Assyrians knew this nation as *Tabal*. They are the old Tibarenians. In the Scriptures they are almost regularly associated with Meshech; cf. Ezek. 27:13; 32:26; 38:2, 3; 39:1. In Isa. 66:19 with Javan.

"Meshech" are known to Herodotus as Μόσχοι. They dwelt at the southwestern corner of the Black Sea. The Assyrians knew them as *Muskâya* or coupled them on the monuments with Tubal, thus: *Tabali* and *Muški* (in Sargon's inscription).

"Tiras" seems to refer to Pelasgians of the Aegean Sea, a pirate nation known as Τορσηνοί, who terrorized the whole neighborhood. They might be identified with the later E-trus-cans of Italy.

Now, indeed, these are all names of individuals, who are to be regarded as founders of the various nationalities bearing their names.

3. **And the sons of Gomer: Ashkenaz and Riphath and Togarmah.**

"Ashkenaz" might be identified with Ascanius, the name of a sea in Bithynia. Assyriologists point to the name *Ašguza*, people who settled near Lake Urumia. In any case, Jewish tradition identifies this name with the Germans, for whom (or for the German Jews) it is used to this day. Perhaps more truth inheres in this tradition than men are wont to admit. From their old seat in Asia Minor these Indo-Europeans may have migrated to Germany, a thought found even in Luther.

"Riphath," most likely, refers to the Paphlagonians who dwelt by the river Rhebas ('Ρήβας). Others would place them farther west near the Bosphorus.

"Togarmah" is identified by Delitzsch with *Tilgarimmu* in Cappadocia.

4. **And the sons of Javan: Elishah and Tarshish, Kittim and Dodanim.**

If Javan be the Ionians, then these are all kin to the Greeks. "Elishah" should then be referred to the district Elis. Many reject this; but "modern opinion is greatly divided." *Alašia* on Cyprus, referred to in the Tell-el-Amarna tablets, seems most satisfactory to some.

"Tarshish" must be the old city of Tartessus in southern Spain. The name occurs frequently in the Scriptures. Tarsus in Cilicia seems an ill-founded suggestion.

"Kittim" is a plural noun referring to those who dwelt on the east coast of Cyprus. This name, too, is found rather frequently in the Scriptures; cf. Num. 24:24; Jer. 2:10; Ezek. 27:6 etc.

"Dodanim" is another plural noun. Perhaps the ancient seat of the oracle at Dodona gives us a clue to the locality, which we should then seek in northern Greece. It hardly seems that "Rodanim" (I Chron.

1:7) needs to be considered, for the marginal Keri there too suggests "Dodanim."

So the Japhethites are seen to be spread abroad over a well-defined area extending from Spain to Media and pretty much in one straight line from east to west. The enumeration, however, does not proceed in geographical sequence, apparently for the reason that the descendants are listed according to their age.

5. It is of these that the islands of the nations were populated according to their countries, every man with his own language, according to their class among the nations.

This summarizing verse recalls what portion of the world was really held in possession by the Japhethites. As we said above immediately preceding v. 5, that the territory "from Spain (through Asia Minor) to Media" is involved, so the author says the same thing in the terminology of his day. For "the islands of the nations" are really the Mediterranean coast line (*'iyyey* = *Gestade*, K. W.) including the Black Sea coast line, one broad strip from west to east. To complete this picture the author recalls for us how these Japhethites each had their country and separate language, and were still dwelling in tribal divisions or clans in the midst of their particular nation. Consequently, the *be* before the last word is rather to be taken in its usual sense "in" rather than as a "*be* of norm" as K. S. would make of it (332 r). The emphasis of the initial *me'élleh* is best retained by a rendering like: "It is of these," etc.

b)   The Sons of Ham (6-20)

The following diagram shows at a glance how this list subdivides itself.

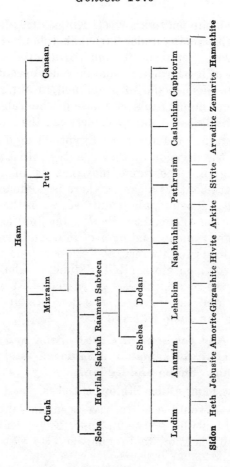

6.   And the sons of Ham: Cush and Mizraim and Put and Canaan.

"Cush," whose various subdivisions are recorded in v. 7, represents the land of Ethiopia to the south of Egypt, but at the same time the Cushites are found extending eastward into Arabia.   However, it seems rather to correspond primarily to the present-day Nubia, (Procksch, Jeremias) which lies north of the country of Ethiopia, as we now know it.   Yet in days of old Cush extended indefinitely to the south.   Just because we happen to know (II Kings 19:9; Isa. 37:9) that the Ethiopians under Tirhakah (about 789 B. C.) clashed with Sennacherib and so definitely came to the notice of the Israelites, that does not exclude earlier knowledge of a people so prominent in antiquity and again offers no clue to a late date of the Table of Nations. The Tell-el-Amarna Tablets call the land *Kashi.*

"Mizraim" definitely is Egypt. The dual form is due to the division of that country into Upper and Lower Egypt. The name may not be of Egyptian origin, but about its meaning there is no doubt.

"Put" is commonly identified with the country known to the ancients as *Punt,* lying in East Africa (Somaliland) and extending over into southern Arabia. It was famous for its incense. Another land is chosen by some commentators (Keil, Skinner), who think of Libya on the northern coast of Africa, west of Egypt.

"Canaan" is, of course, the land of Canaan. The son is the same one referred to in 9:22, 25.

7. And the sons of Cush: Seba and Havilah and Sabtah and Raamah and Sabteca. And the sons of Raamah: Sheba and Dedan.

These must all be Ethiopian tribes.

"Seba" would seem to have been the land around the ancient city of Meroë, in upper Egypt on the Nile, for this city is know to Josephus as Σαβὰ πόλις, the city of Saba.

"Havilah," as a name, means "sandland." It would seem to cover certain Arabic tribes, some of Hamitic extraction, some of Semitic (v. 29), located near "Seba."

"Sabtah" must also be an Ethiopic group, though it is usually identified with the city in Arabia called Sabbatha, famous in days of old for its sixty temples and its trade in incense.

"Raamah" seems to be a tribe of Sabaeans in southwest Arabia.

"Sabteca" represents that branch of the Ethiopians which lay farthest to the east, namely, east of the Persian gulf, where Samuthake (Σαμυθάκη) lay, a name which bears resemblance to Sabteca.

"Sheba," descended from Raamah and thus representing the third generation from Ham, is also mentioned because the kingdom of Sheba was particularly famous; and the land does happen to be referred to rather frequently in the Bible. Southwestern Arabia must again be meant. Incense was also an outstanding product of this land.

"Dedan" is sought in different parts of Arabia, northwest, southeast, southwest. The last seems most likely.

8, 9. Cush begat Nimrod; he was the first tyrant upon earth. He was a mighty hunter in the sight of Yahweh; wherefore it is said: A mighty unter in the sight of Yahweh as Nimrod was.

Here the type of presentation that has prevailed through the chapter to this point is abandoned and a digression is made by the author. Since the first half of the verse already allows itself a different mode of speech than the preceding (*yaladh* = "beget"), this half-verse is promptly stamped as interpolation, the assumption being that no author could have had the least of flexibility of style. For like reasons many hold that with v. 8 b the material must be assigned to J.

In any case, we have here a set of facts about the origin of the Babylonian empire, facts found nowhere else among the records of antiquity. The strangest part about the whole account is that Babylonia and Assyria originated with men of Hamitic descent. When the Bible stands alone in reporting a matter of history, the prevailing tendency is to discredit the Biblical statement. Yet in many other instances statements from other sources are accepted as satisfactory upon the testimony of a single witness. Why discriminate thus against the Scriptures?

The course that our interpretation of these two verses takes will be determined very largely by the meaning of the word "Nimrod." For the meaning of the verbform *nimrodh*, without a doubt, is "let us revolt." Now the other words employed are, if left by themselves, either good or evil in their connotation, depending on the connection in which they appear. *Gibbor* may mean "hero" or "tyrant." "Hunter" *(gibbor tsáyidh)* may be a harmless hunter of the fields, or he may be one who hunts men to enslave them. The phrase, "in the sight of Yahweh," in itself expresses neither approval nor disapproval. But each of these terms acquires a bad sense in the light of the name "Nimrod." The tendency of this Cushite must have been to rise up against, and to attempt to overthrow, all existing order. In fact, he must have used this motto so frequently in exhorting others to rebellion, that finally it was applied to him as a name descriptive of the basic trait of his character. If this be so, then *gibbor* must be rendered "tyrant," or "despot" — a use of the word found also Ps. 52:1, 3; and 120:4, for which passages K. W. justly claims the meaning *Gewaltmensch*. So this inciter to revolt (Nimrod) came to be the first tyrant upon the earth, oppressing others and using them for the furtherance of his own interests.

Now what follows might, perhaps, by itself be taken to refer to hunting in the customary sense, were it not for the phrase "in the sight of Yahweh." For a very questionable meaning results if this phrase *(liphne Yahweh)* be rendered "in the estimation of Yahweh," *nach dem Urteile Yahwehs* (K. C. and others). For such a rendering would in a measure constitute a kind of superlative (K. S. 309 l), but a superlative that bears the meaning that even Yahweh

was impressed by this hunter's prowess and achievements — a thought that strikes us as involving a rather
trivial conception of God. For man's little hunting
exploits are hardly sufficient to rouse the wonder and
admiration of the Almighty. Besides, in this case the
name of Yahweh is used, i. e., the God of mercy and
covenant. So the meaning, claimed also by B D B for
this passage: "in the sight of (estimation)" will have
to be abandoned and the other, offered by B D B
under c) or d) will have to be applied here: either "in
the full (mental) view of" as in 6:13 and Lam. 1:22,
or "openly before" as in I Sam. 12:2 or in Gen. 17:1.
Our objection above applies also to II Kings 5:1, which
refers only to *man's* esteem. What the phrase then
means in this connection is that the gross violation
of men's rights, that this mighty hunter of men became
guilty of, did not elude the watchful eye of Him, who
in mercy regards the welfare of men, Yahweh, but the
fact was openly before Him, even if He did not at once
proceed to take vengeance upon the despot. So the
expression "mighty hunter" does not refer to exploits
in bagging game. In fact, since *gibbor* in v. 8 means
"tyrant" (Meek correctly: "despot"), *gibbor tsáyidh*
of v. 9 should be rendered as "a tyrant or despot of
hunt," which plainly indicates that men and not beasts
were hunted.

Consequently, also the proverbial expression (cf.
I Sam. 19:24; 10:12; Gen. 22:14 etc.) that arose at
this time when, apparently, others too began to engage
in the sport of hunting *men* in order to tyrannize or
enslave them, must be taken in the same sense.

The critical attempts to find Babylonian parallels
for Nimrod are a bit amusing. It is admitted by the
extreme critics, on the one hand, that "a perfectly
convincing Assyriological prototype of the figure of
Nimrod has not as yet been discovered." On the other
hand, Jeremias is so sure that one ought to exist in

the person of Gilgamesch, that he even invents a Babylonian name for him that the Babylonians could have used, *nâmir-uddu,* i. e., "shining light." What an absurd scientific method — manufacturing the desired evidence! Procksch veers into astral myths and makes Nimrod out to be a constellation, Orion — *mirable dictu!*

10-12. The beginning of his kingdom was Babylon, and Erech and Akkad and Calneh in the land of Shinar. From that region he went forth to Assyria and built Nineveh and Rehoboth-ir, and Calah and Resen, between Nineveh and Calah — this is that great city.

Here is the real story of the founding of empires, for that matter, of the first empires. Having the type of character that we find described in v. 8, 9 in the person of Nimrod, we must needs regard both Babylon and Assyria as exponents of the spirit of this world. This attitude over against Babylon is the attitude of the Scriptures in prophetic utterances (cf. Isa. 13, also Isa. 47) as well as in the book of Revelation (18:21). These early kingdoms or empires are, therefore, not to be regarded as useful institutions, guaranteeing law and order in a troubled world, but rather as the achievements of a lawless fellow who taught men to revolt against duly constituted authority.

His first undertaking in this direction is Babylon. Our chief difficulty is to determine the correct relation of this account to the account of the origin of the name Babylon ("confusion"), as set down 11:1-9. Our impression of the matter is this: since v. 11 distinctly says, "he *built* Nineveh," but v. 10 does not ascribe the *building* of Babylon to him, it may well be that Nimrod merely took over the existing city Babel and made it the beginning of his kingdom; then joined the other cities to this mother city. So, in reality, chapter eleven would antedate this portion of chapter ten. If it be claimed that the Babylonian name *Bâbilu* means "gate of God," we need not deny that the Babylonians may have built this more acceptable name upon the one that the Bible offers as connected with the confusion of tongues. Yet, for all that, the truth of the Biblical account on this matter may be regarded as unimpaired.

Now Erech lies southeast of Babylon, a distance of slightly more than one hundred miles. Akkad lies in Northbabylon; Calneh somewhere in the neighborhood, but cuneiform inscriptions do not seem to have identified it. So these four cities in the land of Shinar mark a kind of initial empire. For such cities in days of old regularly had each its own king and therefore counted as so many separate kingdoms. "Shinar" is Babylon, perhaps allied to *Shumir* (Sumerians).

Now A. V. renders v. 11: "Out of that land went forth Asshur and builded Nineveh." Though this translation is grammatically possible, it fails to do justice to what is implied in v. 10, which speaks of the beginning of his kingdom as though it were leading up to the next step of his empire building, which now v. 11 offers. Our rendering of v. 11, then, presupposes that "Asshur" lacks the ending *(ah)* which usually indicates place to which, but is also frequently omitted. It shows Nimrod's second venture in empire building and avoids bringing in a mysterious "Asshur" of whom the Scripture has nothing more to tell. The nucleus of this second undertaking was "Nineveh," known in cuneiform inscriptions as *Ninaa* or *Ninua*, and situated on the upper Tigris opposite the present Mosul. This city, we remark again, was actually founded by Nimrod: he "built" it. But similarly as in the case of Babylon there are sister or daughter cities that make a complex of cities around which the kingdom grows. Of these "Rehoboth-ir" is mentioned first. There is the possibility that this name is used to designate a suburb or suburbs of Nineveh, since the name signifies "broad places of the city"; then it might be the Assyrian *rêbit Ninâ.* The next city of this aggregation is "Calah," identified in cuneiform writing as *Kalchu,* which lay near the confluence of the Tigris and the upper Zab. Then there is "Resen," which according to the text lay between Nineveh and Calah. The author's concluding remark, written by him, no doubt, after Nineveh was already known as a metropolis of no mean proportion, runs thus: "This is that great city." Of course, this refers to Nineveh and shows what component parts went to make it such an outstanding city or city state. This concluding statement fits in so very naturally here, that there is no valid reason for calling these last three words a gloss. With these words the interesting bit of information about this famous Cushite or Ethiopian closes. A valuable bit of information as to the origin of the kingdoms of the world is thus supplied.

13, 14. **And Mizraim begat the Ludim and the Anamim and the Lehabim and the Naphtuchim; and the Pathrusim and the Casluchim (from whom went out the Philistines) and the Kaphtorim.**

Now Mizraim, as pointed out above in v. 6, is Egypt. Consequently, a statement like: "Egypt begat the Ludim," etc., must mean: "from the Egyptians sprang the Ludim," etc. These nations, then, kin to the Egyptians, may have played a more or less important part in days of old but can now in some instances scarcely be identified. The "Ludim" may have dwelt near Egypt, west of the Nile delta. The "Anamim" are usually thought of as having occupied an oasis west of Egypt. The "Lehabim" do seem to bear a name akin to that of the old Libyans, west of Egypt on the north coast of Africa.

For "Naphtuchim" two explanations are given, which, however, arrive at the same result. It is claimed that *naptah* in Egyptian means "the people of Ptah,"

who was revered in Memphis and vicinity (Ebers).
But Brugsch takes the Egyptian word *p-to-(e)m-hit(j)*, which means North-Egypt (cf. K. W. and
B D B).

But the "Pathrusim" must have inhabited South
or Upper Egypt, for *p(ĕ)-tĕ-res* means "south land"
(B D B).

14. The "Casluchim" present difficulties. Some
claim: "not identified." However, the suggestion that
their land is to be sought near Mons Casius, east of
the delta of the Nile, is not out of harmony with what
preceded.

Special difficulty seems to grow out of the fact
that the "Philistines" are now said to have gone out
from the Casluchim. For Amos 9:7 informs us that
the Philistines hail from Caphtor, that is to say, from
the island of Crete. However, the remark of Amos
need not rule out the claim of our passage. Most likely,
Amos lays down the major fact: Crete is primarily
the original home of the Philistines. For that matter,
since according to our explanation the Casluchim are
found just a bit farther along the coast of the Mediterranean, namely toward the southwest, they may originally even have come from Crete. Being near to the
Egyptians, they may have assimilated enough of the
Egyptian mode of life and intermarried with Egyptians
sufficiently to deserve to be classed among the nations
allied to the Egyptians. Then, however, their parallel
affinity to those Cretans settled in the land of Philistia
may have impelled them to "go out" from thence and
settle in Philistia. If Moses reports this, the event
naturally took place before his time. Nor is this assumption at all in conflict with the claim raised by a
number of scholars, namely that both Casluchim and
Philistines are a deposit resulting from swarms of
"maritime nations" (*Seevoelker*, K. W.) that overran
the eastern end of the Mediterranean and even Egypt

in the twelfth century B. C. In fact, successive waves of these nations swooping down from Asia Minor to Crete and beyond are quite reasonably the greatest likelihood. Even more such surging waves may have come than history knows of. That would, then, also help account for the fact that the Philistines after disastrous defeats by Israel keep bobbing up always surprisingly strong. Moses seems to have a complete line of information on all these events involved in the early history of the nations. He also knows that Caphtor (Crete) is chiefly the home of the Philistines and he knows whom they displaced in Canaan: The Avvim (Deut. 2:23). Criticism places too much confidence in its own precarious reconstruction of history and too little confidence in the Biblical records, when it remarks, that this assumption of J that already in Abraham's time (21:32) the Philistines are in the land "is, of course, an anachronism, since they first came there in the twelfth century" (Procksch).

15-19. **And Canaan begat Sidon, his first-born, and Heth and the Jebusite and the Amorite and the Girgashite and the Hivite and the Arkite and the Sinite and the Arvadite and the Zemarite and the Hamathite. And afterward were the families (tribes) of the Canaanites scattered abroad, so that the territory of the Canaanites extended from Sidon toward Gerar as far as Gaza, and over toward Sodom and Gomorrah and Admah and Zeboiyim, even unto Lasha.**

Now the Canaanites are treated, because Moses knew that Israel's associations with these people were destined to be many (cf. 15:16; 46:4 etc.), and Israel must also definitely know who were Canaanites and who not, because of Israel's duty to drive them out of the land of Canaan (Deut. 20:17 and parallels). Statements like the first need not be pressed, where Moses says "Canaan begat Sidon." This may mean that there actually was a son by that name, or that the Sidonites are descended from one of the descendants of Canaan. In this instance the issue is settled by the fact that "Sidon" is described as the "first-born." That clinches the fact that he was an individual and makes it most likely that "Heth," too, was an individual. However, in the list that follows we shall never be able to determine whether names like "Jebusite" involve an ancestor with the actual name of Jebus.

"Sidon" appears as the great Phoenician city of later date. Josh. 11:8; 19:28 it is still "great Zidon" (or "Sidon"). Later Tyre, twenty miles to the south, distinctly overshadows Sidon.

"Heth" is the father of the famous Hittites, who first appear around Hebron in Abraham's time, but the greater number of whom seem to have concentrated around the Orontes River and thence extended over toward the Euphrates, holding the famous city Carchemish. This is the nation whose existence was doubted, though claimed apparently only by the Bible. More recent discoveries have proved not only that the nation existed but that it was a formidable one.

The "Jebusite" (singular, collective, as throughout the rest of the list, K. S. 256 e) centered about Jerusalem.

The "Amorite" dwelled mostly in the mountains, especially around the Lebanon range. The Assyrians called them *Amurri*. They are so prominent at the time of the Conquest that oftentimes all Canaanites are simply called Amorites (cf. Exod. 3:8; 3:17, 13:5 etc.).

The "Girgashite" — not definitely located in Canaan. The "Hivite" mostly in the central portion. The "Arkite" may have dwelt in Arke to the north, *Tell 'Arka*, north of Tripolis, which again lay north of Sidon. The "Sinite" should, no doubt, be placed near the Arkites. The "Arvadite" belongs apparently in the vicinity of the island city Aradus, also north of

Tripolis. Likewise the "Zemarite" may have a remnant of its name in *Tsumra,* north of Tripolis. "Hamathite," without a doubt, must be identified with the ancient and well-known Hamath on the Orontes River; Assyrian: *Emû.*

18 b. While we have thus far seen the original Canaanite tribes and approximately their place of settlement, which was mostly along the coast, we are now informed that they spread out or "were spread abroad" (B D B), *naphótsû,* Nifal from *pûts.* These original "families" or "clans" (*mishpechóth*) now do not seem to have maintained their strength to the north. For the so-called "territory of the Canaanites" extended only from Sidon southward in the direction of the famous stronghold "Gerar," but not entirely toward Gerar but only to Gaza. For "toward Gerar" the Hebrew has an idiom with impersonal use of the second person, namely "as thou goest toward Gerar," (*bo'akhah,* Kal participle: "thou going," K. S. 324 b; 402 a; G. K. 144 h). The suffix of this participle appears written *plene.* But toward the east and south the Canaanite territory extended in the direction of the cities to the southern end of the Dead Sea; "Sodom, Gomorrah, Admah and Zeboiyim." The last two of these are not identified but are merely associated with the overthrow of the whole group in their destruction.

"Lasha" may be on the west shore of the Dead Sea. Jerome, at least, placed it at *Callirhoë,* on the east of the Dead Sea, the site of the later famous "Baths of Herod."

20. **These are the sons of Ham according to their clans and languages in their countries among the nations.**

See v. 5 above. This summarizing verse for the Hamites, differing slightly from v. 5 in its arrangement of terms, is essentially the same as that verse. The original stock to which the parts belonged ("clans") as well as "the languages" were the principles determining the division.

c)   The Sons of Shem (v. 21-31)

21.   **Children were born also to Shem, the father of all the sons of Eber, the elder brother of Japheth.**

According to his custom Moses disposes first of all the matters less relevant to his purpose. His book from this point forward is concerned almost exclusively with Shemites, therefore they must come last in the Table. At once, however, we are also informed of the fact that for the writer the most prominent branch of the Shemites are "the sons of Eber," that is to say, the Hebrews. Yet Hebrews must be regarded as a much broader term than Israelites. For "Eber" as a term primarily means "across" or "the region across the Euphrates River," for it was from this place that Eber himself came (thence his name), even though later such as the Edomites and Ishmaelites bore this name. The term, as we believe Koenig rightly contends (K. W. p. 312), is not identical with the term "Chabiri" mentioned in the Tell-el-Amarna tablets and found making incursions from the south into Canaan in the pre-Israelite days. Besides, though Shem's descendants are mentioned last, we are not on that account to suppose that Shem was the youngest son of Noah. Therefore we read that he was "the elder brother of Japheth." Japheth is mentioned by way of comparison because Shem really had more affinity with Japheth than with Ham.

Shem's descendants are to be graphed as follows:

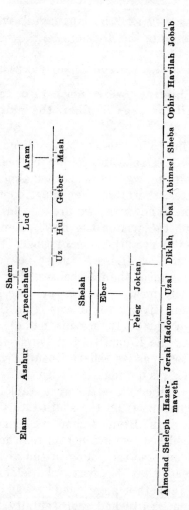

22-24. The sons of Shem: Elam and Asshur and Arpachshad and Lud and Aram. And the sons of Aram: Uz and Hul and Gether and Mash. And Arpachshad begat Shelah, and Shelah begat Eber.

"Elam" is the country east of the Tigris River. The Assyrians speak of it as *Elamtu* meaning "highland." Its ancient capital was Shushan,

"Asshur," used in the Bible sometimes for the personal ancestor, sometimes for the people, sometimes for the land, is Assyria, called Asshur by the old Assyrians themselves. The land originally lay east of the Tigris at the Upper Zab.

"Arpachshad" is usually regarded as referring to the country Arrapachitis on the Upper Zab northeast from Nineveh; Assyrian *Arbacha*.

"Lud" may refer to the Lydians in Asia Minor, of whom Herodotus already reports that they counted themselves to have sprung from Nineveh, a Semite City. Procksch merely makes an untenable statement when he says that for the Lydians in Asia Minor "Semitic origin is simply out of the question."

"Aram" represents the later Aramaeans who dwelt northeast of Palestine. They are in the Bible usually referred to by the name "Syrians." K. C. points out that none of the divisions which later became known as being Aramaeans are listed here, such as: Aram-dammeseq, Aram-Soba, Aram-beth-rechob, Aram-maacha. We should consider this fact an indication of the great age of this table.

23. Under the persons (or lands, or peoples) derived from Aram are listed:

"Uz," concerning which name we know practically only that it represents a division of Aramaeans. Concerning "Gether" and "Hul" the situation is the same. "Mash" might be *Mons Masius*, "north of Nisibis (between Armenia and Mesopotamia)."

Then the line of Arpachshad is traced through several successive generations apparently: "Shelah," of whom we know nothing, "Eber," discussed above on v. 21. Eber has two sons. The first is Peleg, the second Joktan.

25. **And unto Eber there were born two sons, the name of the one was Peleg — for in his time**

the earth was divided — and the name of his brother, Joktan.

A verse such as this makes it highly probable that in the lists of the various descendants, that we have had thus far, the names used actually were the names of individual persons. For here Peleg and Joktan are distinctly called "sons," and one is said to be the "brother" of the other. "Peleg" means "division," for he lived at the time when the earth was divided *(niphlegah)* and the name given to the man is in memory of this event. The event referred to in chapter eleven must be the one under consideration — the Confusion of Tongues. Nothing more is told about Peleg. He may have been the father of a people, he may not. However, "Joktan" was the father of numerous offspring, all of whom appear to be founders of Arabic tribes, especially those of Yemen. Aside from this fact very little is known concerning the tribe names about to be given in v. 26-29.

26-29. And Joktan begat Almodad and Sheleph and Hazarmaveth and Jerah; and Hadoram and Uzal and Diklah; and Obal and Abimael and Sheba; and Ophir and Havilah and Jobab; all these were the sons of Joktan.

"Almodad" is some south-Arabic people. The *"al"* may represent the Hebrew "el," i. e., God. So the name may mean Modad is God. "Sheleph" belongs into the same neighborhood. "Hazarmaveth" seems to be a form derived from Hadramant, which lies in southeastern Arabia, a region from which myrrh used to be exported. "Jerah" again may be another name for the moon, and so the name of a tribe that worshipped the moon-god.

27. "Hadoram" must have represented some other group in Arabia, toward the south. "Uzal" is claimed to have been an old name of the capital city of the district Yemen. Since "Diklah" is allied to the

Arabic name for a date-palm, this name may refer
to a tribe that dwelt in a region where date-palms
abounded.

28. About "Obal" and "Abimael" we know nothing except that they must belong somewhere in Arabia.
"Sheba," as to form, is identical with the Sheba of
v. 7. Since we there located it in southwestern Arabia,
though involving a Hamite group, we must admit the
suitability of this location for a Semitic tribe. In some
manner that we cannot now determine there must have
been a blending of the Hamitic and the Semitic in
this people.

29. "Ophir," then, would seem to belong, as do
all these other sons of Shem, into southern Arabia,
not in India, as is commonly conjectured, nor in East
Africa. "Havilah," mentioned in v. 7 also, must present
a situation analogous to that of Sheba — a blending
of the Hamitic and the Semitic element. "Jobab," not
located, is the last member of the group. Since thirteen
descendants of one man is a surprisingly large number,
the verse closes by reassuring us that these all actually
were descended from Joktan.

30. **The section inhabited by them extended
from Mesha in the direction of Sephar, to the eastern
mountains.**

The Hebrew expression literally runs thus: "And
their dwellings were from Mesha as thou goest to
Sephar." In present-day English that must mean
something like what our rendering presents. On "as
thou goest" see v. 19. Though both "Mesha" and
"Sephar" must lie in southern Arabia, we know too
little about their location to be able to understand the
bearing of the verse.

31. **These are the sons of Shem according to
their clans and languages in their lands according to
their nations.**

In substance this verse agrees with v. 20.

32. These are the tribes of the sons of Noah according to their branches among their various nationalities. From these were the nations of the earth spread abroad after the flood.

This final summary binds together the three main branches *(tôledôth)* of the human race. Apparently, the last statement leaves us under the impression that all the nations of the earth spreading abroad after the Flood came from this stock. How such racial groups as the Mongolians or Chinese or North American Indians and the like fit into this picture has not yet been discerned. Some count exactly seventy descendants of Noah in this list (Delitzsch). Others arrive at a total of sixty-eight. Koenig counts seventy-one. To insist on the symbolical number seventy is hardly warranted.

HOMILETICAL SUGGESTIONS

It may very well be questioned whether a man should ever preach on a chapter such as this. It could be expounded in adult Bible class study, and even then a summary view of the whole chapter and its purpose might meet all needs. Perhaps the section v. 8-11 could be used on occasion to set forth the story of the origin of the kingdoms of this world and their basic character. But such a sermon might have too little gospel content and be largely negative in character, showing what the kingdom of God is *not*.

CHAPTER XI

d)   **The Confusion of Tongues** (11:1-9)

This is the last item to be reported under the head of the "History of the sons of Noah," which began 10:1. When this item is disposed of, the general history of mankind will be concluded, and the author may begin to center on the line of promise in Shem (11:10). That the author was intending right along to treat of this confusion of tongues appears from 10:25, where in connection with Peleg it is mentioned that "in his days was the earth divided."

If the author's brief history of all mankind is to be at least relatively complete, it must deal with all the major factors that help explain the present state of the world. Besides a knowledge of the origin of sin and its divisive effects in general; besides a knowledge of the first great judgment upon the earth — the Flood; besides a summary account of the diffusion of the various nations after the Flood, we need, indeed, also some explanation of the great variety of different languages and dialects that are found in the world and how these languages originated. The story of their origin was known to Moses and was by him written down as an inspired and an instructive account, which finds no worthy parallel in the literature of earliest antiquity.

It is now conceded that a cuneiform account of the confusion of tongues is not available. Jeremias claims to have demonstrated the error of the opinion that a parallel was available. A few rather late parallels are to be found, which Jeremias conveniently lists *(Das Alte Testament im Lichte des alten Orients,*

(381)

p. 175 ff.). These are found in the Sibylline oracles, a pseudepigraphic writing, whose earliest parts reach back only to the second century B. C., or again in Alexander Polyhistor, of the first century B. C.; also in writings of Moses of Chorene, an Armenian of the fifth century A. D., and lastly in the Ethiopic book of Jubilees, perhaps a still later work. Mankind does not pride itself on faithful remembrance of the things of its history that are less honorable. Scripture records all important events with strict impartiality.

The time of this event is about one hundred years after the Flood, since Peleg (10:25) receives his name, which signifies "division," in memory of this event, and Peleg was born 1757 after the Creation, and so one hundred years after the Flood (1656). If it be thought that one hundred years is too short a time to allow for the increase of the human race to sufficient strength to be able to undertake a work of such magnitude, the computations of Keil have shown that the human race might have grown to a total of about 30,000 persons on the supposition that the families ordinarily had about eight children, a reasonable assumption for those times. Besides, it must be recalled that practically the whole human race participated in this project.

If, then, the account as a whole shows the confusion of tongues to be the outgrowth of human presumption and disobedience, the practical lesson of the story must be primarily this, that the present resultant confusion that is upon us must serve as a constant reminder of the inclination of the human heart to arrogance and disobedience. The multiplicity of languages upon the face of the earth is a monument not to human ingenuity but to human sin.

Naturally, this account of the confusion of tongues is not a second attempt to set forth, as criticism claims, what had already been covered in chapter ten. For the tenth chapter describes only the various racial

groups into which the human family *naturally* divided
itself. Our chapter shows how an unnatural dispersion
was caused by human sin on the basis of distinct
languages. Chapter ten describes progressive development; chapter eleven records a divine judgment. As
usual, this historical account is libelled by the critics as
being "a mythical and legendary account."

1, 2. **And all the inhabitants of the earth had
one language and one and the same vocabulary.
And it came to pass as they journeyed eastward
that they discovered a broad plain in the land of
Shinar and settled down there.**

If all the inhabitants of the postdiluvian world
are, as the Scriptures teach, descended from Noah, they
must, indeed, have used one and the same language.
Of this very natural fact the writer makes us aware
by dwelling besides upon the fact that the one
"language" (*saphah*, literally: "lip") had not yet become differentiated into various dialects; for the word
"lip" apparently emphasizes that the lips of all were
shaped alike in uttering words. In addition, the very
"words" *(debharim)* were of one sort *'achadhim,* "one
and the same" (B D B). We should say, all had "the
same vocabulary." *Debharim 'achadhim* cannot mean
"few words" (Meek), as though we were here dealing
with a crude type of primitive man. For though the
plural *'achadhim* does in some instances mean "few,"
that cannot be the case where *'e(ch)chad* ("one") —
the singular of the same word — appears in parallel
use in the same sentence. In the early days after the
Flood such a complete speech unity was, indeed, an
indication of a deeper spiritual and cultural unity.
But at the point where our chapter begins the inner
unity was already a thing of the past. Ham and Canaan represent the strongest manifestation of a divergent spirit. The word "earth" must here by metonomy
represent "the inhabitants of the earth." *Wayhi* is

masculine, though *ha'arets* is feminine, since the sentence usually begins with the neutral Hebrew form, i. e., the masculine (G. K. 145 d).

2. The region of Ararat (8:4) was the center from which the human race began to spread abroad upon the earth, all fanciful claims to the contrary notwithstanding. From this cradle of the human race men "journeyed (*nasa'* — lit. "to pull up stakes") eastward." Though *miqqédem* would seem to mean "from the east" and so apparently "westward," yet the usage of the term in 2:8; 3:24; 12:8 and 13:11 indicates that "eastward" must be the correct rendering. Since "eastward" includes southeastward, this interpretation is doubly established by the simple fact that Babylon (Shinar) lies southeast of Ararat. "Shinar," though including, perhaps, more than the land of Babylon (cf. on 10:10), is yet that extremely fertile land that the ancients praised so highly, attributing to it two hundred fold fertility and more. We can readily see what attracted them to this "broad plain" *(biq'ah)*. For though this word is also rendered "valley," it signifies a broad plain rather than a narrow gorge, though both plain and gorge are bounded by mountains. So fertile a land invites men to "settle down" permanently (*yashabh*, originally only: "to sit down").

3, 4. **And they said, one to another: Come, let us make bricks and let us burn them well. And they used brick in place of stone and bitumen in place of mortar. And they said: Come, let us build for ourselves a city and especially a tower whose top shall reach to heaven, and let us make for ourselves a name, lest we be scattered abroad upon the face of the whole earth.**

Some time after having become established in the land of Shinar — no one can say how long after — they who constituted the human race resolved upon building a city and a tower. As many remains in this region show, such towers were regular adjuncts to the cities. They were called *zikkurats* and were temple-towers. Nothing indicates that the venture described in our chapter is a temple-tower. Besides, everything seems to indicate that this is the first tower ever attempted. It would, then, seem as though all these later towers, in spite of the divine judgment upon the first, are imitations of the first to an extent; but at the same time they appear to constitute an attempt to deflect any possibility of divine punishment by consecrating them to the guardian divinity of the city.

To make the scene as vivid as possible the writer takes us back to the first counsels that were held as the titanic project got under way. With great eagerness of spirit they encourage one another: note the "come" (Whitelaw: "come on") in v. 3 and again in v. 4. *Habhah,* imperative, strong form, from *yahabh,* though second person, used with the hortative first person (K. S. 355 g). First they encourage one another to the arduous task of making the bricks and laying them. One almost sees the originators of the plan start from their seats and mutually ("one to another") exhort one another to get under way. *Nilbenah lebhenîm* involves a cognate object, like the parallel Assyrian *labânu libittu.* The verbs have the hortative ending *ah.* "Let us burn well" uses the expression *nisrephah lisrepha,* "let us burn to a burning," which may be rendered as followed by a dative of product, or merely by an adverbial phrase. In any case, it must mean: "burn well." Here Moses inserts an explanatory statement before he lets us hear the rest of their purpose by dwelling upon the unique nature of the materials used — unique for such as are in rocky Palestine with its innumerable stones. For the builders purpose to use their burnt brick in place of stone and bitumen for mortar. Abundant remains of similar structures display how very accurate the author is in his statement.

For more substantial buildings not the sun-dried but
the kiln-dried bricks were used, and bitumen sealed
the joints.   Such structures cohere very firmly to this
present day.   To a non-Babylonian such a mode of
building would seem strange as well as particularly
worthy of notice.   This explains the insertion of the
parenthesis.   Critics fail to discern the propriety of
this parenthesis at this point and to find evidence of
divergent accounts.   The strangest claim of the critics
is that here in this simple and coherent narrative two
original and divergent accounts, a city story and a
tower story, were woven into one.

4.   The purpose of the first exhortation to burn
bricks (v. 3), of course, is that therewith structures
might be reared.   These structures are to be "a city
and especially a tower."   The original says *"and* a
tower," but without a doubt, the major purpose was
the tower, therefore we have here the so-called *waw
speciale* = "and in particular."   The explanation of the
builders as to the purpose of the tower reveals clearly
the ungodly purpose that motivated the entire undertaking.   In fact, several ungodly purposes are here
intimately intertwined.   First of all, in reference to the
tower *(mighdal)* they say: "whose top shall reach to
heaven."   Now, indeed, in other uses of the phrase "to
heaven" (cf. Deut. 1:28; 9:1; Ps. 107:26) a hyperbole
is plainly involved, yet, if we take into consideration
the defiant spirit of the rest of the statement, we can
hardly go wrong if we interpret the phrase as meant
literally here.   This already is an ungodly purpose.
But we dare hardly make it involve a dethroning of
God, because such a purpose, if harbored, would apparently have found expression at this point.   Nor is
there any sense in letting these builders appear as
providing a safety measure against another Flood.
For the word guaranteeing the non-recurrence of the
Flood was, without a doubt, well known; and, in the

second place, our verse gives full expression to their purpose. Besides, such fantastic reports about a tower which was actually raised to a height of nine miles and was then destroyed by a strong wind, deserve the sharp condemnation that Luther already bestowed on them. The preposition in *bashshamáyim* is the "Beth of contact," used with verbs of touching.

The first part of the purpose expressed is: "let us make for ourselves a name." So, then, the statement: "let us make a tower whose top shall reach to heaven" is only auxiliary to this part, the making of a name. "Making a name" *(na'aseh shem)* signifies to acquire fame or a reputation. The passages claimed for the use of the word "name" for "monument" (cf. II Sam. 8:13; Isa. 55:13) hardly establish that meaning here. These builders are, for one thing, strenuously determined to achieve fame. No effort is to be spared. If stones are not available, they must be manufactured. Nothing shall deter these men, so greedy of enhancing the glory of their own name. This also is a part of their ungodly purpose.

The major purpose of these defiant builders lies in the word which represents the climax of their endeavors: "lest we be scattered abroad upon the face of the whole earth." This word breathes defiance of God. After the Flood God had bidden Noah (9:1) and his sons "to replenish the earth." This, of necessity, involved spreading abroad. These Babylonian builders were sensing that now, as their inner oneness of purpose was lost — for they were no longer one in the fear of God — they might sooner or later scatter after all. They preferred to remain a closely welded unit and to refuse to obey God's injunction. The tower was to provide the rallying point and to be at the same time a token of their oneness of purpose. So it, of necessity, becomes the symbol of defiance of God. From this historic incident it appears that later tales like those of the heaven-storming Titans originated. At the same time nothing could more flagrantly display how little of the unity of faith remained in humankind. Since God does not for them supply that which draws their hearts into a unity of purpose, so vain a thing as this inanimate, useless tower is to weld them into a unity. Such a concentrated spirit of opposition to God is sufficiently serious to call for divine intervention. It was the climax of the ungodly purpose involved in this entire venture.

5. **And Yahweh came down to see the city and particularly the tower which the children of men built.**

The anthropomorphic expression Yahweh "came down" *(yaradh)* is a vivid way of stating that God interposed. Where He had till now, as so often in the affairs of the children of men, simply allowed things to take their course, now He manifestly intervenes and takes the situation in hand. His judicial control and regulation is His coming down. Therefore the expression is not the same here as in Exod. 19:20; 34:5; Num. 11:25; 12:5, where Yahweh actually descended in visible fashion to deal with men face to face. It is rather to be likened to similar instances like Exod. 3:8; Num. 11:17, or, involving a different expression, 17:22; 35:13. Crude conceptions of such coming down are rendered impossible by such passage of Scripture as I Kings 8:17; Ps. 139; Prov. 15:3. The Targum, as usual, paraphrases the expression: "Yahweh revealed Himself."

The work had progressed very definitely at this time when God intervened, as the perfect form of the word *banû* indicates. For this cannot here mean "had completed," but merely: "had built to this point." Besides, the use of the verb "go down," here as well as in v. 7, does not point to a twofold going down with a return to heaven intervening; or, as some would have, first a more remote approach, then a closer approach. The simplest solution of the problem is that offered by Strack: the typical style of Hebrew narrative is being followed, first a general statement, newspaper-heading-like, covers the case, then follow the details. *Lir'oth* = infinitive of purpose (K. S. 407 a).

6. **And Yahweh said: Behold, the people are one and they all have one language, and this is merely the beginning of what they do, and now from nothing that they devise to do will they desist. Come, let us go down and there confuse their language so that one man will not be able to understand another's speech.**

God is spoken of as Yahweh because of the mercy He displays in preventing mankind from carrying out its pernicious purpose. The root of the trouble lies very largely in the fact that "the people" on the earth are but "one" and are bound together into a strong unity by "one language." This is to an extent an incongruity. Inner enmity is no longer a fact, why should outward unity be? It cannot but work harm to let this situation continue. As little as sinful man deserves a habitation like the garden of Eden, so little does a disunited human family deserve the unifying medium of one language. Though mankind have the one language, good cannot come from the possession of it. This is the very line of argument followed by the divine word, for God charges: "this is merely the beginning of what they do." As long as the medium of one language is theirs, just so long will they be able to carry through reasonable though ungodly projects that they may happen to take in hand. God discerns that similar undertakings will follow upon this one. "This is the beginning of their doing" means that more will be undertaken after this first enterprise. "From nothing that they devise to do will they desist." If, however, the only unity which they still possess is disturbed — the unity of language — then all such ungodly endeavors of the future will be cancelled. *Hachchillam*, Hifil infinitive with double reduplication, irregular, from *Challal*.

So pitting His divine resolution against theirs in a hortatory *habhah*, calculated to offset that of mankind in v. 3 and v. 4, Yahweh determines "to go down," that is, actively to interfere in what He has winked at thus far, and to "confuse their language." The result of this is going to be what is expressed as the divine purpose, "so that one man will not be able to understand another's speech." Exactly how this was accomplished we cannot now determine. Whether, as some contend, the organ of hearing was wrought upon; or, as others claim, a modification of speech was involved; or whether, as still others believe, the inner character, of which speech is a reflex, was so modified that it expressed itself otherwise than heretofore, no man will ever be able to determine. Whether the effects were immediate or whether they began to appear gradually, even this we can scarcely guess at. Besides, not every last person was at once alienated from every other person. Enough to know that divine Wisdom determined upon this effective means of checking man's impudence and that this device was adequate for its purpose.

The plural, "let *us* go down" *(neredhah),* is spoken out of the fulness of the character of God, who is called by the plural name *'Elohîm* and who possesses unbounded resources and potentialities. Though not a direct reference to the Holy Trinity, the plural here involves that too. The same plural in 1:26 and 3:22.

8, 9. So Yahweh scattered them abroad from thence all over the earth and they left off building the city. Wherefore its name is called Babel be-

cause there Yahweh made a babble of the languages of all the earth, and from thence Yahweh scattered them abroad all over the earth.

With astounding ease God has wrought the confusion of His enemies and made them desist from their purpose. Not only that, they must even obey His command, "replenish the earth," though they certainly never intended to do so. Yet where that viewpoint naturally suggests itself, Moses regards the whole transaction rather as a demonstration of the mercy of God — God defeated man's purpose so as to prevent man from injuring himself further — as the use of the divine name Yahweh, three times in these two verses, suggests. The term "city" is used for the whole project, for, naturally, the tower was abandoned also — a legitimate synecdoche.

9. Since the verb *balal* means "to confuse" and from it the form *balbel*, contracted to *Babel* is derived, we have here the actual origin of the name of this famed city. Meek conveys the paronomasia involved very effectively by a rendering which we have followed above: . . . . "Called *Babel* because there Yahweh made a *babble*" . . . Whatever other interpretation the Babylonians themselves may have put upon this name (cf. 10:10 *supra*), this Biblical interpretation is the original and it remains valid. The play upon words which the Hebrew allows does not, however, now give warrant to deduce the claim, held by theologians ancient and modern, that Hebrew was the original language of mankind, for, as we have shown above, this same play upon words is reproducible just as effectively in English. The verb *qara'* presents a good illustration of the use of impersonal verbs, "one called" = "men called," or, passive "is called," (K. S. 324 c). Though *men* scatter because of their inability to co-operate,

this result is very properly ascribed to Yahweh, "*He* scattered them abroad."

Much interest centers on the question whether the ruins of the Tower of Babel are still extant. Two rival claimants for the distinction stand out: a) the site of the ruins of the temple of Nebo at Borsippa usually called *Birs Nimrûd* and situated southwest of Babylon on the west bank of the Euphrates; here is a tower of seven stages, each stage of a different color. Beginning at the top, the first is silver (for the moon), the second, dark blue (for Mercury), the third, a whitish yellow (for Venus), the fourth, golden (for the sun), the fifth, rose red (for Mars), the sixth, brownish red (for Jupiter), the seventh, black (for Saturn). The ruins of the tower still tower fifty yards above the rest of the mass of ruins. b) The second contestant for the honor is the place of the temple of Marduk in Babylon, called *Esagil* and having a tower called *E-temen-an-ki*. Though this last-mentioned tower has the advantage of being in the city, whereas the former is at some distance from it (about fifteen miles), yet it will be noted that the city and the tower are mentioned separately in v. 4. Besides, the very significant fact is recorded by history that when Nebuchadnezzar (604-562 B. C.) determined to repair the Birs-Nimrud tower *he provided it with a peak,* which it had before apparently not possessed. Though the opinions of scholars are still quite sharply divided on this question, we cast our vote for the site of the Nebo tower at Borsippa. Yet we do not claim that the seven stages of the tower dedicated to the seven planets and so also to the seven major deities were at the time of the first building already appointed to these idols; because we do not believe that idolatry had developed to such an extent at that time. Nor have we any means of knowing how many stages of the tower had been completed at the time the work was interrupted. Nor do we know for a certainty that the Birs-Nimrud tower is actually the Tower of Babel.

V. The History of Shem (v. 10-26)

In 9:26 the particular blessedness that Shem should enjoy is indicated. We showed that the statement involved Messianic import. Now the author traces out the line of Shem until he comes to that point where the chosen line begins to develop into one distinct people. There is a fine propriety about the above heading: Shem's history is primarily the story of his descendants.

Moses is still following very consistently the plan carried through the entire book of Genesis: he disposes briefly of the less relevant (history of Shem) that he might treat at length the more essential (history of Terah).

10, 11. This is the history (see on 2:4) **of Shem. Shem was a hundred years old and begat Arpachshad two years after the Flood. And Shem lived, after he begat Arpachshad, five hundred years, and begat sons and daughters.**

12, 13. And Arpachshad lived thirty-five years and begat Shelah. And Arpachshad lived, after he begat Shelah, four hundred and three years, and begat sons and daughters.

14, 15. And Shelah lived thirty years and begat Eber. And Shelah lived, after he begat Eber, four hundred and three years, and begat sons and daughters.

16, 17. And Eber lived thirty-four years and begat Peleg. And Eber lived, after he begat Peleg, four hundred and thirty years, and begat sons and daughters.

18, 19. And Peleg lived thirty years and begat Reu. And Peleg lived, after he begat Reu, two

**hundred and nine years, and he begat sons and
daughters.**

20, 21.   **And Reu lived thirty-two years and begat Serug.   And Reu lived, after he begat Serug,
two hundred and seven years, and begat sons and
daughters.**

22, 23.   **And Serug lived thirty years and begat
Nahor.   And Serug lived, after he begat Nahor, two
hundred years, and begat sons and daughters.**

24, 25.   **And Nahor lived twenty-nine years
and begat Terah.   And Nahor lived, after he begat
Terah, a hundred and nineteen years, and begat sons
and daughters.**

26.   **And Terah lived seventy years and begat
Abraham and Nahor and Haran.**

On this history of Shem as a whole we must
remark that it differs as to the pattern followed from
chapter five in but one respect, namely in that it
gives no separate statement of the total age of the
individual, nor of the fact that he died. Equally apparent is the gradual decline of the span of human
life: the first child is born earlier, and the rest of life
is a shorter period.

However, a few details demand attention. So in
v. 10 the one phrase that is added is only a variation
from the strict pattern of regular form throughout
the entire *toledôth,* viz., the phrase "two years after
the Flood." To us the simplest explanation of this
phrase lies in the fact that, according to 10:22, Shem
had two other sons before Arpachshad, namely Elam
and Asshur. If, then, these three children were born
in rapid succession, it would not be a physical impossibility to have Arpachshad "begotten" two years after
the Flood. Other explanations offered are not as simple
as this one.

We believe the following tabular representation
will set forth the facts involved more clearly than any
other mode of representation.

	Age at birth of first son	*Year of birth*	*Years after birth of first son*	*Total age*	*Year of death*
Shem	100	1556	500	600	2156
Arpachshad	35	1658	403	438	2096
Shelah	30	1693	403	433	2126
Eber	34	1723	430	473	2187
Peleg	30	1757	209	239	1996
Reu	32	1787	207	239	2026
Serug	30	1819	200	230	2049
Nahor	29	1849	119	148	1997
Terah	70	1878	135	205	2083
Abraham	100	1948	75	175	2123
Isaac	60	2048	120	180	2228
Jacob	....	2108	......	130	....

For convenience' sake we have appended three
names for which the requisite information is not found
in our chapter. A comparison yields the following
interesting facts. Since Noah died 2006, he lived fifty-
eight years after the birth of Abraham. Shem, for
that matter, did not die till Jacob was forty-eight
years old. Furthermore, Shem outlived even Abraham,
as did also Eber. No doubt, there was a divine providence behind this matter of ages. Men like Noah and
Shem were granted great length of life that, being
historic personages and survivors of the Flood, they
might by their very presence as well as by their testimony offer warning to their godless successors. For
Luther, no doubt, argues correctly when he deduces
from the activity of the godless in their ungodly projects, that the true children of God will on their part
also have proved themselves active in upholding righteousness and in directing the Old Testament church.
These godly patriarchs were the repositories of sound

tradition and pillars and bulwarks of the truth over against the corruption wrought by error.

We see at this point, too, how very few links there actually were in the chain of tradition from Adam to Abraham. For since Adam lived to the time of Methuselah (or Lamech), and Methuselah lived to the time of Shem, and Shem lived to the time of Jacob, the original truth which Adam possessed was transmitted through but three links of the chain till it came into Jacob's possession. When we consider besides how these men were all renowed for their piety and their fidelity, we may readily concede that they must have watched over the preservation of truth with zealous care.

Part of the ground of this genealogy, as far as Peleg, was covered by the preceding chapter. See 10:25. One especially noteworthy fact in reference to Peleg is that with him the span of human life dropped to almost half of what it had been attaining to before. But Peleg happened to be the one in whose time the confusion of tongues took place (10:25).

It is rather difficult to determine definitely just what some of the proper names of this list may mean. No doubt, after the analogy of "Peleg," they were names with a distinct meaning. Above, on 10:22, we indicated that "Arpachshad" may be another name for a district northeast of Nineveh. So, likewise, the Assyrian name *Sarûg* may be identical with our "*Serug.*" *Sarûg* is a district in Mesopotamia. From this it appears that these individuals in our list will in some cases at least have given their name to the district which they or their desendants occupied. "Eber" may mean "the man from across," i. e., the river Euphrates. Such meaning may quite naturally attach itself to a man, and K. C., therefore, concludes too hastily that these names may not all refer properly to persons. "Terah" may mean a type of ibex, a mountain goat. But, on the other hand, K. C. very correctly points out

that because of names like Terah we are not by any
means justified in concluding that a totemistic stage
of religion was characteristic of men of this time.

Somewhat like the history of Adam (5:32) this
history of Shem concludes with the three sons of the
last member of the list.

VI.   The History of Terah (11:27-25:11)

27, 28.   **This is the history of Terah.   Terah
begat Abram and Nahor and Haran.   And Haran
begat Lot.   And Haran died before Terah, his
father, in the land of his birth, in Ur of Chaldees.**

It is a rather remarkable fact that this history of
Terah, which deals but very briefly with Terah himself,
covers the entire history of Abraham, so that no
separate history of Abraham occurs in a book in which
he may well be said to be the chief character.   Perhaps
the following suggestion might cover the case: Joshua
24:2 Terah, the father of Israel, is said to have served
other gods beyond the River (Euphrates), yet 11:31
Terah leaves Ur, a center of idolatry, with Abraham.
Perhaps this departure of his represents a break with
idolatry, as Luther, too, supposes, a break which was
completely realized in Abraham, so that Abraham
can be said to complete the movement Terah began,
that is to say, "the history of Terah."

The three sons mentioned in v. 26 are again listed
in v. 27, for this is a new "story" and here the fortunes
of these three are to be treated in detail.   Haran is
disposed of first because he dies after having begotten
a son, Lot.   This death occurs "before Terah," i. e.,
during Terah's lifetime.   Apparently, this was the first
instance where a man of the race of godly men died
during his father's lifetime.   No doubt, this death
caused Terah great grief, but yet this obvious fact does
not give us warrant to translate '*al-peney* in the
sense: "to the great grief of."   Special mention is made

of the fact that he died in Ur of Chaldees, because Terah and the rest of his family were soon going to leave Ur of Chaldees behind. But Ur was "the land of his birth." Consequently, Terah lived there before Haran was born.

As to the location of Ur again two principal locations contend for pre-eminence. Some maintain that it must lie north or northwest of Haran. Others, and by far the majority, in a spot identified as Uru, 125 miles southeast of Babylon, south of the lower Euphrates, a spot where extensive excavations have been made, (cf. C. Leonard Wooley's "Ur of Chaldees") and where the worship of the moongod Sin prevailed. It is called in the original *Ur Kasdîm*. Now, as K. W. maintains, a phonetic law of the Babylonians would transmute the form *Kasdîm* into *Kaldu*, as also the LXX translate: Χαλδαῖοι. These Chaldeans, at first merely a prominent tribe, later become the dominant group in Babylon(Hab. 1:6). This Ur is also called *Muqajjar* at present, meaning "asphaltized." Some spell it *Muqayyar*.

29, 30. Now Abram and Nahor married: the name of Abram's wife was Sarai, and the name of Nahor's wife was Milcah, the daughter of Haran, the father of Milcah and of Yiscah. But Sarai was barren; she had no children.

"To take a wife" *(laqach 'ishshah)* is the technical Hebrew expression for getting married. The marriage as well as the wives of Abraham and Nahor are of importance for the rest of this history, therefore they are here formally reported. Abraham's wife bears the name "Sarai" (Heb. *Saray* — with an old feminine ending — meaning "princess"), and she must, according to her name, have been a woman of a measure of social standing. She cannot be identical with the Yiscah mentioned in this verse, as Jewish commentators in particular have long contended, even though we may not be

able to discover why this unknown Yiscah should have
been introduced at this point. For Sarai, according to
20:12, was indeed Abraham's sister, that is daughter
of the same father but not of the same mother, and,
therefore, really half-sister; but Yiscah's father was
Haran. We dare not, however, judge relations such
as these — which would now be properly termed incestuous — according to the standards of the present
time. As long as it pleased God to let the human race
descend from one pair, it must be conceded that for a
time marriage between brothers and sisters was a
necessity. It may well take quite a time before a sense
of the impropriety of such a relation arose. Nahor
marries Milcah, his niece, of whom we shall hear later.
The Hebrew repeats the term "father" thus: "the
father of Milcah and the father of Yiscah" because of
a tendency to avoid a succession of dependent nouns
(K. S. 276 a).

30. Since Sarai's barrenness is to figure rather
prominently in the succeeding events, attention is
drawn to it emphatically at this point already, also by
the parallel statement: "she had no children." The
Hebrew idiom prefers the singular, where we use the
plural; for the Hebrew says: "she had no child,"
waladh, unusual for *yéledh.* Other cases where special
mention of barrenness is made are: 16:2; 25:21;
29:31; Judg. 13:2; I Sam. 1:5; 2:5.

"Abram" may mean "the exalted father" or "the
Exalted One is my father." The meaning of "Nahor"
is obscure. "Haran" would seem to mean "moun-
taineer." "Sarai," according to its root, cannot be the
same as *Sharra* and so related to *Sharratu,* the goddess
of Charran, the wife of the moongod *Sin.* Such efforts
to make historical personages indentical with mythological figures degrade Biblical history.

**31, 32. Now Terah took his son, Abram, and
his grandson, Lot, the son of Haran, and Sarai, his**

daughter-in-law, the wife of his son Abram, and they went forth with them from Ur of Chaldees to go to the land of Canaan; and they came to Haran and settled down there. And the days of Terah were two hundred and five years, and Terah died in Haran.

In connection with v. 27 we discussed the reason why Terah may have left Ur. We believe that what we said goes deeper into the case than does the supposition that this was a step in conformity with certain other movements of the time, as, for example, the going forth of the Phœnicians toward the sea. Not all of Terah's clan go with him. Nahor and Milcah stay behind, although they too are afterward found in Mesopotamia (24:10). Those mentioned as taken along by Terah are Abram, Sarai, and Lot, his orphaned grandson. Why Canaan was definitely fixed upon as goal at the time of the departure from Ur cannot be determined. It may then already have counted as a land flowing with milk and honey. Apparently, the trip straight west across the desert would have been impossible with flocks and herds. So the first stage of the journey went northwest to Mesopotamia to the city of Haran in Padan Aram, a distance of about 600 miles. Nor will we ever be able to determine why they all "settled down (*yashabh* = originally, "to sit down") there." Did Terah feel that he was far enough removed from the pernicious influences of idolatry? Did the land as such appeal to him? In spite of what we said on v. 27 above, it must be remarked that, according to Josh. 24:2, Terah served other gods "beyond the river." Haran lies beyond the river. Even if our original contention was correct, Terah apparently did not successfully carry through the break with idolatry, as it was practiced in those lands. The Jewish tradition asserts that the original summons, like unto that found 12:1 ff., came to Terah in Ur of Chaldees, but that Terah failed to obey it;

Abraham, however, did offer the requisite obedience. We cannot help but feel in sympathy with this approach to the problem, as we shall show especially at the beginning of chapter twelve.

'Artsah has the old ending *ah* locative to express place to which (K. S. 330 a). *Yetse'û, "they* went forth," has as its subject Terah and Abraham; "with *them"* means: Sarai and Lot.

32. Terah's history closes with the statement of his age, 205 years. His death occurred in Haran. A difficulty must be touched upon here. Acts 7:4, Stephen, in an inspired address (cf. Acts 6:10), tells us that Abraham left, "when his father was dead." Yet it appears that Terah lived sixty years after Abram's departure from Haran. For his total age was 205 years, and Abraham was born when Terah was seventy (v. 26) and was seventy-five when he left Haran (12:4) : 205-145 = 60. How can Stephen say, Abram left "when his father was dead"? The question is a very difficult one. Luther once expressed the thought that he would be exceedingly grateful for a man sufficiently clever to offer the solution. One attempt at solution makes the statement of v. 26 place Abram first because of his great importance, but claims that Nahor and Haran were both older — or at least Nahor, for Abram's son marries Nahor's granddaughter. But this last reason is covered already by the mere fact that Abram's son was begotten very late and so would naturally be a contemporary with Rebecca, Nahor's grandchild. A second explanation takes the words of Acts 7:4: "his father was dead" in the spiritual sense. But all other such statements as well as the connection make this interpretation seem unlikely. Though allied to this last interpretation, the one that we suggest and favor takes the expression "was dead" in the sense "was dead to him." Because of Terah's adherence to idolatry he was as good as dead for Abram, and so Abram could leave him behind, sorry, indeed, for his

father's lot but separated from him already as from one dead. Should none of these explanations satisfy, it should be borne in mind that similar perplexities are found in connection with problems in secular history, but difficulties do not necessarily spell error. We are simply too far removed from these events to be able to decipher how details dovetail together.

HOMILETICAL SUGGESTIONS

In our judgment the only section that can be used to advantage as a text is that of v. 1-9, which may appear under the familiar heading, "The Confusion of Tongues." A specific turn in another direction is given to the entire treatment if the theme takes on the form: "The Confusion wrought by Sin." A good point of departure in any case might be the legend preserved among the ancients concerning the heaven-storming Titans. The fable offered by the legend is merely a distorted form of the truth which the Bible account gives in these verses. One should not neglect to point out very definitely in this connection that the gift of Pentecost cancels the harm done by the sinful pride of man, for there the speaking in other tongues signifies that the Holy Spirit repairs by the one language of the Gospel the sad confusion wrought by sin.

CHAPTER XII

The Life of Abraham (12:1-25:11)

Up to this point the universal history of mankind has been under consideration. Now the account narrows down to the history of the Kingdom of God. For if the mighty of this earth establish kingdoms (cf. 10:10), in a far more real sense does God Himself set up a kingdom, a kingdom which differs point for point from the kingdoms of this world but which is none the less real, in fact, is the only reality. History, as Moses now writes it, traces the development of this kingdom. In fact, the Ruler of the destinies of history so shapes history that it may serve to aid in the development of His kingdom.

As far as the life of Abram, which now follows, is concerned, it is usually divided into about four different periods, each supposedly set off by the appearance of God to Abram. Now if the individual instances of the appearing of God to Abram be listed as well as the instances where the word of the Lord came unto Abram, it will be found that these experiences make a total of eight, or, counting the original word in Ur of Chaldees according to Acts 7:2, nine. But the distinction between the mere coming of the Word to Abram (12:1; 13:14; 21:12; 22:1) and the vision (15:1) or the appearance of the Lord (12:7; 17:1; 18:1), is largely artificial. Even when the word of the Lord came to Abram, the Lord may have appeared to Abram even where there is no specific mention made of His appearing. These separate instances of God's appearing to Abram are not said by the Scriptures to have been marks indicating new stages of development in Abram's life. The truth rather appears to have

been this: when God's Word or His appearance to
Abram became a necessity, then God manifested Himself. Such an appearance, then, does not necessarily
mean that Abram had grown or developed to a certain
point or was about to grow or to develop in a certain
direction. We are, therefore, inclined to divide
Abram's life into three parts: a) his early life prior
to the time of the first call in Ur of Chaldees — concerning which period we know absolutely nothing except that Abram took Sarai to wife; b) the period
lying between God's first promise of posterity and the
actual birth of this seed, Isaac (12:1-21:7); c) the
events after the birth of Isaac (21:8-25:11).

In connection with the question where the first
call of God came to Abram there are a few things to
be added to what has thus far been said in reference
to Terah. Even though the account of Moses does not
indicate the possibility of a call earlier than the one
of 12:1, yet the correct scriptural tradition knows of
the coming of this first call in Ur of Chaldees. Gen.
15:7 and Neh. 9:7 might perhaps be so construed as
to mean that Abram's leaving of Ur stood under God's
special providence; but Acts 7:2 definitely asserts that
God's first call to Abram came in Ur, "before he came
to Haran." As our previous explanation indicated,
we believe that this call included Terah but did not
succeed in weaning him from idolatry. Again, on the
question whether Terah's household only or also Abram
were involved in the "serving of other gods," of which
Josh. 24:2 speaks, we cannot assert definitely just
what Abram's position was. To us it seems most natural to assume that on Abram's part there had been
only the incipient stages of idolatry, which were abandoned when God called him forth. Consequently, it
would appear that this initial summons was merely by
the mercy of Him that called and not upon the strength
of the merits of the one who was called, as Luther also
rightly contends.

This faith, however, which God's grace engendered, proved to be a faith of such exemplary character that all that are of faith are classified as "sons of Abram" (Gal. 3:7), and so Abram truly becomes the father of all believers. Only when we regard this record of Abram's life as a record of a life of faith, do we justice to it.

Unfortunately, much confusion has been introduced into the subject of the lives of the patriarchs by certain untenable theories on the basis of which far-reaching reconstructions have been attempted. We shall list the major of these theories and indicate briefly how they do violence to the available evidence. For a more thoroughgoing presentation of the case we must refer to the works of Eduard Koenig, especially his *Geschichte der alttestamentlichen Religion,* and his *Geschichte des Reiches Gottes,* as well as to his *Genesis Commentary.* For this able scholar has blasted these futile theories into the smallest of atoms by his devastating attack upon them.

One more general mode of approach is that which roughly classifies all the historical material of Genesis as *purely legendary.* Dillmann gives a somewhat naive statement of the case when he says: "Nowadays, of course, everybody quite takes it for granted that all these tales about the fathers do not belong into the realm of strict history but into that of legend." Aside from the presumption which regards all the opponents of this view as nobodies, the assumption prevails that Israel must in all respects be like other nations. If other nations had tales from their early history which were purely legendary, so must Israel's record be. Aside from being a begging of the principle, critics of this stripe are ready to concede Israel's distinct superiority in the matter of religion. Why cannot the rest of the life of this people furnish material superior to that found in other nations?

One of the most popular methods of dealing with patriarchal history is to approach it on the basis of the so-called *tribal theory (Stammtheorie)*. This theory assumes that the patriarchs were not actual historical characters but fictitious characters which are to serve to explain the origin of certain tribes. When Abram goes to Egypt, the tribe in reality went in its earlier days, etc. The patriarchs are eponymous characters to whom is ascribed what befell the tribe. The grain of truth involved in this theory is that, in reality, certain of the names mentioned in the Table of Nations, chapter ten, are tribal names and not names of persons. However, in such cases (10:13, 14, 16, 17, 18) tribal names are used ("Amorite, Girgashite," etc.), and no attempt is made to make them appear as individuals. The claim by which the tribal theory is chiefly supported is that ethnology has no instances on record where nations descended from an individual, as, for example, Israel from Abram. However, on this score the Biblical records happen to have preserved facts which ethnology no longer has available. But how a nation may descend from an individual is traced step for step in the Biblical record.

Besides, the Genesis records in their detailed accounts bear too much of the stamp of records concerning characters of flesh and blood as we have it. Dillmann may make light of this fact and say: "We need nowadays no longer prove that the wealth of picturesque details of the narrative is not in itself a proof of the historicity of the things narrated but is, on the contrary, a characteristic mark of the legend." But though legends do usually abound in picturesque details, the things narrated in Genesis very evidently bear the stamp of sober truth. Christ and the apostles recognized the patriarchs as historical characters; cf. such remarks as John 8:56 and the almost two dozen references of Christ to Abraham alone.

More farfetched than either of the two theories
described thus far is the *astral-myth theory*. Briefly
stated, it amounts to this: even as Greek mythology
had certain tales by way of explanation of the origin
of the signs of the zodiac, so did the Babylonians, and
so, of necessity, must Israel. An illustration: Sarah's
going down to Egypt as a sterile woman is the Israelitish way of stating the Babylonian myth of the
descent of the goddess Ishtar into the underworld
to receive the boon of fertility. Even though the
story primarily tells of Abram's going to Egypt, and
though Egypt has to be taken to signify the underworld — a thing utterly without parallel in the Scriptures — and even though Sarai must be interpreted
to be an adaptation of the name of the Babylonian
goddess *Sharratu,* the wife of the moon god, in spite
of all these forms of unwarranted treatment of the
text, the adherents of this theory fail to see its folly.
We cannot but label such a theory as an attempt to
discredit Scripture.

A fourth mode of misinterpreting the sacred narrative is the attempt to account for it on the basis of
what we might term the *Beduin-ideal theory*. Briefly,
this involves the notion that the writer or the writers
of the patriarchal history were in reality setting forth
the type of Beduin life as found in patriarchal times
as an ideal for a later more civilized and more degenerate age. The writer is supposed to be enthusiastic
for the Beduin type of life and to see in it the cure
for the social ills of his time. So the Beduin religion
is also set forth as an ideal of monotheistic religion.
Incidentally, that utter simplicity supposed to be set
forth by this type of life is hardly characteristic of
the patriarchs, for already men like Abram are in
possession of much goods and great wealth and are in
a position to give rich gifts such as jewels to close
friends or prospective wives.

In reading how Gunkel, an ardent advocate of the purely legendary or mythical theory, manipulates his theory, one is almost tempted to speak of still another theory, namely the theory which glorifies the clever pranks of the patriarchs. For in writing particularly of the devices employed by Jacob in taking advantage of Esau or of Laban, he writes as if the readers of these tales gloated over them as a humorous glorification of a crafty ancestor. On other occasions he writes with a pitying disdain of the very crude and elementary conceptions of the deity held by these early writers. Again the effort to deflate the conception of the Scriptures is manifest, and a Biblical book is reduced to the level of a collection of amusing anecdotes.

Parallel with all these faulty theories runs the erroneous conception of the patriarchal religion. Here again we may refer to prevelant theories. We shall do no more, however, than to list briefly the erroneous conceptions we are referring to. Prominent among these is the attitude which describes the early religion of Israel as *totemism*. This endeavors to prove that certain types of creatures were deemed sacred and were worshipped by certain tribes. Proof for this view is deduced, for example, in the case of Terah from the fact that his name may signify a type of mountain goat. The proof grows very top-heavy, when so elaborate a conclusion is built upon an accidental possibility.

A second, equally grievous misconception is that which describes the religion of the patriarchs as *ancestor* worship. In proof of this mention is made, for example, of the fact that certain graves are mentioned, like that of Deborah, (Gen. 35:8) in connection with which an "oak of weeping" is referred to, or where, it is asserted, sacrifices to the dead were made. Nowhere are the statements found, however, that would actually prove that the spirits of the dead were thought of as gods. The whole conception is as shallow and as unscientific as it can be.

Then even *fetishism* has been attributed to the patriarchs. Israel's religion is supposed to give indications that holy hills were reverenced as a fetish; so, too, fountains, trees, and stones. Yet even the unlearned will be able to detect quite readily that these strange reconstructions of the text must be read into the text in a manner which does violence to all sober and honest interpretation of the text. The thought lying behind all such attempts is, of course, this: since such lower levels of religion are seen on the part of many other nations, therefore they must be characteristic of Israel's religion in its earlier stages — a faulty style of argument.

1. The Call of Abram and the Exodus from Haran
(v. 1-9)

1. And Yahweh said unto Abram: Depart from thy country, from thy relatives and from thy father's house unto a land which I will show thee.

"Get thee out" (A. V.), though entirely correct, sounds too sharply imperative in the English of our day; for *lekh-lekha* is a mild "go for thyself," *lekha* being either a dative of interest or merely an ethical dative (K. S. 35), its force being like the English: "do go" or the German: *"geh doch."* This command is attributed to *Yahweh,* whose mercy controls all that he does in this connection in singling out an individual who is to become the ancestor of the Savior's line. The extent of the sacrifice asked of Abram covers three items which draw an ever narrowing circle until the last makes the extent of the sacrifice most keenly felt. The "country" *('erets)* which is to be left is, of course, the country which according to 11:31 had become the new home of Terah's group. For this verse (v. 1) attaches itself to the preceding situation by a *waw* "and." So 12:1 intends by this device to build up on 11:31, 32. Consequently, the A. V. translation is not justified in rendering, "Now the Lord *had* said" — a rendering made, no doubt, to harmonize with Acts 7:2. As the new country (Haran) still offered too many dangers to this man whom God's grace singled out, so also did his "relatives" *(môlédheth)*, those who were tied to him by blood and were exerting a more subtle and powerful influence than the individual usually realizes. But strongest of all was the influence of his "father's house," and hardest, the sacrifice of breaking these dearest ties. Apparently, in both these latter terms a larger complex of persons is involved than those mentioned in 11:31. Under "relatives" we must, no doubt, include Nahor's household, which must have emigrated from Ur shortly after Terah's departure.

Usually either too much or too little is put into the clause: "unto a land which I will show thee." Too little, if it be assumed that Abram did not even have an idea in what direction or toward what land he should go. For v. 5 says "they went forth to go into the land of Canaan." Besides, according to 11:31 the destination of Terah was Canaan at the first. On the other hand, too much is presupposed if it be assumed that Abram actually knew that Canaan was to be his ultimate destination. The happy mean in this case, then, would be that Abram well knew that he should first bend his steps toward Canaan. But the land that God intended to show him was yet to be revealed. In other words, only after Abram had actually arrived in Canaan did God also reveal to him that Canaan was the land where he was to take up his dwelling permanently.

So the whole issue still is very definitely one of faith. With a general knowledge of the direction in which he is to turn, this man still must venture out in faith in the providence of God, trusting that in God's own good time his ultimate goal would be made apparent to him. It is this exemplary faith which the

author of Hebrews extols when he says (11:8) : "By
faith Abram, when he was called, obeyed to go out
unto a place which he was to receive for an inheritance;
and he went out, not knowing whither he went." The
last part of this statement may well be understood as
being in harmony with our interpretation above:
Abram knew the direction, but he did not know the
specific inheritance.

In the final *'ar'ekka* the suffix is attached more
closely by the use of a *nun energicum* (G. K. 58 i).

> 2. **I will make of thee a great nation,**
> **And I will bless thee,**
> **And I will make thy name great,**
> **And be thou a blessing;**
> **And I will bless them that bless thee,**
> **And I will curse him that curseth thee.**

> 3. **And in thee shall all the families of the**
> **earth be blessed.**

For parallels see 18:18; 22:18; 26:4; 28:14.

We have arranged the various items of these two
verses thus in order to make the constituent parts as
readily apparent as possible. Much energy is expended
in trying to determine how many parts constitute this
blessing laid upon Abram. Some arrive at three parts,
some at four, some at five. We feel that each is distinct
by itself, and, therefore, the covenant number seven
prevails here, even though there is no explicit covenant
involved. In a sense, one element of v. 1 might be
drawn upon, viz., "the land I will show thee," as being
still another promise of God, but these words are only
indirectly a blessing. So, then, for the one act of
sacrifice on Abram's part there is to be a sevenfold
reward on Yahweh's.

The first promise runs thus: "I will make of thee
a great nation." The word for "nation" is *gôy*, usually
used of the heathen nations, but here, as in 35:11 and

Exod. 19:6, in reference to Israel, to signify that, as nations go, Israel shall be great. "Great nation," of course, implies more than great numbers. Since the greatness is of God's making, it involves true greatness in every sense. If ever there was a great nation, it was Israel. The force of this word must naturally be reckoned over against the fact that at the time when it was spoken Abram had no son.

The second promise runs thus: "I will bless thee." This statement, then, does not refer to the nation but to Abram alone. A man is blessed when due to the gracious working of God all goes well with him (cf. 39:5); the things that he undertakes thrive; and true success crowns all his endeavors. This certainly is a promise that was realized in Abram's life.

The third item: "I will make thy name great." Abram personally is to become famous. The various names that are given to Abram display a part of this fame. So he is called "the father of a multitude" (17:5), a prince of God (23:6); the man in God's confidence (18:17-19); a prophet (20:7); the servant of God (Ps. 105:6); and the friend of God (20:7). Even without such names he could still be famous. But this fame is not a personal achievement of his but a divinely wrought favor.

The fourth: "And be thou a blessing." The form in which this item of the promise appears differs materially from that of all the rest. Instead of being an imperfect hortative, it is the imperative, "and be thou" *(wehyeh)*. Now it is true enough that an imperative may be joined to a hortative (K. S. 364 n), but it cannot be denied that this is "strange" (K. S. 203) in this case. Merely to make this imperative just one more promise strips it too utterly of its peculiar character, as does A. V.: "and thou shalt be a blessing." The fact of the matter is that it, indeed, expresses something that God does: God is the One, who in the last analysis makes Abram to be a true blessing unto others. But at the same time, a moral responsibility of Abram's is involved: he should do his part that he may become a blessing to others. Consequently the imperative, "be thou a blessing." He personally should aim to live such a life that others are blessed by it.

The fifth item: "I will bless them that bless thee." So intimately is God concerned in having men take the proper attitude toward this prophet and servant of His that whoever wishes Abram well, to him will God do good. For this difference between God's blessing (item 2 above) and man's blessing in the second half of this fifth item is that man's blessings are the wishing of good, God's blessings the impartation of good. Besides, it should be noted that divine grace presupposes that there will be *many* that wish Abram well; therefore *mebharekhê'kha,* plural, "thy blessers."

The sixth item: "And I will curse him that curseth thee." The Hebrew uses two different verbs — *'arar* for God's judicial cursing and *galal* for man's injudicious or blasphemous cursing. Again divine grace presupposes that there will not be many that wish this friend of God ill: therefore *meqallelkha,* singular, "thy curser." The deeper reason behind all this is that Abram will be so closely identified with the good work of God, that to curse him comes to be almost the equivalent of cursing God.

The seventh item: "And in thee shall all the families of the earth be blessed." This word reaches back to the divided "families" (10:5, 20, 31) of the earth, divided by their sins, as well as to the curse of 3:17 which is now to be replaced by a blessing. A blessing so great that its effect shall extend to "all the families of the earth" can be thought of only in connection with the promised Savior. This word, therefore, is definitely Messianic and determines that the Messiah is to emerge from the line of Abram. Negative criticism, consciously or unconsciously bent on removing the Messianic element from the Old Testament, attempts to cancel the specifically Messianic thought of the passage by modifying the meaning of the verb "be blessed," *nibhrekhû*. This stem is Nifal and so passive. Now the claim is raised that the inherent idea of the Nifal is reflexive; therefore the Nifal should be rendered as a reflexive, as the parallel Hithpaels of 22:18 and 26:4 suggest. Besides, it is claimed, the verb *barakh* has a passive in the Pual form which is extensively used. Yet the truth of the matter is that the passive of the Nifal stem should be adhered to as the normal thing, unless the passive sense actually is impossible. The Nifal is passive rather than reflexive. In the second place, a careful study of the Pual will reveal that it is used of blessings on the lower levels — blessings on the house, the name, the inheritance, the person, the land, or the generation of the upright. Or when the verb is used in reference to "the name of the Lord" (Job 1:21), it refers to blessings that man bestows upon it — human blessings, not divine. In our passage the case is different. Here the reference is to blessings divinely bestowed. Therefore a distinctive verb is sought. The Hithpaels of 22:18 and 26:4 merely add another aspect of the case, namely that men shall wish for themselves (reflexive) the blessing of the seed of Abram. These two passages, therefore, are not an interpretation of ours but merely a thought supplementary to this original promise. Besides, the usual interpretation given by critics to the fourth item ("be thou a blessing") would cover the last or seventh, and so instead of having a word that mounts to a climax, they have a weak repetition that is to no purpose. Even Procksch feels constrained to admit that "only in the idea of the Messiah does the depth of the thought (of this word) adequately display itself." The old conservative interpretation is well established in every way. It alone meets the needs of the case.

The object *meqallelkha* is not placed first so much
for emphasis as to make possible a chiastic arrangement of clauses.

4. **So Abram went forth as Yahweh told him,
and Lot went forth with him; and Abram was
seventy-five years old when he went forth from
Haran.**

Abram's obedience rendered in faith is stressed
primarily in this word: as he has been bidden to do,
so he does; Yahweh's word must be fulfilled. Whether
there was any struggle with the reluctant flesh or not,
we are not told. The important thing is: Abram's
faith yielded obedience. The pain of separation is eased
in part by the coming along of Abram's nephew Lot.
God's mercy is displayed in this fact, for He it was,
no doubt, who disposed Lot's heart to desire to accompany Abram. There must have been something of a
spiritual kinship between these two men, even if Lot
afterwards proves far inferior to Abram. Important
for our understanding the situation correctly is our
knowledge of the age of Abram. For if he is seventy-
five years old, he is even according to the standards of
that time a middle-aged man. So decisive a step as his
would hardly come so easily at his age as at an earlier
period in his life. So the mention of Abram's age
helps us to put a more correct estimate upon the heroic
quality of this act of faith. Criticism claims that v. 4 b
as well as v. 5 are traceable to a different source,
namely to P, whereas the rest of the chapter dates
from J. Luther, especially apt on discerning the character of faith, remarks on this act of Abram's: "Faith
is a lively and powerful thing; it is not merely a
drowsy and idle thought; nor does it float somewhere
upon the heart as a duck upon the water, but it is
like water warmed through and through by a good
warm fire."

Age is expressed in Hebrew by the idiom, "a child of so-and-so-many years" (G. K. 128 o).

5. And Abram took Sarai his wife and Lot his nephew and all their acquisition which they had acquired and the persons that they had gotten in Haran, and they went forth to go to the land of Canaan, and (in due course of time) they arrived in the land of Canaan.

Quite in conformity with the patriarchal mode of life, where the patriarch himself enjoys a rare measure of authority over the whole clan, the departure is attributed entirely to Abram: *he* took the persons and the goods. We have translated above, "acquisition which they had acquired," to indicate the cognate object which the Hebrew expresses *rakhash rekhush*. *Rakhash* really covers all movable possessions, *Fahrhabe* (K. W.). It is not a distinctive word of P; it is not an indication that a particular author is writing, but a word used when possessions have to be referred to. Here, in particular, it is becoming apparent that we are dealing with a very rich man. He has not only chattels but also a great retinue. These persons the Hebrew refers to by the very general word "souls" (collective singular, *néphesh*), which is about the equivalent of "persons." The verb used with this word is *'asah*, meaning originally "to make"; here "to get," as in 31:1. These "persons" include not only the children born of this large retinue of servants but the many servants that had been acquired by purchase.

Mark that the immediate and definite objective is "the land of Canaan," as indicated above. We have inserted parenthetically "in due course of time" because such, largely obvious, phrases are for the most part taken for granted in Hebrew. English would have actually expressed this idea. In characteristic fashion Moses passes by all the details that might have been connected with this long journey. Nothing essential to the author's purpose occurred on the way.

Though '*artsah* ("to the land") has the old locative
ending, this does not prevent the attaching of the
noun "Canaan" to produce the construct relationship
(K. S. 273).

**6, 7. And Abram passed through the land as
far as the place Shechem to the terebinth of Moreh,
and the Canaanites were in the land at that time.
And Yahweh appeared unto Abram and said:
To thy seed will I give this land. And he built an
altar there unto Yahweh who had appeared unto
him.**

This verse agrees well with our interpretation of
v. 1. Abram "passes through" the land without being
definitely aware what part or how much of it is
destined for him. The first place where a stop worthy
of record is made is "the place Shechem." The thing
that makes this place important is the fact that God
there appears to Abram. The word "place" *(maqôm)*
simply means "town" or "locality," a meaning of the
word also with us. This meaning is both natural and
in harmony with the established uses of the word. The
technical meaning, adopted by some, "the holy place"
or "the sanctuary" is not well established. Nor do
passages like 28:11; 35:7; Deut. 12:13 establish this
technical meaning. That such a use attaches to the
Arabic *maqâm* is not sufficient ground for demanding
a like Hebrew usage. Besides, in the nature of the case
it seems very unlikely that any of the Canaanite high-
places could have been centres of worship of Yahweh,
the only true God. Besides, Abram, just called forth
from idolatrous connections, may well be regarded as
a man who for conscience' sake would have avoided
the sites sacred to Canaanitish idols, lest he himself
appear as an idolater. The same objection applies to
Jacob in 28:11. "Shechem," as Skinner too points
out, was important already in the Tell-Amarna period
(1480-1460 B. C.) and may well have been a prominent

city when Abram arrived there. Usually the cities
which became prominent later were of importance
already long before, as excavations revealing pre-
Canaanite levels clearly prove. "Shechem," then, is
not here used proleptically for "the site of the later
Shechem." Its prominent position could well have
made it one of the outstanding towns of this early
date. The author does not only weave these references
to certain towns into his narrative in order to lend to
these places a measure of sanctity for later time (such
a purpose, of course, is perfectly permissible) ; but he
primarily records the event as an event, because it
actually transpired and was of moment in the life of
Abram.

The historical importance of the event can in part
be displayed by likening this appearance of Yahweh's
to Abram to a gracious welcome and reception tendered
by the Lord to Abram as he definitely arrives in the
center of the land destined for his descendants. At the
same time the appearance of God to Abram is a reward for his fidelity in obeying the Lord's behest. Not
everyone may be honored by such divine favors.

Besides, when God says: "I will give this land
to thy seed," it is sufficiently apparent that Abram
himself is not destined to receive it. So this is another
one of the divine words calculated to exercise faith.

But the generous character of the promise should
be noted very particularly. Abram had merely been
bidden to go to a land that God would show him. There
was in that word no intimation that Abram's seed
would inherit that land. So God is seen actually to give
more then He promised. After such a fashion does
God keep His word.

One more aspect of the case should be considered.
For the development of God's purposes in the seed of
Abram it is essential that a definite land be available
within which this seed comes to its normal develop-

ment. So the promise of the land as held in safekeeping by God for Abram's seed is not a capricious promise but one that ties up definitely with the needs of the case. From this point on it will be seen that every new promise fits into the development of God's purposes as into an organic whole which is going through a normal process of growth.

However, two things more had been recorded before the appearance of God is mentioned. First, that at Shechem (which lay between Ebal and Gerizim, not quite at the site of the present Nablus) Abram encamped by an ancient landmark, "the terebinth of Moreh." '*Elôn* without a doubt means a big tree and very likely the turpentine tree, or terebinth, rather than the oak. "Moreh" may be a proper name (e. g. A. V.). It may be that, since the word also means "teacher, "instructor," some renowned person, apt at giving counsel to the people, had held forth under this tree. But all suppositions, such as that the words ought to be rendered "oracle-terebinth," or that we here have indications of an animistic religion on the part of the patriarchs, are guesses. It is just as possible that in days of old some worshipper of Yahweh had under this oak admonished and instructed the people. In the absense of anything definite our translation above has much to commend it.

Then Moses records: "the Canaanites were in the land at that time." This is stated in preparation for the promise about to be given to Abram. For no one can fully realize the greatness of the thing promised to Abram until he remembers that the land promised to the posterity of Abram was already occupied by the Canaanites. But Abram's faith is not daunted by this seeming difficulty. Almost unanimously criticism makes this clause manifestly post-Mosaic. However, it does not require great ingenuity to understand that Moses could have written thus. Even Koenig fails to see clearly on this point. Note: the singular, "the

Canaanite," used for a term usually found in the plural
(K. S. 256 e).

7. God's brief word spoken on the occasion of
this appearance is: "To thy seed will I give this land."
Abram himself was to possess only a burial ground.
Faith had to accept "things not seen." A word from
God requires a response on the part of man. Abram
felt himself impelled to give personal public testimony
to God's mercy displayed in this appearance. So he
built an altar. This statement is misconstrued by
criticism in its attempt to find as many distinctions
as possible between so-called sources. This passage,
being ascribed to J, is said to mean that J never records
instances of actual sacrifices by the patriarchs. That
is the argument from silence, and it is inconclusive
because the word for altar is *mizbéach,* meaning "a
place for slaughter." The manifest intention of the
author must be that "a place for slaughter" was made
in order to slaughter a victim. Altars become altars
when the victim is slain. A mere altar of stones would
have been a formalistic gesture on Abram's part — a
gesture like falling on one's knees to pray but omitting
the prayer. The soul of the patriarchal religion was
sacrifice. The critics find matters, which no one before
their time dreamed of. The altar is said to be built
"unto Yahweh" to emphasize the undeserved mercy of
His promise.

8. **And he journeyed onward toward the hills
to the east of Bethel, and he pitched his tent with
Bethel to the west and Ai to the east; and there
he built an altar unto Yahweh and called upon the
name of Yahweh.**

Still largely nomadic in his habits, upon his first
arrival in the land Abram next pitched his tent near
"Bethel," here so called proleptically, see 28:19. Moses
diligently records such well-authenticated events of
Abram's life in order to awaken an anticipation for the

land in the hearts of the Israelites who are journeying toward this land, as well as to let historic spots be vested with sacred memories after Israel has come into possession of the land. "Ai" has the article, being derived from a common noun meaning "heap of stones." As the noun in usage becomes a proper noun, the article still clings to it. Again an altar is built and, of course, sacrifice made together with public invocation of Yahweh's name, an act which could hardly be performed without proclaiming the works and the character of Yahweh — a fact which leads Luther to translate: "he *preached* concerning the name of the Lord." For a full discussion of this expression, which specifically means "to use the name of the Lord in worhsip" (B D B) see above on 4:26. The *beth* used in the expression is the *Beth of interest* (K. S. 212 c). On *wayyett* see G. K. 76 c.

9. **And Abram pulled up stakes and kept on moving toward the Negeb.**

Nasa' actually means "to pull up stakes," a natural expression in nomadic days. To convey the idea that this kept on for quite a while the absolute infinitive *(nasôa')* is joined to the finite verb, as well as the absolute infinitive of the verb "to go" *(halôkh)* which almost equals our adverb "continually." (K. S. 329 v; G. K. 113 u). The "Negeb" is the region of Palestine that lies south of Hebron. It is an arid region in parts of which isolated flocks may be tended, at least down as far south as Beersheba. It may have been less desiccated in patriarchal days. Often the word merely indicated the direction, south.

2. **The Trip to Egypt During a Famine** (v. 10-21)

Now follows an episode that is less attractive. Abram does not appear to good advantage in it. With impartial truth Moses records what Abram did. If the account remains entirely objective without the addition of a subjective opinion or estimate of the ethical value of Abram's conduct, this can readily be seen to be offset by the fact that the narrative as such in its unvarnished truth so plainly sets forth the unworthy sentiments that animated the patriarch, that the sympathetic reader is almost made to blush for the thing done by the man of God. The charge of the critics is decidedly unfair when they say: "There is no suggestion that either the untruthfulness or the selfish cowardice of the request (of Abram) was severely reprobated by the ethical code to which the narrative appealed." Prochsch sees the situation more nearly as it actually is when he asserts: "It is quite impossible here not to notice the narrator's sarcasm," and adds that this step that Abram took "is most sharply condemned" by the writer.

Comparing chapters twenty and twenty-six, we find two situations that constitute a close parallel to the one under consideration. Strange as such recurrences may strike us, it should be remembered that life often brings us into situations that are practically duplicates of what transpired at an earlier date; and he that marvels that a patriarch sinned a second time after a definite rebuke, let him remember how often he himself may repeat a sin for which a stern admonition had been addressed to him.

To say this must have been "a very popular story in ancient Israel" hardly does justice to the facts of the case. Why should Israel have deemed the failings of its patriarchs material for "popular" stories? The recording of three such instances is explicable only on the score of the strict impartiality of the author.

10. **Now there was a famine in the land and Abram went down to Egypt to sojourn there, for the famine was heavy in the land.**

In Canaan famines have been periodic since times immemorial. They still recur. In addition to being

practically a homeless stranger, Abram incurs the
difficulty of subsisting with all his household and his
flocks during days when men can make but a precarious
livelihood. The account does not dwell upon the difficulties of the position. They who faithfully obey
God's behests are not promptly rewarded by God in all
things. Particular difficulties may arise as an outgrowth of their oedience.

To go down to Egypt at such a time, to the granary
of antiquity, is quite in conformity with what monumental inscriptions portray. There are found scenes
depicting "the admission of Semites to the rich pas-
tures of Egypt." The expression "to sojourn there"
indicates that nothing more is intended than a temporary stay. To this day the Beduins are not grievously
disturbed by the necessity of departing for a time from
their accustomed dwelling places when famine prevails.
"Go down" *(yaradh)* is the proper verb for going from
the mountains of Palestine to the lower levels of Egypt.

**11-13. And it came to pass when he was at
the point of entering Egypt, he said unto Sarai, his
wife: See, now, I know that thou art a woman of
beautiful appearance, and it shall come to pass if
any of the Egyptian men see thee, they will say,
That is his wife; so they will slay me but spare thy
life. Please say that thout art my sister, in order
that it may go well with me for thy sake, and my
life be spared because of thee.**

According to 20:13 Abram and Sarai agreed to
employ the deception here described whenever they got
into a difficulty such as this. So v. 11-13 must be
regarded in the light of a reminder on Abram's part
to live up to the standing agreement. This was done
when they "were at the point of entering Egypt." The
Hebrew idiom, however, states the case thus: "he drew
near *(hiqrîbh)* to enter toward Egypt." The *le* before
bô' makes the equivalent of a direct object of *hiqrîbh,*

(K. S. 399 n). *Yadhá'ti* is not to be rendered as a past, being a *perfectum resultativum* — as a result of the full knowledge of the case that he has he now "knows" (present) (K. S. 127). The next Hebrew idiom runs thus "a woman, beautiful in respect to appearance," *mar'eh* being an accusative of specification, known also as *Temjiz accusative* (K. S. 336 h).

12. Abram knows how little the rights of foreigners were respected in olden times. He also knows how beautiful women would be sought out when they came to a foreign land. He also understands that marriage was respected sufficiently that men felt they must dispose of the husband before they could take his wife. Egyptian parallels prove that men had no hesitation about committing murder in an effort to secure their object. There was nothing beside the point in the estimate that he makes of the situation except the morals of the patriarch. Though 20:12 indicates that the literal truth was being told, there is yet the possibility of telling it with the intent to deceive; and so it becomes a lie. In addition, there is something cowardly and mean about expecting Sarai to encounter the hazards in order that Abram might avoid danger. The heroic is noticeably absent in this request.

If the question arise: "How can Sarai be deemed beautiful enough at the age of sixty-five to allow for the complimentary terms here used (on her age cf. 17:17 and 12:4; she died at the age of 127, see 23:1)?" it must be remembered that according to the limits of longevity of those times she was only middle-aged. Middle-aged women may have retained their beauty, especially if they have not borne many children. On Pharaoh's part the taking of a woman into his harem may be largely a political expedient to enhance his own influence. *Hammitsrîm* are not "all," but "any of the Egyptian men" (Procksch).

13. The particle *na'* with the imperative gives a milder tone to the imperative, like our "please." Abram knows that if anyone takes Sarai on the supposition that she is Abram's sister, Abram as the honored brother will be an object of respectful treatment. Fully aware of the fact that such a course may involve the sacrifice of Sarai's honor in order that he himself might fare well, he nevertheless asks Sarai to make the sacrifice. Abram never sank lower, as far as we know, than when he made this request. Sarai's acquiescence, however, seems to grow out of the idea that there actually is no other safe course to follow. She was as sadly deficient in faith as he himself on this occasion. Luther's labored efforts to justify Abram's course do not meet with our approval.

14, 15. And it came to pass as Abram came to Egypt, Egyptian men saw the woman that she was exceedingly beautiful. Also the princes of Pharaoh saw her and praised her to Pharaoh, and the woman was taken into Pharaoh's house.

That Abram had not been dealing with a hypothetical case appears from the sequel. It is immediately apparent that at least the Hebrew women of this time — as, of course, in later times also — did not go about veiled. See v. 12 for our rendering "Egyptian men." In their efforts to set so-called sources at variance with one another as much as possible, the critics here freely accept that Sarai must have been beautiful but claim that this view of the case clashes with the divergent view of 17:17. On the weaving together of chief and subordinate clauses ("the woman" really belongs into the subordinate clause) see K. S. 414 b.

15. "The princes of Pharaoh" are practically his "courtiers" (Meek). They seek to ingratiate themselves with Pharaoh by recommending this woman of exceptional beauty. On the form *halallû* see G. K. 10 g. *Beth* ("house") is used without a preposition

or locative ending — a common use (K. S. 330 c). The more nearly absolute authority of the king of those times is indicated by the fact that whatsoever woman he desires is promptly brought to him.

16. **And he bestowed favors upon Abram for her sake, and he (Abram) possessed sheep and cattle and asses and menservants and maidservants and she-asses and camels.**

That the move of taking the supposed sister of Abram had also political implications appears from the fact that Pharaoh now grants favors to his new brother-in-law, as he begins to deem Abram. The somewhat colorless verb *hêtibh,* "to do well," is used to express the idea of "bestowing favors." When, then, the things are listed that Abram possessed, the sense of the passage cannot be that Pharaoh's gift included all these elements but rather that, partly as a result of Pharaoh's gift, Abram's wealth was made up of the constituent parts here listed. The order of these parts is somewhat puzzling: "menservants and maidservants" inserted before "she-asses and camels." However, this must have been the original order of the items in the text, for not only the Masoretic text but the Greek and the Syrian versions give this order. One possible explanation would be that the items are listed in the order of their acquisition. First Abram specialized in the acquisition of "sheep and cattle and asses." Then he recognized the need of more "servants" and proceeded to acquire more such. Lastly he branched out in the direction of "she-asses and camels." In this instance, too, textual alterations can offer nothing more than conjectures. Though it is commonly admitted that "camels" do not appear among the items specialized in by the Egyptians up to this time — for they are not indicated on early monumental inscriptions — yet nothing could prevent a man like Abram from bringing his own camels along, if he already possessed them. The verse does not say that Pharaoh gave all these gifts to Abram; it merely lists the totals of his possessions. Meek mistranslates when he renders: Abram "was the recipient of sheep," etc.

17. **And Yahweh laid heavy afflictions upon Pharaoh and upon his household because of Sarai, Abram's wife.**

It is very clear that all this is reported as an instance of God's undeserved favor bestowed upon Abram. Comparatively speaking, Pharaoh was in the right over against Abram, for Pharaoh had acted in good faith, and Abram had practiced deception. Potentially, Pharaoh may have been as much in the wrong as Abram — a thing usually overlooked — for had Abram admitted that he was Sarai's husband, Pharaoh might have had him killed. In any case, Abram's lie does not make him a worthy recipient of divine mercy. But God's mercy outruns man's merit, as the Pentateuch emphasizes with particular instances. Since Abram is the father of the seed of promise, Sarai, the mother, must be safeguarded. Man's sin almost defeats God's purpose, but God's mercy prevails. The Hebrew expression for "laying heavy afflictions" upon Pharaoh is "to strike with strokes" *(nigga' negha'im)* G. K. 117 q. What these afflictions were we shall never be able to determine; an analogy can be seen in 20:18. Apparently they were intended to be of a kind that would prevent Pharaoh from approaching Sarai, for the Piel of *nagha'* is used "only of smiting with disease." Procksch, therefore, is far more specific than the evidence allows when he says: "sexual ailments of Pharaoh."

18, 19. **And Pharaoh called Abram and said: What is this that thou hast done to me? Why didst thou not tell me that she was thy wife? Why didst**

**thou say: She is my sister? And so I took her to
myself to wife. And now, there is thy wife; take
her and go.**

Again, in this condensed account we have no
means of determining exactly how Pharaoh became
aware of the fact that Yahweh brought on his affliction
for Sarai's sake. It may have been that he had something of the fear of God in his heart and felt that he
must have done something to incur the affliction. He
may then have consulted with Sarai and found out
what the actual situation was. We shall give him the
benefit of the doubt when he represents himself as
entirely in the right and implies that Abram would
have suffered no harm had he actually stepped up at
once as Sarai's husband. It appears that Pharaoh
gives the statement of the case that represents him
in as favorable a light as possible. Yet he seems justified in his vexation, at least in part. The first clause
has been well translated: "What a way for you to
treat me!" (Meek). Yet a part of the protest seems
overdone. When he inquires why Abram did this, he
asks concerning a matter that he understood well
enough, as parallels from Egyptian sources indicate
only too clearly. The rebuke that Abram deserves he
receives at the hands of one who is not even a worshipper of Yahweh. It consists in a rather curt dismissal. The fact that Abram receives it in silence indicates that Abram was aware of his deserving to be
rebuked; and so, by representing the case thus, the
author indicates where the right and the wrong of the
matter lay.

20. **And Pharaoh appointed men over him and
they escorted him away and his wife and all that
he had.**

'*Anashîm* means "a number of men" (K. S. 74).
The business of this group was to serve as bodyguard
and to escort Abram to the border (*yeshallechû* means

"dismiss" in a milder sense, or "escort"). Pharaoh has been duly impressed. He would not venture to do Abram harm. The appointing of men of his own to guard the sojourner is a tacit admission to the effect that serious danger really threatened. Besides, since God has made it plain that His favor rests upon Abram, Pharaoh feels that God might take vengeance upon him if he let evil befall Abram. Pharaoh recognized that he had been "reproved" by God (Ps. 105:14, 15). Since God never could administer undeserved reproof, this psalm passage proves that the construction we put upon Pharaoh's deed as involving a measure of guilt was not wrong.

HOMILETICAL SUGGESTIONS

The first section offering itself for treatment in this chapter is v. 1-9. Here the general theme of the Pentateuch may be treated, "the Greatness of God's Mercy," for this thought certainly overtops every other in this pericope. Yet other approaches to this text are permissible. If the New Testament (Heb. 11:8-10) here makes an issue of the "Faith of Abraham," why could we not hold fast the same point of view? For that matter, one might center attention on the Messianic thought, and in that event v. 1-3 might constitute enough of a text, with a remarkable climax in the Messianic thought of 3b. In no case should this Messianic feature be submerged or treated but briefly. Then there remains the second unit section of the text v. 10-20. To this different approaches are admissible. Again the theme of God's undeserved mercy may be put into the forefront. That would still have to be the case to an extent even if the theme were used: "The Frailty of God's Saints." Even a more general subject is permissible, such as, "The Unimpeachable Honesty of the Bible." If the last subject be used, it would be necessary to have the text furnish the one notable example. Other examples would be entitled to no more than very brief, passing notice.

CHAPTER XIII

3. Separation from Lot (v. 1-18)

We have only begun to penetrate into the life of
Abram and into the depth of faith displayed by that
life. The last incident, it is true, may have led to a less
favorable estimate of his character. What immediately
follows tends to give a more adequate measure of this,
one of the rarest of characters in the Scriptures. Besides, there will be occasions when divine wisdom will
deem it expedient to have a direct word from on high
granted to Abram. The rich development of divine
mercy that follows the steps of this venerable patriarch
especially deserves to be traced through its progressive
development.

The separation from Lot is a necessity growing
out of deeper reasons than those usually cited. Lot is
an element that is not suited to be an integral part of
the chosen people, as his later deterioration shows.
Circumstances soon arise which make it eminently
desirable to remove this unsuitable material as early
as possible. Behind the outward separation lies a
deeper motivation.

At the same time, this incident has always served
in the church as a typical case of how to deal in a
practical way with the problem of incompatibility. If
persons simply cannot get along together, nothing is
gained by attempting to force the issue or by discussing
the point till a solution is reached. Incompatibility is
best dealt with by separation: let those that cannot
agree get out of one another's way. To Ambrose is
attributed the saying *divide ut maneat amicitia*, a
procedure which does not merit the criticism, "a
wretched but practicable rule" (Delitzsch).

(430)

1, 2. And Abram went up from Egypt toward the Negeb, he and his wife and all that he possessed, and Lot was with him. And Abram was very rich in cattle, in silver and in gold.

"Went up" is the correct expression regularly used for going up from the land of Egypt which lay on a lower level than mountainous Palestine. Since his route was mostly northward, A. V. does not do well to render *hannegbah* "into the south." It should rather be "into the South-country" — always so called from the standpoint of central Palestine — or else "into the Negeb." See above 12:9. Now it is specially mentioned that "his wife" was with him, to recall to mind that through his folly he had almost lost her. Incidentally it is recalled that Lot had gone along, for Lot is about to figure in the following incident.

2. Besides, the great wealth of Abram is most conveniently mentioned here that we may at once visualize the patriarch as abounding in manifold possession. The Hebrew aptly says *Kabhedh*, "heavy," for rich. Critics fail to see the simple connection between v. 1 and v. 2 and place v. 2 behind v. 4. *Miqneh* means acquisition, but in the nomadic type of existence it came to mean primarily "cattle." Apparently, "gold and silver" in abundance were not among the common possessions of nomads like Abram. Consequently, separate mention is made of this form of wealth. A good bit of this latter form of wealth may have just been acquired in Egypt. However, to make Abram wealthy chiefly as the result of rich gifts from Pharaoh is hardly correct. God had abundantly blessed the man; and wealth as such is not an evil nor incompatible with holiness of life. The word for gold, *zahabh*, used, as Procksch points out also by Aramaeans and Arabians, is not the word employed by Canaanites and Babylonians, viz., *charats* (cf. χρυσός). This would seem to point to different sources of the

gold for these different groups. The article with
"cattle, silver and gold" is the article used with familiar objects, like our English, "the weeds are growing
all over our garden"; cf. G. K. 126 m; K. S. 297 a.

3, 4. **So he went in stages from the Negeb to
Bethel, to the place where his tent had been in the
previous instance between Bethel and Ai, to the
place of the altar which he had formerly made there.
And there Abram called upon the name of the
Lord.**

This "going in stages" is a good description of the
nomadic mode of travel: periodic stops are made that
the flocks may not be overdriven (cf. 33:13). Since
Abram and Lot are traversing practically the same
route as the one they followed down to Egypt, the
expression *lemassa'aw,* meaning "by *his* stages," most
likely indicates that he used practically the same stages
that had been suitable on the downward journey. So
also the Septuagint and the Vulgate. According to
12:8 his tent had been pitched between Bethel and Ai
"in the previous instance," *battechilah* = "in the beginning." The word "place" (*maqôm*) means "the
native sanctuary" as little here as in 12:6. It was
the place of Abram's altar not the place where
Canaanite altars had marked a sanctuary, as 4a plainly says. The last clause is not to be rendered as a
relative: "where Abram," etc., because the repetition
of the subject Abram especially aims to emphasize that
this clause is co-ordinate and states the important
transaction at this spot: the public worship of the
name of the Lord (cf. 4:26 and 12:8). Apparently,
this worship was to Abram a matter of personal necessity as well as of public testimony. Of personal necessity, for he desired to express his penitence at his
lapse from truth as well as his gratitude for the undeserved protection of himself and his wife by Yahweh.
At the same time this public act proclaimed the honor

of Yahweh, the true and faithful, to whom alone Abram
ascribed his safe return.

**5-7. Lot, also, who was going along with
Abram, had flocks and herds and tents.** **And the
land was not able to support them so that they might
have dwelt together, for their possessions were so
great that they were not able to dwell together.
And so there was strife between the keepers of
Abram's cattle and the keepers of Lot's cattle, and
(besides) the Canaanite and the Perizzite were
dwelling in the land at that time.**

Nothing has thus far indicated that Lot also was
a man of means. Apparently, he first acquired greater
wealth after he was in Abram's company and the Lord
was blessing them both. His wealth was hardly as
extensive as Abram's; for "flocks and herds" are included under the "cattle" ascribed to Abram (v. 2).
That Abram had a great retinue of servants goes without saying. "Tents," like the parallel "houses," is
no doubt used by metonomy for the people that dwelt
in them. It would seem that Lot had made special
efforts to accumulate "tents"; otherwise these would
hardly have been mentioned separately.

The participle *holekh* has the article because the
noun which it modifies is a proper noun and so is
definite (K. S. 333 z).

6. Naturally, since nomadic life demands ample
pasturage, such large flocks put a heavy drain upon
the natural resources along this line. In reality, "the
land was not able to support them," (*nasa'* as in 36:7)
so as actually to make it possible for them "to dwell
together." *La* before the infinitive *shébheth* to express result. *Yachdaw* with a fossilized or at least
indefinite (K. S. 324 e) pronominal suffix. The verse
closes with a palindromic *result* clause after *result*
and cause had been stated previously — a rather common construction, cf. 3:19; 6:5 f; 7:22; 11:9. How-

ever, v. 6 dare not be set over against v. 5 with the claim that v. 6 (ascribed to P) makes scant pasturage the ground of separation, whereas v. 5 (ascribed to J) together with v. 7 speaks of strife. For the critics are acting upon the assumption that in life one simple cause must underlie one simple result. Life is far more complex than to allow for such an inadequate approach. Nor do the words that Dillmann lists as marks of P (or A): "possessions," "support," "land of Canaan," "the cities of the oval," constitute a stylistic peculiarity. Such words grow out of the nature of the story that is being narrated.

7. "Strife" between the respective shepherds is unavoidable when in many a case situations will arise as to whom priority belongs in reference to a certain pasturage. Strife had actually begun to break out between the shepherds. An additional fact (note our parenthetical "besides" in the translation) bore upon the case and must be mentioned if an adequate picture of the situation is to be won, namely: "The Canaanite and the Perizzite were dwelling in the land at that time." Everyone might know that such was the case but might forget to reckon with it for the moment. For since both these groups also held parts of the land by virtue of long residence, Abram and Lot could only lay claim to the unoccupied areas. This additional statement does not, therefore, give indication of a time when Canaanites and Perizzites were no longer in the land, and does not, therefore, originate with a writer of a later date than Moses, as critics keep reiterating. Delitzsch, a critic, rightly classes the remark as "one necessary to give an adequate picture of the situation." Another thought lies involved in the statement about the original inhabitants: it was hardly a fitting situation to have the men who followed the true God falling into quarrels with one another in the sight of the idolatrous inhabitants of

the land. The "Canaanites," apparently, dwelt largely
in fortified cities. The "Perizzites," akin apparently
to *perazi*, "the hamlet-dweller," lived more in the open
country, and they may have been of the original inhabitants of Canaan, but were not of the stock of Ham
(cf. 10:15-18). They are also listed in 34:30 and Judg.
1:4, 5 together with the Canaanites, and were also of
the nations to be dispossessed by Israel (Gen. 15:20;
Exod. 3:17, and 17 times).

**8, 9. And Abram said to Lot: Please do not
let strife arise between me and thee, between my
shepherds and thy shepherds; for we are brethren.
Is not all the land open before thee? Please part
from me. If thou goest to the left, I will go to the
right; and if thou goest to the right, I will go to
the left.**

As Luther aptly remarks on the subject, after
Abram had given an excellent demonstration of faith
in the previous chapter, he now gives a good example
of the type of works that faith produces. The true
magnanimity of faith is here displayed. How readily
Abram might have insisted on his rights: he was the
elder; he had come to this country at God's behest,
not Lot; to Abram's seed the land had been promised.
With utter selflessness and in true faith, which knows
that God cannot fail in the keeping of His promise,
Abram takes the difficulty in hand. In the wisdom of
faith he acts before the peace between him and Lot
has been marred. In the courtesy of faith he speaks
very kindly: note the double "please," (*na'*) which
softens even the kindly suggestions. With the tactful-
ness of faith he appeals to proper motives: "for we
are brethren" (Heb. "we are men that are brethren"
— a noun used for an adjective: *'achchîm = verbrue-
dert*, K. S. 306 r). "Brother" is used in the wider
sense in this case, as 24:27: Bethuel and Abram; and
29:12: Jacob and Laban. Meek's rendering of the

opening sentence is admirable: "There simply must be no quarrel between you and me."

9. The question here, as aften, is the equivalent of a strong assertion. "Before thee" means "open before thee," though the Hebrew has only *lephanêkha*. The nifal *hipparedh* is here used reflexively: separate yourself = "part." "Left" and "right" here apparently refer to the East and the West respectively, not to the North and the South (Targum). The choice lies wholly with Lot. He may take whatsoever he will. *Hashshemo'l* is a locative; *'eyminah* is a Hifil denominated from *yamîn*, "right-hand." The same relation holds good for the last two forms, only in reverse order: *yamîn* being used as locative and *'ashme'îlah* as Hifil.

10, 11. **Then Lot lifted up his eyes and beheld all the Round of the Jordan that it was well-watered, every part of it, before Yahweh destroyed Sodom and Gomorrah; in fact, it was as the garden of Yahweh, or at least even as the land of Egypt, in the vicinity of Zoar. So Lot chose for himself the whole Round of the Jordan, and Lot departed eastward; and so they parted one from another.**

Lot prepares to make his choice and to this end "lifts up his eyes" that he might evaluate the surrounding country as it presented itself to the eye. We make Lot a moral degenerate when we say that he looked about "with a look of eager, lustful greed" (Whitelaw). Again, we judge him far too leniently when we call this "a work of righteousness, because he walked in faith" (Luther). The truth lies between these two opinions. The gradual degeneracy of a relatively good character begins at this point. It is little to Lot's credit that he immediately takes full advantage of Abram's bighearted offer. Of course, since Canaan was still in reality "a land flowing with milk and honey," we are not confronted with the

grievous evil of having only a very undesirable portion
of the land left for Abram. Of two acceptable portions Lot takes the perhaps more acceptable. There
is nothing mean about Lot's choice. Nevertheless, it
is an act devoid of all finer impulses. The portion
Lot chooses is called the *kikkar* of the Jordan. This
term implies something round, here "a round district."
It is not the whole basin of the Jordan from the Lake
of Gennesareth to the Dead Sea but only that portion
which extends from about Jericho down to and including the northern end of the Dead Sea to Zoar. So
much only, according to the various uses of the term
kikkar where it appears in the Scriptures. In the
vicinity of Bethel, at a spot a few minutes to the southeast of the village, is an eminence called *Burg Beitin,*
of which it is said that it is undoubtedly "one of the
greatest viewpoints of Palestine" from which, in fact,
the Jordan valley and the northern end of the Dead
Sea are distinctly to be seen. This region was "well-
watered" at that time and therefore both fertile and
provided with ample pasturage.

Now when Moses reminds us that this region was
so attractive "before Yahweh destroyed Sodom and
Gomorrah," he clearly implies that in his time the
region was sadly altered. One question will perhaps
never be determined at this point and that is how far
the devastating effects of the overthrow of Sodom and
Gomorrah affected the rest of the Dead Sea region.
Some hold that the Bible indicates that the entire
Dead Sea is the result of that cataclysmic overthrow.
We personally believe that indeed only the southern
shallow end of the Dead Sea became covered with
water as a result of the overthrow of these cities, as
also Kyle's investigations seem to substantiate. But
at the same time it appears that more or less of a
blight settled upon the whole *kikkar*. For the author
here goes on to describe that it once was as "the gar-

den of Yahweh" by which he must mean the garden
of Eden which was in a special sense Yahweh's handiwork. The comparison must have been suitable, else
Moses would not have used it. It is true that, nevertheless, the simile is a bit strong. Consequently, it
is toned down by a second simile that has a fine propriety about it from another point of view: "as the
land of Egypt." To indicate that this second comparison steps to a lower level we inserted the explanatory
words: "or at least as." The special propriety of this
latter simile lies in this that the region is like Egypt
in that a deeper lying river winds through a fertile
plain enclosed by mountains on either side. The last
phrase, "in the vicinity of Zoar," attaches itself not
to "Egypt" but the word "well-watered," and so
selects what may have been the most pleasant spot of
the now blasted area. All the explanation offered is
in place only on the supposition that a tremendous
deterioration of the whole "round" has taken place,
and this is exactly what the writer wishes to convey. Again critics fail to catch the import of the statement when they assert that "the last half of the
verse seems greatly overloaded" (Skinner). "In the
vicinity" (*bo'akhah*) in Hebrew literally = "as thou
goest."

11. When Lot chooses for himself "the whole
Round of the Jordan," he is planning in reference to
his herds which will require ample pasturage. Consequently, he makes his choice by going "eastward."
Mikkédem used as in 11:2. So the separation between the two is complete. The heterogeneous element
has been removed. *Abram* is alone, as providence at
this time intended that he should be; cf. Isa. 51:2;
Ezek. 33:24; Mal. 2:15.

12, 13. **And Abram dwelt in the land of
Canaan whereas Lot dwelt in the cities of the Round,
and pitched tent even as far as Sodom. And the**

men of Sodom were wicked and very sinful in the sight of Yahweh.

To make it apparent that the separation effected was very definite we are informed that Canaan proper was Abram's habitation. Lot, on the other hand, (*waw* adversative) is found in the cities of the Round (*kikkar* practically a proper name, K. S. 295 g). Hengstenberg, no doubt, is correct when he makes the observation (*Geschichte des alten Bundes*) that Lot's successive deterioration of character is being described. Apparently, at the outset Lot turned to this region because the quiet tenor of a godly life in the company of Abram was not sufficiently attractive for him. He craved the diversions and the excitement offered by city life. So first he turns toward the Round; then he is found in "the cities of the Round"; then he even touches the city notorious for its wickedness, "Sodom." For when the explanatory phrase is added that Sodom's men were "wicked and very sinful in the sight of Yahweh," this is done not only in anticipation of the things to be found in chapter nineteen but chiefly in reference to Lot. If the moral character of these cities was so pronouncedly unsavory, then a godly man should rather have shunned association with the inhabitants. We finally, however, find the man enrolled among the inhabitants of wicked Sodom. He may not have shared their sins; but, apparently, he was not so entirely averse to them as a godly man should be. The expression "very sinful" is made especially strong in Hebrew by the use of the noun for the adjective "sinners exceedingly." The additional phrase "in the sight of Yahweh" is more than a Hebrew superlative — a view rejected by Luther on verse 10, "garden of Yahweh." As we indicated in connection with 10:9, "before Yahweh" means "openly before," "in the full mental view of." Yahweh, the Faithful One, was not ignorant of the danger that threatened His own from the side of the ungodliness of these sinners. Naturally, then, of the two terms, "wicked and very sinful in the sight of Yahweh," the second one marks a decided advance upon the first. Not without reason the expression that ascribes to Sodom sinfulness that "cries out to heaven" quite properly grew out of descriptions such as those of our verse. Yahweh's faithfulness demands that He take cognizance of such extreme iniquity and rebuke it for the sake of His true children, lest they suffer harm.

14, 15. But Yahweh on His part said unto Abram after Lot had parted from him: Lift up now thine eyes and look about from the place where thou art to the north, to the south, to the east, and to the west; for all the land at which thou art looking, to thee will I give it and to thy seed for a long time.

"Yahweh on His part" (noun first, for emphasis) had not been unaware of what His friend had passed through. Abram had by Lot's separation been rendered still more alone. No doubt, the godly patriarch grieved over the necessary separation. But Abram himself had kept himself without sin throughout this test, and this indeed pleased God, who loves to encourage His own in welldoing and rewards them wherever circumstances allow such a course. Rationalistic workrighteousness is reflected in Dillmann's statement of the case: "Abram had through his magnanimous conduct made himself worthy of further favor." But God does love to reward with rewards of grace those who truly serve Him. That this act in this instance is to be viewed from this point of view appears from the addition of the clause, "after Lot had parted from him."

There is, indeed, a contrast between the lifting up of the eyes on Abram's part here and that of Lot

v. 10, where selfish interest motivated the act. Abram
is to regard the land in every direction with the eyes
of faith. From certain eminences of Palestine much
of the land can actually be seen. Abram, however,
is to regard it all not only a certain portion as his
own. What he has seemingly lost by not having regard to his material advantage is more than offset by
what God bestows upon him. In this case this principle
holds good even in regard to material possessions.
True, Abram becomes possessor only in his seed —
"to thy seed I will give it." But such possession is
none the less real. Such possession is guaranteed by
God as extending *'ahh 'ôlam,* "for a long time." We
have preferred to render this expression thus, because
it actually implies nothing more than for an indefinitely
long season whose end cannot yet be determined,
being derived from *'alam,* "to be hidden." Under circumstances the expression may mean actual eternity.
On the other hand, it may imply no more than for
the rest of a man's lifetime (Exod. 21:6). Now,
surely, as commentators of all times have clearly
pointed out, especially already Luther and Calvin, this
promise to Abram is conditional, requiring faith.
God cannot give rich promises of good which mate-
rialize even when men have cast off His Savior. History is the best commentary on how this promise is
meant. When the Jews definitely cast off Christ, they
were definitely as a nation expelled from the land. All
who fall back upon this promise as guaranteeing a
restoration of Palestine to the Jews before the end
of time have laid into it a meaning which the words
simply do not convey. A very accurate rendering
of *'adh 'ôlam* is given by K. C., *bis in dunkle Zukunft,* "unto the dark future." "For all time" (Meek)
is, of course, wrong. So is "forever" (A. V.).
Luther's commentary is correct: "a long time."

The participle *ro'eh,* "art looking," lends color to the situation, indicating that as soon as Abram was bidden to look about, he proceeded to do so, and while he was looking, the promise was amplified.

16, 17. And I shall make thy seed as the dust of the earth, so that if a man be able to count the dust of the earth, then shall thy seed be counted. Come, walk abroad in the land according to its length and breadth; for to thee I do give it.

What a challenge to the faith of a childless old man! Yet, also, how rich a promise. Each new word spoken by God to Abram — and this is now the third word — marks some distinct advance upon the preceding. True, in its literal meaning the promise is a hyperbole, as are many other statements in the Scripture, but, of course, a perfectly legitimate form of emphatic statement. Dust of the earth simply cannot be counted. But no one would ever think of ascribing exaggeration to the statement because it bears its own restriction: "as the dust" insofar as dust cannot be counted.

17. Abram is at once to give evidence of his faith in this rich and gracious promise by "walking abroad," literally *hithhallekh* = "go for one's self." In cheerful faith and anticipation of the future possession of the land by his seed Abram is to roam about freely through the land, rejoicing in its many advantages. *Qûm,* "arise," is not to be taken literally, as addressed only to persons in a sitting posture. It has come to be practically only an interjection like "come," as is also indicated in part by the asyndeton. "Come, walk abroad." K. S. labels this a "conventional asyndeton" (357 l). The solemn repetition, after v. 15, of the promise "to thee do I give it" (*lekha 'ettenénnah*) is quite in place, because the promise of God is all that faith has to cling to under the circumstances, and

so these promises must stand out' distinctly with emphasis.

18. And Abram kept moving his tent along and came and dwelt by the terebinths of Mamre, which are in Hebron; and he built an altar there unto Yahweh.

It seems that *ye'ehal,* "he tented," in this instance aims to show Abram's response to God's summons to go about through the land; therefore we have rendered: "he kept moving his tent along." Then, apparently, after the joyful inspection of the land was finished, he came to Hebron and made his more nearly permanent home there. For Hebron was the city near which the patriarchs particularly delighted to dwell. "Hebron" (*chebhrôn*) according to the root-meaning of the name seems to mean a place where a treaty or covenant was made (cf. the German *Buenden* in compounds of city names). Whether the city then occupied the site that present-day Hebron does may well be questioned; nor is there any trace left of "the terebinths of Mamre." On "terebinths" cf. 12:6. "Mamre," apparently, was a noted man of that time; see 14:13. This new permanent home is to be sanctified by an altar for sacrifices to Yahweh, and is to have in that altar a means of worship as well as a testimony to all men that Abram had nothing in common with the Canaanites and their idolatrous worship.

HOMILETICAL SUGGESTIONS

This chapter also has two sections for homiletical use. The first includes v. 1-13. Since faith is the outstanding characteristic of Abraham, it would be quite proper to preach at this point on the subject of the "Magnanimity of Faith." If one should desire to dwell on the more practical angle of the case, even such a subject as the "Wisdom of the Separation" of friends could suggest a proper mode of approach. For the remaining verses (14-18) we suggest some such theme as "the Reward of

Grace," because God is plainly rewarding Abraham for what he lost in his bighearted attitude toward Lot.   Yet it is just as clear that this reward is utterly unmerited on Abraham's part. Consequently, the paradoxical phrase "reward of grace" applies here.   Material rewards do loom up rather prominently in the Pentateuch.   By way of explanation it should be remembered that on the Old Testament level many clear revelations that we now enjoy had not yet been received.   Therefore visible tangible evidences of divine favor may be regarded as more of a necessity. Yet even on the New Testament level this subject is in place as the very clear parallel Matt. 19:29 from the Savior's own lips indicates.   Whatever is done for Christ's sake meets with a suitable reward.

CHAPTER XIV

4. The Defeat of the Kings by Abram (14:1-24)

We now see Abram in an entirely new capacity. He appears in contact with the kings of this world and in contrast with them to some extent. Indeed, in part his unselfishness is still further demonstrated. But at the same time we are shown how courageous true faith makes this man. As prominent a fact as any revealed by the chapter is how the man whom God has honored by rare promises of mercy is a man who enjoys honor also among men: he moves at ease among kings, easily the equal of any of them. However, not one of these facts dare be stressed at the expense of the rest, as though any of them fully expressed the purpose of the chapter.

Criticism misinterprets an honest record when it represents the whole narrative as a bit of fiction written in order to magnify the hero. Equally unfair is the approach which says: since elsewhere matters of this sort are not narrated concerning Abram, therefore this cannot be true.

Source criticism finds itself sorely beset by difficulties at this point, inasmuch as the customary sources usually assigned for Genesis fail to prove adequate for this chapter: here are neither E, J, or P. About four terms are discovered that are usually assigned to P, but with that the similarity ceases. The very obvious fact concerning the vocabulary of this chapter, namely, that it is somewhat different from other chapters merely because it deals with a different type of subject — this obvious fact does not seem to occur to the critics. As a result much learning is

(445)

expended on the questions: from what source are the facts narrated derived; are they oral tradition; do they come from some Canaanite or some Babylonian clay tablets; etc.? It cannot be denied that parenthetical explanations abound throughout the chapter: e. g., v. 2, "the same is Zoar"; v. 3, "the same is the Salt Sea"; v. 7, "the same is Kadesh"; v. 15, "which is on the left hand of Damascus"; v. 17, "the same is the King's Vale." These are most readily accounted for on the score that the old names current at the time this event transpired in a number of instances required an explanation by the time when Moses wrote the account for his contemporaries.

Before taking in hand the various proper names of the kings mentioned particularly in v. 1, we wish to draw attention to a general fact in regard to all of them. The claims raised in regard to all of them range from one extreme to the other. Whereas some students leave the impression that just about each one of the four mentioned has been positively identified by Babylonian evidence of clay tablets or monuments; others just as decidedly seek to create the impression that not one has been or can be identified. In fact, for that matter they contend that the historical situation here described is quite out of harmony with what an accurate study of history reveals.

As so often, the truth lies between the two extremes. Some of the kings in question may have been identified by other historical evidence; at least, the names involved are names quite possible for these lands and these times. In other words, what the chapter contains is in reality neither proved nor disproved by sound historical research, just as little as grounds exist for questioning the reliability of any item in the chapter.

1. **And it came to pass in the days of Amraphel, king of Shinar, and Arioch, king of Ellasar,**

Chedorlaomer, king of Elam, and Tidal, king of Goyim.

"Amraphel" first demands attention. It is customary to identify him with the famous Hammurabi. Yet it cannot be denied that the identification is far from convincing. The chief difficulty centers in the final "l," for the assumed Babylonian original has no equivalent for it. This is freely admitted by many (cf. Procksch and Koenig). But the difficulty is disposed of by the assumption that some Jewish copyist must have made a mistake. But how unscientific: I seek to establish the identity of a certain name; the identity fails to become clear and convincing; therefore, *I* am not wrong but the *name* is. K. C. adopts the device of a longer form which he claims is once used for Hammurabi, viz., *Chammurapi - ilu,* that is, "Chammurapi is a God." But that is a complete sentence, not a name! Besides, Hammurabi, according to Michell's accurate computations, first ascended the throne in 2068 B. C.; whereas Chedorlaomer's famous expedition had occurred twenty years earlier in 2088 B. C. Now the Shinar over which he reigned was Babylon, as we noted on 10:10.

Certainly "Arioch" is analogous to Eri-Aku, whom some identify with Rim-Sin, King of Larsa, which last name certainly resembles "Ellasar," an old Babylonian city a bit to the north of the lower Euphrates, a place now called *Senkereh*. At this point the identification is highly probable, for Rim-Sin actually came to the throne about 2098 B. C.

In the case of "Chedorlaomer" everything again becomes highly problematic. For a Babylonian name like *Kudur-Lathgumal,* or as others construe it: *Kudur-lagomar,* is possible but has never been discovered. So the Babylonian source-material fails to prove adequate for identification. "Elam" is, of course, to the east of the middle Tigris and south

of *Assyria,* corresponding roughly with the later Persia
(cf. 10:22).

As far as "Tidal" is concerned, it may be that he
is identical with *Tudkhula* who made an attack upon
Babylon together with the Elamites. But the words
following his name present difficulty. "Goyim" may
simply mean "nations" (A. V.). In that event Tidal
would have been the head of a more or less mixed group
composed of various nationalities. There is the more
remote possibility that "Goyim" is another way of
writing *Guti,* a people on the Upper Zab.

The noun "days" has a succession of nouns in
the construct relationship following; cf. K. S. 276 b.

**2. They made war with Bera, king of Sodom,
and Birsha, king of Gomorrah, Shinab, king of
Admah, and Shemeber, king of Zeboyim; and the
king of Bela (that is, Zoar).**

It is true that there is a slight break in the construction at this point: strictly speaking, the four
proper nouns, i. e., the names of the kings preceding,
are not subjects of the verb "made" but genitives dependent on "days." But in reality these names stand
out so prominently that they may without the slightest
confusion be regarded as the subjects of the verb of
v. 2. To call this "a faulty syntax which a good writer
would have avoided" is unfair. Not one of these five
kings has ever been identified. The Jewish interpretation of their names is entirely fanciful and unlikely,
when it separates the first into *be-ra',* i. e., "in wickedness," and the second into *be-resha',* i. e., "in iniquity."
On the strength of the unreasonableness of such an
etymology critics jump to the conclusion that the
names themselves are fictitious. By comparing parallel
Arabic roots (cf. K. W.) it will be seen that the first
name might mean "Victor," the second, "a sturdy
man," the third, "Sin (the moon god) is father," and
Shemeber, "the name (of God) is mighty." Sodom

and Gomorrah, as we indicated (13:10), apparently lay at the southern end or lagoon of what is now the Dead Sea. "Admah" and "Zeboyim" are mentioned, aside from this chapter, only in Deut. 29:23 and Hos. 11:8, where their overthrow together with Sodom and Gomorrah is implied, though their destruction is not reported in chapter nineteen. They must have been rather near the two more familiar cities, yet sufficiently distinct from them to allow for having a separate king. "Bela," or "Zoar," had best be placed at the southeast corner of the Dead Sea.

Note the unconnected perfect *'asû* after the introductory *wayhi* of v. 1 (K. S. 370 b).

3. **All these allied themselves for an expedition to the valley of Siddim (that is, the Salt Sea).**

Though the construction of the sentence is somewhat loose and this verse might possibly refer to an act of the kings of v. 2, it seems quite a bit more likely that as in v. 2 the kings of v. 1 were regarded as grammatical subjects, so in v. 3 the same subjects are still under consideration. These kings from the East "allied themselves (*chabherû*) for an expedition to (all covered by *'el* in a pregnant construction) the valley of Siddim." The name of this valley may be allied with the noun *sidh*, "chalk," and so no reason exists for changing *Siddim* to *Shedhîm*, (Kittel) i. e., "evil spirits." The parenthetical remark "that is, the Salt Sea," does not commit the author of it, as commentators so frequently assert at this point, to the view that the entire Dead Sea is the result of the catastrophe reported in chapter nineteen. For, since the bottom of the northern two-thirds of the sea lies in some instances as much as 1,300 feet beneath the surface level, which in turn already lies 1,300 feet beneath the sea level, it seems most likely that this part of the lake was in existence from days of old. An author well aware of this, as Moses no

doubt was, would then mean his remark in the sense:
Valley of Siddim = *the southern end* of the Salt
Sea — a synecdoche, the whole for the part.

**4-6. Twelve years they had remained sub-
ject to Chedorlaomer and in the thirteenth year they
revolted; and in the fourteenth year came Chedorlaomer and the kings allied with him and smote the
Rephaim at Ashteroth-Qarnayim and the Zuzim at
Ham and the Emim in the plain of Qiryathayim;
and the Horites in their mountains, namely those
of Seir, as far as El Paran which is by the wilderness.**

A concise account is given as to how the war
mentioned in v. 2 originated, or rather, why Chedorlaomer and his confederates undertook the punitive expedition which gave rise to the chief episode
of our chapter. Elamite and Babylonian domination
of Palestine had been effective for twelve years.
Chedorlaomer the Elamite was at the time in question sovereign also over Babylon, a fact with which
historical records agree. For reasons not revealed
at this point the five kings listed in v. 2 decided
to revolt. When the customary tribute as token of
submission failed to be paid, Chedorlaomer decided
that the rebels needed to be brought to time. This
punitive step was feasible in the fourteenth year.
Though it be said that "Chedorlaomer came," that does
not of necessity involve personal participation. In
the language of the monuments expeditions sent out
at the king's behest are ascribed to him, at least if
they are successful. At this point we may well note
how it came to pass, perhaps, that no record of this
expedition has come to us. Egyptian and Babylonian
kings were not wont to have chronicles made of their
defeats, and this expedition ended disastrously for
Chedorlaomer. The kings of Shinar and Larsa must
identify their cause with that of Chedorlaomer: he

himself, no doubt, compelled them, as did also a community of interests. The cardinal numerals are used for the ordinals (G. K. 134, o).

5 b. Now the route taken by these Mesopotamian forces is interesting. It reveals a wide sweep to the east and south and then around to the southwest; then northeast to the western side of the Dead Sea, and lastly the troops swarm down upon their final objective, the cities in the Vale of Siddim. All manner of fault has been found with this route taken by Chedorlaomer. Because the reason for it is not given in this brief account, the critics feel they may with impunity make light of any explanation that we may offer, as though it must needs be trivial. Again and again a very reasonable explanation has been suggested to them, only to be brushed aside. The simplest of all explanations is that the army coming from the east wanted to eliminate the possibility of an attack from the rear by unfriendly groups. These unfriendly groups were either unsubdued opponents or subjugated opponents known to be restive and inclined to side with other revolters. The author of our chapter is not under necessity of giving a full account of all that transpires and of the motives behind every act. For the building-up of the narrative, what is related is very effective. It shows the line being drawn closer and closer about Sodom and Gomorrah. We are made to sense the apprehension of the revolting cities; and they turn around from point to point as reports come pouring in about the defeat of the groups being attacked.

The first ones subdued are "Rephaim," who are overcome at Ashteroth-Qarnayim. The only thing we are safe in saying about the Rephaim is that they belonged to the earlier level of inhabitants of the land. They are found on both sides of the Jordan. Since they are associated with other races that may have

been of the giants, it is not impossible that they themselves were of gigantic stature. "Asteroth" seems to be
the old capital of Bashan, of which ruins still remain
under the name of *Tell 'Aschtera,* nearly twenty miles
east of the Sea of Galilee. The name itself is that
of the goddess Astarte, and Qarnayim means "of the
two horns"; perhaps Astarte as goddess of the moon
(whose crescent has two horns) may in this town
have been known as "Astarte of the twin horns." At
any event, there the first major victory was achieved.

In regard to the "Zuzim" it seems best to accept
the suggestion that this is merely another form of
Zamzummim who are mentioned in Deut. 2:20. The
Ammonites dispossessed them, apparently, and so they
would have dwelt to the south of the Rephaim. The
Greek translators already were at a loss to identify
them and so translated the term "strong peoples"
(ἔθνη ἰσχυρά). The scene of their defeat, "Ham," is
not known. Since it lay in Ammonite territory, it
could well have been Rabba of the Ammonites (cf.
Deut. 3:11), as Keil suggests; for this was apparently
the capital city.

The "Emim" also belonged to the aboriginal inhabitants of Canaan. Something unusual was associated with them apparently, for their name seems
to signify "terrors" (B D B). They had formerly
possessed the land of the Moabites (Deut. 2:10, 11).
The scene of their defeat was in the plain of "Qiryathayim." The name of this town, being dual, perhaps signifies "double town." The modern *Kurêyât*
about 1¼ miles southeast of Mt. Attarus and 6¾ miles
north-northwest from Dibon seems to serve pretty well
as identification. This would be a location about seven
miles east and a bit to the north of the middle of
the Dead Sea. These conquests of Chedorlaomer seem
to mark almost a straight line to the south.

From Qiryathayim the punitive expedition made somewhat of a circuit around the chief rebels and first proceeded to deal out punishment to the south, in fact, due south of the Dead Sea, in the land or the mountains of Seir, later Edom. Here dwelt the "Horites." This name means "cave-dwellers," it would seem (*chor* = "hole"). This meaning may be regarded as almost established by the expression following, viz., "in their mountains." "As far as El Paran" is a concise expression which is best taken to mean that the pursuit after the vanquished Horites extended to this point. Some seek to identify this El Paran with Elath on the Gulf of Akaba. In that case *'eyl*, which means "terebinth" or "large tree" generally, would seem to indicate that originally El or Elath was marked by a large grove of perhaps terebinths. But Paran is the name of the wilderness in the northern half of the Sinai peninsula, and so it would seem more likely that El Paran lay on its borders.

7. And they returned and came to En Mishpat (that is, Kadesh) and smote all the field of the Amalekites and also the Amorites that were dwelling in Hazazon Tamar.

El Paran must have marked the farthest point reached, for after reaching it, the host "returned" in the direction of "En Mishpat." This spot is explained to be Kadesh. Now, without a doubt, Kadesh Barnea is meant, the famous stopping place of Israel during the wilderness wanderings. Hardly any scholars nowadays doubt that this must be what is now known as Ain Kadeis, a famous oasis. "En" (Hebrew: *'eyn* = 'Ain) = "well." Originally this spot had been called "the Well of Judgment" (*mishpat*). It may, therefore, originally have been a sacred spot where judgment was sought or given, or where some famous seer had held forth. "Kadesh" means "holy."

So the later name would indicate that some type of
sanctuary had been found here. In any case, it was
a prominent spot even in those days. Apparently,
from this point the host proceeded to smite an area
that lay to the west, namely "the field of the Amalekites." Now the Amalekites are descended from Ama-
lek, a grandson of Esau (36:12). Consequently there
could be none at Abram's time. Therefore the unusual
expression is used, *"the field* (or plain) of the Amalekites" in the proleptic sense of "the field which later
was occupied by the Amalekites." Moses could not
be guilty of so crude an anachronism as to say that
the Amalekites were smitten. However, he does not
indicate what name this desert tribe bore.

The last group attacked and vanquished are the
"Amorites," who dwelt as far north as Lebanon but
were scattered all through Palestine and were really
the most prominent of the Canaanites. In Chedorlaomer's time they were established at "Hazazon Tamar."
This name would mean "the sandy country of palms."
According to II Chron. 20:2 this was Engedi on the
western shore of the Dead Sea, still a beautiful spot.
This seems to have been the last foe that needed to
be disposed of. Though the approach to Sodom is
very difficult from this point, Sodom was next taken
in hand, although it is not said that a direct approach
was made to it from Engedi.

8, 9. **And there went forth the king of Sodom
and the king of Gomorrah and the king of Admah
and the king of Zeboyim and the king of Bela (that
is, Zoar), and they drew up in battle array against
them in the valley of Siddim, that is against Chedorlaomer, king of Elam, and Tidal, king of Goyim, and
Amraphel, king of Shinar, and Arioch, king of Ellasar — four kings against five.**

Governed by the nearest subject, as so often in
Hebrew, we have a singular verb *yetse'*, though other

subjects of the same verb follow. The style of narrative is a bit diffuse, as is often the case in epic poetry. That the kings of the Dead Sea region did not turn out sooner to encounter the foe of whose approach they had long been aware, indicates either lack of ability and enterprise, or lack of courage, or, perhaps, the illusory hope on their part that their enemies would not venture against them. It seems most in harmony with the facts of the case to argue that the debauched mode of life characteristic of this group had debased their courage so that they only took up arms when actually compelled to and then put up but a pitiable defense. That "they drew up in battle array in the valley of Siddim" seems to be a further indication that this portion, which is now the southern third of the Dead Sea, was in those days not yet inundated by the waters of this sea.

The different order of the names of the attacking kings (or of their armies, perhaps, if the kings were not actually present in person) that appears in v. 9 over against v. 1, may have been occasioned by the relative importance of these kings at this point of the campaign. The dominant factor, no doubt, was Chedorlaomer; cf. also v. 4 and 5. Next in order came Tidal.

10. **Now the valley of Siddim was full of bitumen pits, and as the kings of Sodom and of Gomorrah fled some leaped into the pits, and the rest fled into the mountains.**

The Hebrew way of saying "full of bitumen pits" is: "pits, pits of bitumen." Repetition expresses abundance, plentitude, etc. (G. K. 123 e; K. S. 88). Now, indeed, *yippelû shammah* might mean: "they fell there" = "perished." Strictly applied to the subjects expressed, namely the kings of Sodom and Gomorrah, this would mean: they perished. However, this assumption would create a difficulty in v. 17

where the king of Sodom is still alive. In any case, in v. 17 a new king of Sodom could hardly be met with so soon, for opportunity for the choice of one had hardly been given. But the verb *naphal* may mean "to get down hastily" (cf. 24:64). So we have the somewhat disgraceful situation of a number of defeated kings hastily crawling into bitumen pits, and their defeated army taking refuge in the mountains. The word "king" before "Sodom" and "Gomorrah" does not mean that one king governed both cities but is a concise way of saying "kings." "Some" has to be supplied before "leaped" because immediately a "rest" is spoken of (Meek).

11, 12. **And they took all the goods of Sodom and Gomorrah and all their foodstuffs and went away. They also captured Lot, Abram's brother's son, and his goods before they left, for he was living in Sodom.**

The victors, though not last mentioned, are naturally the subject of the verb "took." Hebrew rhetoric does not require to have the subject specifically indicated to prevent ambiguity. In true marauder style the victors take along all that can feasibly be transported — "all the goods," *rekhush*, a word supposed to belong to P's vocabulary. Since their own food supply has run low, they also replenish their stock by taking practically all that the people of these towns had laid up in store. Lot, of whom we last had heard that he was approaching Sodom more closely, now had actually taken up residence within its gates — a very puzzling act. Somehow he was not in the army, or if he was, he was unfortunate enough to be taken captive, and at this point now we are shown how this event involved Abram, for he was "Abram's brother's son." This familiar fact is merely stated to recall how all this had its bearing upon Abram. The man who had been willing to cast

in his lot with Abram's at the time of the latter's
departure from Haran was now certainly exposed to
as wretched a fate as could befall men in ancient times,
that of a prisoner of war.

**13, 14. And a fugitive came and told Abram,
the man from across the river, who was dwelling
by the terebinths of Mamre, the Amorite, the brother
of Eshcol and Aner, who were bound by covenant
to Abram. And Abram heard that his kinsman had
been taken captive and he led forth his trained men,
born in his own household, three hundred and
eighteen of them and went in pursuit as far as Dan.**

Now follows the story of Abram's prompt action.
A fugitive from the Sodomite catastrophe appears,
"*the* fugitive" in Hebrew; generic article; this may
cover any number of fugitives (K. S. 300 a).   He
informs Abram regarding what transpired.   In apposition with Abram stands in Hebrew the word "the
Hebrew," which we have rendered, according to its
meaning: "the man from across the river," i. e., the
Euphrates.   The term ultimately practically denotes
nationality and is used in particular in contrast with
other nationalities (cf. 43:32; Exod. 1:15; 2:11; 21:2;
Deut. 15:12; I Sam. 13:3).   The contrast is here with
the Amorites who are about to be named.   Abram still
is where the close of the previous chapter left him;
and this fact should be mentioned that we may understand that Abram was readily accessible and in a
position to inaugurate immediate pursuit.   So, too,
the brothers, or perhaps kinsmen, of Mamre are also
mentioned here, Eshcol and Aner, who are to be referred to before the incident is entirely concluded.
For these men were "bound by a covenant" to
Abram, an expression for which the Hebrew uses the
terms "masters of a covenant" — *ba'aley berîth* —
ba'al being used in that familiar, broad sense of merely expressing some type of relation, (K. S. 306 g).

Strange to say, criticism is surprised that three men should be mentioned here, who bear names identical with place names, and says, "it is hard to believe" that this should be the case (Procksch). However, that difficulty is easily removed. A frequent identity of personal names and place names is found. An equal difficulty to many seems to be the writer's failure to mention here that Mamre, Eshcol and Aner at once took part in the expedition about to be inaugurated. But is not that already definitely implied in the mention of the fact that these men were "bound by covenant to Abram"?

As soon as Abram hears of the capture of "his kinsman" (Hebrew: "brother" — the broader use of the word), he takes measures to rescue him. The inconsiderate treatment of Abram by Lot is not counted against the captive. The dangers and difficulties are not allowed to stand in the way of brotherly duty. Courageous as he is, Abram recognizes that a resolute surprise attack, wisely timed, may offset the lack of numbers. Though, of course, we encounter Abram here engaged in war, it is most evident that he was not venturing abroad for honor's sake or to achieve some personal advantage. The safety of others led him on this unselfish undertaking. Luther mentions, by way of contrast, the exploits of Alexander and Scipio. We translate the *hapax legomenon chanîkh* as "trained men" — practically the same as A. V. and A. R. V. These were all of them servants "born in his own household" and therefore more apt to be dependable under all circumstances. We are amazed at the number of them —318. This points to a body of servants easily numbering a thousand and gives us some idea of the size of the flocks as well as of the influence of the man. The hardy courage that urged him to "go in pursuit" calls forth our admiration; for, besides, Abram was no longer young.

Almost without exception commentators locate "Dan" at the site of Dan Laish, about ten miles almost due north of Lake Merom, that is the town frequently referred to in the expression "from Dan even unto Beersheba." This town, as all know, first received the name Dan in the days of the Judges; see Judg. 18:7, 29. The use of the term at this point would then clearly be post-Mosaic and evidence of authorship of the book later than the time of the Judges. Critics are so ready to accept this view that by almost universal consent they ignore the other possible location of Dan so entirely as though it were not even worthy of consideration. For another Dan in Gilead (see Deut. 34:1), mentioned apparently in II Sam. 24:6 as "Dan Jaan," excellently meets the needs of the case, for that matter even better than does Dan Laish. For Dan Jaan must lie, according to Deut. 34:1, on the northern edge of Gilead and therefore about east, perhaps fifteen or twenty miles from the southern end of the Dead Sea, and therefore along the route that an army retreating to Babylon and Elam would be most likely to take in approaching Damascus. Dan Laish lies too far north and presents difficulties for men in flight, who would hardly turn toward Damascus in flight because of intervening rivers. Consequently, we have here no post-Mosaic terms and everything conforms excellently with the idea of Mosaic authorship.

15, 16. **And he divided his forces and made an assault upon them by night, he and his servants, and he defeated them and he pursued them as far as Hobah which lies to the north of Damascus; and he brought back all the goods and also Lot, his kinsman, and his goods did he bring back, as well as the wives and the soldiers.**

A pregnant construction opens the verse: "he divided himself upon" = "he divided his forces and

made an assault upon." The fact that he comes "by
night" (adverbial accusative, K. S. 331 b) shows that
Abram recognized the need of some very strong
strategy like a surprise attack. One can visualize
the manner in which the victorious army returning
back home lay scattered about, secure in the thought
of having none to attack them, flushed with victory
and, perhaps, with drink; no sentinels posted; nothing farther from the thoughts of all than the idea of
an attack. Other instances of dividing forces for
an attack are recorded in Judg. 7:16; I Sam. 11:11;
13:17; Job 1:17. Apparently the statement "he and
his servants" indicates that Abram personally participated in the assault and did not merely direct the
strategy. Many instances are on record, also in the
Scriptures, how oriental armies were thrown into a
wild rout by some such device as the one employed
here. Though, of course, in point of numbers Abram's
force must have been far inferior to that of the con-
federate kings, we create a badly distorted picture of
the situation if we claim (with Dillmann) that Abram
encountered only such scattered bands as trailed behind. For how, then, could he have retrieved all the
people of Sodom, merely to mention this one outstanding fact. Unusual as it may seem, the whole army was
routed. God was permitting Abram to meet with success in his bold venture. To make the defeat as
effective as possible and to guard against a return
attack, the assailants pressed their pursuit rather far,
as we are expressly told, going even as far as "Hobah,"
north of Damascus. A fountain by this name was
identified by Wetzstein about eighty miles northeast of
Damascus. Of course, the expression *missemo'l,* "to
the left," means "to the north of," because the Hebrew
gets his bearings by facing the "east" (*qédhem* =
"before" = "east"). *Damméseq* is the ancient city

of Damascus, known also later from the Amarna tablets as *Dimaški.*

16.   That Abram did a very thorough and effect- ive piece of work in an effort to rehabilitate the poor people of Sodom appears from all that he recaptured. For one thing, he brought back all the goods, which were, indeed, a necessity for the Sodomites. For- tunately, "Lot, his kinsman," had suffered no harm and could be freed as well as his goods restored. Then since "women" were the special objects of capture, it lay in Abram's purpose to liberate these unfor- tunates.   Lastly he set free and brought back also *ha'am,* literally, "the people."   But this expression signifies the "people bearing arms" (B D B), as ap- pears from passages such as I Sam. 11:11; I Kings 20:10; sometimes they are called by the fuller title *'am hammilchamah,* "people of war," (Josh. 8:1, 3; 10:7; 11:7).   So here it is better not to translate "rest of the people" (Strack, Meek) but "the soldiers," (K. W., *Mannschaft*).

Let this yet be said in justification of Abram's step.   Without a doubt, the four kings of the East cannot with any show of right lay claim to the con- trol of the five kings of the Valley of Siddim.   Abram was, therefore, championing the cause of those who had been unjustly oppressed.

17.   **And the king of Sodom went forth to meet him in the Valley of Shaveh (that is, the King's Valley) after his return from the defeat of Chedor- laomer and the kings who were with him.**

Now Abram is a hero and a public benefactor. It appears that those were doing him honor who pre- viously had scarcely deigned to notice him.   "The king of Sodom," whom we last saw taking precipitate refuge in the bitumen pits, now again has come forth and desires to acknowledge publicly the inestimable benefit that Abram has bestowed upon him.   Critics

again attempt to invalidate the story by stating that
this verse conflicts with verse 10, claiming that there
the king of Sodom died, here he is resurrected. In
all fairness they ought to offer to their readers the
simple explanation given above, that v. 10 may mean
they hastily hid in the pits. The canons of criticism
employed by critics are often so sharp that no writings, not even their own, could pass muster in the
face of them. A positive identification of "the Valley
of Shaveh" is no longer possible, though, no doubt,
the explanation "the King's Valley" marked it definitely for the early readers. The name itself indicates
that it was a "level" valley. The name "King's Valley"
seems to come from the fact that kings, especially
Melchizedek met with Abram there on this historic
occasion. As a rule, expositors seek this valley northeast of Jerusalem, in the valley of the Kidron. Nor
is it improbable that the king of Sodom should
encounter Abram so far from the south end of the
Salt See. Circumstances would have made it eminently proper for the king of Sodom to express his gratitude by coming quite a distance to meet Abram.

The infinitive *shûbhó* preceded by "after" (*'acharey*) is the equivalent of an adverbial clause of time
(K. S. 401 c). On *hakkôth* see G. K. 76 c.

**18. And Melchizedek, the king of Salem,
brought forth bread and wine, and he was a priest
of El Elyon.**

Another prominent personage appeared at this
juncture, Melchizedek. To make the fact of his coming forth specially emphatic, this verse does not, as
usual, place the verb first, but the subject, Melchizedek, a deft touch of emphasis which can hardly be
produced in translation, being something like: "Even
Melchizedek came forth." In view of the explanation
of 7:2 the meaning of the name is fully established:
"king of righteousness." All other attempts at inter-

pretation such as, "My king is righteousness" (K. C.),
or "My king is *Tsedheq*" (B D B *et al.*) are to be
rejected, especially where the latter understands
Tsedheq to be some native god. The ending *î* of
Melchî is to be regarded as merely conjunctive, not
possessive, first person (contra K. S. 272 a). Since
this man is a priest of *'El'Elyon*, i. e., "God Most
High," and this is a name of Yahweh, found indeed only in Ps. 78:35 but in many similar combinations quite frequently, we are compelled to regard this
venerable king-priest as a worshipper and publicly an
adherent of the true religion of Yahweh as handed
down from the sounder tradition of the times of the
Flood. That this was the actual course of development of religions, and that monotheism definitely preceded polytheism may now be regarded as fully demonstrated by works such as Samuel Zwemer's *The Origin
of Religion.* However, "Salem" is merely a shortened form of "Jerusalem," the *Urusalim* of the
Amarna tablets; the same short form appears in
Ps. 76:2. What further confirms this identification
is the fact that proper names are frequently used in
an abbreviated form in the Scriptures. Besides,
Abram is regarded as having practically returned
from the expedition: Jerusalem is not so far from
Hebron. The identification of Salem with other sites,
as near Scythopolis, almost up at the Sea of Galilee,
is, therefore, not very satisfactory.

Melchizedek "brings forth bread and wine." He
does this as one who wants to be seen to offer his support to such good men, who do such laudable things
as Abram had just done. He recognizes that a generous offer of rations for the troops was at this time
the prime physical necessity. Nothing more should be
sought in this act of Melchizedek's. He expresses
his friendship and perhaps his religious kinship with
Abram by offering the most common form of meat

and drink, "bread and wine." Attempts to find here a type of the Holy Sacrament have been consistently and rightly rejected by Protestant commentators after the example of Luther.

All they who, following a Jewish tradition, attempt to identify Melchizedek with Shem, the son of Noah, who, it is true, was still living at this time, must do so on the strength of the merest supposition, for no scriptural evidence points in this direction. All that can be said in favor of this interpretation is that it makes the figure of the priest-king more glamorous. Of true value is that which the author of Hebrews sees in Melchizedek that, inasmuch as he combines in himself two offices which were not even combined in the commonwealth of Israel, namely those of priest and king, he is a type of Christ of a higher order even than Aaron (Heb. 7:11 ff.).

But what of the striking parallel to Heb. 7:3 offered by the formula repeated several times in the Amarna letters by the king of Jerusalem writing to the Pharaoh, Amenophis IV, where he says: "Neither my father nor my mother set me in this place; the mighty arm of the king established me in my father's house," (vs. "without father, without mother," Heb. 7:3)? Viewed soberly, the parallel is striking but quite superficial and in the last analysis purely accidental. The words written in the Amarna tablets are merely diplomatic flattery: he owes his position, he claims, entirely to his Egyptian overlord not to heredity from father and mother. The author of Hebrews sees in the fact that father and mother of this mysterious king of old are not mentioned a parallel to Christ's spiritual position: He owes nothing in this exalted priesthood to father or mother. Here is a case where archaeology, though offering an accidental word parallel, in reality contributes nothing to the case under consideration.

The dative *le* after "priest" necessitates rendering "*a* priest" and forbids "*the* priest" (K. S. 280 l) ; correct, ἱερεὺς τοῦ θεοῦ (LXX).

19, 20. And he blessed him, saying:
Blessed be Abram of El Elyon, the Creator of heaven and earth,
And blessed be El Elyon, who has delivered thine enemies into thy hands.
Thereupon he gave him a tithe of all.

As one who as priest ranks above Abram, Melchizedek bestows a blessing; for "the less is blessed of the greater" (Heb. 7:7). The *le* before the divine name does not mean "to" but "of" or "by" (K. S. 104; B D B 5 d, sub *le*). The priest defines who he considers El Elyon to be, namely, "the Creator of heaven and earth" — a strictly monotheistic conception and entirely correct. Though we only assume that Melchizedek came into possession of the truth concerning God by way of the tradition that still prevailed pure and true in a few instances at this late date after the Flood, there is nothing that conflicts with such an assumption except an evolution theory of history, which at this point, as so often, conflicts with facts. The verb for "Creator" (for "Creator" is a participle) is not the customary *bara'*, as the usual Hebrew tradition knows it, but the less common *qanah* — a further indication that Melchizedek had a religious background different from Abram's. In fact, it would seem that Melchizedek is not in possession of as full a measure of the truth as is Abram; for, apparently, Melchizedek does not know God as Yahweh, though the correctness of the conception "God Most High" cannot be denied. "Heaven and earth" stand without an article — poetic style (K. S. 292 a).

20. Melchizedek's blessing is in every way what it should be: it ascribes the glory to God and lets

Abram appear merely as what he is, an instrument God deigned to use — so the second half of the blessing. The first half had represented Abram as standing in need of the blessing of El Elyon and therefore bestowed that blessing from the hands of the Omnipotent Creator. As Luther beautifully points out in this connection, this comprehensive blessing is quite exhaustive and gives a true and adequate presentation of truth. In fact, since it contains so much of truth, Luther calls it *eine sehr lange Predigt,* and actually believes that Melchizedek set forth the substance of what is here stated in a much more detailed fashion. There can be no doubt about it that whether long or short this blessing was a clear-cut confession of him who gave it and a strong testimony to the truth, given at a solemn moment under memorable circumstances also in the ears of an ungodly and unbelieving group of neighbors. No doubt, on Moses' part the object of recording so memorable a piece of history connected with one of the major cities of the blessed land, was to impress the people with the glorious record that truth had had in the earliest day in some of these venerable cities.

The "tithe" given by Abram is, no doubt, rendered to Melchizedek in his capacity as priest and for the sanctuary at Salem. By this act Abram expressed his gratitude to God, Who alone had prospered his venture. Strictly speaking, *ma'aser* should be rendered merely "*a* tenth part," for it was not identical with *the* tenth part or tithe which the Mosaic law required.

21-24. And the king of Sodom said unto Abram: Give me the people and take the goods for yourself. But Abram said to the king of Sodom: I have lifted up my hand to Yahweh, El Elyon, the Creator of heaven and earth, not to take anything of all that belongs to thee, from a thread to a shoe-

string, lest thou shouldest say, It is I who made
Abram rich. Quite apart from me (let this matter
be settled). Only what the young men have eaten
(will I accept). But as for the portion of the men
who accompanied me, Aner, Eshcol and Mamre, let
them take their own portion.

A second king now addresses Abram, apparently
at the same spot, "the King's Vale," this king, however, thinks in entirely different terms, in terms of
things purely material. As king he naturally expects
to have his people restored to him. He recognizes,
however, how enormously he is indebted to Abram
and seeks to give expression to his sense of indebted-
ness by asking Abram to take all the goods recaptured,
i. e., *rekhush,* "the movable chattels," such as precious garments, all gold and silver, weapons, cattle.
No one can deny that Abram could have kept these
as his due. The king of Sodom is ready to give his
full sanction to such an act. Abram, however, cannot do such a thing. He is not covetous, the thought
of the acquisition of wealth never entered into the
undertaking of the expedition. But another weightier
consideration enters into the case: Abram desires
to stand out clearly as a man who prospers only because of God's blessing. Hitherto this status of his
had been unmistakably clear; Abram had never sought
wealth, nor resorted to questionable methods of getting it; nor had anyone contributed to his wealth.
Least of all could Abram accept a generous bestowal
from a man of the calibre of the king of Sodom, a
purely sensual materialist and idolater. The acceptance of the gift would have impugned Abram's spiritual standing. Consequently, Abram summarily
rejects the proposal. Firmness but not "proud and
almost disdainful magnanimity" characterizes this
action. So far-reaching are the spiritual consequences
which Abram sees involved in this step that he had

already taken an oath by "lifting up his hand to Yahweh" (cf. for the same formula of oath Exod. 6:8; Num. 14:30; Deut. 32:40; Ezek. 20:23; Dan. 12:7). No doubt, Abram knew the king of Sodom to be just such a character who would afterward distort the facts of the case in such a fashion as to claim: "I made Abram rich."

By calling Yahweh by the name employed by Melchizedek (v. 19), "El Elyon, the Creator of heaven and earth," Abram bears testimony to the fact that his God and Melchizedek's are one and the same person, even though, in reality, Melchizedek's conception of Him may be less deep. *'Im* introduces a negative oath (K. S. 391 b; G. K. 149 c). By the way, this is the first oath recorded in the Bible.

23. Abram makes his point in the refusal emphatic by the statement that he would not even take "a thread or a shoestring." We might have said "a piece of string" for the first item. The second, strictly speaking, is a sandal thong. *We* before *'adh* strengthens the form (K. S. 376 c.)

24. The initial *bil'adhay,* means literally, "not up to me." We believe this meaning may be retained (as K. C. suggests) in an ellipsis, "Quite apart from me," that is to say, "Leave me out of the adjustments to be made on the question of goods."

Frankly, we cannot understand why men should ever have claimed that "an earlier writer would perhaps not have understood this scruple." This claim merely injects the claim of gradual evolutionistic growth of spiritual apprehension. Was Abram so far above his time that even a sympathetic recorder of the things he did could not appreciate the finer traits in his character? Equally strange to us is the attempt to make contradictions where everything harmonizes, by claiming that Abram who disclaimed a right to the spoils for himself could not possibly have bestowed a tenth on Melchizedek. The least bit of effort to understand would show that a religious tenth reveals the same spirit as the refusal for personal use.

One natural exception must be made: something of that which was taken from the vanquished enemy had to be used to feed the deliverers. Abram wanted it understood that he felt justified in having appropriated this much. His confederates, Aner, Eshcol and Mamre, were, of course, not to be bound by his own conscientious scruples. These men were at liberty to make whatever adjustment they desired with the king of Sodom.

So closes this chapter that throws a delightful sidelight on Abram's character, more particularly on the faith of the patriarch; for it was a faith that made Abram both courageous and extremely considerate for the honor of Yahweh. It was a faith utterly selfless.

HOMILETICAL SUGGESTIONS

The entire chapter is a unit text. Surely, v. 1-12 could hardly be used alone; for who would care to preach about campaigns, as the kings of this earth conduct them? Even v. 1-16 would be unsatisfactory, for some of the finest things essential to the proper understanding of Abraham's victory would be passed by. In any case, the remaining portion v. 17-24 would also hardly constitute a unit that is satisfactory in itself. The major point in our approach to this chapter would suggest a theme such as "The Dignity of the Father of Believers." Very proper also would be the theme "The Courage of Faith," if one desires to carry through consistently the idea that Abram is above all else a man of faith.

Could v. 18-20 be used for a sermon on "Melchizedek — a Type of Christ"? Why not? The letter to the Hebrews would in that case suggest the points of view that must predominate. Yet Hebrews points only to the material found in this pericope. Consequently v. 18-20 gives occasion for a good sermon on "Christ—our Priest-King."

CHAPTER XV

5. God's Covenant with Abram (15:1-21)

In a very particular sense this is a monumental chapter, monumental in the testimony that it bears to saving truth. It is for this reason that Paul alludes to a word from this chapter when he establishes the truth concerning salvation (Rom. 4:3; Gal. 3:6). It is nothing short of amazing to find in the patriarchal age so clear-cut an answer to the question: How can a man be justified in the sight of God? The way of salvation was one and the same in the old covenant as well as in the new.

At the same time, this chapter demonstrates in particular how God's treatment of Abram moved along from step to step in conformity with the patriarch's needs. As new problems arose, a new course of procedure was inaugurated by God. The more severely Abram's faith was put to the test during the period of waiting for the son who was to be born, the more substantial became the support that God offered to Abram's faith. If hitherto numerous offspring had been assured, and a land promised in which his seed might multiply, now the assurance is given that Abram's own seed and not that of another should be his heir, and the promise is established in a covenant.

At the same time we find in this chapter as positive a type of evidence as anyone might desire of the high level and the distinct character of the patriarchal religion. Even when men accept the separation of the Pentateuch into various sources (a thing we definitely reject as unscientific), even these sources give indication of very accurate transmission of the facts of early history. The Hebrews had a keen sense for preserving tradition reliably. This accurate tradition of theirs also indicates very definitely that Israel's religion did not first originate with the literary prophets. Nor did it first take its beginning with Moses and the exodus from Egypt. But, as this chapter very clearly indicates, Israel's religion appeared in the patriarchs as a religion essentially the same as it is found to be in the eighth century, yet in the matter of details sufficiently different to allow for our classifying it as the patriarchal stage of Israel's religion; and having as its heart and core faith in a faithful God.

This revelation of God to Abram is the fifth granted to the patriarch.

At the very outset we must remark that no one is now in a position to tell just how God manifested Himself to men in visions; but such revelations of God must have come with an emphatic distinctness to men, so that the recipient could not be in doubt whether or not God was actually speaking.

1. **After these things the word of Yahweh came to Abram in a vision, thus: Be not afraid, Abram; I am thy shield, thy exceeding great reward.**

The accurate report of what transpired in Abram's life indicates that in point of time this vision came after the defeat of the kings. The particular word used for "vision" (*machazeh*) is not a common one, being found besides only in Num. 24:4, 16 and Ezek. 13:7. It is used with the article because the type of vision accompanying divine revelation is implied (the article with things customary — K. S. 299 b). But since the chapter presents a unit, one part naturally attaching itself to the other, the statement at the head, that this revelation came in a vision, covers the entire chapter.

The denial of this simple fact works confusion. Such a denial grows out of a restriction of the idea of a "vision," as though as soon as some form of action takes place, the vision must be terminated. The truth of the matter is that the ecstatic state which renders the mind receptive to divine revelation may allow for "seeing" (*machazeh*, from *chazah*, "to see") God speak and for seeing one's self do various things and God, too, do things as well as speak. "Visions," like dreams, allow for a wide latitude of experiences for him that has them, though the vision and the dream are by no means identical. Standing at the opening of the chapter, the term "vision" is designed to cover the entire complex experience that follows.

A major difficulty is encountered in determining why Abram was addressed: "Fear not." What caused Abram's fears? Looking backward, as might be suggested by the phrase "after these things," we might prefer to hold that Abram feared retribution at the hand of the Eastern kings after the surprise defeat he had inflicted upon them. So the Jewish commentators largely believed. This view seems to meet additional support in the rest of the divine communication: "I am thy shield." Now, it cannot be denied that Abram was human enough to be visited by a measure of trepidation at the thought of another punitive expedition from the East. But the rest of the chapter shows beyond the possibility of doubt that such a fear is by no means under consideration, but the fear of remaining childless is what Abram and the Lord alone refer to. Over against that danger God promises that He Himself is the perfectly adequate safeguard and the only reward that Abram needs. From thoughts of what is deemed humanly possible Abram should center all hope in God alone as a God adequate for every need. Since, then, the Lord emphatically points to Himself, we see at once that the second half of the statement must be rendered as we have translated above: "(I am) thy exceeding great reward," and not after the fashion of the Greek translators, who made of this a second clause: "thy reward is very great." For, as Whitelaw rightly suggests, this rendering "fails to give prominence to the thought that the patriarch's reward was to be the all-sufficient Jehovah Himself." With this agrees the emphatic position of *'anokhî*: "It is I who am the shield," etc.

Harbeh, though an absolute infinitive, is, as frequently, used adverbially.

2, 3. And Abram said: Lord Yahweh, what couldest Thou give me, seeing I am going on childless, and the prospective heir of my house is the Damascene, Eliezer? Abram also said: See, to me Thou hast not given offspring; and, look, one belonging to my household will inherit my goods.

Holding these two responses of Abram together and noting that each is separately introduced by "and Abram said," we gain the impression that Abram spoke twice before God answered. Apparently, this was exactly the way this event transpired. Before God applies the new comfort that He is about to administer to Abram, He gives Abram full opportunity to give vent to the thoughts that oppress him, in order that the divine comfort may operate the more effectively.

Abram's first mild complaint, expressing what has long burdened his soul and caused fear (v. 1 b), begins: "Lord Yahweh," i. e., *'adhonay yahweh.* *'Adhonay* signifies *Allherr,* i. e., "Lord of all"; coupled with *Yahweh,* it represents a very respectful and reverent address and shows Abram as one who was by no means doubtful of God's omnipotence. But, at the same time, Abram voices the natural misgivings of the limited human understanding when he says: *ma(h)t-titten-lî.* This should not be ren-

dered: "What wilt thou give me?" God had not
just concluded promising him anything. But rather:
"What couldest thou give me?" For, to tell the truth,
Abram does not see what God could give. Abram
was "going on" through life (*holekh* not here in the
sense of "perish") "childless" (*'arîrî* = "stripped,"
i. e., of children). What we have rendered as "prospective heir" is a typically Hebrew expression: "son
of possession" (*ben-mésheq*), i. e., the one who will
possess. The rest of the statement is also unusual:
"is Damascus Eliezer." (*Eli'ezer* = "God is help").
Apparently, Eliezer was from Damascus. By metonomy, Abram says, "my heir is Damascus, i. e., Eliezer." This says no more than that Eliezer seems
to have hailed from this ancient city. To make the
statement imply that he would ultimately take all of
Abram's goods back to that city certainly stretches
the point.

It seems that out of this harmless reference to
Eliezer's connection with Damascus has grown the
entirely unfounded legend about Abram's residence in
Damascus and his being king of that city. Luther
misreads *ben-mésheq* and gives Eliezer a son. In this
verse *'adhonay* appears for the first time in Genesis;
it is rarely coupled with Yahweh.

3. This verse presents Abram's misgivings more
strongly; note the vivid double interjection *hen* and
hinneh, "see" and "look." These give to the statement the tone of an implied plea — not of impatience
or of unbelief but of eager request. "One belonging
to my household" is again a typical Hebrew expression
with the broad use of the word "son"; for it runs
thus: *ben bethî*, "son of my house." What we have
rendered "will inherit my goods" literally = "he will
be heir to me," *er wird mich beerben*. Tragic as all
this is for Abram, the situation reflected speaks well
for the status of servants in Abram's day and house-

hold. After the master's children the children of the headservant were counted as heirs.

A practical point may be considered here. Abram had in the previous chapter acquitted himself nobly and sought no selfish advantage. Such are not always or promptly rewarded by God. There may come seeming neglect or indifference on God's part after a man has served Him unselfishly. So must the true love of God's own be put to the test.

Note: Here the participle takes the object not as a pronominal suffix but with the sign of the accusative, *yoresh 'othî*, K. S. 240 b, also a common construction.

4, 5. And, lo, the word of Yahweh came unto him thus: This man shall not be thine heir, but one born of thine own body, he shall be thine heir. And He led him forth outside and He said: Look, now, at the heavens and count the stars, if thou canst count them. Then He said to him: So numerous shall thy offspring be.

With the same statement as furnished in v. 1 for the communication of a divine revelation God's answer to Abram is introduced. A "lo" (*hinneh*) accompanies the introductory remark, because a divine word is always a very noteworthy event. *Yahweh*, who displays mercy also in what He promises in this case, and who also clearly foresees the course events will take, informs him that Eliezer will not be heir to Abram, but a direct descendant of his own. *Mimme'êkha* means "from thy belly," euphemistically for the generative organs. From this point onward Abram is enabled to see clearly that when God speaks of Abram's offspring, He means the term very literally. Besides, *hû'* resumes the subject emphatically: "that very one shall be heir" (K. S. 340 a).

5. To make the fact as such doubly impressive Yahweh brings Abram outside, that is to say, in the

vision, and bids him gaze upon the stars and count them. "So" (*koh*, which usually points backward) therefore "so numerous" shall Abram's "offspring" (Heb. *zéra'* — "seed") be. The uncounted multitude is the point of the comparison. The point made by the comparison would come home to the patriarch with all the greater emphasis under the Oriental skies where the stars gleam far more distinctly and so appear more numerous. The fact that present day astronomers happen to chart the heavens, listing all stars and counting them, detracts nothing from the force of the comparison as it was originally made by God for Abram, who would never have thought of attempting to count all. The same comparison is used in 22:17; 26:4 and Exod. 32:13. Dods departs from the point at issue by letting God's control of the stars, His calling them by name and so proving Himself a God who "has designs of infinite sweep and comprehension," be the point of the comparison, whereas Yahweh had distinctly referred to their being countless, as the point at issue.

If one compares 13:16 ("dust of the earth") with this promise, one notices that at least in one point a distinct advance is marked and that may be allowed for here. The comparison now stresses not only numbers, but a noble sort of multitude will God bring into being.

The *na'* after *habbet* gives a kindly tone to the imperative (K. S. 355 b). On *koh* as retrospective see K. S. 332 b.

6. **And he believed in Yahweh, and He counted it to him for righteousness.**

The biggest word in the chapter, one of the greatest in the Old Testament! Here is the first instance of the use of the word "believe" in the Scriptures. *He'emîn*, Hifil of *'aman*, "to confirm" and "support," means "trust," "believe," implying *fiducia* rather than *assensus*. It is construed with *be,* as here, or with *le*. The form is unusual, perfect with *waw,* not as one would expect, imperfect with *waw conversive*. Apparently, by this device the author would indicate that the permanence of this attitude is to be stressed: not only: Abram believed just this once, but: Abram proved constant in his faith, *er bewaehrte sich als Glaeubiger* (K. S. 367 i). Kittel's correction *wayya'amîn* blurs the fine distinction.

But at once we are moved to ask in what way can it be detected that Abram did believe and what indication have we that his faith was counted to him for righteousness? The first answer must be that this grand truth was revealed to the author, Moses, by the Spirit of inspiration; for of himself no man would ever have discovered such a possibility. But on the other hand, such revelations are never made in the abstract: they grow out of situations that clearly demonstrate them. So here, particularly from what follows, when God asks Abram to carry out certain orders and Abram unhesitatingly obeys; this attitude displays his faith. Again, the response of God to Abram's implicit obedience shows that Abram met with God's favor: he was justified; his faith had been counted to him for righteousness.

Perhaps the most marvelous thing about this word is the clearness with which it rules out all efforts and attainments of man as contributory factors in the justification. Workrighteousness is completely eliminated, a fact which again human reason might never have discerned but for divine exposition as granted to inspired men (Rom. 4; Gal. 3). But the only factor that counts in this transaction is faith, and even faith only in so far as it grasps God's promise, not faith as an achievement of man.

The expression "and He counted it to him for righteousness" involves a purely forensic act. "Righteousness," well defined (K. W.) as "normalcy in reference to the obligations of an individual," is the equivalent of measuring up to the demands of God. What God demands and expects of a sinful mortal is faith. He that has faith measures up to God's requirements, is declared to have manifested the normal attitude pleasing to God; against such a one God has no wrath or displeasure. He counts him innocent; He gives him a verdict of "Not guilty." Meek seems to stand entirely on the basis of workrighteousness when he renders: He "counted it to his credit." Such translations, modern enough in expression, are unsatisfactory and wrong.

Now the question arises, Is Abram's faith different from the justifying faith of the New Testament believer? We answer unhesitatingly and emphatically, No. The very issue in this chapter has been Abram's seed. But Abram cannot as a spiritual man have thought of this seed only as numerous descendants; for already in 12:3 b that seed had been shown as involving the one who would bring salvation to mankind ("all families of the earth blessed"). How could Abram have overlooked or undervalued this chief item? The remark of Hunnius (quoted by Delitzsch) certainly is correct: *sub innumerabili illa posteritate latebat Christus.* Abram believed that God would send this Savior for his own good as well as for the whole world. Naturally, however, such faith may not possess full understanding of the details of the redemptive work and the atoning sacrifice. Yet in essence it is trust in the Savior sent by God.

To this must be added the question raised by Luther whether Abram had been justified by faith before this time, or whether only at this point his faith began to be counted to him for righteousness. Naturally, the answer has to be that Abram was justified by faith as soon as this faith began to manifest it-

self, which must have been years before this time.
But why first record the justification here? We feel
our answer must take the same form as Luther's, who
points out that justification by faith is first indicated
in the Scriptures in a connection where the Savior is
definitely involved, in order that none might venture
to dissociate justification from Him.

Note the rapid change of subject in the short compound sentence — a common observation in Hebrew
(K. S. 399 b). The feminine suffix on the verb
"count" represents the neuter "it" (K. S. 12; G. K.
112 q).

**7. And He said to Him: I am Yahweh who
brought thee forth from Ur of the Chaldees to give
thee this land for a possession.**

The "vision" is not concluded. It has further
revelation of import to Abram. To this purpose God
goes on to remind Abram first of all that He is the
one who called him forth from Ur of the Chaldees
(cf. 11:28). This reminder recalls the whole of God's
plan in reference to Abram and his descendants, which
plan took its beginning with the Exodus from Ur.
Abram is now to be shown what things must yet
transpire before God will bring this plan to a complete realization. Critics find this self-introduction of
Yahweh "to be natural only at the commencement of
an "interview" and here "difficult to reconcile with the
assumption of the unity of the narrative."

**8. And he said: Lord Yahweh, whereby shall
I know that I shall possess it?**

Again the same reverent address as in v. 2 in
token of his faith in God's ability to perform what
He promises. But this faith seeks legitimate tokens;
it is anxious to have still fuller assurance. So Abram
asks, not in a spirit of doubt but with the purpose
to be more solidly established in its conviction. We

find Gideon's prayer analogous (Judg. 6:17ff.), or
the question of the Virgin Mary (Luk. 1:34). "Whereby" = *bammah* = "by what."

9, 10. **And He said to him: Take me a three-
year-old heifer, a three-year-old she-goat, a three-
year-old ram and a turtledove and a young pigeon.
And he took him all these and he cut them in two
and he put them in order each part over against
its corresponding part, but the birds he did not cut
in two.**

A covenant is to be established. God condescends
to let it be made after the fashion of covenants made
in those days, particularly among the Chaldeans. K.
C. points to the historical evidence of the use of the
same ceremony when the North Syrian Mati'lu is put
under obligation to Aschschurnirari. The covenanting
parties would pass between the halves of the beasts,
and this may have implied that a similar lot, viz., being killed, was to befall their own cattle in the event
of their violating the covenant. But a modification
of the procedure is involved in this case: neither do
both parties pass between the halves, nor is the threat
implied.

The proceeding, therefore, is not a sacrifice, even
though animals that are at a later date ordained for
sacrifice are employed. The requirement of creatures
three years old has no further significance than that
they are to be of full strength and beauty. *Meshul-
lésheth,* a pual feminine participle, does not mean
"three" of each (Targum) but three years old. No
particular significance attaches to the number of
creatures used. For the count of them is difficult in
any case. They seem to be five; yet, if the halves
are laid over against one another and the turtledove
over against the young pigeon, four pairs appear on

the scene. We cannot even be sure of this arrangement of the birds. The animals used are simply those that are most suitable for sacrifice among the domesticated animals, as also the Mosaic law provided that these only were suitable for sacrifice.

It should also be noted that without receiving specific directions Abram understands what the Lord intends and proceeds on his own accord to cut up the victims into parts. It is also very much in place to observe that on the level of the practices of patriarchal religion the mode of procedure is quite different from the mode of offering sacrifices as prescribed by the book of Leviticus. For there Moses prescribes burning of sacrifices with fire (Lev. 1). Yet regarding the points of contact between both modes note also the practice of not cutting up the smaller birds (Lev. 1:17). But again: Abram did not offer a sacrifice in this instance.

The article is used with *tsippor* (here collective) because the birds have been previously mentioned ("the article of relative familiarity," K. S. 298 b). The datives "take me" (*lî*) and "he took him" (*lô*) are datives of interest merging into ethical datives. The final *bathar* does not appear with *waw* conversive as imperfect because the object intruded for emphasis after the conjunction (K. S. 368 t).

The various acts of Abram here recorded must be regarded, according to v. 1, as having transpired in the course of the "vision." What do we know about visions that allows us to claim such acts cannot be part of a vision?

11, 12. The birds of prey came down upon the carcases, but Abram drove them away. And the sun was about to go down, and a deep sleep fell upon Abram and, lo, terror and great darkness was falling upon him.

Wherever carcases are, birds of prey promptly congregate — here *'ayit,* used collectively. Since these victims have thus been prepared for the solemnization of a sacred covenant, Abram drives off the foul birds that might pollute them. This is but natural. To suggest that Abram regarded the appearance of birds of prey as an ill omen, just because certain Arabic tribes still suppose the mere sight of buzzards to be an ill omen, is a purely gratuitous assumption attributing to one nation what is characteristic of another. Israel's legitimate religion, whether on the patriarchal, Mosaic, or prophetic level, never acknowledges omens or superstitions.

The article with *'ayit* is the categorical article, (K. S. 300 a). The further meaning of this feature of the vision will be touched upon below.

12. As far as the vision itself is concerned, it transpires in such a fashion that in the course of it Abram sees the sun at the point of setting, about as a man might dream he sees the sun setting. Such a dream or vision might occur morning, noon or night. Attempts to compute the length of time over which the experience extended by the expressions used such as "the sun was about to go down," would lead to an unnaturally long lapse of time. The setting of the sun in the vision prepares for the falling of darkness upon him. But first of all comes a "deep sleep" (*tardemah*) which is as little a "trance" here as it was in 2:21 (which see). The "terror and the great darkness" that fall upon him are the terror which the ancestor experiences in the vision at the revelation of the sufferings which his descendants must endure. In the vision he feels these things in anticipation, even before the revelation is imparted to him that his descendants are destined to this particular form of misery. Perhaps the relation of *'êmah chashekhah gedholah* (without conjunction), would be expressed

best by a rendering like: "terror and an awful gloom."
The difference between the verb *naphelah* and the
particle *nopheleth* should be noted: the deep sleep *fell*,
i. e., quickly as a single act, but the terror and awful
gloom *kept falling,* or settling upon him and were still
enfolding him more fully when the rest of the revelation came (K. S. 237 e explains a bit differently).

Wayhi (masculine) begins the sentence, as often
when the gender of the subject to follow has not yet
been revealed; this does not, however, make *hashshémesh* masculine (K. S. 345 c). Note *wayhi le* =
"was about to" (K. S. 234; G. K. 114 h, i). The
"deep sleep" (v. 12) is not in conflict with the "vision"
(v. 1) as though the one term were the Elohist's way
of putting it, the other the Yahwist's (e. g. Procksch).
The "deep sleep" takes place within the "vision."

13-16. **And He said to Abram: Thou shalt
know of a surety that thy descendants shall be
sojourners in a land which is not theirs, where they
shall be enslaved and oppressed for four hundred
years. But I in turn will judge that nation to whom
they are enslaved, and afterwards they shall go
forth with great possessions. But thou on thy part
shalt go unto thy fathers in peace and shalt be
buried at a ripe old age. And the fourth generation
shall return here; for the guilt of the Amorites is
not yet complete.**

Now comes the revelation in words apart from
the symbolic act, which here is made to represent the
same facts, but it can only be understood after the
revelation thus offered by word and by symbol makes
the fact involved doubly impressive; and, surely, there
was need of unusual emphasis, for this word was
largely to furnish the much needed light during the
dark ages of the period here described.

The knowledge provided for Abram is of a very
definite and positive sort: "thou shalt know of a

surety," Hebrew: "knowing thou shalt know," verb
plus its absolute infinitive (G. K. 113, o). *Zéra'* =
"seed," "descendants." The *ger*, "sojourner," is one
whose stay in certain territory is only temporary. We
could translate: "a temporary resident." Nothing for
the present indicates that the land involved is Egypt.
Perhaps this is not revealed lest Abram's descendants
conceive an undue prejudice against this land. This
first part of the revelation involves nothing grievous.
Abram himself, for that matter, was a sojourner in
the land of Canaan when he received this revelation.
The next two terms, however, cover the unpleasant
side of the experience: "they (Israel) shall serve
them" (Egyptians), which we have rendered for purposes of easier construction: "where they shall be
enslaved." Then, with a quick change of person:
"they" now = Egyptians — "they (Egyptians) shall
oppress them." This is the hardest part which Israel
will have to endure. The whole experience of being
sojourner, being enslaved, and being oppressed shall
involve "four hundred years." To make the whole
sojourn one continuous oppression is completely at
variance with the facts. In fact, computing according
to the life of Moses, we should be nearest the truth
if we allot the last century to the oppression.

The four hundred years mentioned are, of course,
a round number, which is given more exactly in Exod.
12:40, as 430 years. Michell's computations agree
with these figures, making the year of Jacob's going
down into Egypt to be 1879 B. C. and the year of
the Exodus 1449. Since this latter year, or perhaps
1447 B. C., is now quite commonly accepted, we may
let these dates stand as sufficiently exact for all practical purposes. How Moses arrives at the computation
430 in Exod. 12:40 need not here concern us. Other
instances of exact predictions in numbers of years are

found in Jer. 25:11; 29:20, in reference to seventy years; and Isa. 16:14, for a matter of three years.

Note: *lo' lahem* is a relative clause with the customary relative omitted (G. K. 115 e).

14. The participle *dan*, according to the context, points to the future: "I will judge." "Judging" here implies "punishing." Here it is also revealed at once that Israel shall not be the poorer for its experience. By way of compensation for the affliction suffered the nation shall "go forth with great possessions." *Rekhûsh* is again used for "possessions" because they are movable. The choice of the word, here too, is not a mark of P but the natural term to use, for Israel was not to be rich in real estate but in *rekhûsh*. Criticism fails to discover such simple proprieties. *Beth of accompaniment* with *rekhûsh* (K. S. 402 s).

So in v. 13, 14 a great basic principle, applying to God's people, has been revealed: they must through much tribulation enter into the Kingdom of God (Acts 14:22), even as did the Captain of their salvation (Luke 24:26) ; but, on the other hand, God will often offset their losses and reimburse them so that their needs will be marvelously supplied. At the same time a correct conception of God as the Judge of the nations is clearly reflected at this point. Even in the patriarchal age a clear conception, correct in all its parts, prevailed in reference to Yahweh.

15. Since the natural question must arise in the patriarch's mind, whether the things predicted will begin to come to pass during his lifetime, God assures him that such shall not be the case. An emphatic "thou" (*'attah*) reinforces the subject: "thou on thy part." The expression "go unto thy fathers" must involve more than having his own dead body laid beside the dead bodies of the fathers. So we find here a clear testimony to belief in an eternal life in the

patriarchal age. Coupled with this revelation from
God is the assurance of a decent burial at a ripe old
age, a thing desired especially in Israel and, for that
matter, among most of the nations of antiquity. On
the question of "going to thy fathers" Whitelaw rightly remarks that it must involve more than burial, because Abram's ancestors were not entombed in
Canaan, where his own sepulchre was (Gen. 25:9).

16. Some regard *dôr rebhî'î* as an accusative of
condition: "as fourth generation" they shall return.
It seems even simpler to us to make it the plain subject: "the fourth generation" shall return. Since four
generations cover more than four hundred years, we
see that the word reckons a hundred years to a generation, according to the computation prevalent at the
time of speaking. Such a computation, according to
chapter eleven, is not out of place, especially if one
considers that Abram himself lived to the age of 175
years.

Another factor enters into these computations
and readjustments — "the guilt of the Amorites." All
the inhabitants of Canaan are referred to by the term
"Amorites," the most important family of the Canaanites (see on 10:16). The term is similarly used in
48:22; Num. 13:29; 21:21, etc.; Deut. 1:7, 19. These
aboriginal inhabitants of Canaan had heaped up a
measure of "guilt" (*'awon*) by this time. The
measure was not yet "complete" (*shalem*), that is,
they were nearing the point where divine tolerance
could bear with them no longer, but they had not yet
arrived at this point. God's foreknowledge discerned
that in a few more centuries these wicked nations
would have forfeited their right to live, and then He
would replace them in the land of Canaan by the
Israelites. Passages bearing on the iniquity of the
Canaanites are Lev. 18:24 ff.; 20:22 ff.; Deut. 18:9 ff.
So God will allow the children of Israel to be absent

from the land while the Canaanites continue in their evil ways. When He can bear with the Canaanites no longer, He will have another nation ready wherewith to replace them. Thus far we have encountered no direct evidence of Canaanite iniquity but shall soon see the startling examples offered by Sodom.

17, 18 a. And it came to pass when the sun had set and dense darkness prevailed, that, lo, a smoking firepot and a flaming torch passed between these pieces. On that day Yahweh made a covenant with Abram,

In the vision in the sequence of events the sun finally sets; it was on the verge of doing so v. 12. The quick change of the Orient from daylight to intense darkness (*'alaṭah*) follows. This darkness makes the next phenomenon, which is one of fire, all the more distinct by contrast. What Abram sees is of a character to occasion surprise ("lo" — *hinneh*), for it is first of all a *tannûr*, a portable clay oven, a couple of feet high, more or less like an inverted bowl, with a hole on the upper side for draft purposes. This "firepot" has the fire within it kindled and flaming out of the top of the oven like a "torch" (*lappîdh*). This firepot plus the flaming torch above pass in between the pieces that Abram had made of the animals that he had been commanded to take.

18 a. All this would be worse than puzzling if it were not for the fact that the much needed explanation at once, as so often, follows: "on this day Yahweh made a covenant with Abram." This "smoking firepot and flaming torch" represented Yahweh passing between the halves of the victims and so concluding the covenant. Nor is this mode of designating Yahweh's presence unsuitable or inappropriate. He who at Horeb appeared in the burning bush (Exod. 3:2-6) and on Mount Sinai in a consuming fire (Exod.

19:18) and throughout the time of the wilderness wanderings in a pillar of fire (Exod. 13:21), now appears as a fire, only the guise of it was the most frequent form in which fire appeared to the nomads of that day, the portable "firepot." So men of Abram's type and age were wont usually to behold fire.

Now the whole typical representation is clear to us: the divided beasts represent Israel; the birds of prey who would have devoured them are the oppressing nation; Abram drives these birds away, that is, the blessing of God laid upon the nation for its great ancestor's sake drives away all harm; the fire passing between the parts represents the ever present God who concludes a covenant with His people and vouchsafes His continual presence to them. That is as far as we dare go in interpreting the symbolism involved. In regard to the first point we believe this explanation will set our minds at rest: the commonly known clean animals represent Israel, the clean nation among the many unclean.

Still a word about the covenant God concluded with Abram. Considered in the abstract, a covenant is unnecessary. God's word is so sure that no special guarantees are needed to confirm it. That word had been given to Abram. But in order to make Abram sure and give him all the support his faith needs during the time of severe trial, God employs means that men might use to make assurance doubly sure. For, as time drags on, Abram's faith in reference to the promised seed and heir is being tried always more severely.

The word for "covenant," *berîth*, does not originally mean "law," as some claim; and the expression *karath berîth*, "to *cut* a covenant," results from the butchering of the victims that were slain in the ceremonies attendant upon the conclusion of a covenant.

In v. 17 the use of *hayah* (masculine) with the feminine subject *'alatah* is accounted for by the adaptation of the construction to that immediately preceding: *wayhi* (masculine) *hashshémesh* (feminine). (K. S. 350 e).

Lastly, it should not be forgotten that the covenants God makes with men are not mutual agreements as between man and man. They are rather agreements emanating from God. For in the nature of the case here are not two parties who stand on an equal footing. In fact, in the instance under consideration God binds Himself to the fulfillment of certain obligations; Abram is bound to no obligations whatsoever. God's priority is a prominent feature of the covenants of this type.

18b-21. Saying: To thy descendants do I give this land from the River of Egypt to the Great River, the River Euphrates; the Kenites, and the Kenizzites, and the Kadmonites; and the Hittites, and the Perizzites, and the Rephaim; and the Amorites, and the Canaanites, and the Girgashites and the Jebusites.

We misconstrue the whole situation if we suppose v. 18 to mean that after all that had preceded in the vision now also there came the concluding of a covenant. The passing of the "firepot" between the pieces was the actual concluding of the covenant on God's part; and so v. 18 is best taken in the sense: So on that day God made a covenant with Abram. Again we misconstrue v. 18 b if we take its words to be the sole substance of the covenant. Rather all that had been revealed in this chapter as favors promised to Abram was the substance of the covenant. Of all that is thus promised v. 18 b really constitutes a good summary and so sums up v. 4 and v. 7 and provides a good conclusion to v. 16. The emphasis of

v. 18 b-21 lies, however, chiefly on the extent of the territory promised to Abram's descendants.

The perfect "I have given," *nathâttî*, is the perfect used in solemn basic assurances and is best rendered by a present "I do give" (K. S. 131 b; G. K. 106 m). "The River of Egypt" could hardly be the Wady el 'Arish (Rhinocolura), for that insignificant winter torrent could hardly be set in contrast to the "Great River, the River Euphrates." Consequently, "the River of Egypt" is the Nile. However, that does not necessarily mean that Israelitish territory will some day actually extend directly to the Nile. But these two major rivers were the easiest way of designating within what limits Israel's boundaries should lie. Twice during Israel's history this extent of territory was realized, during the reign of Solomon (I Kings 8:65) as well as in the days of Jereboam II of Israel (II Kings 14:25). The failure to see it fulfilled on other occasions was due, of course, to Israel's disobedience. However, such a measure of territory definitely put Israel into the category of the first-class nations of the world, even though but temporarily.

The heart of this vast territory is being occupied by the nations here enumerated, ten in number. This number may vary. In the various instances where the enumeration occurs sometimes three nations are mentioned as representative of all (Exod. 23:28), sometimes five (Exod. 3:17), or six; but most usually seven (Josh. 24:11). Not always are the same names used. Here some of the names listed occur for the only time that they are found in the Bible like "Kenizzites" and "Kadmonites." The reason for the use of different names now from later may well be that at Abram's time, four centuries before the occupation, a different group of nations will have been in evidence.

The "Kenites" originally dwelt to the south, for Moses' brother-in-law was a Kenite (Judg. 1:16). Later they are still found but in the northern part of Canaan (Judg. 4:11). The "Kenizzites" seem to have been to the south also. The "Kadmonites," as their name indicates (*qadhmonî,* cf. *qédem,* "east"), were more toward the east. For the "Hittites "see our remarks on 10:15. For the "Perizzites" on 13:7. For the "Rephaim," cf. 14:5. For the "Amorites," "Canaanites," "Girgashites," and "Jebusites" see the remarks on 10:15, 16. The total number ten here indicates that a complete piece of territory is going to be given into the hands of Abram's seed.

We should list the analysis of the chapter as attempted by critics in order to demonstrate how the assured results of modern criticism are far from convincing. Skinner admits the "insurmountable difficulties" and lists Gunkel's solution: for J, 1 a, b γ, 2 a, 3 b, 4, 6, 9, 10, 12 a α, b, 17, 18 a, b α. Compare what Procksch assigns to J: 1, 3, 4, (7), 8-11, 12 a α b, 17, 18, 19, 20, 21. Or for E, — Gunkel: 1 b α β, 3 a [2 b ?], 5, 11, 12 a β, 13 a, 14, and the rest to the Redactor. But Procksch gives E: 1 b γ, 2, 5, 6, 12 a β, 13 a, 14 a, 16, 15. Yet Cornill once said there was no *tastendes Waehlen,* i. e., "uncertain selecting."

HOMILETICAL SUGGESTIONS

Here is a fine opportunity to preach a good sermon on justification by faith. For this purpose the section v. 1-6 is appropriate. The opening verses describe the situation that prevailed; v. 6 is the grand climax and theme. The New Testament gives full warrant for such a use of the text. Therefore also, we should make it entirely plain that Christ the Savior was definitely involved also in the faith of Abraham.

Though v. 7-11 leads up to the section v. 12-21, yet we feel that it presents difficulties from the present day point of view.

In a Bible Class one could explain the problems involved. In a sermon this can be done less conveniently. Therefore we should suggest as a second text from this chapter v. 12-21. Here the future of God's people is revealed and, as it happens, in such a way as to present certain constant truths: such as the hostility of the world; the consequent sufferings of the church; and the ultimate triumph of God's own. For this purpose v. 12-16 might suffice. But sound Bible knowledge can be built up by the use of fuller texts, and so we recommend the longer portion, v. 12-21.

CHAPTER XVI

6. The Birth of Ishmael (16:1-16)

The period of waiting appointed for Abram is not yet at an end. The fact that the promise of God does not become a reality leads Abram and his wife to take recourse to human ingenuity. God, however, wants it to be clearly understood that the child involved is in every sense to be a child of promise. Yahweh's grace will give him, man can contribute nothing. The experience of this chapter makes this fact most clearly apparent to Abram and to Sarai.

When in days of old reverence for the venerable patriarchs led commentators to make attempts completely to exonerate these holy men of God from all guilt or blame in connection with an episode such as this, the present day lack of reverence for the Word and for the worthy men of antiquity results in expositions that impute the cheapest of motives to the characters involved and that evaluate their individual deeds at as low a value as possible. The truth does not really ·lie between these two extremes, for a prophetic word (Mal. 2:15) ascribes a good motive to Abram for his share in this case: he sought the seed promised of God. There is no reason for excluding Sarai from having a share in such a good motive. Consequently, we shall be justified in our approach to the problem involved to aim to put the best construction on everything, and by so doing we shall not lay ourselves open to the charge of unseemly partiality. Calvin's summary of the case is quite commendable: "The faith of both was defective; not, indeed, with regard to the substance

of the promise, but with regard to the method in
which they proceeded." Luther's attitude is the same.

1, 2. **Now Sarai, Abram's wife, bore him no
children, but she had an Egyptian maid, whose
name was Hagar. So Sarai said to Abram: Behold, now, the Lord has prevented me from having
children; suppose you marry my maid; perhaps our
household would be built through her. And Abram
approved of Sarai's suggestion.**

As is evident from v. 16, Abram had been in the
land about ten years. If we consider the advanced
age of both Abram and Sarai, they had surely waited
a long time. The Hebrew uses the verb without an
object in stating the case: "She did not bear for
him" (*lo' yaledhah lô*). To Sarai the thought comes
that perhaps customary devices may be resorted to.
Women of standing like Sarai had their personal
maids, who were their own in a special sense. They
were the personal property of the wife and were
appointed specially to wait upon her. The maid under
consideration here happened to be an Egyptian, having been acquired, no doubt, during the brief stay
in Egypt (12:10 ff.). The custom of those days
allowed in a case of this sort that the wife give her
maid to her husband as a secondary wife in the hope
that the new union would be blessed with offspring,
which offspring would then promptly be claimed and
adopted by the mistress. No stigma attached to the
position of the maid: she was a wife, though not,
indeed, of the same social standing as the first wife.
For Sarai to take such a step certainly involved self-
denial, even a kind of self-effacement. It was this
rather noble mode of procedure on Sarai's part that
may in part have blinded the patriarch's eyes so that
he failed to discern the actual issues involved. Then,
also, if we consider the chief servant, Eliezer, and the

excellent faith he later displays, we may well suppose
that the chief maid may well have been a woman who
was indeed imbued with the faith that reigned in the
household and may modestly have been desirous of
having a part in the achievement of the high purpose
to which this household was destined.

Yet, in spite of all that may be said by way of
extenuating the fault of the parties involved, it was
still a double fault and sin. First, it clashed with the
true conception of monogamous marriage, which alone
is acceptable with God. Secondly, it involved the employ-
ment of human devices seemingly to bolster up a
divine purpose which was in any case destined to be
achieved as God had originally ordained. In so far
the fault involved was unbelief.

"Hagar," from the root "to flee," stamps her as
"the fugitive," apparently because of the later event
when she fled from her mistress. This later name,
then, must have replaced a former one now unknown.

How keenly barrenness was felt to be a curse and
how highly offspring were prized as a manifestation
of divine favor, appears from a comparison of the
following passages: 19:31; 31:1; 23 with 21:6; 24:60;
Exod. 23:26; Deut. 7:14.

2. Correctly Sarai ascribes her failure to bear
children to Yahweh's not having given them to her.
Literally translated, the Hebrew says: "Yahweh hath
shut me up, or restrained me, (A. V.) from bearing,"
the *min* with *lédheth* here constituting the equivalent
of a negative clause of result (K. S. 406n; G. K. 119x).
Bo-na' 'el, "Go, pray, unto," etc., is a euphemism, to
which the *na'* imparts a certain mildness of suggestion, which Meek has cleverly reproduced in colloquial
English: "Suppose you marry." A very distinct
Hebrew idiom lies at the basis of what we have rendered: "perhaps my household would be built through

her"; for the Hebrew says: "perhaps I may be built up through her." The verb *'ibbaneh,* from *banah,* "build," rests on the root *ben,* "son." "To be built up," therefore, is the same idea as "to have children" or "build up a family," (Meek). *'Ibbaneh* is potential (K. S. 186). The *min* of agent (K. S. 107) appears in *mimménnah.* When Abram "hearkens" (*shama'*) to his wife's "voice" (*qôl*), he "approves of Sarai's suggestion." No doubt, the patriarch was impressed by Sarai's utter selflessness.

3. **So Sarai, Abram's wife, took Hagar, her Egyptian maid, after ten years of Abram's dwelling in the land of Canaan, and gave her in marriage to Abram, her husband.**

The somewhat more circumstantial style of the verse is manifestly a device for making it the more apparent what it cost Sarai to take such a step; for she was "Abram's wife," and Hagar was only "her Egyptian maid"; and, for all that, Abram was still "her husband." Besides, to indicate that these good people had really waited quite patiently, at this point the author indicates how long Abram had dwelt in Canaan — a full ten years. So the particular character of the verse on purely literary grounds appears to be quite readily accounted for. However, according to the critics, who seem to lack appreciation for all niceties of a good and flexible style, every instance where the style grows more circumstantial is supposed to mark the insertion of a portion from P.

The infinitive *shébheth* here functions as a noun in the construct state (K. S. 229 f.). *Lô le'ishshah,* "to him for wife," is a condensed purpose clause (K. S. 407 d). It must be quite apparent that "to give as wife" must mean "to give in marriage." Here was no concubinage but a formal marital union, though Hagar was but the second wife.

4. **And he went in unto Hagar and she conceived. When she saw that she had conceived, her mistress was lightly esteemed in her eyes.**

The plan works out, apparently according to schedule. *Bo''el,* "to go in unto," is a delicate euphemism.

Now at this point the evils of polygamy begin to rear their ugly head. It is always bound to be the fruitful mother of envy, jealousy, and strife. The baser elements in man are unleashed by it. Each of the three characters now appears to disadvantage. Yet we are not compelled now to suppose that such extremes resulted as Jamieson suggests — "bursts of temper, or blows." The fine praise that Peter bestows upon Sarai (I Pet. 3:6) hardly allows us to think of her as degenerating into a shrew. When it is remarked of Hagar that "her mistress was lightly esteemed in her eyes," that need involve nothing more than that she thought that God had bestowed upon her what He had denied Sarai, and so she thought herself superior to her mistress and showed her disdain in certain ways. This attitude was bound to pain Sarai, who was, no doubt, a woman of high position, while Hagar was only an Egyptian slave.

5. **Then Sarai said to Abram: The wrong done to me is your fault. I gave my maid into your arms, and when she saw that she had conceived, I became lightly esteemed in her eyes. May Yahweh judge between me and thee.**

Now Sarai's judgment becomes impaired by the bitter feelings roused in her. Hagar's wrong leads Sarai to do further wrong. Sin grows more involved. Sarai blames Abram for doing what she had in reality suggested. At least, so it seems. Luther attempts to avoid so crude a charge on her part by supposing that she rather charges Abram with showing certain prefer-

ences and honors to Hagar and so becoming the cause
of her arrogance. Then her charge would be correct:
"The wrong done to me is your fault." But the explanation that follows does not interpret the wrong
thus. So we shall do better to call hers an unreason-
able charge growing out of her wounded pride. Our
translation here corresponds with the Greek rendering,
ἀδικοῦμαι ἐκ σοῦ. *Chamaṣi*, "my wrong," must mean
"the wrong done to me," the pronominal suffix being
an objective genitive (K. S. 37). To supply the verb
"may it be" results in an idle repetition; for afterward
she says: "Yahweh judge between me and thee." So
instead of making the clause voluntative ("may"), we
make it indicative: "My wrong is on thee" = "The
wrong done me is your fault." The statement: "May
Yahweh judge between me and thee," is rightly explained (K. W.) "to decide the controversy at issue
between two parties."

The injustice of the charge made by Sarai might
well have roused Abram to a heated reply. Indeed,
with excellent self-control he replies moderately (v. 6).

In the last word of the verse the second *yodh* is
redundant.

6. **But Abram said to Sarai: See, thy maid
is in thy power; do to her what pleases thee. So
Sarai humbled her, and she fled from her.**

Some charge Abram at this point with being
"strangely unchivalrous" (Procksch). He is not suggesting cruelty to Sarai nor condoning it. He is merely suggesting the natural solution of the problem. In
reality, Sarai is still Hagar's mistress. That relation
has not really been cancelled. Abram suggests that
she use her right as mistress. He does, however, not
suggest the use of cruelty or injustice. It is not really
said that Sarai did what is unjustifiable. Nor should
it be forgotten that Hagar had begun to do wrong and

required correction. Apparently also, according to the custom of the times, Abram had no jurisdiction over Hagar directly, for she was esteemed Sarai's maid. The Hebrew idiom "do what is good in thine eyes" is our: "do what pleases thee."

Here, we believe, Sarai is usually wronged. Of the various meanings of *'innah* the more severe are chosen, like "deal hardly with" (A. V.), or "treated cruelly" (Meek). Luther may well be followed: *wollte sie demuetigen* = "wanted to humble her." When the problem is thus approached, Sarai is merely regarded as having taken steps to bring Hagar to realize that she had begun to be somewhat presumptuous, such as making her to live with the servants and perform more menial tasks. But, of course, we must allow for sinful excesses also on her part. Sarai may not have proceeded with due tact and consideration. In suggesting such a course Abram may too have failed to counsel due caution. Every actor in this domestic drama may have given evidence of shortcomings in one way or another. Hagar, on her part, being somewhat self-willed and independent, refused to accept correction and "fled from her."

7. But the Angel of the Lord found her by the spring of water in the wilderness, by the fountain on the road to Shur.

A singular honor is conferred upon Hagar by the appearance of the Angel of the Lord. This would seem to lend added weight to our contention that Hagar was a woman of godly disposition, and one who may have given evidence of such a disposition by prayer to the God of Abram, made at the time of her present difficulty. Luther's suggestion may also be approved of, when he suggests that after Hagar's flight Abram and Sarai made prayer to God in behalf of the fugitive. The Hebrew text says he found her "by *the* spring," not "*a* spring." This is best understood

as the article applied to the customary, (*der Connexi-
tuet*, K. S. 299 b), that is, the spring where travellers
on the way to Shur were wont to stop. "Shur" is
regarded by many as meaning "wall," a meaning quite
possible according to the Aramaic. In that event it
may be the name of a line of fortresses erected by
the Egyptian king, perhaps at the Isthmus of Suez, to
keep out Asiatic invaders. In that case Hagar quite
naturally was on the way back to her home country,
Egypt. Having come to this well, she had come far
enough away from Abram's home, which may at this
time have been at Hebron, to allow for the settling of
her thoughts and feelings, and she may already have
begun to view the situation a bit more soberly and
justly than she did at the time when she first resolved
upon flight. So the Angel's approach appears to be
well timed.

But the angel of the Lord (*mal'akh Yahweh*),
who was He? We believe Hengstenberg and Keil
demonstrated adequately both that He was divine and
that He is to be regarded as a kind of pre-incarnation
of the Messiah — using the term "pre-incarnation"
as indeed open to criticism if pressed too closely.
For our passage His identity with Yahweh is fully
established by v. 13. For the present we offer Whitelaw's five arguments (condensed) for this position.
The Angel of the Lord is not a created being but
the Divine Being Himself; for

1.   He explicitly identifies Himself with Yahweh
on various occasions.

2.   Those to whom He makes His presence known
recognize Him as divine.

3.   The Biblical writers call Him Yahweh.

4.   The doctrine here implied of a plurality of
persons in the Godhead is in complete accordance with
earlier foreshadowing.

5. The organic unity of Scripture would be broken if it could be proved that the central point in the Old Testament revelation was a creature angel, while that of the New is the incarnation of the God-Man.

K. C. attempts to dispose of all such arguments by the too simple explanation that an ambassador most readily makes a transition into the words of the one who commissioned him. Granting that such a thing might be done by ordinary human ambassadors — a thing of which we personally are still very doubtful — we feel that the Almighty stands too far above the creature, even an angel, to allow for such a piece of presumption on the part of His representatives. If Exod. 3:6 be examined, as one of the passages bearing upon the case, one could hardly venture to say that such a transition from one person to another takes place. The claim to being none other than Yahweh Himself is too distinct.

The attempted translation *"an* angel of the Lord" is rightly rejected by K. S. 304 e. This Angel of the Lord is in a class by Himself and distinctly recognized as a superior being by the writers of the Old Testament books.

8. **And He said: Hagar, Sarai's maid, whence hast thou come and whither art thou going? And she said: Away from Sarai, my mistress, I am (now) fleeing.**

In what form or under what guise Hagar saw Him who now addressed her we are not told. It is most likely that to her it seemed most like an angel. His mode of address is calculated to rouse an awareness in Hagar's mind that her flight has not altered her position or her duty, nor has her state of pregnancy caused any such alteration: Hagar is still "Sarai's maid." So the Angel of the Lord still esteems her. The question following does not have the purpose of eliciting information but again addresses itself to the conscience of the fugitive. From a spiritually favored home she is setting out in flight to a very uncertain future. Apparently, the mode of address succeeds in producing the desired state of mind: Hagar acknowledges that she is fleeing from her "mistress." By the use of that title for Sarai Hagar admits that the original relation is not cancelled. The pronoun with the participle (*'anokhî boráchath*) describes a progressive act: "I am (now) fleeing."

9, 10. **And the Angel of Yahweh said unto her: Return to thy mistress and submit thyself under her hands. Besides, the Angel of Yahweh said unto her: I will greatly multiply thy descendants so that they cannot be counted for multitude.**

Before Hagar does anything else she should correct the existing wrong of her life, her self-willed departure from her regular place in life. She must return to her mistress; for Sarai still is mistress, even upon Hagar's express admission (v. 8). No man should rashly abandon his place in life unless he have a distinct indication from the Lord to do so. *Hith'annî* need not here be rendered by so strong a verb as "humble oneself." Plain, dutiful submission in the fulfillment of her duties is sufficient for Hagar. Nor would Sarai, after this experience with the Angel became known, have asked any more. Therefore render: "submit thyself." Our idiom might substitute "under her authority" for "under her hands." We have retained the Hebrew idiom, because it cannot be misunderstood.

10. Three times consecutive verses (v. 9, 10, 11) begin, "And the Angel of Yahweh said unto her." In fact, three distinct facts are revealed to Hagar. So after the first word we do well to translate

"Again," or "besides," or "furthermore," "He said,"
etc. Criticism does not understand the simple reason
for the unusual repetition, which aims only to make
each of the three words stand out separately, and
claims that such repetition is a proof of interpolation
and so discards v. 9, 10.

The second revelation now made to Hagar by
the omniscient Angel is that of countless offspring.
The Hebrew absolute infinitive functions here: "multiplying I will multiply" = "I will greatly multiply."
So it comes to pass that two vast nations, the Jews
and the Ishmaelites, are descended from Abraham.
No further spiritual advantage is attached to the
advantage of numbers.

**11, 12. Besides, the Angel of Yahweh said to
her: Behold thou art with child and wilt bear a
son, and thou shalt call his name Ishmael (God
hears), for Yahweh hath heard thy distress. And
he will be a wild ass of a man. His hand shall be
against every man and every man's hand against
him, and he will dwell over against all his brethren.**

Now the revelation of the Angel of Yahweh concerns itself specifically with the son that is to be born
to Hagar. The child to be born God knows to be a
son, and He ordains that this child shall bear a name
that shall always be a reminder to him as well as
to his mother that God in a very signal way gave
ear to the cry of this woman in her distress. For
yishma'e'l means "God hears." When God ordains
this name, He makes provision for keeping mother
and son close to Himself. There is a divine pedagogy behind this name. Besides, when God says that
He hears, the inference is almost unavoidable that
the mother had cried unto Yahweh in her distress.
The words used might allow for the thought that her
"distress" (*'onyekh*) had constituted a plea for
mercy with God, for we read, "Yahweh hath heard

thy *distress*," not thy *prayer*. However, by metonomy "distress" may signify "cry of distress." At the same time, God would hardly have honored with His personal appearance a woman who did not even know how to call upon Him in the day of trouble.

N. B. *Yoladht* is a mixed form, half perfect, half participle, used as future after *hinneh*; see G. K. 94 f. *Harah* with the same word is a participle pointing to the present — (K. S. 237 f.). In *h'innakh* the suffix is an object.

12. In this interview, in which Hagar is highly honored by receiving such extensive revelation, the less complimentary revelation concerning her son is not made with the idea of humiliating the mother, but, most likely, that in her training of her son she may take proper steps to curb the wild and lawless elements of his nature. The first fact communicated to her concerning his nature is that he will be by disposition a *pére' 'adham*, "a wild ass of a man," the second noun in the construct relationship with the first (K. S. 337 c). A similar construction appears Prov. 15:20, "a fool of a man" = "a foolish man." The unrestrained love of liberty on the part of these wild desert animals is further depicted, Job 39:5-8. Ishmael's descendants, the Arabs, roving over the wide expanses of the desert lands adjacent to Bible lands, are still characterized by this trait. In addition, he cannot be said to be distinguished for amiability and love of peace. He personally shall be the aggressor against all others (*hakkol* with the article of totality, K. S. 301 a), and as a result "every man's hand shall be against him." This idiom, of course, conveys the idea of being continually at loggerheads with others. Even in the matter of a dwellingplace, this antagonistic spirit, brooking no restraint or interference, shall express itself in his dwelling "over against all his brethren." *'Al-peney*

may signify "to the east of." But here, apparently,
more than mere direction is involved, for the phrase
means "upon the face of" or "against the face of,"
and that plainly involves hostility, as it does Job 1:11.
Apparently, the fellow himself as well as his descendants will not be of a peaceable disposition. We should
say, he will carry a chip on his shoulder and have his
finger on the trigger.

13. **And she called the name of Yahweh who
spoke unto her, Thou art El Roi (a God of seeing);
for she said: Have I indeed here been permitted
to look after Him who sees me?**

Such a rare experience as Hagar here had calls
for a response, first for an immediate reaction, then
for the reaction of obedience. The immediate reaction
is recorded here. Since the full revelation that is
ours was not yet available in early days, each new
revelation of God's character and being was memorial-
ized in a new name or by some remark that epitom-
ized the experience. So here Hagar very aptly invents the name for Yahweh — *'El Ro'î,* "a God of
seeing," = a God "who sees" (B D B). For "see"
may also mean "consider," "have regard to," "concern oneself about," *sich kümmern um* (K. W.), as
is indicated by Gen. 39:23; Exod. 4:31; I Kings 12:16;
Isa. 5:12, etc. Hitherto Hagar's position had been
growing increasingly difficult. Yahweh had done
nothing to relieve her when she cried unto Him. She
thought she had been abandoned. Now comes not only
hope but a glorious revelation of the future and a personal appearance of the Angel of the Lord. Now she
knows that Yahweh cares, He looks after her, He is
"a God who sees." This is more intimately expressed
as a prayer in a direct address to Him: "Thou art
El Roi." She herself offers the explanation for this
appropriate name, in that she says in a question that
reflects the astonishment that is still strong upon

her: "Have I indeed here been permitted to look after Him who sees me?" Literally this statement begins, "Have I indeed here seen?" But that expresses surprise at such a rare privilege. Hagar well knew that God's manifestations had been very rare in the history of the human race. That she had thus been honored is recognized as a rare privilege. Therefore, "have I indeed seen?" must certainly mean: "have I indeed here *been permitted to see?*" as K. C. happily suggests. But really *ra'îthî 'acharey* is not so much "see" as "look after," as we have translated. For no mortal to whom God appeared ventured to look directly into or upon the glorious countenance of the Lord. Even Moses in answer to his special request could not venture to take such a step (Exod. 33:23). So here very tersely Hagar described what happened in her case. When Yahweh appeared, she indeed conversed with Him; but only as He departed did she "look after Him." So at least she appears to have understood that no sinful mortal can see God's countenance directly and live (see Exod. 33:20). So she did not even attempt so rash a thing. But to her God now is a God "who sees me," i. e., "cares for me." Therefore we construe the final *ro'î* as participle active *ro'eh* with object suffix, "my seer"="who sees me." If it were to be taken as a pausal form of the *rŏ'î* (with short "o" — the noun "seeing") found in the middle of the verse, the accent would have to stand on the penult, as Job 33:21 indicates.

Consequently we feel constrained to abandon the views of Hengstenberg (in his "Christology") and of Keil (*ad loc.*) which render: "Have I also seen here after seeing" in the sense: "Am I still alive and able to see after having looked upon God?" Keil, usually very conservative about textual changes, ad- admits that he must shift the accent of the last word in order to translate thus. However, at best, Hagar would have chosen a very involved way of expressing her thought, as for example Procksch's treatment of the case indicates. For in an effort to make the text say this, he makes three major insertions in the text — with the license of the critic — and then secures this rendering: "Thou art a God whom one can see *and live.* For she said: Have I really been able to see God and *stay alive* after seeing Him?" It takes almost too many insertions to secure this thought. Besides, the text ought to read thus. But it does not. Hagar's problem is not so much the more theological one concerning the possibility of seeing God and surviving but the more practical one: Does God see me? does God really care?

Some press the *halom* ("here") unduly. It merely makes the statement of the case more vivid by recalling the scene of the experience — "here." When drawn to the beginning of a statement as here, such adverbs are used in a more general sense, not usually with emphasis (cf. K. S. 339t). So the statement refuses to yield the sense, quite foreign to the whole connection, that Hagar is chiefly surprised that God appeared to her *here* and not at the place of Abram's dwelling-place, as though God had already been appearing there to her and to many others. No, she is surprised that he appears at all.

Ro'i, the final word, is a participle treated primarily as noun, object of "after" (K. S. 241 a).

14. **Therefore the well came to be called Beer-lahai-roi (a well of the Living One who seeth me). Behold, it is between Kadesh and Bered.**

Previously called a "spring" (v.7), it is here called a "well," because, perhaps, the water did spring forth but was walled in in a well more or less deep.

The experience of Hagar became known, and, in memory of what she had said, the well came to bear a name indicative of this experience — "it was called"

— *gara'* impersonal: "one called," *man nannte*. This slight difference appears in the name of the well: God is called "the Living One." Quite properly so, because the fact that He has regard for the needs of those who call upon Him, stamps Him as truly a Living God and not a dead conception. He "seeth me" is used exactly as in v. 13. Similar forms of the divine name appear in Josh. 3:10; Hos. 1:10; Ps. 42:2; 84:2; II Kings 19:4, 16. For those living at Moses' time the well is located more definitely. The "Behold" is another way of saying: "See" (if you wish to locate it) it is, etc. "Kadesh" is the site usually designated Kadesh Barnea, forty miles due south and a bit to the west of Beersheba. "Bered" has never been located. Skinner believes the well must be *'Ain-Muweilih*, "a caravan station about twelve miles to the west of Kadesh." A *hû'* ("it is") is omitted in the statement as self-evident.

15, 16. **And Hagar bore Abram a son; and Abram called the name of the son whom Hagar bore, Ishmael. And Abram was a man eighty-six years old when Hagar bore Ishmael to Abram.**

Hagar's return to Abram's dwellingplace in obedience to the specific command of the Angel was so self-evident that it is not specially mentioned. The author appears to feel that men will understand that a good woman of Hagar's disposition would never think of doing otherwise than returning under such circumstances. Abram is strictly obedient to the divine injunction and gives the assigned name. His giving of the name implies the formal acknowledgment of the son as his own, and this could hardly have been taken care of by Sarai, and consequently it cannot be a mark of a particular author's way of stating the case (as though in J the mother gave the name [cf. v. 11] and in P the father v. 15). In v. 11 the mother is commissioned because she alone is present; in v. 15 the father carries out the commission because he acknowledges his son. These are plain facts not stylistic peculiarities.

16. Quite appropriately we are told how old Abram was when Ishmael was born. Had the writer not told us, we might justly have charged him with failure to satisfy our justifiable inquiry. Again the customary claim that a verse like 16 must belong to P, because it conveys an exact formal statement statistical in character, must yield to the needs of the case, which indicate that such a statement is almost essential to the completeness of the narrative.

Observe the idiomatic use of *ben* to express age: "a *son* of eighty-six years." Also, the repetition of the word "year" with compound numbers, like "eighty-six." In the last word of the verse the pronoun is displaced by the less common noun (K. S. 4).

On the chapter as a whole it may yet briefly be observed that the critical analysis wavers, revealing how the results of criticism are far from "assured." Skinner makes J the author of all except vv. 1 a, 3, 15, 16, which are given to P; vv. 8, 9 are interpolated. Koenig gives vv. 1-15 to J and only v. 16 to P. Procksch reconstructs: 20:1; then chapter 16; then 25:18; though he, too, assigns vv. 1 a, 3, 15, and 16 to P. Strack is uncertain about v. 1 a.

Many, in order to uphold their theory, call the whole chapter another version of Hagar's expulsion (21:18 ff.).

HOMILETICAL SUGGESTIONS

The big themes of Genesis should be employed as copiously as possible. They are God's mercy and man's faith. So in the case of this chapter the tendency to dwell upon the frailty and the human failings should recede into the background. Not that Abram's and Sarai's weakness should be made light of. But these failings of God's frail children merely offer the background against which God's mercy is displayed the more gloriously. In this particular instance that aspect of the case which receives strongest emphasis is the "Strength of God's Covenant." Grievous as the patriarch's sin is, and though it might appear as though it might annul God's gracious promises, yet that covenant survives and God even deals graciously with the person involved more indirectly—with Hagar, and that, for Abraham's sake, with whom He has made a covenant. Points of view such as these should predominate. Then there will be less danger of falling into a trivial mode of treatment of these portions of the sacred narrative.

CHAPTER XVII

7. **The Covenant Sealed by New Names and Circumcision (17:1-27)**

The basic fact to be observed for a proper approach to this chapter is that the covenant referred to is not a new one. For 15:18 reports the establishment of the covenant, whose essential provisions are the same as those here outlined. Consequently this chapter marks an advance in this direction that the things previously guaranteed are now foretold as finally coming to pass: the one covenant promises certain blessings, the other the realization of these blessings when their appointed time has come.

Criticism confuses issues by claiming that our chapter gives P's account of the covenant which was covered by J's account in the somewhat different fashion in chapter 15. Consequently it need not be wondered at that the critical approach continually magnifies incidental differences and tries to set these two chapters at variance with one another.

Furthermore, the distinct importance of our chapter is readily discerned. A man who has long been obliged to wait in unwavering faith certainly requires clear promises of God upon which to build such faith. For faith must have a foundation. Here these promises, covering the essentials of numerous posterity and possession of the land, and involving by implication the Messianic features found in v. 12, now specify Sarai as the mother who is to bear the son, and also establish a covenant sign. Immediately before the birth of the son of promise these distinct features are, of course, most in place. Aside from this, to have all these promises featured as parts of the covenant seals everything for the faith of Abram which is now under necessity of hoping and believing against all hope.

1, 2. When Abram was a man of ninety-nine years, Yahweh appeared to Abram and said: I am El Shadday; walk before me and be thou perfect. And I will establish my covenant between me and thee, and will multiply thee exceedingly.

If we are to understand rightly the things about to be reported, it is essential to know at what juncture of Abram's life they took place, that is to say, how old Abram was. This very natural consideration calls for the statement of Abram's age at this point. Consequently, to begin to note here the precise style of P who is supposed to love exact statistical information is a misreading of a very simple and natural statement. The Hebrew idiom "a son of" (*ben*) for "a man of" appears here. The dative construction "to Abram" here is not the customary *le* but *'el* (K. S., p. 263, Note 1).

The divine name *'El Shadday* here demands attention. "God Almighty," or "Almigthy God," (A. V.), is a very satisfactory translation. So other versions: Luther — *der allmaechtige Gott*; Vulgate — usually, *omnipotens*. It would appear that this name *Shadday* comes from the root *shadad*, which may mean, "deal violently," but would in reference to God signify "to display power." This derivation is so natural and the sense so satisfactory that efforts to lay inferior and unworthy meanings into this divine name should not have been made. Very unsatisfactory is the evidence which would impress the meaning of "hurler of lightnings," "mountain god," "demon," or "thunder god" upon the title; and behind such efforts lies the attempt to degrade the patriarchal religion to the level of contemporary heathen religions. But neither can we lend our approval to the queer Jewish etymology of the name, which makes *sh* = "who," and *day* = "sufficiently"; therefore "the self-sufficient," cf. the Septuagint rendering ἱκανός. The name is common in Job, where the Greek translators usually render it παντοκράτωρ, "the Almighty."

To the critics the use of this name is a sure index of the style of P. But quite apart from the fact that the argument in a circle functions in the proof — first these passages are because of the name assigned to P, then the name is again extracted from the passages as proof of P's use of it — of the six passages thus assigned to P one is admitted to be touched up by a redactor (Gen. 43:14) ; and besides, the first verse of our chapter bears the name "Yahweh," which also is then conveniently assigned to another redactor, and lastly, the name appears also in Num. 24:4, 16, assigned to JE.

Of far more importance is the remark by Delitzsch which indicates the propriety of the use of this name here: he claims that El Shadday designates "the God who compels nature to do what is contrary to itself and subdues it to bow and minister to grace." So in the last analysis it should not be regarded as a stylistic peculiarity or as a favorite divine name regularly used by some one author, but as the most appropriate divine name for the circumstances under consideration at this point. It is *Yahweh*, according to the text, who says: "*I* am El Shadday" — not P.

Abram is by no means to desist from the type of life which wholeheartedly aims to please God. Though he has been obliged to wait long and patiently for the Lord, conscientious conduct is still the most manifest characteristic of him who is called a true servant of His. Therefore says Yahweh: "Walk before me and be thou perfect." The one command demands a God-conscious life of the best type; the other, faithful observance of all duties. The one is sound mysticism; the other, conscientious conduct. The one is the soul of true religion; the other, the practice of it. "Walk before me" is a very expressive description of how a believer realizes the very real presence of God. "Perfect" (*tamim*), of course, involves not complete moral perfection; but since it involves the idea of "complete" and "sound," it implies that no vital feature of a godly life is absent. Such a demand does not ask Abram to make himself fit to receive divine blessings, but it does warn him against doing those things whereby he renders himself unfit.

2. God's covenant was seen to have been established by God already 15:18. Consequently, *nathan berîth* cannot here mean "to set up a covenant," but rather to put into force, or to make operative, the one that is in force. It is in this sense that we used the hardly adequate rendering "I will establish." God is simply assuring Abram that the time has now come to let the promised things begin to take place. That must mean for Abram: a son will be born. That, too, is exactly what lies in the divine promise: "I will multiply thee exceedingly." God speaks in terms of the ultimate results. Abram for the present thinks primarily in terms of the immediate realization. *Bim'odh me'odh* constitutes, as usual in such repetitions, a kind of superlative (K. S. 318 f.). Strack has a translation that covers the idea involved very acceptably from one point of view: "I will let my promise made to thee become a reality."

3. **And Abram fell upon his face, and God continued to speak to him and said:**

Abram's response to the gracious divine promise is humble adoration, which leads him who recognizes how unworthy he is to receive such a promise to fall face downward to the ground. Since this displays the proper attitude on Abram's part, God goes on to address him.

From this point onward through the chapter the divine name *'Elohîm* is used, the Creator-God. *Yahweh* (v. 1) marked the divine manifestation about to be reported as a token of gracious favor. *'El Shadday* emphasized that God was about to display His power in making nature subservient to grace. *'Elohîm* covers the idea adequately from this point onward, for the Creator is about to do a creative work in enabling Sarai to bring forth.

4, 5. As for me, behold my covenant with thee stands, and thou shalt become a father of a multitude of nations. So thy name shall no longer be called Abram, but thy name shall be Abraham; because as a father of a multitude of nations have I appointed thee.

The emphatic "I" (*'anî*) at the beginning of the verse introduces significantly what God purposes to do and stands in contrast with the obligations Abram is to meet, which are preceded by a prominent emphatic "thou" (*'attah*) v. 9. The pronoun of v. 4 which is thus made emphatic by an independent pronominal form is the possessive attached to *berîthî*, "*my* covenant," (K. S. 341 g). The initial statement lacks a verb: "my covenant with thee," necessitating that some verb like "stands" be supplied in translating. As previously remarked, the covenant of chapter 15 is regarded as unassailable. The promise of v. 2 which still only guaranteed numerous offspring is now elucidated as involving "a multitude of nations." To be the ancestor of one prominent nation would be a gracious prospect. To become the ancestor of a multitude of nations is almost without precedent, except in the case of Noah's sons. As a matter of fact the Ishmaelites and the sons of

Ketura, as well as all Israelites acknowledge him as father. Besides, he becomes "heir of the world" (Rom. 4:13) by virtue of all true believers of all nations, who through faith become his children.

5. In token of this new fact Abram's name is changed by God. Many question this fact in spite of the plain statement here recorded and reckon the account nothing more than an attempt to explain how men changed Abram's name. But the integrity of a writer like Moses dare not be questioned; for he is nowhere found inventing episodes such as this one. It may not be a strict etymology, for the second half, *raham*, could hardly be derived from *hamôn*, "multitude." Consequently the criticisms of Procksch, who calls the efforts "clumsy," or of Dillmann, who labels it "hardly an etymology" are untenable. The simple facts seem to be these: the altered name is to appear as one but little different from the original. However, *raham*, "multitude," is very close to *ram*, "exalted," but since the root is not in use in Hebrew but only in Arabic (*ruhâm*) but apparently was understood in Hebrew, it suggests itself as usable; only its equivalent must be given in a truly Hebrew word "multitude" = *hamôn*. The attempts to extract other meanings from the name, which the text adequately explains, must therefore be dismissed as hypercritical. So, too, the explanation that the inserted *h* really only represents the long vowel within the word — a practice nowhere met with in Hebrew.

The sign of the accusative *'eth* before the virtual subject *shimkha* is to be explained by the fact that in adopting the *passive* verb the retained object practically becomes the subject (K. S. 109). The conjunction *waw* before *hayah* is adversative (K. S. 360 b; cf. Gen. 42:10).

6. And I will make thee exceedingly prolific, and make nations of thee and kings shall come forth from thee.

The promise of v. 4 is unfolded as to the further honors it embraces. Again critics lose this feature by trying to describe the legal style of P, of which this is only a further example. V. 4 had only assured "a multitude of nations." This promise could be construed to mean small nations. Our verse now construes it to mean very populous nations; for "I will make thee exceedingly prolific." *Hiphréthî* strictly means "I will make fruitful," but our idiom prefers "prolific" (Meek). Between the two new features of the promise stands "I will make nations of thee," the original promise whose possibilities are being unfolded. The second new feature mentioned is: "Kings shall come forth from thee." The future nations descended from Abraham are to produce out of their own midst their own competent heads worthy of the name of "Kings."

Note both an accusative and a dative (really factative) object after *nathan* (K. S. 327 t).

7. And I shall uphold my covenant between me and between thee and thy seed after thee for generations to come as a covenant reaching into the hidden future, to be God to thee and to thy seed after thee.

This verse dwells more specifically on the covenant proper. The verb *qûm*, here used in the Hifil, may mean "make a covenant," or "uphold a covenant," depending on the connection. Here the latter must be meant. But the new thing unfolded is that the covenant is to continue in force graciously also for his descendants "for generations" — literally "for their generations" — as a *berîth 'ôlam*. Though this expression is usually translated "an everlasting covenant" (A. V.), really the force of *'ôlam* car-

ries no farther than "into the hidden future" (*bis
in dunkle Zukunft*, K. C.). It may on occasion actually signify eternity. At times it does not reach
beyond the limits of a lifetime. The vital soul of
the covenant is also specifically mentioned: He will
"be God" (*le'lohîm* = "for God") to Abraham and
to his descendants, that means He will fulfill those
obligations to which He pledges Himself by becoming party to a covenant. All that one might rightly
expect of God will be realized. God can really promise
no more than that He will be God to men.

Here critics make the most valiant attempt to
make this so-called covenant of P radically different
from the covenants mentioned elsewhere. For in the
passages relating to covenants according to P, as
they say, Exod. 6:7; 29:45; Lev. 11:45, as well as
in our passage, the statement, "I will be their God,"
is not matched by another which says: "they shall
be my people." So "a reciprocal act of choice on
man's part" is not an "essential feature of the relation." However, the passages cited above as well as
those listed together with them attributed to Ph,
like Lev. 22:33; 25:38; 26:12, 45; Num. 15:41,
though they do not contain the very words referred
to, still always stress the equivalent, namely, walking in a manner worthy of God. The only thing
missing is the set form of words. How hard and
futile are the labors of critics to set part against
part in Holy Writ.

Note the plural suffix "to *their* generations" referring back to the collective singular seed (K. S. 346 p).

8. **And I will give to thee and to thy seed
after thee the land of thy sojournings, namely the
entire land of Canaan for a possession in the hidden
future, and I will be God to them.**

The land had been promised to Abraham and
his descendants before this; see 12:7 and 15:18.

In the almost twenty-five years that had elapsed
hitherto no trace of the fulfillment of this promise
was discernible. Consequently it was quite in order
to renew this promise too in an all-embracing covenant. To make the statement as broad as possible the
promise is added that this possession of the land is
to be for long years to come. But the future is not
to resolve itself into any such thing as mere outward possessions, even though it be of a good land.
So the promise definitely adds that in these long
years to come God will be God to Abraham's seed.

Our translation of *'ôlam* in this verse and the
preceding as "in (or into) the hidden future" provides whatever corrective may be needed for the extra-
vagant opinion that Canaan is to be the inalienable
possession of Israel, perhaps even into the Millennium.
Long endurance of this possession is guaranteed by
this expression but not eternal possession.

The plural *meghurîm,* "sojournings," is one of
the plurals of extent common with nouns picturing
various conditions (K. S. 261 a). "Possession of the
hidden future" for "future possession" is a characteristic example of the use of nouns for adjectives (K.
S. 306 a).

9, 10. **And God said unto Abraham: But as
for thee, thou shalt keep my covenant, thou and
thy descendants after thee throughout their generations. This is the covenant-sign which ye shall
observe between me and yourselves and (between)
thy descendants after thee: all of your males shall
be circumcised:**

Abraham gets a clear outline of his obligations
which the covenant imposes upon him and his descendants for all times to come: "thou shalt keep
my covenant." This general statement implies quite
a bit. It imposes the broad duty upon Abraham and
all his descendants to live in a manner befitting those

who are bound by God's covenant. All this is really
so self-evident that for the present no further specifications are required. Besides, v. 1 had very clearly
covered these obligations in the word: "Walk before me and be thou perfect."

10. But a new feature is appended to the covenant, which is so distinctly a part of it that at first
the statement merely runs thus: "This is the covenant"
(*berîth*). However, since the thing demanded as
being the covenant immediately follows, and is circumcision, the word "covenant" must here be used
by metonomy for "covenant-sign," or "covenant-
condition" (K. C.). This "covenant-sign" is laid as
a duty upon Abraham and upon his offspring. The
commandment as such is the Nifal absolute infinitive
himmôl, for infinitives may be used as imperatives
when they stand unconnected as here. Cf. Exod.
12:48. The further specification "all males" is not
self-evident; for, in the first place, it allows for no
exceptions, and, in the second place, it exempts all
females, for circumcision of females in ancient times
as well as at the present is a regular custom among
some races or tribes.

It cannot be denied that such a custom distinctly
appointed for so holy a purpose is apt to strike us
as exceedingly strange. Nor can such purely utilita-
rian considerations as a sanitary expedient appeal to
us as having been the primary purpose behind the
rite. A deeper meaning must be sought. The two
chief considerations that require investigation here
are: first, the rite as such represents a putting away
of evil, a kind of purification, in fact, more specifically it points to the necessity of the purification of
life at its very source. It is not a sacrament effica-
cious in supplying the needed grace and the desired
effect. But it suggests in a type or symbol what
obligations are laid upon those who stand in covenant

relation with God, namely primarily to put away the
foreskin of their hearts (Jer. 4:4), to circumcise the
heart and "be no longer stiffnecked" (Deut. 10:16),
an effect which, strictly speaking, only the Lord's
grace can achieve in man (Deut. 30:6), which, therefore, man in seeking to accomplish must seek from
the Lord.   Secondly, this rite is tied up closely with
the Messianic hope.   For if it indicates the purification of life at its source, it in the last analysis points
forward to Him through whom all such purification is to be achieved, who is Himself also to be born
by a woman, but is to be He in whom for the
first time that which circumcision prefigures will be
actually realized.

Here it should be remembered that this rite,
even as it is not a sacrament, so, too, is not a divinely
ordained instrumentality for initiation into the people
of God, at least not for a native Israelite.   He was
a member of the people of God by virtue of birth.
By circumcision he was made aware of his covenant
obligations and received a perpetual badge or reminder of these obligations.   That circumcision fore-
shadows baptism is, of course, undeniable.

11-13.   **Namely, ye shall be circumcised in the
flesh of your foreskin, and this shall be for a sign
of a covenant between me and you.   Namely, when
a child is eight days old, then shall all males be
circumcised for all generations to come: as well the
children born in the house as also those bought for
money of any foreigner whatsoever, who does not
happen to be of your race.   Invariably ye shall circumcise these (slave children) born in your house
or bought for money; and so my covenant shall be
in your flesh for a covenant enduring into the far
distant future.**

These necessary explanations how the rite of circumcision is to be put into practice fit together far

more smoothly than a cursory reading of the original
text or even of our familiar version seems to indicate. For the initial "and" of v. 11 and v. 12 really
is a "namely," the German *und zwar* (K. C.). Consequently, the things implied in the initial statement
(v. 10) are being unfolded. Yet how could a rite
of this sort be inaugurated at all in a satisfactory
manner without clear directions a) as to what manner of operation it was to be (v. 11); or b) as to
at what age it was to be administered (v. 12 a);
or c) as to who falls under its provisions, whether
only the direct descendants of Abraham or also the
slaves of the household (v. 12 b); or d) as to the
absolute or relative necessity of this rite for all those
enumerated (v. 13). To impose the rite and leave
all these problems open would merely have caused
grievous perplexity to those entrusted with the duty
of circumcision. Consequently, all such critical remarks as "the legal style of this section is so pronounced that it reads like a stray leaf from the book
of Leviticus," are just another case where the nature
of the circumstances that call for just such a presentation is confused with the problem of style. The
question of various authors (J, E. and P) does not
enter in at this point. No matter who the author
is, the case in question calls for this kind of presentation of the necessary details.

So then, first of all, since a mark in the flesh
might be cut into various parts of the body, the
divine command specifies what man's thoughts might
well have deemed improbable, that this cutting was
to be "in the flesh" — euphemism — of their foreskin. Such a περιτομή will then certainly be "a sign of
a covenant" between God and a member of the
covenant people. So little does the unsanctified mind
appreciate the issues involved, that in the eyes of

the Gentiles circumcision was merely an occasion for ridicule of the Jews.

The converted Kal perfect attaches itself naturally to an infinitive absolute used as an imperative (K. S. 367 t). The sign of the accusative *'eth* here stands not with a definite object but with an accusative of specification (*besar*). The subject of *hayah* has to be supplied *ad sensum* from the preceding, and so we have inserted a "this," or we could have supplied the subject "circumcision."

12. In so important a rite it is not to be left to man's discretion when it is to be administered. "Eight days" is the proper age. Apparently, as the law regards the young cattle as beginning their independent existence with their eighth day (see Exod. 22:30), so a child may be viewed from the same angle. That rule is to hold good "for all generations to come," literally: "according to your generations," a phrase which makes poor English. Such specific regulations, which divine wisdom stoops to give, must have satisfied those to whom the administration of the rite was entrusted. They knew step for step how to regulate its application.

Besides, had even Abraham been left to his own devices, he might well have been puzzled as to whether he might regard the slave children as candidates for this rite. Again, the added question might have arisen, whether here a distinction was to be made between children born of slaves who belonged to the household at the time of the birth of the children (on these children the master had special claim — Exod. 21:2-6) and those children, on the other hand, who had been born of slave parents before these parents passed into control of the Hebrew master. In the case of Abraham's very large household such cases would be numerous. God Himself

proves His estimate of the importance of the rite by
regulating these details.

It certainly is passing strange to find critics referring to this solemn and sacred rite which God ordained
as a "taboo" — "the taboo of the household required
the circumcision" of the purchased slave child
(Procksch). Taboos are superstitious practices; here
is one of the most solemn divine institutions of the
Old Testament.

But now the further question: "Were such circumcised slaves and slave children by this rite incorporated into the chosen race?" We believe that the
answer must be, "Yes." Israel certainly never had
a separate slave class, who were deemed inferior
beings and mere chattels. What then became of the
slaves that originally were part of the household
establishment and went down into Egypt at Jacob's
time? The answer seems to be: "They were naturally absorbed by the Israelites and blended with the
Israelite stock, adopting the Israelite religion." So
with all its necessary exclusiveness Israel was at the
same time broader in its attitude than many assume.
But there certainly could be little hesitation about
letting circumcised slaves be merged with the
chosen race.

The final *hû'* stands in a somewhat unusual position after the subject and the predicate.

13. The injunction is made exceptionally strong
by the absolute infinitive, joined with its corresponding verb: "circumcising you shall circumcise"="You
shall invariably circumcise." A final emphatic summary serves to strengthen the impression of the importance of the rite ordained.

14. **The uncircumcised male, one who shall not
be circumcised in the flesh of his foreskin, such a
person shall be cut from his people; he has broken
my covenant.**

The eventuality has yet to be dealt with, what to do with the one who might refuse to receive this badge of the covenant relation. The penalty demanded is severe: "such a person (literally: "this soul") shall be cut off from his people" (*'ammêha = seine Volksgenossen*). The mooted question just how this penalty is to be defined is settled most satisfactorily, in view of passages where practically the same expression occurs — Exod. 12:15, 19; Lev. 7:20, 21, 25; 17:9, 10 — as allowing for two possibilities. In some instances, where neglect of the important divine ordinance was marked by a spirit of rebellious defiance, the proper authorities were expected to take the offender in hand, and after a just trial, which might establish his stubborn contempt, to put away such iniquity from Israel. On the other hand, there were cases of less flagrant neglect, which due to modifying circumstances might not call for interference on the part of the authorities; and yet the offender was not to regard his offense lightly. The thing threatened for such a case then appeared to be that God Himself would take it in hand and "cut off" such a person, according to tradition "by an early death before such a one had begotten offspring" (Delitzsch).

On *hephar* (with *a*) see G. K. 67 v. The asyndeton of the last clause marks the writer's (or speaker's) indignation. In *wenikhretha* the converted perfect follows after a nominative absolute (K. S. 367, 8).

15, 16. Then God said unto Abraham: As for Sarai thy wife, thou shalt no longer call her Sarai, but Sarah shall be her name. And I shall bless her and shall also give thee a son from her, and as a result of my blessing she shall be a mother of nations; kings of peoples shall spring from her.

No specific word from God had hitherto indicated that Sarai was actually to bring forth the long promised son. This word is now spoken. On the strength of the implications of monogamous marriage this fact had actually been presupposed, excepting, of course, the possibility that Sarai should have died before Abraham had such a son. In anticipation of this event Sarai is given a new name, *Sarah,* which bears no different meaning from her former name but marks an added dignity nevertheless because of the circumstances involved. "Sarah" means "princess," or the "princely one." Without a special divine blessing it would, of course, have been a physical impossibility for Sarah to bring forth this son. Consequently, this potent blessing of God is twice referred to: once in connection with this son, then in relation to the "kings of peoples" that shall in the course of time spring from this son. But she who thus becomes the mother of kings certainly merits the name "Princess." The meaning that some attach to the name, when they say it signifies "the Contender" (*Kaempferin,* Luther), is less appropriate and natural.

Nathátti is a promissory perfect, as in v. 20. The *kî* of v. 15 is adversative as usual after a negative.

To catch the full scope of the last part of this promise it should be carefully weighed that Sarah herself is to become "a mother of nations." The original has only "she shall be unto nations," which, however, A. V. already felt free to render: "she shall be a *mother of* nations." This promise cannot have the Ishmaelites or the sons of Ketura (25:2 ff) in mind: they are not of Sarah. The Israelites descended from her, however, are only *one* nation. Consequently "the posterity of Abraham embraces the spiritual posterity also, i. e., all nations who are grafted ἐκ πίστεως 'Αβραάμ into the seed of Abraham (Rom. 4:11, 12, 16, 17). So Abraham becomes 'heir of the world' (Rom 4:13) through the spiritual Israel" (Keil).

17. **Then Abraham fell upon his face and laughed, and he said to himself: Shall a child be born to a man a hundred years old? or shall Sarah — shall a woman of ninety years bring forth a child?**

From what follows it becomes very clear that Abraham's attitude in no wise lays him open to blame. Nothing is indicative of doubt or misgivings in his reply. Consequently, when he falls upon his face, this is an act of worshipful adoration. Also his laughter is the laughter of joy and surprise. A host of glad feelings is called forth in him at this precious promise. So, too, the questions express no doubt but happy wonder. For saying "to himself" the Hebrew uses the more expressive *belibbô,* "in his heart." That he who is a hundred years old should have a son does indicate that he realizes that he has not lost his vitality; for afterward he becomes father of a number of children (25:2 ff.). But that he at the age of a hundred years should have a son out of a hitherto childless union is, indeed, quite remarkable. His strong joy over Sarah's good fortune finds expression in the double interrogative particle (*'im* and *ha*) in the resumption of the question thus: "Shall Sarah — shall a woman," etc. Whereas we say, "a woman of ninety years," the Hebrew says, "a daughter of ninety," etc., employing the word *bath* for this and many other such relationships.

18. **And Abraham said unto God: Would that Ishmael might live before Thee!**

This plea means: Would that Ishmael might live in thy favor! This plea is not a substitute suggestion for what God offered in v. 16. God's answer v. 19 and 20 makes such an interpretation impossible.

Not a substitute suggestion but an additional plea
Abraham offers. When he observes that God's new
promise passes by Ishmael completely, he seeks a
favor from God for him, that he too might have God's
good will directed toward him.

19, 20. **And God said, Most assuredly Sarah
thy wife shall bring forth a son for thee and thou
shalt call his name Isaac; and I will establish my
covenant with him as a covenant for the hidden
future for his seed after him. Also in reference to
Ishmael have I heard thee: behold, I shall bless him
and make him fruitful and shall make him grow
exceedingly numerous; twelve princes shall his line
produce, and I appoint him to be a great nation.**

The good approach of A. V. and Luther is here
lost by the A. R. V., which renders the initial *'abhal.*
"Nay but." So also B D B, but as a result of a
false exegesis. Since nothing in Abraham's remark
suggests a substitute suggestion, God has nothing
to reject. He confirms what Abraham's joyful faith
accepted: "Most assuredly Sarah shall bring forth
a son," and appoints a name for this son, commemo-
rative of the father's joy, "Isaac," Hebrew: *yits-
chaq* = "he laughs," or more appropriately "glad,"
"happy," Koenig: *heiter, froehlich.* He is, besides,
definitely indicated as the one with whom God's
covenant is to be established after Abraham: he carries on the line of promise in a special relation to
God. *Yolédheth* reaches distinctly into the future in
this case: she "will be bringing forth."

20. Now God's response to the plea for Ishmael.
He has accepted the plea and agrees to answer it:
"I have heard thee." *Le* introduces a dative of
reference: "as for Ishmael." Since all depends on
God's blessing as to whether a man has any future,
God agrees to bestow His blessing, which will appear
in a fourfold form. First, He purposes to make

Ishmael "fruitful," the same word that we rendered
"prolific," (v. 6). Secondly, this will result in his
being "exceedingly numerous." Thirdly, he specifically predicts that in the course of the history of the
nation "twelve princes" shall successively appear. The
faithful historian records the fulfillment of this
promise 25:12-16. Some nations might have called
such rulers "kings." Ishmaelites preferred the title
"princes." Fourthly — and this is practically the
inevitable result of all that preceded — they shall
become "a great nation." Certainly, God gave a
very generous response to Abraham's petition in
Ishmael's behalf. Spiritual prerogatives are not included, inasmuch as this nation had no capacity nor
destiny in this field.

Berákhti is a promissory perfect (K. S. 131).
Shenêm appears as a constant irregular form, a *Keri
perpetuum* (G. K. 97 d).

**21. But my covenant I establish with Isaac
whom Sarah shall bear unto thee at this set time
in the next year.**

This word is as explicit as it can be in ruling
out Ishmael from the prospect of continuing in the
covenant. The emphatic position of the word "my
covenant" necessitates regarding the statement as
adversative. Ishmael, a child brought into the world
according to human devices, is not of grace as is
the covenant. But Isaac is a child purely of grace.
With him the covenant may be coupled. Besides, the
lapse of only one more year is appointed before the
fulfillment of the promise appears.

**22. And He finished speaking with him and
God went up from Abraham.**

The interview is definitely terminated by God.
Whether now Abraham saw Him who appeared to
Him actually ascend upward, or whether the correct

statement that God ascended upward from the earth is merely made by the author Moses as a more highly descriptive way of telling of God's departure, matters little. God's abode is higher than the earth, and the Scriptures consistently describe it as being thus: therefore — "God went up." When Meek translates *wayyá'al* as a pale "he left," that is a typical modernistic translation which levels off what is distinctive in revelation as found in the Scriptures. On *killah le* see G. K. 114 m.

23. **Then Abraham took Ishmael his son, and those servants that had been born in his house as well as those that had been purchased for money — every male in Abraham's household — and circumcised the flesh of their foreskin on that very day, just as God had told him to do.**

The excellent obedience of the faith of Abraham prompts him to carry out the divine injunction in regard to circumcision immediately. Now there are at least two ways of reporting such an act of faith. Either a summary statement to this effect may be made, or else a detailed statement repeating portion for portion the salient features of the command. The author prefers the latter mode, dwelling with loving attention upon every detail, as, no doubt, Abraham himself did while carrying out what had been enjoined upon him. This mode of representation may be regarded as quite effective, at least in the esteem of those who enter into the spirit of the account sympathetically. But, strange to say, such a representation earns for the author a bit of adverse criticism on the part of modern scholars, who even speak of the "pedantic and redundant circumstantiality of narration" here displayed.

So also Ishmael's circumcision is by such regarded as an inconsistency; for "the rite is a sign of the covenant, from which Ishmael is excluded."

Why manufacture baseless charges? All men can see that Ishmael is excluded merely from being the one whose descendants shall personally carry on the line of promise from which the Deliverer will ultimately come. He is by no means to be excluded from sharing in the blessings that are to spring from that promised Deliverer, neither he himself, nor even the servants of the household. He is to consider himself a candidate for a share in these blessings. Circumcision constitutes an invitation for him and the others circumcised to regard themselves such candidates. He and they may afterward reject such spiritual opportunities, even though they continue the custom of circumcision. The loss, then, in such an event is their own fault. The initial circumcision threw open the door of gracious invitation.

The conscientious obedience of Abraham is reflected most strongly in the statement that he did all this "on that very day" — a thing God had not even demanded in so many words.

24, 25. And Abraham was a man of ninety-nine years when he was circumcised in the flesh of his foreskin; whereas Ishmael, his son, was a lad of thirteen years when he was circumcised in the flesh of his foreskin.

The event is of sufficient importance to have the age of the chief characters brought to our attention, though v. 1 had already reported Abraham's age. The thought conveyed by the emphatic repetition of this fact suggests very prominently again Abraham's faith: the man who had waited so long for the son of promise had not as a result of long waiting grown weak in the faith, so that God's words are now, perhaps, regarded somewhat lightly. Rather, in perfect trust Abraham yields implicit obedience to every word, no matter how strange it may seem to human reason. "Man of" and "lad of" are one expression in Hebrew: *ben*.

It has been observed that the Arab descendants of Ishmael still choose the age of about thirteen for the circumcising of their children. Such a practice could well base itself on the recollection of their ancestor's age at the time of his circumcision. However, to let the notice here given count merely as a statement "based on the knowledge of this custom" in just one more attempt to label Biblical statements as manufactured rather than historical.

26, 27. On this very day Abraham and Ishmael, his son, were circumcised, as well as all the men of his household, those born in the house and those purchased for money from foreigners, who were circumcised with him.

This is the closing statement in the elaborate detailed account of what because of its importance deserved and required to be recorded with minute exactitude. This is not an account of a man (P) whose style is circumstantial and pedantic. This account comes from Moses who suits his style to the needs of the case with a fine sense of propriety.

HOMILETICAL SUGGESTIONS

It seems to us that only the portions v. 1-8 and v. 15-21 are suitable for use as texts, and perhaps these two had better serve as *one* text. The sections concerning circumcision are not adapted to use in a sermon. The other portions speak emphatically of the greatness of God's mercy toward Abraham, which includes unusual blessings for Sarah as well as for Hagar. Care should be taken in treating all such portions of Abraham's story to indicate how each new divine word marks a distinct advance upon the preceding words. The details of what the covenant implies are here the matter under particular consideration.

CHAPTER XVIII

8. The Manifestation of Yahweh at Mamre
(18:1-33)

The time of the birth of the promised son has
drawn very near and may definitely be revealed. Besides, Sarah, whose share in the experience should
be more than a purely natural and physical one, needs
to be so directed that her faith may enable her to
take her part in a manner truly worthy of the event.
In addition, the faith of Abraham is to be given an
opportunity to express its unselfishness, that a clear
revelation of the nature of the faith of a true saint
of God may be offered. When God manifests Himself to
Abraham at Mamre, the first two of these issues are
disposed of in connection with His promise concerning
the early birth of the son, and the third, in connection with the revelation of His purpose to take the
case of wicked Sodom in hand.

Criticism feels that the entire chapter should be
assigned to J. One argument in support of the contention is the use of the divine name Yahweh. However, the suitability of this name for this chapter
and the next is immediately apparent. It is Yahweh,
the faithful covenant God, who is concerned about
the matter of having the child of promise come in
due season to believing parents. But at the same
time, it is a part of the faithful care of Yahweh for
the covenant people that leads Him to resort to acts
of retributive and punitive justice in order to clear
the path for the normal development of His people.

Some critics still prefer to follow Wellhausen's
lead in making v. 17-19, 22 b-33 a editorial inser-

tions. Dillmann, however, claims that neither language, nor material arguments justify such a contention. Any man reading along naturally will see that the verdicts which decree that certain verses are later insertions are highly subjective opinions, which no amount of learning can prove.

If the story of the visit of the Almighty with Abraham is seen to have striking parallels in heathen mythology, we naturally explain this coincidence by the simple observation that the truth of this experience penetrated far into other nations and there suffered such modifications as we now observe, for example, in the legend of Philemon and Baucis. To invert the course of procedure and make Israel the borrower, would do violence to the fidelity with which Israel guarded its sacred tradition, and so would be unjustifiable.

1. And Yahweh appeared unto him by the terebinths of Mamre as he was sitting in the door of the tent in the heat of the day.

The site marked by this experience was "by the terebinths of Mamre." Mamre here, too, as in 14:13, appears to be the Amorite who stood on a friendly footing with Abraham. Knowing what we do of Abraham, we conclude that this Amorite must have been of a nobler sort than the average run of his tribe. The terebinths may have been a larger grove near Hebron, which Mamre allowed Abraham to put to use for encamping in their shade. The time indicated for this experience was the heat of day, when the Orientals of these lands must observe a period of rest because of the dangerous heat of the sun. *Ke* with the infinitive *chom* is a temporal phrase. The article with *yôm* ("day") is the article for the customary thing — such heat as marked days regularly. The participle *yoshebh* marks the sitting as a process of some duration — durative participle. *Wehû' yoshebh* is a circumstantial clause (G. K. 141 e).

The assertion of this first verse, that it was "Yahweh" who appeared to Abraham here, must be held fast in determining the identity of the three visitors. This first verse furnishes the basic statement. This statement cannot be meant in the rather loose sense that Yahweh made His appearance by sending some three men. If that sense were to be conveyed, v. 1 would have made a very unsatisfactory statement of the case. *Péthach* is an accusative of place (G. K. 118 g).

2. **And he lifted up his eyes and looked, and, behold, three men were standing over against him; and when he saw them, he ran to meet them from the door of his tent and bowed down to the earth.**

The "behold," which plainly marks something unusual, has been strained needlessly in several directions. Some let Abraham drouse in the noonday heat, and let him discover the men as he awakes. That is too prosy. Others insist that the "behold" indicates the sudden and miraculous appearing of the three. That's an exaggeration. The truth lies between the two claims. The men have approached quite naturally along the road to the tent. Abraham may have been deep in thought in the quiet of noon. To be confronted by three strangers whose approach one did not observe is quite unusual, and it calls for a *hinneh* to mark Abraham's surprise. These three are "standing" (*nitstsabhîm* — Niphal, durative participle). Oriental courtesy makes this gesture practically the equivalent of our knocking. There can be no thought of drawing nearer until the one standing has been invited to do so. They stood *'alayu'*, literally, "above him," for he was sitting. We should say, "over against him." Again, demonstrative oriental courtesy requires "to run" (*rûts*), or at least to hasten to meet such. The customary elaborate greeting by prostration follows. This act need not involve worship except in the case where it is done before God as adoration, when the gesture remains the same. For the present those approaching are called "three men," for such they seemed to Abraham to be.

3-5. And he said: My lord, if I have found favor in thy sight, please do not pass by thy servant. Let a bit of water, pray, be brought and wash your feet and rest under this tree; and let me fetch you a morsel of bread and refresh yourselves; afterwards you may pass on; for on this account have you passed over before your servant. And they said: Do as you said.

The first problem is whether "my lord" should have been rendered "my Lord." So the Hebrew vowelpoints suggest (*'adhonāy*). However, the same consonants could be pointed *'adhonî*, "my lord," or *'adhonay* (short "a"), "my lords." The last (Meek) will not do because the address continues in the singular, "*thy* sight." The divine character of the chief figure is displayed in v. 13. That the two accompanying Him are angels is revealed 19:1. Had Abraham at once discerned His divine character, he could not have offered food. Besides, all three were taking part in the conversation according to 5 b and 9 a. So the relative truth of the pointing of the text lies in this that He truly was the Lord (*'adhonāy*). The error lies in this that Abraham did not yet address Him as such.

With fine courtesy ("If I have found favor in thy sight") he begs these passers-by not to continue on their way without stopping. For the first person pronoun he uses the title expressive of humility — "thy servant."

4. Washing of feet was the first offering of hospitality; cf. 19:2; 24:32; 43:24. The urgency of

the invitation finds expression in the successive use
of *na'*. The imperfects are jussives (K. E. 355 b).
Yuqqach is Hofal (G. K. 66 g). "Rest" is really
the verb *sha'an,* meaning to lie down propped on an
elbow. Of course, this posture has nothing to say
as to the posture assumed while eating, for then the
meal was still perhaps more than an hour distant
in the future. "This tree" is an attempt to render
the article *ha'ets,* which is here the article for the
customary thing — the tree that was wont to stand
near the tent door or under whose shade the tent was
pitched (K. S. 299 b).

5. With unostentatious humility the prospective
host refers to the meal he proposes to offer as a "bit
of bread." The Hebrew idiom for "refresh yourselves" is to "brace your hearts" (*sa'adhû*). Finally,
the statement: "for this account have you passed"
indicates that the speaker regards the fact that they
did pass his tent as a providential opportunity for
him to display courtesy. We well recognize, as
B D B p. 475 b shows, that the expression *kî 'al
khen* does often mean "inasmuch as." Yet even
the discussion of B D B shows that the rendering
we have employed ("for on this account") is also
permissible. Here, in fact, it is the crowning touch
of a sincere courtesy.

Oriental courtesy is wont to be elaborate; and
though parallels from experiences of travellers may
be cited to show Abraham to have been a typical
nomad, yet what stands out in the Biblical narrative
is the absolute sincerity of this fine courtesy. (Heb.
13:2 refers to this occasion.) The courtesy of a sincere faith is here portrayed in an inimitable fashion.

6-8. **And Abraham hastened into the tent to
Sarah and said: Quick, three measures of fine flour,
knead it and make cakes. Out to the herd ran
Abraham and took a heifer, tender and good, and**

gave it to the servant, and he made haste to prepare it.   Then he took sour milk and sweet milk and the heifer which he had had prepared and set it before them, while he himself stood by them under the tree; and they ate.

In the Orient bread is never prepared at any other time than immediately before it is eaten. So bread must be prepared by Sarah for these guests. Though the guests number only three, the simple food offered will be presented in lavish abundance. -"Three measures" have been computed to make four and a half pecks (Skinner). What is left over can be disposed of with ease by the servants of so large an establishment as the one Abraham had. The quick command is elliptic; it implies: "Make haste (and take) three measures," etc. Meek renders *maharî* well: "quick." Then literally: three seahs, flour, fine flour." "Cakes" — *'ugôth* — "are usually fried twice in fat or milk and are a finer product than *léchem* ('bread')" — Procksch.

7.   "To the herd" stands first in the sentence to indicate how rapidly Abraham turns from one task to the next. The *ben baqar*, "son of the cow," might be a calf or a heifer. He selects of his best — "tender and good" — personally superintending every step of the preparation. The slaying, flaying and roasting is attended to by the *na'ar* ("boy" or "young man"). The style of roasting is described by some as taking smaller portions and roasting them individually on skewers or small spits. Among people who ate meat but rarely such a dish is especially delectable. *Yema(h)her* here, as frequently, functions practically as an adverb, "quickly," and the following infinitive *'sôth* functions as a main verb (G. K. 114 m). Of course, one may translate: "he made haste to prepare it." The subject of the verb is, without doubt, the servant.

8. *Chem'ah* is "sour milk," or "curds," a refreshing drink deemed particularly healthful. *Chalabh* is "sweet milk," whether of camels, cows, or goats. The bread is not separately mentioned as having been set before the guests; the use of the thin bread to fold about portions of the meat as they are taken in hand is too obvious to require special mention. The idiom "stand by," *'amadh 'al,* implies to stand by to be of service, and could even be rendered "and he served them." Cf. I Sam. 16:22; I Kings 1:2; I Kings 17:1, in the expression "stand before."

The eating of the three heavenly guests — "and they ate" — is marvelous indeed. We must declare this eating to have been real but rather by accommodation than of necessity. Augustine's word still stands as a classic explanation: "That He ate, was rather of power than of necessity. The earth absorbs water by drinking it in. Different is the mode of absorption by the glowing ray of the sun. The one is because of need, the other by virtue of power." The eating on the part of the glorified Christ after the resurrection serves as an explanatory parallel to this incident. The Almighty sought to draw near to Abraham in intimate contact. The friendliest and most intimate contacts among the sons of men are oft made over a friendly meal.

9, 10. **And they said to him: Where is Sarah, thy wife? And he said: Behold, in the tent. And He said: I will certainly return to thee again after a year, and behold Sarah, thy wife, shall have a son. Now Sarah was listening at the door of the tent, and this (door) was behind Him.**

Oriental courtesy perhaps in those days already forbade to all except intimates to inquire after a wife. These visitors give indication of their authority by making the inquiry. Besides, their coming is con-

cerned vitally with a most remarkable experience that
is about to befall Sarah. Then, too, Sarah's faith
needs to be raised to the proper level to do justice
to the experience. Abraham must have sensed the
note of authority in what the speakers said. Still this
statement must be correct: "*they* said." Either all
spoke or else they displayed such interest in the
question that it was as though all had spoken. Now
Sarah was where wives were usually found when
guests were outside the tent — in the tent. The "behold" in this case amounts to little more than, "Inside the tent *there*" (Meek). Without circumlocution
the visitor, the outstanding one among the three,
assumes sole control of the conversation and delivers
the promise He has come to give. This promise conveys the definite assurance, "Sarah shall have a son."
The time for this event is fixed — "after a year."
For *ka'eth chayyah* = "according to this time when
it revives" = "when this time of the year returns" =
"after a year." This is still a satisfactory translation and one that is quite unforced. "According to
the time of a pregnant woman" is hardly to be extracted from the passage. *"So ich lebe,"* (Luther),
i. e., "as I live," is still more impossible. Then, also,
the word definitely indicates that God alone will bring
this miracle to pass: "I will certainly return," i. e.,
it shall not come to pass of itself but through my
intervention. Since this returning of the Lord is
nowhere recorded, it appears most suitable to regard
the event as such as the manner in which God came
to Abraham and to Sarah. The article in *ka'eth* is
the article of familiar things, *Artikel der Connexitaet*
(K. S. 387 e): "As the familiar time revives."

Now Sarah did not merely "hear" this (A. V.)
as she stood behind the door, for *shomá'ath* is
feminine participle, "she was hearing," i. e., "she
was listening." Nor could Yahweh see her or any

trace of her, for "this door was behind Him." This is plainly stated here so that what He next says may be seen to be the evidence of His omniscience not of His observation.

The points over *'elayw* in v. 9 have not been explained satisfactorily.

11, 12. Now Abraham and Sarah were old and well along in years, and it had ceased to be with Sarah after the manner of women. So Sarah laughed to herself and said: After I have become worn out, have I enjoyed sexual delight and my lord too is an old man?

The seemingly insurmountable physical obstacle in the way of the fulfillment of this divine promise is now drawn to our attention. Capacity for procreation and conception was extinct. Sarah's case at least must have seemed irremediable. The woman's periods had ceased with the so-called change of life and with them the capacity to conceive. The promise seems laughable to the carnal thoughts of Sarah, and she actually laughs "to herself," i. e., "within her midst" — Hebrew idiom for the reflexive pronoun. In a question without an interrogative particle Sarah expresses her wonder at the thought: she is worn out, so is Abraham. Viewing the matter from the angle of a thing already accomplished, though she does not believe that it will transpire, she says: "Have I enjoyed sexual delight?" The matter is not put very delicately by Sarah. I Pet. 3:6 rightly deduces from her address ("lord") that she respected her husband.

This laughter on Sarah's part was the laughter of incredulity and so a form of unbelief. It bore no trace of scoffing. Jamieson ought not to have spoken of a "silent sneer."

13-15. And Yahweh said unto Abraham: Why then did Sarah laugh saying: Shall I really

bear a child seeing I have grown old? Is anything too difficult for Yahweh? At the appointed time after a year I will return to thee and Sarah shall have a son. But Sarah denied, saying: I did not laugh — for she was afraid. But He said: No, but thou didst laugh.

Here the chief of the visitors displays His character by revealing His omniscience. He is therefore very appropriately called "Yahweh" at this point, the author taking up the clue which he offered in v. 1. He addresses the rebuke to Abraham, for there would have been a mild impropriety about calling out to the woman in the other compartment of the tent. Yahweh specifically tells Sarah through this address to Abraham what she did. Imagine the astounding nature of this revelation to Sarah: her secret thoughts have been correctly read; the very motive she had referred to, namely that she had grown old, is also displayed to her. This attitude is rebuked by Yahweh as being the equivalent of saying that something is "too difficult for Yahweh." Such an opinion, of course, is patent unbelief. *Yippale'* does originally signify, "to be wonderful." Here it must bear the derived meaning "too difficult." The preposition *min* following the verb makes a comparative whose original form would have been: "anything more difficult than Yahweh could perform." As it now stands, *miyyahweh* is the equivalent of a negative result clause (K. S. 406 l; cf. also 308 b; G. K. 133 c; 102 m). *Dabhar* here is the equivalent of an indefinite pronoun: "thing" = "anything." (K. S. 80 c). We still cannot fathom how anyone should ever have ventured to say, "As the narrative stands, the sentence does not imply identity between the speaker and Yahweh" (Skinner). Verse 14 alone might have left the question open, but v. 13 had identified the speaker beforehand.

Yahweh simply reiterates His promise. Above
(v. 10) the time within which the son was to be
born had been appointed; and so it is now referred
to as "the appointed time" (*mô'edh*), and the limit
of a year is repeated — "when this time revives" =
"after a year," as in v. 10 above.

15. In fear at so remarkable a visitor Sarah
attempts self-defense, which under the circumstances
can take only one form — a lie, a downright lie: "I
did not laugh." The brief reply of the Almighty
stamps her defense as unworthy of further consideration. She is rebuked and dismissed with an authoritative: "No, but thou didst lie." The usual negative *lo'* here amounts to "no." The *kî* is adversative,
"but."

The second half of the chapter begins at this
point — what transpired near Mamre after the
guests had been escorted along the road for a short
distance.

16. **And the men rose up from thence and
directed their gaze in the direction of Sodom and
Abraham went with them to escort them (for a part
of the way).**

The first part of their mission being disposed
of, the "men (*'anashîm*) arise" from the meal and
make preparations to depart from that place (*mishsham*). The Hebrew expression is very concise:
"they rose up from thence." They give indication
of being on the way to Sodom, because they direct
their gaze in the direction of "Sodom." Originally
in the Hifil *shaqaph* means "to look out and down,"
also with *'al peney*, i. e., "upon the faces of." This
is a very appropriate verb in this instance, because
from the region of Hebron one would "look out and
down" toward Sodom. The sincere courtesy of

Abraham prompts him besides to "escort them" —
shallecham = "to send them along." Tradition has
it that he went several miles (*ca.* three) to a place
called by Jerome *Caphar Barucha,* but now known
as *Janum* or *Beni Naim,* at which point the Dead
Sea comes into view and perhaps also the site of
Sodom. The expression *'al - peney* can hardly mean
"toward the plain of" (Keil). It means "toward" or
"in the direction of."

**17-19. And Yahweh said: Am I going to hide
from Abraham what I purpose to do, seeing that
Abraham is surely going to become a great and
strong nation, and in him all the nations of the earth
are going to be blessed? For I acknowledge him to
be my intimate friend to the end that he may enjoin
upon his children and his household after him to
keep the way of Yahweh to do what is just and right,
in order that Yahweh may bring upon Abraham that
which he promised him.**

It seems best to assume that this soliloquy of
Yahweh was spoken softly yet audibly. It was
truly a soliloquy. It was just as certainly intended
for Abraham's ears. Here, certainly, in a most
definite sense Abraham is treated as a trusted friend
and initiated into the counsels of God. From a passage such as this can grow the Scriptural designation
of Abraham as "friend of God"; cf. Isa. 41:8;
II Chron. 20:7; James 2:23. Even the Arabs know
and use this title of Abraham. It would be unseemly to explain this revelation on the score that
since Abraham is heir to this land, God will do nothing involving one of the cities without informing
Abraham of His purpose. The words here spoken
indicate a twofold reason for making the revelation.
First, Abraham is Yahweh's intimate friend. Secondly, this notable destruction, which is about to transpire, should be faithfully transmitted to Abraham's

posterity as a warning example for all times to come. The second of these reasons is the major; the first is auxiliary to the second.

Of course, Yahweh's deliberations about making this revelation to Abraham are not recorded to convey the impression that Yahweh was momentarily in a quandary, but to give us an insight into Yahweh's reasons for making this revelation and also to reveal drastically the intimacy of the relation between God and His saints.

The participle *mekhaśśeh*, "am I *hiding?*" must mean: "Am I *going to hide?*" The following participle is distinctly future progressive, i. e., *'oseh* = "what I *purpose* to do." Yahweh makes His revelation in conformity with Abraham's destiny, which is "to become a great and strong nation" and to have "all the nations of the earth blessed in him." This unmistakably refers to the Messianic blessing to be realized in the seed of Abraham. On *nibhrekhû* — "be blessed" — see 12:3; it does not mean "feel blessed" (Strack).

19. The *yadha'* here regularly comes in for its share of discussion. The root does primarily mean "know." But a bare "know" will hardly meet the needs of the case here. This fact has driven some to the extreme position of rendering "I have chosen" (Strack). But allusion to the Scriptures Hos. 13:5; Amos 3:2; Ps. 1:6 will hardly establish such a use. In cases such as these the meaning prevails "to acknowledge one as an intimate friend" — *als guten Bekannten anerkennen* (K. W.). "To enter into personal relations with" (Skinner) amounts to about the same thing.

Now God did thus acknowledge Abraham as His intimate friend, not for Abraham's sake only but, as He specifically says, that what is thus conveyed to him might be passed on to posterity. In fact, it was to be delivered as a solemn injunction (*yetsawweh* = "he may enjoin") to his own children as well as to the entire household. For though no specific ordinance is involved, nevertheless, the dreadful fate of wicked Sodom is in itself a solemn reminder to shun Sodom's wicked ways and "to keep the way of Yahweh." The expression "way of Yahweh" (*dérekh yahweh*) requires "Yahweh" to be construed as a subjective genitive: "the way which Yahweh desires." This is further defined as involving "to do what is just (*tsedhaqah*) and right" (*mishpat*). Procksch nicely distinguishes between these two terms, making the former signify inner, the latter outer righteousness. So Yahweh describes a salutary effect as going out from the correct knowledge of the overthrow of Sodom and Gomorrah because of their iniquity. The blasted site and the true story of how divine justice blasted it constituted a lasting memorial of solemn import to Israel. To give heed to this divine lesson was essential, for only then would Yahweh "bring upon Abraham that which He promised him." Though Yahweh speaks, He says "that *Yahweh* may bring," referring to Himself by His proper title to make the assurance more solemn (K. S. 5). *Weshamerû* — "and they shall keep" — here must be construed as a consecutive final clause, "that they may keep" or "to keep."

It will be observed that neither here nor in v. 20, 21 does God directly say that He will destroy these wicked cities. But from what He does say and from what Abraham knew about them, it was possible for Abraham to arrive at but one conclusion and that was: Yahweh is come to destroy these cities.

20, 21. And Yahweh said: The outcry over Sodom and Gomorrah — surely it is great, and their sin — surely it is exceedingly grievous. I am going down now to see whether they have done altogether

**according to the cry over it which has come unto
me; and if not, I will know.**

This is all that Yahweh reveals about His purpose. There is an "outcry (forward for empasis)
over Sodom and Gomorrah" (objective genitive). *Kî*
does mean *"that."* Here the thought implied is:
"it is a fact *that."* That certainly allows for the
meaning "surely." Then we have two very emphatic
statements about the extreme wickedness of the
cities. When sins are said to cry out to heaven, that
surely is a drastic way of saying that they call for
divine interference. On *kî* see K. S. 351 c.

21. "I am going down" in this case involves a
mere descent from the higher spot where these words
were spoken to the low-lying cities. In reality only
the two angels (19:1) go directly to the city. The
statements of the verse in no wise imply that God's
omniscience is curtailed and that so He is under
necessity of securing information as men might. God
chooses this mode of procedure to make apparent the
fact that He, as Just Judge of all the earth, does
nothing without first being in full possession of all
facts. The subsequent experience of the angels in
Sodom displays the moral state of Sodom far more
effectually than could many an explanation besides.
God practically claims that the facts of the case
have come up before Him already. But He does
nothing until facts warrant interference. "The cry
over it" is again an objective genitive (K. S. 37).
'Er'eh as imperfect takes the place of the voluntative (G. K. 75 l). *Kalah,* a noun, "completion,"
here appears to be used as an adverbial accusative,
"altogether."

22. **And the men turned from thence and
went toward Sodom, but Abraham was still standing
before Yahweh.**

Here already those who specifically count as men (*'anashîm*) or later more specifically as angels (19:1) separate themselves from the group, and the one remaining behind is described very plainly as Yahweh. In the light of this clear analysis of the case we reject all statements that claim: "In what way the narrator conceived that Yahweh was present in the three men, we can hardly tell" (Skinner). An opportunity is to be given to Abraham for a free unforced expression of his broader sympathies. Intercession, if it is to have any value, surely must come unsolicited. But Abraham will emerge from the test with a rare revelation of his deep unselfishness.

23-25. And Abraham drew near and said: Wilt Thou indeed snatch away the righteous with the wicked? Perchance there may be fifty righteous men within the city. Wilt Thou indeed snatch away and not grant pardon to the place for the sake of the fifty righteous which are in the midst of it? Far be it from Thee to do such a thing, to kill the righteous man together with the wicked, and so righteous and wicked be treated alike; far be it from Thee; shall not the Judge of all the earth deal righteously?

Abraham, well informed as to Sodom's extreme wickedness, has no doubt what God must purpose to do. So he "draws near." Though in specific connections this expression (*naghash*) means prayer, in this case it describes only the act preparatory to prayer, for it does not even say: he drew near *to God*.

The boldness of faith betrayed by this intercession may well astound us. It surely is not based on the assumption that God might deal unjustly. Nor would it ever have occurred to Abraham that he himself might be more compassionate than Yahweh. But Abraham recognized that there was a possibility of the perishing of righteous men in this impending cata-

strophe, even his own relatives also. Much as he hopes
that Lot and his family might be rescued, he is not
so narrow or selfish as to think only of these. One
might almost say that with a heart kindled by the
love that God imparts to faith Abraham ventures to
plead the case of God's love over against God's righteousness. We may never know how these attributes
of God are reconciled to one another, except in so far
as they blend in Christ. But the boldness of this act
of faith is acceptable with God inasmuch as it is
really born out of God's heart. This attitude is the
"importunity" Christ refers to in the parable of
Luke 11:8.

But who would "righteous men" — *tsaddiqîm* —
be in this instance? We should say, such who have
made the proper use of the truth they have, whether
it be much or little, and have let it have its work on
their heart, yielding to it not by their own powers but
under the influence of this truth. On the level of the
truth on which they stand they would have dealt fairly
and honestly. Apparently for the whole complex of
five cities the sum "fifty" is assigned. "Place"
(*maqôm*) above apparently means as much as region.

When the opening question is addressed to God:
"Wilt thou snatch away (*saphah* = 'cut off,' 'break
off') the righteous with the wicked?" Abraham, no
doubt, recalls that in major calamities this sometimes
happens. But whatever may be pleaded for the righteous, that plea he wishes to make. So his prayer constitutes a kind of wrestling with God. A man who
has himself received mercy seeks to secure mercy
for others.

Another fact appears in this connection, namely,
that the ungodly are frequently spared for the sake
of the righteous, though, of course, there is a limit
to what they may thus achieve for others.

In v. 23 the singular *tsaddiq* is a case of the use of a singular noun in place of the more regular plural (K. S. 256 d). In v. 24 *saphah* is used without an object, though it is a transitive verb usually appearing with an object (K. S. 209 b). The article with *tsaddiqîm* is occasioned by the earlier use of the word; these "righteous" are relatively familiar (*relative Bekanntheit*, K. S. 298 b).

25) Most amazing is the free address of faith at this point. Yet, though it strikes a responsive chord in every heart, hardly anyone would be capable of venturing to address God thus. Behind it lies absolute confidence in God's fairness. Besides, that grand and correct conception of God that was characteristic of the patriarchs appears very definitely here. God is far from being a tribal God; He is "the Judge of *all the earth.*" The critics have failed to evaluate this fact properly.

Chalilah, really a noun, an adverbial accusative here, *ad profanum,* we can render only by some such phrase as "far be it." With *Wehayah* the construction passes over from the infinitive to the use of the finite verb (G. K. 114 r; K. S. 413 a; 367 u).

26. And Yahweh said: If I find in Sodom fifty righteous men within the city, I will spare the whole place for their sake.

Yahweh cannot be displeased with what Abraham said. He grants Abraham's petition. Everything for the present is cast into the anthropomorphic mold of thought. God knows how many righteous are in the city. It will not be requisite for Him first to make an extended investigation. We still believe that "Sodom" is mentioned by synecdoche for all the places to be destroyed. The two separate phrases "in Sodom" and "within the city" simply hold apart what we usually would combine in the phrase "with the city of Sodom" (Meek). The apodosis is introduced emphatically by *waw* ("and") (K. S. 415 v). The word for "guilt" (*'awôn*) usually used after *nasa'*, in the phrase "to pardon the guilt" is here missing.

27, 28. And Abraham answered and said: Behold, now, I have begun to speak unto 'Adonay (the Lord) and I but dust and ashes. Perhaps five may be wanting of the fifty righteous; wilt thou destroy all the city on account of the five? And He said: I will not destroy it if I find there forty and five.

Abraham speaks with a due sense of his unworthiness and is fully aware of the boldness of his act. He recognizes that God is *'Adonay*, Lord of all, and that he on his part is but "dust and ashes" — "dust in origin, ashes in the end." Respectfully Abraham also substitutes the majestic title *'Adonay* for the familiar "Thou." Also very cautiously he drops but "five" from the first stipulated "fifty." Interceding love is ingenious: surely, the lack of five could hardly constitute a ground for destroying the city. God acknowledges the validity of the plea. *Yachserûn* has the old ending *ûn* for *û* (G. K. 47 m).

29-32. And he again proceeded to speak to Him and said: Perhaps there will be found there forty? And He replied: Not will I do it for the sake of the forty. And he said: I pray, let not 'Adonay be angry if I speak — perhaps there will be found there thirty. And He replied: Not will I do it if I find thirty there. And he said: Behold, now, I have begun to speak unto 'Adonay, perhaps there will be found there twenty. And He replied: I will not destroy it, for the sake of the twenty. And he said: I pray, let not 'Adonay be angry if I speak only this once — perhaps there will be found there ten. And He replied: I will not destroy it for the sake of the ten.

Before our astounded gaze are unfolded the details of a plea that stands without parallel in the annals of history. Never mortal prayed as this mortal. At the same time the writer relates the story with consummate skill, letting the tension grow with each successive plea. Never does Abraham wax presumptuous. Well aware of his unworthiness, he pleads his case carefully. But with the wisdom born of faith he discerns that by asking more than his last plea did he would no longer be pleading according to the will of God. Besides, any lower number would have degraded a worthy intercession into a narrow plea for one's relatives only.

30. *Yi'char*, masculine, is used for the neuter. In *happá'am* the article is used with the old demonstrative force, or (according to K. S. 299 a) it is the *Artikel der Connexitaet*. *Wa'adhabberah* is the emphatic cohortative, "would that I might," called also the *yaqtul gravatum* (K. S. 198 b).

33. **And Yahweh went away after He had finished speaking with Abraham, and Abraham returned to his place.**

The scene closes abruptly: Yahweh goes away (*wayyélekh*), and Abraham returns home. There is no need of saying where Yahweh went. Everyone knows that. Also in Abraham's case a very general expression is used: "to his place." This brief closing remark serves to mark a lull in the action of the story. Some calamity is impending, and the thread of the narrative is about to resume with the unfinished part.

HOMILETICAL SUGGESTIONS

A chapter with a wealth of human interest for the preacher! Two distinct episodes stand out: v. 1-15 and v. 16-33. In treating the former several points of view are permissible. The more general thought of "God's Loving-kindness toward His Children" may come to the forefront when we observe the paternal friendly approach of the Lord. When the faith-difficulty of Sarah is taken in hand, then the point of view of v. 14 may predominate, suggesting the theme: "Is anything too hard for the Lord?" Then there is the further possibility of regarding what we see of Abraham as a manifestation of faith from still a different angle. Then we might treat of the "True Courtesy of True Faith"—a subject which we personally regard as by no means trivial. The second half of the chapter, v. 16-33, can be treated under heads such as "The Boldness of Faith," or "Intercessory Prayer at its Best." We also deem that approach appropriate which views this portion from the point of view of "Ye are my Friends." Then v. 19 suggests still another approach along the line: "The Memory of God's Judgment is to be Kept Alive."

CHAPTER XIX

9. Guilt and Destruction of Sodom — Sequel: Lot's Degeneracy (19:1-38)

Though strictly speaking this chapter is not a portion of the history of the chosen people, yet it relates an occurrence that was to teach the chosen people a lesson for all times to come; for the site of this calamity was upon the borders of the land of promise. Besides, the chapter shows how even a portion of the relatives of Abraham undergoes a rather rapid deterioration.

From another point of view this chapter is not an independent one but marks the sequel to the preceding. The facts of the previous chapter lead inevitably to this one, and so both are usually treated together under one caption.

There is hardly a more horrible account anywhere on the pages of Holy Writ. Both the degeneracy here described as well as the catastrophic overthrow of the cities involved are calculated to startle by their lurid and gruesome details. Luther confessed that he could not read the chapter without a feeling of deep revulsion (*es geht mir durch mein ganzes Herz*).

Nor should we overlook the fact that the destruction of Sodom is a type of the final overthrow of the wicked and impenitent in the final judgment, as well as of the deliverance of the righteous. Conditions such as are depicted here may be expected to repeat themselves in increasing measure before the end of time.

1, 2. **And the two angels came to Sodom at evening time, as Lot was sitting in the gate of Sodom; and when Lot noticed them, he arose to meet them, and bowed with his face to the ground. And he said: Behold now, sirs, turn aside, I pray, unto the house of your servant, and spend the night, and wash your feet, and ye shall arise early and be on your way. And they said: No, for we shall pass the night in the broad place (of the city).**

A. V. translates erroneously: "there came two angels" — omitting the definite article. The Hebrew must be rendered: *"The* two angels came." They are the same two who in 18:22 turned away and went toward Sodom. Criticism for some unknown reason erases "angels" and substitutes "men." The text merely grows more specific at this point. Those who first appeared merely as "men" are now clearly revealed to be angels. If they arrived "at evening time," having left Hebron perhaps early in the afternoon, they had covered a distance of at least thirty-five miles in six hours, that is to say, in about half the time it would have taken men. The article with "evening" is the article of customary things — *Artikel der Connexitaet* — (K. S. 299 b) ; that is, *the* evening that must follow after the day which is under consideration.

The "gate" of the city where Lot is at the time is the common resort of all men, especially of the elders of a city. There legal matters are adjudicated, transactions closed, bargains made, and affairs discussed. Lot's presence here will hardly be accounted for on the assumption that he was on the lookout for guests in order to afford his hospitality an opportunity to welcome chance strangers. Strangers cannot have been so common in those days. Rather, Lot's presence in the gate constitutes a reproach to the otherwise good and "righteous" man (II Pet. 2:8). After having first moved down into the Plain of Sodom (13:11),

he presently chose Sodom itself as his dwelling place
(13:12) ; and now finally he has arrived at the point
where the activities, the bustle and stir are looked
upon with a more or less tolerant interest. This
much cannot be denied in reference to Lot, that when
the approach of the strangers was noticed by him, he
promptly advances to them with a gracious invitation. He is not ignorant of the danger that threatens
chance visitors in such a town. He arises to meet
them and bows with the customary respectful oriental
salutation, bowing with his face to the ground.
'Appáyim is an adverbial accusative of manner (K. S.
402 h). The same type of excellent courtesy observed in Abraham still marks the nephew. With
urgency, ("behold now" — "turn aside, I pray"), he
presses his invitation. With humility he designates
himself as their "servant." With anxiety for their
welfare — for he knows what men in the open must
face — and, perhaps, consciously at no small risk to
himself he makes his invitation as attractive as possible
("wash your feet," "spend the night"). "Arise early"
(*shakham*) originally meant "to raise the burden to
the shoulder," perhaps from nomadic customs of getting underway with the caravans at daybreak.

The angels refuse, but not because they wished
to make a test of Lot's sincerity; for the spirit of
the invitation must have been immediately apparent.
The reason rather seems to have been, as Luther
already suggests, that persons truly humble are very
modest and unassuming. Since the angels come in the
guise of simple, modest persons, it behooves them to
manifest corresponding qualities. Yet what they do
serves to display rather prominently the basic difference between this one man, Lot, and the rest of the
people of his city.

The purpose stated by the angels — "we shall pass
the night in the broad place" — was not so unusual.

The climate permitted such a course: wrapped in their robe, travellers frequently spend the night lying on the street. "The broad place" (*rechôbh*) is an enlarged area just within the city gate, serving as a market place and for the concourse of all manner of people. Usually it is little more than the widening out of the street that connects with the gate. *Lo'*, "not," is used as "No," (K. S. 352 f). Note the *dagesh forte* conjunctive in the "l."

3. **But he urged them strongly; so they turned aside after him and entered into his house; and he made a feast for them and baked unleavened bread, and they did eat.**

Lot's hospitality is no mere oriental gesture; it is entirely sincere. So he adds entreaty to his invitation, without doubt because he knows these men to be good men, and knows the danger that awaits them. Lot's address *'adhonay*, which we rendered "sirs," is, according to our interpretation of 18:3, the same as that used by Abraham. We, therefore, consider that at first both Abraham and Lot considered their visitors to be merely good and worthy men. The conclusion drawn by many at this point, that Lot lacked the deeper discernment of Abraham, is without warrant. Perhaps *mishteh*, which usually means "feast," should here be kept in the primary meaning "drink," because unleavened bread is mentioned after. However, then Lot's hospitality would have been somewhat niggardly — a cup of wine and bread. For though Lot is a city-dweller, he still, no doubt, was owner of the large herds that had been his when he separated from Abraham. Consequently, the supposition that he was living in reduced circumstances hardly seems warranted.

4, 5. **Before they retired, the men of the city, men of Sodom that they were, surrounded the house, young men and old, all the folk without exception,**

**and they cried out to Lot, saying to him: Where
are the men who have come to you this night?
Bring them forth to us that we may have intercourse
with them.**

So eager are the people of Sodom to be about
their unholy practices that they are already assembled
and ready for mischief before Lot's guests have retired. The expression, "men of Sodom," is no gloss
(Kit., etc.), but it rather seems to have been a proverbial designation for outstanding exponents of the
vice of sodomy, even while the city yet stood. Therefore we have rendered it "men of Sodom that they
were." The horrible proportions to which the vice
had grown is indicated, first, by the fact that "young
men and old" (Hebrew: "from young to old"), put
in their appearance. The fires of unnatural lust
burned unabated even in the aged. To make this
point unmistakably clear two further modifying
phrases are added: the apposition, "all the people,"
and the phrase, "without exception." This latter
expression (*miqqatseh*) is better understood to mean
"without end" (K. W.), i. e., "without exception,"
the *min* being a *min separationis*, and not "from the
end," i. e., from the utmost limits of the city; for
such cities were but small. Secondly, the enormity
of the prevalent vice was indicated by the fact that
the sacred duty of hospitality was so completely replaced by the eagerness to practice vile lust that even
strangers would be sacrificed to wholesale abuse —
a treatment most likely to terminate in death. The
events of this evening display a shocking depravity.
The facts of the case are now apparent to all the
world whether these people "have done altogether
according to the cry" which had come unto the
Lord. The euphemism, "that we may know them"
(*nedhe'ah*), is not born out of delicacy, for they
shout forth their libidinous desires aloud in the streets

of the city, cf. Isa. 3:9; Judg. 19:22. The article with
"night" is of the same type as that used in v. 1 with
"evening," and it could here as there be rendered
as demonstrative; here: "this night." *Nedhe'ah* is
cohortative (K. S. 198 b) and really stronger than
our translation can readily reproduce, viz., "O that
we might know." Note also how the imperative is
followed by the cohortative in the last two verbs (K.
S. 364 n; G. K. 108 d). The particle *térem* (v. 4),
as usual, is followed by the imperfect (G. K.
107 c).

**6-8. And Lot went out of the doorway and
shut the door after him, and said: I pray you, my
brethren, do not act so wickedly. See, I have two
daughters, who have never had intercourse with a
man; let me, I pray you, bring them out to you,
and do to them as you please. Only as far as these
men are concerned, do not do anything to them.
For therefore have they come under the protection
of my roof.**

Lot is not devoid of courage. He himself faces
the mob after he has shut the door behind him for the
safeguarding of his guests.

7. He uses a kindly address, which can hardly
be entirely sincere, "brethren." Perhaps, however,
it would be better to describe his attitude as meek
tolerance.

8. The kindest interpretation of Lot's willing-
ness to sacrifice his daughters to the depraved lusts
of these evildoers stresses that it was done with the
intent of guarding his guests. To that certainly must
be added the fact that under the circumstances Lot
was laboring under a certain confusion. But
Delitzsch's summary still covers the truth, when
he describes Lot's mistake as being an attempt to
avoid sin by sin. In days of old, when an exaggerated
emphasis on hospitality prevailed, we might have

understood how such a sacrifice could be made by a father. But in our day we cannot but feel the strongest aversion to so unpaternal an attitude. Luther's attempts to vindicate Lot's character are quite unconvincing: for Lot could hardly have anticipated with a certain shrewdness that the Sodomites were so bent on this particular form of vileness as to refuse any substitutes. In fact, their refusal to accept Lot's substitute argues for an intensity of evil purpose that surpasses all comprehension.

Note the enclitic *na'*, intensifying or adding vividness to a jussive in v. 7 and to a hortative in v. 8 (K. S. 355 b). *Dabhar* takes the place of the indefinite pronoun, "anything." "For on that account" here, as in 18:5, is best rendered by the old A. V. translation "for therefore." The substitute "inasmuch as" says far less; cf. the remarks on 18:5. *Ha'el* for *ha'elleh* is found eight times in the Pentateuch.

9. **And they said: You just come here! And they went on to say: This one fellow came in here merely to sojourn and he has been playing the part of the judge all this while! Now we will deal worse with you than with them. And they pressed hard upon the man, Lot, and they drew near to break down the door.**

Gash hale'ah does not mean, "Stand back" (A. V., etc.), for *naghash* means the opposite, "draw near." Luther is correct: *Komm hierher*. B D B, which tries to make it mean "approach thither, i. e., move away," does an unwarranted thing. We believe the force of the expression to be quite adequately covered by our colloquial, "You just come here!" The article before *'e(ch)chadh* again has demonstrative force: the expression is somewhat derogatory: "this one fellow." By the expression *yishpot* (with absolute infinitive) used with *waw* conversive

the expression is made to refer to the past, not to
the future: "he will needs be judge" (A. V.) or
"now he would make himself judge" (Meek). The
Sodomites are complaining of what the man has been
doing right along: "he has been playing the part of
the judge all this while." This shows Lot at his
best: he had been Lot the Censor. He had been
wont to reprove them for their iniquitous ways. Till
now they tolerated it, because they felt that through
Abraham they had been delivered for Lot's sake
(14:13 ff.). Now in their exasperation they threaten
to deal worse with Lot than with his guests. In fact,
they intend to harm him as well as them, for they
"draw near to break down the door."

The second *wayyó'mer* at the beginning of the
verse needs merely be rendered "and they went on
to say" and all difficulties are removed (K. S. 368 c).
On *gesh* as a form see G. K. 66 b; of course, it is
an imperative from *naghash*.

10, 11. **And the men stretched forth their
hands and drew Lot in to them into the house, and
closed the door. But the men that were outside
the door of the house, they smote with blindness,
young and old, so that they wore themselves out trying to find the door.**

The angels are here described as "men," because
till now they have done or said nothing to indicate
their higher character. Consequently Lot's conduct
toward them appears to best advantage, for it could
not have been motivated by the knowledge that they
were angels. Apparently, the door could not be
opened from without. Consequently the angels had
to open it if Lot was to gain the safety afforded
by his house. His hospitality here receives a full
and adequate recompense.

11. "The blindness" (article expressing the idea:
that well-know affliction, article of familiar objects,

Artikel der absoluten Bekanntheit, K. S. 297 b), which
comes as punishment and restraint upon these evildoers, is not blindness in the usual sense. It involves
a specific delusion (cf. II Kings 6:18) : they can see,
but they cannot discover the door. Therefore Keil
calls it a "mental blindness," adding that it is "a
punishment for their utter moral blindness." For in
all such punitive measures of God a deeper propriety
is always discernible in reference to the very form
of punishment that befalls one. By this act the
heavenly character and the power of Lot's guests are
made apparent to him. For he must presently have
discovered what these heavenly messengers had done.

The provisions made for the deliverance of Lot
and the members of his immediate relationship are
now to be described.

**12, 13. Then the men said unto Lot: Whom
hast thou here besides? a son-in-law or thy sons or
thy daughters, or anyone else who belongs to thee
in the city. Bring such a one out from the place.
For we are about to destroy this place, because great
is the outcry over them before the face of Yahweh;
and Yahweh has sent us to destroy it.**

The account still continues to describe Lot's
visitors as "men," for, apparently, their appearance
continued as it had from the first. They indicate
to Lot that he will be privileged to forewarn any
such as may be of his relationship, who may be
spared for Lot's sake. Apparently, the ungodly owe
more to the godly in this respect than is usually conceded. The enumeration of persons who might be
approached begins with "son-in-law." Apparently
that is as remote a connection as will be allowed. But
then the obvious ones are also mentioned: "thy sons
or thy daughters or anyone else that belongs" to
Lot. *Chathan,* therefore, does not need to be deleted,
or its position altered, nor need it be supplied with

a suffix. Note: we have translated *mî* as interrogative, "who," because the indefinite sense "anyone" does not seem sufficiently established (K. S. 72). Lot's wife is not enumerated as one to be rescued, because that is too obvious.

13. By the summons of v. 12 Lot's mind has been prepared for the announcement of the impending disaster. So the angels with great kindliness temper the appalling announcement. But when their announcement is made, there is no ambiguity about it: the place is to be destroyed; they themselves are to be the agents of this destruction; the cause that makes this destruction imperative is therefore that the outcry over the inhabitants of the city has reached the point where Yahweh Himself must interfere, in fact, He is the one who has directly commissioned these His agents. Note the participle to describe an impending action (*mashchitîm*). The suffix *am* (outcry — *theirs*) though plural has the noun "place" (*maqôm*) as its antecedent, a kind of collective (K. S. 346 f).

14. **And Lot went out and spoke to his sons-in-law who had married his daughters, and he said: Rise, go forth from this place; for Yahweh is about to destroy the city. But in the eyes of his sons-in-law he was as one who jests.**

The mob having dispersed round about his house, Lot felt that the marvelous protection afforded him a short time before would guarantee his safety on this new mission of mercy. The young men addressed are called "sons-in-law," not by anticipation but because they were such in fact. The participle *loqechey* should, therefore, not be taken in the less likely sense of "who were about to take." The fact that Lot's daughters are not separately mentioned as having been appealed to and warned by their father is explained as being too self-evident to require mention, even as Lot's wife is not mentioned in v. 12. These daughters must, therefore, be regarded as having fully adopted the attitude of their unbelieving husbands. Lot makes his summons urgent: "Rise, go forth" — effective asyndeton. He states the impending danger concisely, and, so, urgently. The sons-in-law regard the matter as a huge joke. They are types of all such as have had all sense of justice and of judgment erased by growing callous in sin. The nearer the judgment comes, the less will men believe it to be impending.

The account tells nothing of the anxiety in which the inmates of Lot's house spent the night, nor of the heavy forebodings that must have weighted down their minds.

15, 16. When dawn appeared, the angels urged Lot, saying: Up, take thy wife and thy two daughters that are with thee, lest thou be swept away in the punishment of the city. But he lingered; so the men took him, his wife, and his two daughters by the hand, because Yahweh was sparing him; and they brought them forth and set them outside the city.

Lot, though a saint, is a specimen of weak godliness. He lacks the decision and the wholehearted obedience of Abraham. The thought of sacrificing house and home and all his goods makes departure difficult. Yet in the last analysis what are material possessions in an hour of such impending disaster? Lot, who should have acted promptly upon having merely received information, must be exhorted and finally taken by the hand and led forth. In v. 15 the two visitors are called "angels," in v. 16 "men." Both appellations apply, one covering what they in reality are, the other how they actually appear. *Bechemlath* is the infinitive of *chamal*, here expressing cause (K. S. 403 a). *Hannimtsa'ôth* — "the

ones found" — *Nifal* participle, could hardly be used
with propriety if some of Lot's daughters did not
happen to be found in the house at the moment. This
is one of the major arguments for interpreting *loqechey* (v. 14) as referring to the past and not to the
future.

17. **And it came to pass when they had
brought them forth outside the city that one of
them said: Flee for your life; do not look behind
you; and do not stop in all this Round (of the Jordan); to the mountains take your flight lest you be
swept away.**

Very specific instructions are given to the fugitives at this point. One in particular gives the commandments to be observed, therefore *wayyo'mer,*
singular, with indefinite subject (K. S. 324 d). Again
the suggestion of the early versions to make the verb
a plural is quite unnecessary. Consequently also, the
singular is no indication that the Lord is speaking
through the angel. Lot's delay has made unbending
haste a necessity. *Nephesh,* usually "soul," is used
in the sense of life, as often, especially in the expression "flee for your life." The command not to
"look behind them" is primarily for the purpose of
demonstrating the necessity of utmost haste. The
third behest forbids stopping anywhere in the so-called
Round (*kikkar*) of the Jordan, sometimes rendered
"the Plain of the Jordan" (see 13:10). Difficult though
it will make the flight, they must take their course
"to the mountains" — the fourth direction — lest they
be swept away. Because the command not to look
around is met with in heathen legends (cf. Orpheus
and Eurydice), that fact does not yet make every
command of that sort in Israelitish history a part
of a legendary account. We ourselves may on occasion
bid another not to look around without being on our
part involved in some legendary transaction.

18-20. And Lot said to them: O no, sirs! See, I pray, thy servant has found favor in your sight, and thou hast displayed great kindness toward me in sparing my life, and I, for my part, am not able to flee to the mountains, lest evil overtake me and I die; look, here is this town near at hand to flee thither — and it is but a tiny place — let me flee to it, pray; (is it not but a tiny place?) that I may escape alive.

Here is a somewhat presumptuous plea by a weak and timid man. He does not seem to realize his extremity, nor to value sufficiently the undeserved favor bestowed upon him. He bargains for further consideration. One is almost tempted to expect that the angels would have given him an impatient and curt refusal. The change of number in the pronouns used ("thy," "your," "thou") seems to spring from Lot's trepidation: sometimes he addresses both; at times he directs his words to the one who had spoken last. Lot bases his plea on the favor that has been bestowed on him. He reinforces it by a plea of physical inability to reach the mountains. He claims the evil from which God is delivering him will overtake him nevertheless — not a very commendable attitude. Finally, he makes the smallness of the place that he has in mind a plea for sparing it, in case he flees thither. It almost taxes the reader's patience to bear with this long-winded plea at a moment of such extreme danger. Lot appreciated but little what was being done for him. The *'adhonay* of v. 18 is a pausal form with *qamets* instead of *pathach* and is not to be read as "Lord," for nothing indicates that Lot had recognized the Lord in these angels. In fact, the Lord had not come down with them to Sodom. On the form *'ûkhal* see G. K. 69 r. The suffix object on *tidhbaqáni* (v. 19) takes the place of a preposi-tional object (K. S. 22). In v. 20 the question introduced by "*ha* interrogative," takes the place of an adverbial clause of cause (K. S. 373 f). The nifal *'immaletah* has "i" under the prefix (cf. G. K. 51 p). The "and" clause, *wattechi*, is final (G. K. 109 f.).

21, 22. And he said to him: Behold, I have accepted thee also in regard to this matter not to overthrow the town of which thou hast spoken. Flee there quickly, for I can do nothing until thou hast come there. Therefore the name of the place is called Zoar ("tiny place").

The stress of circumstances does not allow time for argument and counterargument: Lot's request is granted in a spirit of remarkable patience and long-suffering. The small town is exempted from the calamity to which it had been destined. The angel speaks with a measure of authority which has been granted him as Yahweh's agent. On the other hand, it is apparent that he is under certain restrictions: he can do nothing until Lot is safe. *Zo'ar*, the resultant name, builds on the root of the word for "tiny place" (*mits'ar*) which Lot uses twice. *Maher* is used as an equivalent of the adverb "quickly" (G. K. 120 g).

Now follows an account of one of the most horrifying events of all history.

23-25. As the sun rose upon the earth, Lot came to Zoar, and Yahweh rained upon Sodom and upon Gomorrah sulphur and fire from Yahweh from the heavens; and He overthrew those cities and the entire Round and all the inhabitants of the cities and all that sprang forth from the ground.

The catastrophies wrought by God are fully under His control. This one is not unleashed until Lot has safely reached Zoar. But by that time the sun is fully risen. Although only Sodom and Gomorrah are mentioned, we learn from Deut. 29:23; cf. Hos. 11:8, that

Admah and Zeboiim were involved as well. By adding Zoar to the group we have the so-called Five Cities, i. e., Pentapolis; cf. 14:2, 9. Of course, Zoar was spared.

The means causing the destruction are said to be "sulphur and fire" which Yahweh brought down so plentifully upon these places that He is said to have "rained" them upon Sodom and Gomorrah. On this point the account is very concise. Whatever attempt is made to discover more nearly the details of what transpired, such an attempt must stay strictly within the limits of the textual statements. Nothing points directly to a volcanic eruption; nor do lava remains happen to be found in the immediate vicinity (K. C.). Nor does the expression "overthrew" necessarily point to an earthquake. The "fire" which rained down from heaven may have been lightning. The "sulphur" may have been miraculously wrought and so have rained down together with the lightnings, although there is the other possibility that a huge explosion of highly inflammable materials, including sulphur, deposited in the ground (cf. the "bitumen pits" of 14:10) may have cast these materials, especially the sulphur, high into the air so that they rained upon these cities, causing a vast conflagration. Besides, it seems quite likely that after these combustible materials once took fire, the very site of the cities was literally burnt away to quite a depth, and so the waters of the northern part of the Dead Sea filled in the burnt-out area. For it is a well-known fact that the southern end of the Dead Sea hardly exceeds a depth of twelve feet and usually runs much less, i. e., three or four feet. In fact, at certain points it is by no means difficult to wade across the lake. On the other hand, the northern portion reaches a maximum depth of 1300 feet. To assume, then, that the entire lake is the result of this "overthrow," as some have, hardly seems

reasonable or in conformity with the Biblical account.
A conflagration that would have burnt out the ground
to a depth of 1,300 feet cannot be conceived. An
earthquake, causing so deep and so broad a fissure in
the earth's crust, would at least have called for the
use of the term "earthquake" in this connection, for,
apparently, in violence it would have surpassed all
earthquakes of which man has a record. Equally
difficult would be the assumption that the Jordan once
flowed through this delightful valley of the Pentapolis and poured its water into the Elanitic Gulf.

The most significant term used to describe what
God did is He "overthrew" (*haphakh*). The noun
derived from this verb root (*mahpekhah*) comes to
be the standing designation of the catastrophe in the
Scriptures; cf. Deut. 29:23; Amos 4:11; Jer. 49:18;
50:40; Isa. 13:19. Only that which stands up can
be "overthrown." Consequently the verb connotes
something of the idea of proud men and institutions
being brought low by the Lord who "throws down
the mighty from their seats" and lays iniquity
prostrate.

But what construction shall we put upon the
statement, "Yahweh rained . . . . from Yahweh
from the heavens"? We consider Meek's translation
an evasion of the difficulty by alteration of the text,
when he renders: "The Lord rained . . . . from
the sky." Kit., instead of striking out "from Yahweh," deletes "from the heavens." However, there
is much truth in the claim that the name of God
or Yahweh is often used in solemn or emphatic utterances in place of the pronoun that would normally
be expected. K. C. lists the instances of this sort
that have been met with in Genesis up to this point:
1:27 a, 28 a; 5:1 b; 8:21 a; 9:16 b; 11:9b; 12:8 b;
18:17 a; 19:13 b, etc. But that would hardly apply
in this case, for our passage would hardly come under

the list of those where "the divine name is used instead of the pronoun." For how could Moses have written: "Yahweh rained from Himself"? Yet the statement is certainly meant to be emphatic, but not merely emphatic in the sense in which Keil, following Calvin's interpretation, suggests. For both hold that the statement is worded thus to indicate that this was not rain and lightning operating according to "the wonted course of nature" (*non usitato naturae ordine Deus pluerit*), but that it might be stated quite emphatically that more than the ordinary causes of nature were at work. We believe that the mere expression, "God, or Yahweh, rained from heaven," would have served very adequately to convey such an emphatic statement. But in this instance Yahweh was present in and with His angels whom He had delegated to this task and who acted under specific divine mandate. He who had the day before been visibly present with them, was now invisibly with them. When His agents acted, He acted. Consequently we believe that the view which the church held on this problem from days of old is still the simplest and the best: *Pluit Deus filius a Deo patre* = "God the Son brought down the rain from God the Father," as the Council of Sirmium worded the statement. To devaluate the statement of the text to mean less necessitates a similar process of devaluation of a number of other texts like 1:26, and only by such a process can the claim be supported that there are no indications of the doctrine of the Trinity in Genesis. We believe the combined weight of these passages, including Gen. 1:1, 2, makes the conclusion inevitable that the doctrine of the Holy Trinity is in a measure revealed in the Old Testament, and especially in Genesis. Why should not so fundamental a doctrine be made manifest from the beginning? We may see more of this truth than did the Old Testament saints, but the Church has through the ages always held one and the same truth. Luther says: "This expression indicates two persons in the Godhead."

That more than the destruction of all living beings in the whole affected area is meant is indicated by the added object: "and all that sprang forth from the ground," i. e., *tsémach ha'adhamah,* or "that which sprouted from the ground." We need hardly go so far as to assume that the more or less combustible soil burned out to a depth of several feet. Perhaps only the lowlying sites of the cities were entirely burned, and then, as seems particularly proved by Kyle's investigation of the site, as the water level of the lake rose, the area covered by the conflagration was slowly inundated.

26. **And Lot's wife looked back from behind him, and she became a pillar of salt.**

According to the words employed Lot's wife must already at the time of her looking have been "behind him." This indicates that she was not making as determined efforts to escape as were the others. No one can determine whether "longing, pity, or curiosity" (Delitzsch) impelled her to disregard the very plain divine injunction. Evidently her heart was in the city. She appreciated but little what the delivering angels had done for her. Almost escaped, she allowed her vigilance to relax. So she became a warning example to all who do not make a clear-cut break with the life of wickedness, as Jesus' remarkable warning designates her (Luke 17:32). God's punishment overtook her on the spot, apparently through the agents already operative in the destruction. For she may well have been overtaken by the poisonous fumes and the fiery destruction raining down from heaven hard upon the heels of the fugitives. Rather too drastic a use of the imagination is made when the destructive agent is labelled "lava" (Jamieson), or "huge waves of the Salt Sea" (Procksch). But once overcome, there she lay, apparently not reached by the fire but salt-encrusted by the vapors of the Salt Sea. Lot and his daughters could not have seen this at the time, for to look back would have involved them in the same destruction. Their love for the one lost will, no doubt, have driven them after the havoc of the overthrow had subsided to visit the spot, and there they will have found "the pillar of salt." For the words *wattehî* ("and she became") in no wise in themselves demand an instantaneous conversion into such a pillar. Whatever salt formations have since been described as Lot's wife from the time of the apocryphal book of Wisdom (10:7: "the pillar of salt . . . a memorial of the unbelieving soul") to this day must be regarded as purely fictitious. But in the days shortly after the catastrophe the salt-encrusted, crudely pillar-like remains of the unhappy woman were to be seen.

27, 28. **And Abraham rose early and went to the place where he had stood before Yahweh, and looked out upon Sodom and Gomorrah and upon all the land of the (Jordan) Round, and he saw, and, lo, the smoke from the land went up as the smoke of a smelting furnace.**

So sure had Abraham become of the imminence of a catastrophic overthrow of the wicked cities that he felt impelled upon rising to go back to the place where he had "stood before Yahweh" on the preceding day, for from it a panoramic view of the whole region could be obtained. The eye beheld vast volumes of smoke rising from all the region. The expression here used *qîtor ha'árets*, "smoke of the earth," seems to suggest more definitely that the very ground burned. Our rendering above ("smoke from the land") is perhaps, therefore, less correct. To our suggestions above under this head (v. 25) we would add another, namely, the possibility that also petroleum deposits near the surface may have been ignited to cause an enormous conflagration. The comparison employed to make the picture more vivid is "as the smoke of a smelting furnace." *Kibhshan* is by some rendered "kiln," however K. W. appears to offer the more suitable suggestion *Schmelzofen.* So also Buhl.

The article *"the* morning" is the "article of the customary" — the morning that marks the next day. The article with "smelting furnace" is the article used in comparisons (G. K. 126, o).

29. And it came to pass when God overthrew the cities of the (Jordan) Round that God remembered Abraham and conducted Lot out of the midst of the overthrow, when He overthrew the cities in which Lot dwelt.

The "overthrow" is a mighty act of judgment in which God displays powers which lead men to fear Him; therefore "Elohim" and not "Yahweh." Even when the merciful act of deliverance is recorded, where, without a doubt, "Yahweh" could have been used, Moses uses "Elohim," because Lot no doubt felt primarily fear at the great catastrophe which was unleashing itself. But the primary thought of the verse is: God remembered Lot for Abraham's sake. Abraham's prayer, though denied in the form in which it was offered, is, nevertheless, heard insofar as Lot's preservation is concerned. Lot, consequently, was not delivered for his own sake but for Abraham's. "The effectual fervent prayer of the righteous man availeth much." The blessings that go forth from one true-hearted servant of God are incalculable.

30. **And Lot, together with his two daughters, went up out of Zoar and dwelt in the mountains, for he was afraid to dwell in Zoar; and he and his two daughters dwelt in a cave.**

Lot abandons Zoar as a residence because he fears to dwell there longer. This fear may be interpreted as arising from the fact that he as a fugitive from a city destroyed for its wickedness may have been viewed with suspicion by the people of Zoar. But Zoar, a city originally destined for a like destruction, will hardly have had scruples about the moral integrity of a man like Lot. Besides, it would be just as logical to conclude that the Zoarites might have respected him as a special favorite of the Deity. Therefore, the other explanation is much to be preferred which claims that Zoar was dreaded by Lot because he feared it too might ultimately be overthrown. Such an attitude on Lot's part argues for want of faith. God had answered his petition to have it spared. But Lot is a weak saint. He may, indeed, have seen unabated wickedness in Zoar after "the overthrow" and may have become alarmed at the sight of it. Even that would not excuse his fear. For "*a* cave" the Hebrew has "*the* cave," i. e., the cave that was to be expected in a mountainous region where caves abound — the article of "relative familiarity" (K. S. 299 b). The *le* before *shebheth* is the *le relationis,* taking the place of an accusative after "fear."

31, 32. **And the first-born said to the younger: Our father is old, and there is no one in the land to marry us after the manner of all the earth. Come, let us make our father drunk with wine, and lie with him, that we may preserve offspring from our father.**

We here see the sorry spectacle of people of good antecedents badly contaminated by continued

contact with persons of vicious habits. Lot's daughters stoop to incest, it is true, not because of vile
passions, but because they face the disgrace of dying
without issue. When they claim that there "is no
one in all the land to marry" (Hebrew: "to come
in unto") them, as daughters everywhere else are
married, that remark is dictated by the impatience
of unbelief. Had they waited a while longer, a husband might have been found. The scheme devised
to offset the deficiency is one worthy of the depraved
Sodomites, who had cast all sense of decency aside.
Tse'îrah ("little one") in this connection gains the
force of a comparative "the younger." *Lekhah* is
really the feminine imperative, second person, here
used with the first person as a mere expletive (K.
S. 344 g). "To give to drink," (or, "to make drunk")
naturally may take a double object (K. S. 327 m).

33. **And they made their father drunk with
wine that night, and the first-born went in and lay
with her father, and he was not aware that she lay
down or that she rose up.**

It surely is an indication of moral decay when
a man lets himself be made inebriate so readily by
his daughters. One may attribute grief over the
recent catastrophe and over the loss of his wife to
Lot and so seek to account for his readiness to take
a kind of consolation from the cup offered him, but
the moral responsibility cannot be cancelled by such
considerations. We may even be inclined to believe
that by this time the once "righteous" man (II Pet.
2:7) had lapsed from grace. Charity, however, suggests to hold judgment in suspense, because we hear
nothing more of Lot after this sad event. Stranger
still seems the statement that Lot "knew not" (*lo'
yadha'*) of it. However, the appended limitation,
"of her lying down and her rising up," seems to
remove all difficulties, and so suggests our transla-

tion, "was not aware that she lay down," etc. The
unusual point over the last word is apparently an
indication that the Masoretes considered the statement a strange one. Things done in a drunken stupor
may well be regarded as done with badly blurred
consciousness, nor do they leave a distinct imprint
on the memory. The article before *hû'* is perhaps left
off to prevent cacophony (G. K. 126 y).

**34, 35. And it came to pass on the next day
that the first-born said to the younger: Behold, I
lay with my father last night. Let us make him
drunk with wine also tonight; then do thou go in
and lie with him. So we shall preserve offspring
from our father. So they again made their father
drunk that night; and the younger daughter arose
and lay with him, and he was not aware that she
lay down or that she rose up.**

Keil's formulation of Lot's part in the transaction
covers the case; he says: Lot was "not entirely un-
conscious, yet . . . , without clearly knowing what
he was doing." The measure of culpability of Lot
is, of course, far less than it would have been but for
this circumstance. Yet this is a revolting scene and
a tragic one.

**36-38. So both the daughters of Lot were with
child by their father. And the first-born bare a son
and called his name Moab. He is the father of the
present-day Moabites. And the younger daughter,
she too bore a son and called his name Benammi.
He is the father of the present-day Ammonites.**

Again and again critics label this whole story
the outgrowth of a mean prejudice on the part of
Israel against these two neighboring nations, a hostile
fabrication and an attempt to heap disgrace upon
them. Yet passages like Deut. 2:9 surely indicate
that Israel always maintained a friendly spirit to-

ward these brother nations, especially toward the
Moabites. David's history also may serve as an anti-
dote against such slanders. We have here an objective
account of an actual historical occurrence. Nor is
there any occasion for describing these etymologies
as "forced" or unnatural. These are not strict
etymologies but accounts of names that actually reflected the truth involved.

Mô'abh apparently means the same as *me'abh,*
i. e., "from the father." For though, indeed, *mo,*
derived from *mayim* or *mê,* may mean "water," as
a euphemism for "seed," such a derivation seems
almost too blunt. So the name *Benammi,* "son of my
people," contains a veiled allusion to the father's
paternity; the child is the son of her nearest relative. From this name the term Ammonites arose
in the course of time. We believe that Meek has
rendered the expression of the A. V. "unto this day"
very acceptably as "present-day." It is to be pre-
fixed to the nationalities in question.

The chapter as a whole is nowadays regularly
assigned to J, with the exception of v. 29, in which
Elohim is found, and which therefore is ascribed to
P. But v. 29 is so essential for the purpose of tying
up this chapter with the preceding, showing what
bearing Abraham's intercession really had upon the
fortunes of Lot, that it is unthinkable that another
author should have supplied what practically flows
out of the connection of the two chapters and almost
constitutes their very soul. We showed above how
appropriate the divine name Elohim is at this point.
Besides, claims to the effect that "the tautological
circumstantiality of the priestly writer" are clearly
to be discerned here (K. C.) fall to earth as soon
as we discern that the formal character of the verse
is occasioned by the fact that this verse constitutes

a formal conclusion of the incident just narrated. Such conclusions are inclined naturally to adopt a somewhat more formal style.

HOMILETICAL SUGGESTIONS

Not every part of this chapter is suited for homiletical use. It seems to us that v. 1-11 contains several elements that would require explanation and yet cannot be explained without a measure of impropriety. And if there be a difference of opinion under this head, certainly all must agree that v. 30-38, though it certainly serves a good purpose under several heads, cannot be a text for a sermon. That leaves v. 12-22 first of all—a section that may be regarded as exemplifying the Longsuffering Mercy of God, or any similar formulation that demonstrates effectively how much concerned God is for His own, though they may but little deserve His mercy. Here is an unusual case of a judgment which is plainly designed for depraved sinners. To have a godly man perish in the overthrow of such could create the wrong impression. Consequently, God makes a singular exception of the man Lot. Yet, undoubtedly, it is mercy that is here operative. Then there is the section v. 23-29, which, on the one hand, demonstrates the severity of God's judgments, on the other, the fact that the weak may be spared for the sake of the godly—also a vital truth of the Scriptures to be found frequently in the books of Kings where Israel is again and again spared for David's sake.